For Zoë and Biff

CONTENTS

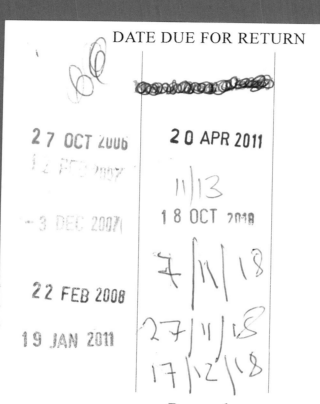

THE ENGLISH BUILDINGS BOOK

Philip Wilkinson and Peter Ashley

ENGLISH HERITAGE

Published by English Heritage
Isambard House, Kemble Drive
Swindon SN2 2GZ

www.english-heritage.org.uk

English Heritage is the Government's
statutory adviser on all aspects of the
historic environment.

Copyright © Philip Wilkinson,
Peter Ashley and English Heritage

Text © Philip Wilkinson

Photographs, unless otherwise stated,
© Peter Ashley

Every effort has been made to trace
copyright holders and we apologise in
advance for any unintentional omissions,
which we would be pleased to correct in
any subsequent edition of this book.

First published 2006

10 9 8 7 6 5 4 3 2 1

ISBN-10 1 85074 969 8
ISBN-13 978 1 85074 969 1

Product code 51078

British Library Cataloguing in
Publication data

A CIP catalogue for this book is available
from the British Library

Edited by Janet Hadley

Brought to publication by
Susan Kelleher and René Rodgers,
English Heritage Publishing

Designed by www.walkerjansseune.co.uk

Printed by Butler and Tanner

Page 2: Selfridges department store, Birmingham.
The glazing reflects the pinnacles of the nearby
church of St Martin in the Bull Ring.

Mounting block, the Talbot, Oundle, Northamptonshire

INTRODUCTION

This country has the richest built environment in the world – there are more interesting buildings per square mile here than anywhere else. And, as a nation we love our old buildings. We are inveterate country house and cathedral visitors, we support world-class conservation bodies (governmental, such as English Heritage, and independent, such as the National Trust), we are avid viewers of heritage programmes on television.

But when we are on pilgrimage to the great architectural shrines, we often ignore the less obvious buildings. Many of these – parish churches, fortifications, shops and markets, factories, schools, theatres, railway stations – all have fascinating stories to tell.

During a visit to a great cathedral, few of us pause to notice the architecture of the railway station as we get off the train or the design of the shop where we buy our souvenirs. So this survey of English buildings is organised, not chronologically like most histories of architecture, but by building type, to highlight some of the structures which we often pass by.

The longest chapters in the book are those on churches and houses. They are long for a reason – houses survive from every period since the Normans, while churches go back even further, to Saxon times. So these parts of the book provide an overview of the history of English architecture, with examples of virtually every period and style.

Many of the architectural icons, such as the cathedral at Canterbury and Castle Howard, are here. But there are also plenty of less familiar buildings. Small houses, for example: we present both the charming cottages of our villages, built in local materials using traditional craft skills, and the terraced houses, those very English creations that line the streets of towns from Burnley to Bridgwater. And you will find a wealth of parish churches: England has more of these than any other country, many of breathtaking beauty or with some feature of historical interest.

There follow chapters on a range of other building types. In each case, by placing the famous next to the little known, we hope to open the reader's eye to entire areas of our absorbing built environment. Along the way, we look at buildings that are built purely to be functional alongside those that aim to be beautiful, at the most lavish next to those built with the slenderest of means.

Our selected railway stations, for example, include the great London termini, with their enormous arching train sheds, triumphs of Victorian engineering and masterpieces in the definition of vast spaces. We also feature lesser, but still impressive stations, where the Victorian talent for decoration was given full rein. But, one of our examples is a station that is little more than two corrugated-iron huts. Although even the corrugated-iron huts were built with pride and a certain visual flair – hence our choice – you would not find them in a history of architecture.

Telephone kiosks are our smallest and least regarded buildings. But these traditional red ones have as interesting a history – and as pleasing an appearance – as many larger structures. They were designed by Giles Gilbert Scott with a domed roof that was probably influenced by the work of the 18th-century architect Sir John Soane.

Building types through the ages

Today we live in a world of specialisation and high technology. We are used to a wide range of building types designed to meet specific purposes. Houses are for living in, factories and offices are work places, a pool is somewhere to swim, and so on. Some of these divisions show signs of breaking down – more and more of us work from home, many schools are used by local communities for all sorts of evening activities. There are also interesting recent multi-purpose buildings, such as leisure complexes and arts centres. The predominant pattern, however, persists: one building, one main purpose.

It has not always been like this. In the Middle Ages most people's lives centred on house and church. They worked in the fields or, if they did not, they most likely had a workshop in their home. More goods were sold from market stalls than from shops, courts were held in castle or church, and hospitals were generally in monasteries. Theatre took place in the street or the inn yard; there were few schools, no factories, no railway stations.

In this world a house was a home and a workplace; a church was a meeting place as well as a place of worship and sometimes it contained a schoolroom too. The archetypal medieval building, the castle, was home, workplace, administrative centre, prison, and place of refuge rolled into one.

In the late Middle Ages the feudal system and its castles began to decline, as did the monasteries, which were destined to be dissolved by Henry VIII in the 1530s. At the same time, partly as a result of stronger and richer middle classes (merchants and artisans), more schools were built, the universities were growing, and markets were provided with more permanent buildings. Soon the theatre began to seek permanent homes (though no buildings of the Shakespearian period survive) and more and more almshouses were set up to care for the elderly.

But multi-purpose buildings were still called for. A typical building of the late medieval, Tudor, and Stuart periods was the combined market house and town hall. These buildings, with an open, arched market space on the ground floor and a meeting room above, still adorn many town centres. They were often built by a prominent craft guild in the town and the officials of the guild held their meetings in the upper room. Such guilds often metamorphosed into town councils, so a guildhall became a town hall. Or the hall could be built from scratch by the town, as a town hall from the start.

In the 18th century there was still more diversity in the built environment – and the increasing tendency to build in brick and stone, combined with the fact that these Georgian buildings are relatively

The Market House at Barnard Castle, County Durham, is an elegant 18th-century solution to the challenge of building a combined town hall and market house. The structure's unusual octagonal shape also helps it act as a focus in the centre of the town.

Late Georgian terraces, like this one in South London, are now highly valued, both for their light, well-proportioned interiors and for the contribution they make to our townscape. But it is still all too easy to ignore examples like these, found on the busy Kennington Park Road.

young, has meant that many buildings, and examples of different types, are still standing. Buildings for national government offices and law courts survive from this time. Advances in science, and acts of philanthropy, led to more hospitals. And prisons, built under the influence of prison reformer John Howard, became another common type of building. The 18th century also saw the biggest change of all, the arrival of the industrial revolution and the construction of the first factories, buildings that overturned the lives of workers, enhanced the wealth of manufacturers, transformed the skyline with structures of a new size and shape, and gave birth to whole industrial towns and cities. The consumer goods market exploded, so countless shops were built or upgraded. And towards the end of the century, inns began to adapt to become hotels.

The Victorians extended this specialisation. The 19th century saw more formalised government at every level, burgeoning industry and commerce, and education for all. New town and city halls, more factories and warehouses, public libraries, and thousands of schools were the result. The high street expanded still further, with the construction of shopping arcades, more shops, and glorious, ornate public houses. Transport took off, and the railway boom that started in the 1840s brought a whole new

architecture with it. Health care advanced further, leading to vast hospitals in cities and smaller rural cottage hospitals. A diversifying entertainment industry added a variety of buildings from music halls to concert halls. And the vast growth of the population and, consequently of Victorian towns and cities, meant these buildings appeared in ever greater numbers.

And the expansion continued into the 20th century, which added such types as airports, cinemas, garages, and specialist kinds of factory and power station to the roster of buildings. No doubt the multiplicity of building types will continue to evolve. And although we may concertina more uses into single buildings once more, holding community events in our churches, designing complexes that combine shopping and sports, or working from home, we will still have a varied built environment for the foreseeable future. Our increasing desire to conserve the best buildings from the past will see to this.

There are still thousands of Victorian school buildings in England's towns and villages, testimony to the far-reaching 19th-century revolution in education. This 'Infants' sign at Roade, Northamptonshire, is a reminder that in the 19th century, education became available at all levels, from elementary to secondary.

During the 19th century there was huge expansion in housing, especially in the late Victorian period. The new dwellings, which ranged from the smallest workers' back-to-back cottages to larger middle-class houses like this one of 1899 at Wigston Fields, Leicestershire, sprawled around the outskirts of cities and into the surrounding villages.

By the 1930s many industrial buildings were showpieces of modern design. The horizontal lines, strip windows, and sweeping curves of the 1930s style were well-suited to structures like this one, at the entrance to the Addis Toothbrush Factory in Hertford.

This capital from the Octagon Chapel in Norwich, based on the Corinthian order, is an example of the use of Classical details in a place of worship.

Looking at buildings

There are many ways of looking at a building, and this book, dealing with a kaleidoscope of buildings, looks at them in several different ways. Being aware of many varied kinds of buildings is partly about noticing the small as well as the large, the minor as well as the major. But it also helps to be aware of the different ways that one can think about buildings. This section of the book introduces a few of these ways. Beginning with the most obvious…

Architecture

Traditional architectural history looks at a chronological succession of styles – Tudor followed by Palladian, Palladian followed by baroque, and so on. Our timeline – *see* pages 364–5 – will help you pin down when such styles were in use. It is a fascinating study, and one that tells much about changing tastes and outlooks, about the relationship between England and Europe, and about the influence of one architect on another. It is especially revealing when applied to large, high-status buildings at the cutting edge of architectural fashion. But it also has its limitations.

Medieval builders, for example, probably did not think in terms of style at all. They adapted previous designs and had no notion of a range of alternative styles. As one master cathedral mason once said to me, 'There is no such thing as style. There are only ways to build.'

Even so, architectural history has much to tell about how these ways to build evolved over time. By looking at similar buildings from different periods one can see clearly how masons, architects, and designers (as well as their clients) responded to changing ideas, fashions, and tastes. Such patterns recur as one turns the pages of this book. And armed with a knowledge of these developing fashions, one can see even familiar groups of structures – the church spires that are much-loved features of the landscape of Northamptonshire, for example – in a different light, perceiving their subtle differences and getting perhaps a little closer to the minds of the people who created them.

What is often interesting is not how buildings conform to architectural style, but how they break the rules. While a great cathedral such as York is a perfect example of Gothic – big windows, pointed arches, vaulted ceiling, flying buttresses, the lot –

a small parish church is very different. Built on a shoestring by a local mason, it will probably have no vaulting or flying buttresses. But the arches will be pointed and the window tracery will be recognisably Gothic – the mason has taken what he can use from the style, adapting it to fit local needs.

Similar things happen when the elements of ancient Classical architecture are applied to later buildings. The Classical orders devised by the Greeks and developed by the Romans rely on certain rules of proportion and on key features – for example, the column, topped by a capital, supporting a feature called the entablature which is made up of three horizontal bands, the architrave, frieze, and cornice. Designers in the 19th century applied this model to all sorts of buildings. As the façade of a country house it can work very well. There are countless houses with entrance porticoes resembling (some more than others) the fronts of Classical temples.

But use the orders to design a shop front and things change dramatically. In a way it works. The entablature becomes the fascia, the part of the front that displays the name of the business. The columns sit on either side of the door and windows. But a shop front more often than not has wide windows and a narrow door, producing unequal gaps between the columns and blowing Classical proportions to smithereens. This is not to decry the efforts to adapt. Small shops and great houses belong to different, but related traditions.

Factories, hospitals, and schools and all sorts of other buildings may also have been designed by architects who had to adapt the prevailing styles to suit a specific building type, often one unheard of when Classical and Gothic architecture was first conceived. These architects were often specialists in this process. Frank Matcham, for example, was the premier theatre architect of the late Victorian and Edwardian period. He adapted Classical elements and baroque interior decoration to suit the curving balconies, shallow-domed ceilings, and proscenium arches of contemporary theatre auditoriums. His interiors, all plaster swags and curlicues and masks, set the tone for theatre-as-fantasy-land, creating magical spaces in which the imagination of the audience could play.

William Bradford was the most successful Victorian brewery architect. His buildings, with their

Museums, often grand buildings full of ancient treasures, were an appropriate place for Classical details, like this Ionic column at Oxford's Ashmolean Museum.

Bunches of fruit, flowers, and foliage – adapted from the rococo style of the 18th century – were popular motifs among designers of 'pleasure buildings' such as the Victorian Wilton's Music Hall in London.

ornate towers, steep roofs, and melange of materials, are nearly as fantastic as Matcham's. The same could be said of a number of 19th-century specialists in pub architecture, the likes of H W Rising and F J Eedle, who created an atmosphere of glittering opulence still enjoyed by many drinkers. All these designers understood their fields intimately, and were able to adapt the vast repertoire of 19th-century structure and ornament to create buildings that still take the breath away. It is one of the aims of this book to highlight some of the buildings created by such experts.

Use

Another approach looks at the uses to which buildings have been put. The plan and entire shape of a building is often the consequence of how it is used. Bottle kilns and water towers, windmills and theatres are all the shape they are to house most effectively the functions they accommodate. The Victorians often built prisons with a radial plan so that all the wings could be seen from a central observation point. Their hospitals had a different kind of layout, to provide maximum fresh air and natural light to the wards. Traditional breweries are

tall buildings, because they house a process that relies on gravity, whereas many factories are long and low, to accommodate horizontal production lines. Stables may be little regarded, and they certainly do not have to be grand. England is full of such careful examples of design where just enough effort has been made to lift a simple structure above the mundane.

Many developments in the design of parish churches were responses to changing religious requirements. A medieval church had many uses but its prime purpose was the celebration of the Divine Office and of the Holy Sacraments, especially Mass. Its most sacred space was the chancel, the preserve of the clergy, where the main altar was situated. The medieval chancel, a place of sacred mystery, was separated and partially hidden from the nave by a screen. In the 17th and 18th centuries, by contrast, the sermon became a more important part of religious services and the churches built in this period have a more open plan, good acoustics, and large pulpits.

Even houses changed dramatically in layout over the centuries because the way people lived in them also changed. In the Middle Ages, most people lived in one room; even a noble family had only a hall

The great church of Beverley Minster in Yorkshire is a good example of a building that grew over time, its architectural style evolving on the way. Its east end, begun in around 1230 is in the Early English Gothic style, with many slim lancet windows. By the time the nave was built in the 14th century, a more ornate form of Gothic had evolved, with complex window tracery. Finally the west front and towers were built in the 15th century.

with a central hearth, a single private room or solar, and a service wing containing rooms such as the pantry. At the end of the Middle Ages, comfort and privacy began to be more important to people, who demanded more smaller rooms with fireplaces. The one-room hall house fell out of fashion. Mark Girouard, in his celebrated book, *Life in the English Country House,* charted such developments in one building type, explaining the social customs that gave rise, for example, to great houses in which suites of rooms interconnected, without corridors.

Evolution

Building designs change with function as well as fashion, and the changes are often there to see, in brick and stone. Another way to look at a building, therefore, is to chart how it has evolved over time, gathering clues about the alterations that have taken place to the structure and finding out why these changes were made.

Sometimes, especially in the Middle Ages, buildings took decades or even hundreds of years to come to their finished form. Medieval technology made building a slow process, and gathering the money for a major project such as a great church could sometimes take generations. So a building such as the Minster in Beverley, East Yorkshire, was begun in one phase of Gothic and finished in another, both style and building evolving as the masons progressed and as one generation succeeded the next, bringing new ideas to the building.

The story of a church such as Beverley is one of ordered evolution. The townspeople probably got roughly the building they expected, even if the style changed over time. But other buildings have evolved in a more haphazard way over the years, in an often complex process of change and remodelling. This is partly a matter of repairs, but also of alterations, responding to the way the building was used. Learn to interpret these alterations, and one can begin to read the history of a building and its users.

The changes can be revealing. The medieval inn, for example, developed into its more luxurious cousin, the hotel. And there are still many hotels that betray their origins as old coaching inns – often there are signs of a blocked arch that originally lead to a stable courtyard and now provides space for the lounge or dining room demanded by hotel

customers. Medieval churches often have aisles or transepts that were added after the main body of the building was completed. These were probably not built to house increasing congregations, as modern visitors sometimes assume. Their most likely purpose was to provide space for extra altars at which priests could say regular Masses for the souls of those who left money to the church.

It is easy to think of the changes wrought to buildings as mainly ones of addition. We are a nation of house extenders, after all. But there have also been changes involving partial demolition and reduction in size. Our ruined monasteries, many left to be plundered, became the Tudor equivalents of architectural salvage yards after Henry VIII broke up the monastic orders and confiscated their wealth. It is sad, in a way, to view this destruction through the perspective of more than 400 years. But it was not many years before people began to look at the remains of the monasteries in a romantic way and by the 18th century, aristocrats were actually building false ruins to adorn their estates. So, as often happens in architectural history, in destruction and change came renewal of a kind.

Change of use

Occasionally the use of a building changes radically. We are used to this today, as the pace of social and economic change makes many buildings useless for their original purpose. Hard times on the farm, and the use of new machinery, has rendered many old barns redundant. So hundreds of barns have been converted for other uses, from light industrial units to luxurious houses. Developments in business and technology leave industrial buildings empty. So flour mills become arts centres and the Bankside Power Station has become London's Tate Modern. Dwindling congregations have abandoned many Nonconformist chapels. Those that have not been demolished do duty as furniture warehouses, auction rooms, or even garages.

We should not think of change of use as a purely modern phenomenon. After the destruction of the monasteries in the 16th century, the buildings of many abbeys were turned into houses by the aristocracy and gentry. The old archbishop's palace at Charing in Kent became a farm in the 17th century. Many a tavern has been turned into a house, and the

This building in East London was originally put up in 1715 as the Ironmongers' Almshouses. In 1910–14 it was converted into the Geffrye Museum, with a series of galleries displaying domestic interiors of different periods.

other way around. Buildings are usually large, long lasting artefacts that require considerable cost and effort to put up. Change of use is very often a better, less costly, and more environmentally friendly alternative to demolition and building anew.

Social history

These approaches, which look at both use and structure, show how buildings also open up avenues of social history, and the social implications of old buildings are yet another facet of their interest. Country house visitors were once all too apt to look at buildings such as Holkham Hall in Norfolk or Castle Howard, North Yorkshire, solely as glorified art galleries, paying attention only to their contents and glorying in the glamour of it all. Things are different now.

The stones of country houses tell all sorts of stories. An Elizabethan house might have been built by a noble family in the hope that the queen might stay there, an event which would increase the status and power of her hosts while it sapped their wealth. Its decoration might be full of motifs that indicate

the builders' aspirations, from heraldic devices to religious symbols. A Palladian or Georgian house might be part residence, part art gallery, a home for a collection of artworks and antiquities collected on that aristocratic rite of passage, the Grand Tour, on which young gentlemen of the 18th and 19th centuries travelled across Europe, picking up fashionable masterpieces. Victorian country houses by contrast, were often devoted to the less rarefied pleasures of the billiard table and the smoking room.

Country houses were communities too. The home of the rich, each estate was also the workplace for dozens – sometimes hundreds – of servants, gardeners, farm labourers, craftsmen, and builders. The 'offices' attached to a large Victorian country house to service it often outnumbered the rooms of the house itself, and comprised a maze of pantries, larders, laundries, still rooms, boot rooms, and lamp rooms. To celebrate a great house should not be to indulge in nostalgia about the privileged lifestyles of pampered grandees, but to appreciate the art, craft, and sheer hard work of those who made it all possible. Mindful of this fact, custodians of country houses are now as likely to display the kitchen complex or stable block or home farm as to show the state rooms. We are beginning, at last, to appreciate the lives of the workers as well as those of the handful of privileged people whom they served.

Even a middle-class London house was once full of servants. The novelist Virginia Woolf remembered the writer Lytton Strachey's house at 46 Gordon Square in the early 20th century: 'Eleven people aged between eight and sixty lived there, and were waited upon by seven servants, while various old women and lame men did odd jobs with rakes and pails by day.'

It is customary – and often helpful – to think of buildings and other artefacts from the past as indicating a lot about the social status of their residents. So big country houses are high status buildings, back-to-back workers' houses are low status, and tall terraced town houses are somewhere in between. All of which is true. But it should never mask the fact that all sorts of other people, such as those who laid the bricks and did the plastering, were intimately involved in the creation of our built heritage. They are the often forgotten creators whose work this book celebrates.

The old Archbishop's
Palace at Charing in
Kent became a farm
more than 300 years
ago. The house still
clearly incorporates
some of the medieval
walls together with
a number of later
additions.

Some of the most interesting fittings in a church are often the monuments. One wall of the chancel of the small parish church of St Mary at Swinbrook, Oxfordshire, is taken up by monuments to the local Fettiplace family. These are the Fettiplaces of the late 17th century, carved by Oxford sculptor William Bird, reclining in comfort on their marble shelves.

The craft of the bricklayer could produce telling details when specially shaped or different-coloured bricks were used. Keble College, Oxford, designed by the Victorian architect William Butterfield, is full of bold brickwork patterns.

Buildings throw light on virtually every area of social history – the rise of industry, the story of education, the development of health care, the history of entertainment – all can be illuminated by the fabric of the buildings that housed these activities. We are lucky that so many such buildings exist. Ruined monasteries reveal the extraordinary importance of religion in medieval times, but can alert us to the way monks provided social services, such as education and health care. Houses in Bournville, Birmingham, and Port Sunlight, Cheshire, show us much about both the values of their philanthropic builders and the way of life of the workers who lived in them. And, should we need reminding, the façades of old buildings often act as displays for carved images of people closely associated with their history: Bluecoat schools with statues of pupils in their uniforms, prison gateways with busts of the great prison reformer John Howard, the images of local heroes who gave buildings to their town. All remind us of the human stories behind our buildings.

Details

It was an architect – the German modernist master Ludwig Mies van der Rohe – who said that God is in the details, and the details of a building can be highly revealing. For one thing, details can be delightfully decorative, and they can be the places to start if one wants to appreciate the art of the craft workers – carvers, plasterers, painters, glaziers, and so on – who add the special touches to all but the most frugal buildings. Discovering the stone carvings in a medieval church, the tiling in a Victorian pub, or the plasterwork in an Edwardian theatre, such things can be among the greatest joys of looking at old buildings.

More than this, such details reveal meanings. A town hall such as the one at Northampton can tell the story of civic prosperity in carved relief panels. The medieval church told Bible stories in wall paintings and stained glass. The stories of forgotten Victorian railway companies are behind symbols that survive on some of our stations. Carvings of comic and tragic masks signpost a theatre, images of extinguished torches indicate a mausoleum.

Fittings

Sometimes, a building may have changed function, but the symbols, or other evocative fittings remain.

And this book pays occasional tribute to the revealing bits and pieces that gather around buildings – old signs or advertisements for forgotten companies; items of packaging and memorabilia bearing the name or image of a building; fixtures and fittings such as station clocks and church pulpits. Such items can transform a building. A structure that is unremarkable as architecture – a small shop, for example, or a rural garage – can be lifted above the mundane by interesting lettering or by signs that have survived from a few decades ago. This is another way in which buildings can add inestimably to the local scene.

Churches are storehouses of fixtures and fittings, such as stained glass, wall paintings, monuments, fonts, and furnishings, which add to the historical interest and to the display of craftsmanship which is one of the joys of parish churches everywhere.

Because some of this material was produced in

a Catholic tradition that was rejected – and indeed despised – by many in the 17th century, much of it has been swept away. Parish churches in the Middle Ages would have been a riot of coloured wall paintings and stained glass, and a church was a three-dimensional metaphor for the City of God, populated with sculptures and carvings of the heavenly host. In a few places one can begin to grasp what this would have been like. The virtually complete set of medieval windows in Fairford, Gloucestershire; the figures of angels that look down from the roofs of East Anglian churches such as March, Cambridgeshire; wall paintings such as the recently restored doom in Coventry – put all these together and one gets some idea of how a medieval church would have been decorated. There are also fascinating survivals, in later churches, including big three-decker pulpits and box pews from the Georgian period.

Objects such as these seem far from the usual fare encountered in books about architecture and building. Yet an ambitious architect very often wants to design everything in a building, from furniture to key escutcheons, and a few of them – Victorians, designers of the Arts and Crafts movement, and modern practitioners – have fulfilled this ambition. They know that such apparent ephemera are more important than they seem. Whether part of an architectural master plan or random add-ons acquired over the years, they are vital clues to the way a building has been used, to the lives of those who have lived, worked, or worshipped there.

Environment

No building is an island, and the position of a building in its surrounding landscape or townscape is another important aspect of our architecture. On one level, this is easy to appreciate. Few objects look more at home in their landscape than a group of farm buildings, constructed from stone or timber from the locality. Small churches, granite in Cornwall, limestone in the Cotswolds, and so on across the country, make a similar impact. Few experiences are more delightful than a walk through the constantly varied vistas of a city such as Oxford. Few marriages of building and setting are as heaven-made as the cathedral close at Salisbury. In each case, building and setting complement each other to perfection.

But the story goes deeper than this because buildings are built where they are for a purpose. The visual effect may be planned, such as a Regency square, or the result of a long evolution, such as a Cornish fishing village. But the placing of each building has its own logic and tells its own tale.

Beautifully planned developments in towns such as Cheltenham, Gloucestershire, serenely peaceful now, are testimony to the rivalries of property speculators. A Yorkshire field barn, apparently in the middle of nowhere, can tell the story of a regime of husbandry in which hay was gathered from nearby meadows and stored on the spot, in the same building where the cattle that ate it also sheltered. A handsome lighthouse is sited at exactly that point on a headland so that its light can be seen for miles. The relationship between building and site can be a matter of livelihood, or of life and death.

Signs and lettering play a huge part in the visual impact of many buildings, especially shops. Bold white capitals stand out on the rich red of the blind pulled down over this butcher's shop window in Uppingham, Rutland. An old RAC car park sign adds to the typographical mix.

At Wigmore Castle, Herefordshire, an innovative conservation scheme was employed by English Heritage. Amongst those involved in the project was an ecologist, who ensured that there was minimal disturbance to the habitats of flora and fauna on and among the building's ruined walls.

Conservation

The condition of our buildings, especially our listed buildings, is a perennial cause for concern. In spite of the national enthusiasm for heritage and the major achievements of pressure groups and conservation bodies, the buildings at risk register maintained by English Heritage usually contains around 1,400 entries. The problem has expanded hugely as we have learned to value relatively recent buildings such as London's Royal Festival Hall as well as those from the distant past.

And conservation is neither cheap nor easy. It entails painstaking research and planning, well honed craft skills, and a vision for the building's future. All of this takes time, too. For a large building, even the preliminary work – the surveys, conservation plans, specialist reports on the state of specific materials or finishes, access studies, costings, grant applications, and the rest – can take years.

If some of our old buildings are in crisis, there is now more support for owners and custodians of historic buildings than ever before. It is heartening that this support starts at the top. The government's statutory body for advising on the historic environment, English Heritage, provides advice,

fosters understanding of the past, and cares for a large portfolio of historic buildings and monuments. It is involved in scholarly research, recording the historic environment, archive keeping, and education.

There are also numerous organisations in the voluntary sector that work for the preservation of historic buildings, supporting research and conservation or actively caring for certain types of building. One of the first was the Society for the Protection of Ancient Buildings (SPAB), founded in the 19th century by the artist and social reformer, William Morris, in response to unsympathetic church restorations. The Society is still active in fostering the most sensitive forms of conservation. Then there is the National Trust, an independent charity set up in 1895 that now owns hundreds of buildings (and vast tracts of countryside), which it cares for and makes accessible to the public.

A number of specialist societies support buildings from particular historical periods. The Georgian Group, the Victorian Society, and the Twentieth Century Society were all set up at different times, when buildings from their chosen era were neglected and unfashionable. Thanks to them, the best architecture from these periods is now in better shape than before, and they continue their work as campaigners, pressure groups, and educators. Individual building types – such as cinemas, theatres, and industrial buildings – all have their support groups. One of the most notable is the Churches Conservation Trust, which looks after scores of churches no longer required for regular worship, buildings that in earlier times might have been demolished.

Another trust, the Landmark Trust, applies lateral thinking to a growing roster of buildings. It takes on threatened structures and converts them into holiday homes, which are let to fund their upkeep. Follies, garden buildings, water towers, industrial buildings, a Martello tower, and many conventional houses have been given the Landmark Trust treatment. They allow people to experience historical buildings at a more intimate level than is possible during a normal visit to a castle or country house. And they increase public awareness and understanding of such buildings as a result.

Such organisations, together with visionary

The former Carreras Cigarette Factory near London's Mornington Crescent tube station is an Egyptian-inspired Art Deco masterpiece of the late 1920s highlighting the company's Black Cat brand of cigarettes. The building, which now contains offices, was beautifully restored in 1999 with the replacement of the black cat statues and reliefs that were part of the original design by M E and O H Collins and A G Porri.

property owners, have the skill and courage to take on the challenges of conservation. All can act decisively if they have the determination and the right vision for the future of their building. For above all, conserved buildings need to have a useful role if they are not to fall rapidly into disrepair once more. So some of the most successful conservation schemes have involved finding new uses for old buildings – converting an old church in Oxford into a college library, turning industrial buildings in Birmingham's jewellery quarter into offices and studios, accommodating shops and art galleries in the warehouses of Liverpool's Albert Dock.

Surprise

Some buildings, though, do not fit easily into any category, and defy any rules we might have about how to look at them. These are mostly the follies – buildings put up to surprise the beholder and enhance the landscape. Often, we are happy to see them purely as examples of some social stereotype like the English eccentric. Mock medieval ruins, Egyptian pavilions, and copies of the Tower of the Winds in Athens certainly seem eccentric enough, although when we know their stories, they usually seem

slightly less bizarre. In fact, these are exemplary buildings because they pull us up short, make us look more closely, force us to ask questions, and show the surrounding landscape in a new light.

So there are many ways of looking at a building, though some buildings yield more interest and information when seen through one set of spectacles than another. This book, therefore, varies its perspective from one building to the next. Some buildings are included because they are key monuments in the history of architecture; some because they are good examples of a specific style or period; some because they are stunningly decorated; some because they reveal aspects of social or industrial history; some because of the way they fit into the landscape; some because, although modest in themselves, they provide one of those uplifting moments of unexpected discovery that make the English scene a constant delight.

This variety means that the buildings are described in different terms. But the intention is always to encourage the reader to look anew, and always to be inquisitive about buildings whether looking at castles or aircraft hangars, palaces or pillboxes, cathedrals or bicycle sheds.

St Lawrence, Diddington, Cambridgeshire

PARISH CHURCHES

Probably no country in the world has a richer stock of old parish churches than Britain, and our churches are among the most interesting of all our ancient buildings. Several thousand of them are medieval, or at least partly so. They are a legacy from the time when England was a Catholic country, affording us a treasury of structures that gives unparalleled insight into the art, crafts, architecture, building techniques, beliefs, and ideas current in England between the Saxon and early Tudor periods.

In the 1530s there was a change in the English position on religion. Henry VIII wanted to divorce his wife, Catherine of Aragon, but the pope would not grant him permission. Henry got around the problem by severing England's links with Rome and appointing himself head of the church in England. There followed several decades of religious dispute and intermittent strife, at the end of which the English church turned its back on its Catholic heritage and became Protestant.

Church design evolved to accommodate Protestant priorities such as the need for good acoustics for sermons, and this change coincided with a turn towards Classical architecture, which was well suited to design plain but elegant box-like churches focused on the pulpit. Catholics meanwhile became a small and persecuted minority until a series of Acts of Parliament gave them back most of their rights in the 18th and 19th centuries. The medieval churches remained in use by the Church of England and only in the 19th century were Catholic churches built again in any numbers.

Although there are some stunning exceptions from all historical periods, most parish churches are small, modest buildings, and most were not built in one go, but have been altered and extended over the centuries. There were a number of reasons for this steady organic growth over the years – changes in liturgical or priestly priorities, repairs to decaying fabric, the need to provide larger accommodation for a growing population, the need for extra altars (for example to say Masses for the souls of specific parishioners), the response to a gift or bequest from a rich family, the continuing desire to improve and beautify a building dedicated to the glory of God.

Benefactions were rarely sufficient to rebuild a whole church, though when they were, the results can be outstanding. But more often than not, the result of all this building activity was an architectural hotchpotch. There are parish churches with a Norman nave, 13th-century chancel, 14th-century spire, aisles and porches added in the 15th century, a collection of 18th-century monuments, and a Victorian vestry.

Medieval parish churches are very much the product of their locality. They were usually built with local materials by local masons and they followed architectural fashions rather than setting them. Many Cornish medieval churches, for example, are built of granite; their carvings are of a different cast to those in regions where there is limestone, a rock much more yielding to the chisel.

But the local influence does not stop there. Regional styles and techniques developed as masons passed on skills to their sons and apprentices. And so specific regions or counties are known for different kinds of church architecture. There was an outstanding group of sculptors at work in Herefordshire churches in the 12th century. Somerset is the county for elegant, late medieval towers, Northamptonshire for spires.

This local distinctiveness was diluted after the Reformation. With the adoption of the Classical style, architects became interested in churches. At the same time communications were becoming better, and styles travelled farther and faster. So churches with Tuscan columns and pediments crop up all over the country. And by Victorian times, church architects were often on the move, taking on restoration work as well as designing new buildings all over the country. They were influenced by the regional styles of their medieval forebears, so that one can find Victorian spires in the Northamptonshire style, poking up amongst the red-brick houses of London suburbs.

The delights of our parish churches are almost endless. In spite of time and the over-zealous efforts of many Victorian restorers (architects are gentler and more circumspect now) much of interest survives. But with small congregations and a system of care and maintenance that places most of the responsibility on local parishes, many of these enjoyable, absorbing, and precious buildings find their fate hanging in the balance. They deserve our interest and our generosity. There is usually a box for visitors' donations near the door.

Saxon parish churches

Christianity spread through Britain as the result of missionary work by churchmen such as Augustine, who was based in Canterbury, and monks such as Benedict Biscop, who founded monasteries at Monkwearmouth (*c* 675) and Jarrow (*c* 685) in County Durham, the latter home to the celebrated historian Bede. Most of their churches were built of wood and have long since perished (one wooden Saxon church remains at Greensted, Essex). But some stone churches were built and a few still stand today. The earliest, which date from the 7th century, are mostly tall, narrow buildings with little

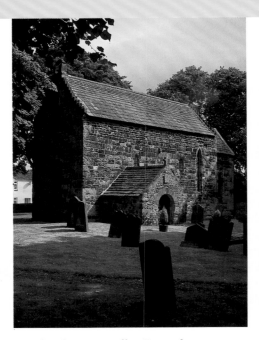

St John the Evangelist, Escomb
County Durham

Tall, narrow and plain, Escomb is the most complete Northumbrian church to survive from the late 7th century. The walls of the nave and tiny chancel are original and are built of massive, well-shaped blocks. Most of the windows are later medieval additions and make the interior much lighter than it would have been in Bede's time. Four small Saxon windows survive, however, set high on the north and south walls, two round-headed and two with straight tops, to give some indication of how the interior would have been lit. The tall, round-headed chancel arch is another impressive original feature.

All Saints, Brixworth
Northamptonshire

The church at Brixworth was built in around 675 by monks from Peterborough. The builders reused thin Roman bricks to make the arches in the nave and the round heads of doorways and windows. In an area where there was little good stone to make voussoirs, these bricks provided a good material to form the curves needed for the arches. In the 10th or 11th century, the church was altered – side chambers (known as porticus) were removed, leaving a series of blocked arches on either side of the nave, and the apse was rebuilt. In addition there was also originally a central crossing tower and, at the west end, where the present tower is located, there was a two-storey entrance porch or narthex.

So although much altered and smaller than it originally was, Brixworth remains one of the most impressive Saxon churches, wider than other surviving churches of the period and keeping something of the atmosphere of the Roman basilicas on which such buildings were based. The church is dominated by many openings – windows, doors, and arches – most of which are round-headed in the typical Saxon manner. It is a very special survival from the time of the famed Mercian king, Offa.

An animal-head corbel of the early 9th century at St Mary, Deerhurst, shows the skill of a Saxon sculptor. The contours of the creature's face are mapped with sweeping lines that show considerable confidence.

in the way of decoration. Later Saxon churches, some rebuilt after attacks by the Vikings in the 9th and 10th centuries, can be more ornate, with decorative features such as pilaster strips relieving otherwise plain walls.

St Mary, Deerhurst
Gloucestershire

This church shows more than one period of Saxon building. Blocked openings abound, pointing to relocated windows and demolished side chambers. But many Saxon features remain, including some interesting carvings and this unusual double, triangular-headed window between the nave and a room in the tower. Triangular-topped openings like this, sometimes also used for doorways, are not uncommon in the late Saxon period, but few display the elegant carving of this example at Deerhurst.

Odda's Chapel, Deerhurst
Gloucestershire

A short walk from the Deerhurst church of St Mary's is Odda's Chapel, a late Saxon building that is uniquely documented. Because of a surviving dedication stone (now in the Ashmolean Museum, Oxford), we know that the chapel was dedicated on 12 April 1056 as a memorial to Aelfric, the brother of Earl Odda, who died in 1053. But at some point after this worship stopped in the chapel and the building was absorbed into the neighbouring farmhouse. It was forgotten until 1885 when builders doing repairs discovered the Saxon round-headed window and long-and-short quoins. The structure of the chapel had been little altered since the 11th century.

All Saints, Earls Barton
Northamptonshire

The tower at Earls Barton shows what late Saxon masons could achieve when given the scope. Details such as the turned shafts in the openings, the vertical pilaster strips, horizontal string-courses, and blind triangular and semicircular arches have been said to be based on contemporary woodworking styles. Perhaps, but another Saxon hallmark, the long-and-short quoin stones at the corners, comes from the vocabulary of the stonemason and makes a decorative feature out of a structural element. Together, these diverse features form a quintessentially late Saxon scheme, unaltered for around a thousand years except for the addition of battlements.

The long-and-short quoins on the tower at All Saints, Earls Barton, are a characteristic detail of high-quality Saxon masonry.

See also

Early Norman parish churches, 28

Early Norman parish churches

The period after the Norman conquest saw a building boom in England. Many of the new structures were churches, built as the Norman invaders made their mark and cemented their power base partly by appointing bishops from across the Channel to run the English church.

No doubt countless Saxon wooden churches were replaced in stone and many new churches were built. As a result, hundreds of English churches still contain some Norman masonry, although most of these have been modified in the succeeding centuries. Early Norman churches show the influence of the

**St Andrew, Winterborne Tomson
Dorset**

The simplest form of early Norman church consists of a single cell or space that contains both nave and chancel. Here the east end is an apse and there is an unusual timber-framed ceiling. The Normans must have built many churches like this, but most have been altered beyond recognition. Rounded chancels were usually extended to make square east ends in the 13th century, and many parish churches were expanded with the addition of aisles. But here, the original shape of the building has survived. There were few alterations – not even an east window – until one wall was pierced

with larger windows in the late Middle Ages and the church was furnished with box pews in the early 18th century. Such buildings are precious survivors. Architect A R Powys – a member of the family that also produced Dorset's celebrated literary sons, the Powys brothers – recognised the building's qualities and restored it for the SPAB in 1931. He is commemorated with a wall plaque in the church.

**St Botolph, Hardham
East Sussex**

Wall paintings from the early 12th century cover nearly all the walls of the church at Hardham. They were painted over at some time in the Middle Ages and were rediscovered and restored in 1866. They have faded, but give an idea of the kind of decoration that would have covered a Norman church. The subjects come from the Bible and show Old Testament characters such as Adam and Eve, plus the Annunciation and Visitation, episodes from the life of Christ, the torments of the damned, and images of the apostles and episodes from the life of St George.

architecture of William the Conqueror's homeland – plain round arches, circular piers with simple capitals and bases, round-headed windows and doorways. Where money and the skill of the masons permitted, there might be a stone ceiling in the form of a rounded barrel vault.

St John's Chapel in the Tower of London is a perfect small place of worship in the early Norman style.

St James, Selham
East Sussex

When the Normans arrived in 1066, architecture did not change overnight. There were still native masons at work, and the buildings of the late 11th and early 12th centuries can sometimes exhibit a bewildering mixture of styles. The chancel arch at Selham is a case in point. The capitals display a variety of motifs. The interlacing snakes and animal head look Saxon, as do the abstract interlace patterns. The spiral design looks more like an attempt at an imperfectly understood Classical motif, such as an Ionic or Composite capital. The arch itself, with its roll-moulding, looks Norman. The resulting mixture is bizarre but full of life.

St Margaret, Hales
Norfolk

This little thatched church, with round tower, nave, and apsidal chancel, looks early Norman in its simplicity. The occasional remaining narrow, round-headed windows like those on the lower levels of the tower also have an early appearance and a blocked window visible inside the tower may even be late Saxon. The round tower itself is quite a common feature in Norfolk, where flint and other small stones lent themselves well to curved walls. Such round towers usually date to the early Middle Ages, and this one is no exception. Like most Norman churches, the building was altered several times later in the Middle Ages, although its isolated position shielded it from the attentions of the more enthusiastic Victorian restorers. The ornate doorway, with its recessed orders, is clearly late Norman, and larger windows were set in the nave walls in the Gothic period to let in more light. Inside are fragments of early wall paintings including an image of St Christopher, a reminder of the once colourful effect of the interior.

Rubble masonry laid in a herringbone pattern is common in the walls of Saxon churches, as here at St James, Selham.

See also

Late Norman parish churches, 30
Norman greater churches, 66
Norman houses, 114
Great towers, 170

Late Norman parish churches

During the 12th century, Norman architecture became more elaborate. Churches display more complex plans, sometimes with a series of spaces – nave, choir, and chancel – separated by arches and leading the eye towards the high altar. Instead of plain or simply moulded arches, the openings were decorated with often extravagant repeated carved motifs. The most common of these motifs was the zigzag or chevron, which appears around doorways, arches and, in the most highly decorated churches,

St Michael, Wadenhoe
Northamptonshire

Late Norman architecture is not all outlandish carving and rich detail. Often, the Normans built simply and economically, with just the odd detail to show the modern observer when they were at work. The late Norman remains at Wadenhoe are mainly in the tower, where the round-headed openings point to a 12th-century date. As usual, this structure has evolved over the years. Further windows with pointed heads were added later, probably in the 13th century, as was the simple saddleback roof.

St Michael, Stewkley
Buckinghamshire

Stewkley is a church of the 1140s with three cells, the nave and square-ended chancel separated by a choir over which is a squat square tower. This is a common late Norman layout but Stewkley is special because it has survived with few alterations – for example there are plenty of round-headed Norman windows still in place, some surrounded by zigzag carving, as here on the west front. There is also a tower, a precious survival because many Norman towers collapsed or became unsafe and were replaced. Inside there are broad arches with zigzags, shafts with scalloped capitals, and a vaulted chancel.

St John, Elkstone
Gloucestershire

Around 1170, the masons completed this small Cotswold church with its tiny cross-vaulted choir and chancel. Low, thick shafts with scalloped capitals support massive arches adorned with zigzags. The pellet motif was used on the hood-mould of the large arch while the masons chose a rare pattern, recalling the crenellations of a castle wall, for the exterior moulding around the east window; inside, it is surrounded by zigzag, to match the chancel arch. Above the choir there was originally a square tower, a small version of the one at Stewkley. But during the Middle Ages this must have collapsed and been taken down.

even windows. Other details, such as capitals, were also more ornate, with designs such as volutes and animal carvings. Even in modest parish churches, the doorway, as the entrance to the sacred space, is often singled out for lavish decorative treatment.

Saints Mary and David, Kilpeck
Herefordshire

The red sandstone church at Kilpeck is perhaps the most dazzling of all smaller Norman buildings. This is because of the perfectly preserved decorative scheme, a riot of carving with figures, mythical beasts, zigzags, beakheads, outlandish corbels, and astrological symbols. Astounding as it seems, it is the masterpiece of a whole school of Herefordshire sculpture, work which survives in smaller fragmentary doses – a font here and carved doorway there – in mostly remote parish churches elsewhere across the county. Scholars have looked far and wide for sources that might have influenced the sculpture at Kilpeck and the other Herefordshire

churches and parallels have been found with carvings in France on the route to the shrine of Santiago de Compostela in northern Spain. Highlights at Kilpeck are the mythical beasts at the west end, the rows of corbels that run around the church below the eaves, and the figures that make up the shafts of the chancel arch. But most magnificent of all is the church's great south doorway. Zigzag, beakhead, and zodiacal symbols adorn its arch. A vigorous flowering plant (a Herefordshire tree of life) fills the semi-circular tympanum. Coiling monsters run up the sides, while the shafts are populated with armed figures who step through a forest of curling stone interlace.

St Mary, Barton on Humber
Lincolnshire

At the end of the 12th century, parish church masons began to be influenced by the Gothic style of architecture that was already taking hold in the cathedrals. They began to use pointed arches instead of the semicircular ones they had long favoured. But they did not always make an abrupt change from one style to another and sometimes liked to keep the more familiar Norman decorative motifs. So some churches were built in a transitional style, in which pointed arches are decorated with zigzag carving. This arcade at Barton on Humber, with its beautifully crisp carving, is a good example of the style.

A corbel table – a row of carved corbels running all the way around the eaves of the building – adorns the upper walls of the church at Kilpeck. These three corbels show the rich mixture of human and animal heads depicted.

See also

Early Norman parish churches, 28
Norman greater churches, 66
Norman houses, 114
Great towers, 170

Early English parish churches

The Gothic style, with its pointed arches, began to be introduced to England in cathedrals such as Canterbury in the late 12th century. By the early 13th century, the style was being used in parish churches too. To begin with it was a style with an emphasis on simplicity – slender, single-light lancet windows were the norm. The extravagant zigzagging ornamentation of the Normans was replaced with more restrained forms and arches were often deeply moulded. Later masons developed larger more complex windows, letting in more light and providing scope for pattern-making with mullions and tracery.

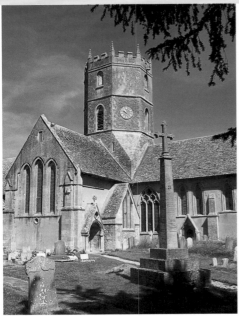

**St Mary, Uffington
Berkshire**

Pairs and triplets of lancet windows dominate the exterior of this church of the mid-13th century. A continuous band of stone runs around much of the church, rising to become the hood-mould above these windows and pulling them together visually. Another band runs just below the windows. A simple device, this use of stone bands must have given the building great unity before the walls were pierced with extra windows to let in more light in the later Middle Ages. Even so, the effect, with pointed-topped buttresses, roundels for consecration crosses, and the group of lancets, is still one of great elegance. The eight-sided tower is a charming and unusual feature.

Its lower storey was originally the base for a spire, but this was destroyed during a storm in the 18th century. Instead of replacing the spire, the 18th-century parishioners opted to extend the tower by another storey – hence the slightly different design of the upper openings. Another unusual feature is the porch in the wall of the south transept. This may indicate a privileged access point from a nearby house belonging to Abingdon Abbey. A moulded arch topped with a quatrefoil and an ornate cross makes a delightful entrance to this porch.

**St Mary, Eaton Bray
Bedfordshire**

Early Gothic architecture is often about lines – lines that lead the eye up piers and shafts and arches towards the roof and towards heaven. In a cathedral, a high vault often provides the climax of this vision, but parish churches are rarely vaulted. But a profusion of shafts and multiple mouldings on the arches can create an equally uplifting effect, as in the interior at Eaton Bray. The aisles here were built in two phases. The south aisle came first, probably in about 1220, and its piers are eight-sided and plain. It was with the north aisle, some 20 years later, that the more elaborate style, with piers clustered with eight shafts each and topped with stiff-leaf capitals, produced the most memorable architecture.

This beam end and corbel at St Mary, Eaton Bray, remind us that medieval parish churches were originally full of colour. The bright painting and gilding is modern, but in keeping with the way colour was used in the Middle Ages.

St Mary, West Walton
Norfolk

St Mary, Stone
Kent

Both the detached tower and the main body of this spacious church are full of high-quality details from around 1240. The porch, with its generous entrance arch, is flanked by eight-sided pinnacles, each topped with a tiny spire and each surrounded with lancet-shaped blind arcading. But its most impressive feature is the profusion of decorative detailing around the archway and along the walls. The entrance arch is made up of deeply cut mouldings, one of which is carved with the dog-tooth pattern that the early Gothic masons favoured. This pattern is repeated on the hood-mould of the arch and between the shafts that support it. The wall on either side is enlivened by blind, lancet-shaped arches.

The detached bell tower at West Walton is a remarkable building in its own right. Apart from the parapet and pinnacles on top it is entirely 13th century and is full of Gothic effects at their grandest. The upper storeys are covered in blind arcading with lancet openings on the first floor. The level above displays openings with the earliest form of tracery, plate tracery, in which a pair of lancets are combined and the space above is pierced with a single quatrefoil.

Few chancels are more glorious than the one at Stone, a church built in the late 13th century, apparently by masons who also worked at Westminster Abbey. Outside there are windows with superb geometrical tracery. Inside, the chancel has arcading with its trefoiled arches and areas covered with spiralling leafy carving; the nave has smaller windows, still in the Early English style.

See also

Early English parish churches, next page
Early English greater churches, 70

Early English parish churches (continued)

Two parts of the parish church received a great deal of attention in the 13th century – the chancel and the tower. The upkeep of the chancel was the responsibility of the clergy (the laity looked after the nave) and in this period liturgy was becoming more complex and priests had to keep their chancels properly equipped with everything from plate to books.

Another important part of the church was the tower and in richer parishes this was sometimes adorned in the 13th century with a spire. Early English spires – developing from chunky near-pyramids to more slender shapes – form a lasting contribution to our landscape and townscape.

St Mary, Barton on Humber
Lincolnshire

This church has a porch with an outstanding opening in the Early English style of around 1275. This is a high-status entrance displaying a variety of motifs from this period of Gothic architecture. On either side is a trio of slim shafts, each topped with weathered capitals with the stiff-leaf carving so loved by masons of the 13th century. These shafts support several orders of arches, deeply moulded to allow the sunlight to pick out their lines as a series of contrasting bands of stone and shadow. One of these orders has extra decoration in the form of dog-tooth moulding.

St Laurence, Wyck Rissington
Gloucestershire

This tiny Cotswold church was consecrated after a major rebuilding of chancel and tower in 1269. The work was commissioned by the monks of Eynsham Abbey in Oxfordshire, who controlled the living. They clearly wanted to follow the 13th-century trend for chancel upgrades in this period and had the resources to produce something more elaborate than a plain wall with a few lancet windows. So this small church contains work of surprising sophistication and originality. The east end is lit with pairs of lancet windows with a star-like window above each pair and a string-course to box them in.

Low buttresses outside give a little extra strength at the corners but are mainly for show. The whole ensemble is a striking and rather unusual piece of Gothic design. Inside, these windows look much more conventional. Because they are deeply recessed and topped with a typical Gothic hood-mould, they look much more unified. The deep splay also helps them to cast more light into the chancel to make a satisfying interior wall – the mason at Wyck Rissington was clearly a skilled designer.

Carved label stops at either end of window hood-moulds gave scope to the Gothic carver at St Laurence, Wyck Rissington.

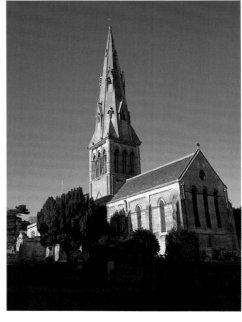

St John the Baptist, Barnack
Northamptonshire

One of the earliest of all English spires was built on top of the Saxon tower at Barnack in the early 13th century. This rather stumpy structure rests on an eight-sided storey, pierced by bell openings with one of the simplest forms of tracery, known as Y-tracery from the pattern made by its bars. These openings are the only place where there is much decoration. The rest – both spire and corner pinnacles – are quite plain. There is only a hint of the scope that masons will later find for making the spire a feature with the most refined decoration.

St Mary, Raunds
Northamptonshire

This church has the most typical 13th-century form of spire. It is called a broach spire because of the four broaches, or half-pyramids, one at each corner of the base. Here the tower is also in the Early English mode, with its blind arcading and twin-light bell openings. The spire itself was rebuilt in the 19th century, but along the original lines. It is lit with tiny traceried windows called lucarnes, which as well as letting in light also ventilate the spire's wooden structure. The mason has given the design added interest by placing the lucarnes on alternate faces of the spire.

St Mary, Ketton
Rutland

This late 13th-century spire is very elegant. The mason has used similar alternating lucarnes to those at St Mary, Raunds, but here they are given much more emphasis – they are quite large in proportion to the spire itself and each has a miniature roof that juts out proudly against the skyline. Bands of stone are used to emphasise the meeting of each face of the spire and to define the ridges of the broaches. Statues in small niches complete the composition. The greater complexity seen in this spire points the way to the 14th century (its building must have straddled the two centuries) and to the still more elaborate spires of the Decorated Gothic style.

See also

Early English parish churches, previous page
Early English greater churches, 70

Decorated parish churches

At the beginning of the 14th century, church architecture began to take a new direction. Although the overall Gothic framework of pointed arches and window tracery remained, buildings took on a more sinuous, organic appearance.

The resulting architecture became known as Decorated, a name that reflects the highly ornate character of many of the buildings, covered as they often are with new kinds of foliage and floral decoration, niches for statuary, and pinnacles

St Patrick, Patrington
East Yorkshire

Few parish churches come close in quality to Patrington, built almost in one go in the first half of the 14th century. It is a cruciform church, with the spacious transepts giving room for extra altars. Outside, curvilinear window tracery and buttresses topped with crocketed pinnacles are the repeated motifs of the Decorated style. These buttresses are important structurally as well as decoratively, because some of the internal spaces are vaulted, and the vaults needed more support than the walls, filled with generous windows, can give. The graceful spire was added later, when the Decorated style had given way to Perpendicular.

St Andrew, Heckington
Lincolnshire

A Decorated church that is virtually all in the one style, Heckington is an aisled building with a west tower. The building is full of the ornate details that typify the Decorated style – a fine spire, elaborate window tracery, buttresses with crockets, and pinnacles. The south porch is one of the most impressive features, the doorway framed by a pair of buttresses incorporating image niches and crockets. The space between doorway and roof line is also filled with carving, with a series of figures leading up to Christ (a replacement figure in front of foliage).

All Saints, Hawton
Nottinghamshire

Here the chancel was rebuilt by Sir Robert de Compton, who died in 1330, to house his tomb. The work is outstanding for the window tracery, which is firmly in the curvilinear mode. More remarkable still is the ensemble of de Compton's tomb, doorway and Easter sepulchre or tomb of Christ, carved with stunning elaboration and clearly strongly influenced by the chancel at St Andrew, Heckington, Lincolnshire. The tomb of Christ was used in celebrations at Easter and on the feast of Corpus Christi. Its carvings show the Ascension at the top and sleeping soldiers at the base, Christ and the Marys in between.

The 12-sided font at St Patrick, Patrington, is contemporary with the church and is covered with decorated motifs such as crocketed openings and leafy decoration.

encrusted with crockets. Much of this work took a battering in the 17th century, when English art suffered from Puritan iconoclasm. But enough remains to show us the scope of both the mason's and the sculptor's art.

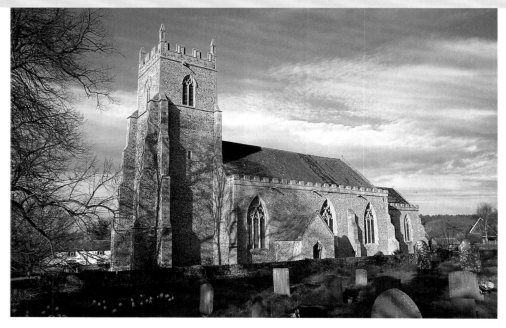

St Mary, Elsing
Norfolk

Elsing church was built of glistening East Anglian flint – combined with larger stones for the buttresses and tower parapet – all in the Decorated style in around 1330 with funds from Sir Hugh Hastings. When Hastings died in 1347, a large memorial brass was set inside the church. It is one of the finest of all brasses, with a life-size figure of the knight. Unusually for this period, the church itself has no aisles, just a wide nave, chancel, and tower with flushwork buttresses. Decorated-style windows throw light across the broad nave.

The tracery in the windows is known as flowing tracery, because its effect is more sinuous than the geometrical designs used in the previous century. It makes Decorated Gothic buildings a delight to the eye, because the range of shapes and patterns is enormous. Inside, stained glass in windows like these produced a jewel-like glow. Most medieval churches lost their old glass in the 17th century, during the Puritans' reaction against religious images. Elsing is fortunate that 14th-century stained-glass figures of the Virgin Mary and three of Christ's apostles remain in the chancel.

St Augustine, Brookland
Kent

Occasionally medieval builders produced something that stands completely outside the normal run of church architecture, as they did with this bizarre, almost modern-looking, detached belfry which dates from the 13th to 15th centuries. It is eight-sided and clad in shingles, and there is no other belfry quite like it, although several Kentish spires have a similar profile. But at 36 ft (11 m) across it is on a much larger scale than the normal church spire. Inside, the belfry is supported by an impressive wooden structure consisting of a network of posts, cross-braces, and arched braces. It is a reminder that the Middle Ages produced skilled carpenters as well as talented masons.

The ogee arch – in which each side has a double curve, going first one way then the opposite – was particularly popular in the early 14th century and the doorway at St Mary, Elsing, is a good example.

See also

Decorated greater churches, 72
Medieval great houses, 120

Perpendicular parish churches

In 1348–9 the Black Death struck. The bubonic plague killed almost half the population of England and the resulting labour shortage brought about an economic crisis. Church building slowed down, and when it picked up again, in the 15th century, the new Perpendicular style of architecture, developed in great churches such as Gloucester Abbey (now the cathedral), was there to inspire churchmen and builders. After the Black Death and its aftermath, there were fortunes to be made by those who were left. The 15th century saw a boom in the textile trade and the cloth merchants funded large

Saints Peter and Paul, Lavenham
Suffolk

One of the largest parish churches in England, Lavenham was rebuilt between about 1480 and 1525 (only the chancel and bell turret are earlier) by local merchants and the Lord of the Manor, the Earl of Oxford. The huge tower dominates the surrounding countryside, but otherwise the main impression is one of rows of windows with their ranks of vertical mullions and their flattened heads that allow nearly the entire surface of the building to be glazed. Even so, between the expanses of glass there was plenty of scope for the sculptor: look closely, and one can see that the buttresses and parapet are richly adorned with

carving. So is the porch, which bears the arms of the Earl of Oxford. Inside, the large clear windows of Lavenham church fill the building with light. It would have been very different in the Middle Ages, when each window would have been a riot of colourful stained glass. The loss, common to virtually every English parish church, is a sad one, but the clear glass enables one fully to appreciate the work of Lavenham's stone carvers, who filled the space between arcade and clerestory with shields, vine motifs, and other ornamentation.

Holy Trinity, Blythburgh
Suffolk

The white, simple interior of Blythburgh dates to the second half of the 15th century. Nave and chancel together form one long space, framed by the gentle rhythm of the tall arches of the arcades with their plain, moulded capitals. The main decorative interest comes from the window tracery and the woodwork. The latter includes the delicate screen that forms the only division between nave and chancel, the painted roof with its large angels, and bench ends carved with items from the medieval vocabulary of morality – figures representing the deadly sins, a man in the stocks, and people going about the business of rural work, from ploughing to hay making.

Perpendicular churches, especially in the wool belt that ran from Somerset to Lincolnshire and in East Anglia. The wool churches, as they are called, have strong exteriors – often with tall towers – and light, spacious interiors.

St Andrew, Cullompton
Devon

Tall piers and matching moulded arches separate the nave from the aisles at Cullompton, and large, four-light windows let in the daylight. The capitals are sculpted with leaves, heads, and figures. All these features make for a complete and satisfying Perpendicular interior. It is enhanced greatly by the woodwork. There is a very handsome timber roof, boarded with lots of cross ribs, and a magnificent wooden screen that runs across the entire width of the church. The colour on the screen (renewed but in keeping with its period) gives an idea of the effect the interior would have made with wall decoration and stained glass in place.

Saints Peter and Paul, Northleach
Gloucestershire

Northleach is one of the finest of the Cotswold wool churches and its two-storied south porch is rich and outstanding. Although the doorway itself is quite plain, it is surrounded by sculptural elaboration. There is a hood-mould in the double-curved ogee shape, inherited from the Decorated style of the century before. There are lots of image niches with crocketed canopies and a number of medieval figures – including the Virgin Mary above the door – have survived. Crocketed pinnacles, the unusual pitched parapet, and the flèche over the stair turret crown it all, combining worldly display with the imagery of piety.

St Wendreda, March
Cambridgeshire

A medieval church was a depiction of the City of God, and nowhere is this clearer than in the roofs of the great East Anglian Perpendicular churches with their hosts of angels. The roof at March is of double hammerbeam construction – in other words there are twin projecting beams in each bay. This kind of construction, alone and undecorated, is an impressive piece of carpentry. But at March angels with outstretched wings are poised on each hammerbeam, and they are joined by more on the corbels and still more near the ridge of the roof. There are over one hundred angels in all, and each seems ready to take flight.

Fan vaulting springs from the tracery in the screen at St Andrew, Cullompton, to make an overhang supporting a multi-layered cornice, richly carved and gilded.

See also

Perpendicular parish churches, next page
Perpendicular greater churches, 74
Early schools and colleges, 268

With the bulk of Perpendicular walls dissolved away to accommodate stained-glass windows, the tower was the largest mass of solid masonry in most 15th-century churches. Towers became places where master masons could best express their skill, and Perpendicular towers remain some of our most beautiful – and also most visible – structures. Bell openings, buttresses, and parapets were three main places where the decorative imagination could blossom, and a few towers are extended

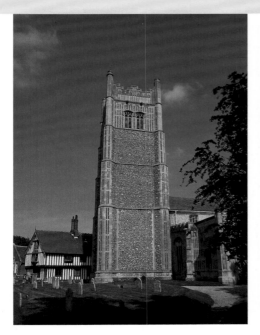

Saints Peter and Paul, Eye
Suffolk

The great Perpendicular churches of East Anglia often have imposing west towers, but building such structures could be difficult in an area where good building stone was thin on the ground. Suffolk masons rose to this challenge by combining locally available flint with dressed stone to make patterns of tracery on the surfaces of exterior walls, a technique known as flushwork. The tower at Eye is one of the best examples, with the lines of Perpendicular mullions reproduced on the walls of the topmost stage – and also on the buttresses and parapet – in stone and flint.

St James, Chipping Campden
Gloucestershire

Gloucestershire's wool churches have grand towers, none more imposing than the one at Chipping Campden, which was added to the church at the end of a series of upgrades at the end of the 15th century. It is a strong design, made original by the three slim pilaster strips that run all the way up the wall from ground to top, where they join in a pair of curvaceous ogee arches at parapet level. Between these strips are set the large west window, some blind panelling, and a pair of bell openings. The strips frame all this detail and lead the viewer's eye upward, emphasising the tower's height.

All Saints, Langtoft
Somerset

Tall and supported by pairs of buttresses at the corners, the tower of All Saints, Langtoft, is one of a large group of Perpendicular towers in Somerset built with similar flair but with local variations in style. In addition to the paired buttresses, most of the Somerset towers have a number of features in common with this one: the tall pinnacles rising above the parapet; the pairs of bell openings filled with stone panels pierced to let out the sound; the very large west window; and the much smaller west door. Niches for images are another common feature. The Somerset group adds up to one of the most significant in English architecture.

heavenward with a spire or lantern. Somerset is the best place to look at 15th-century towers, but there are good examples all over the country, wherever churches were being rebuilt or extended.

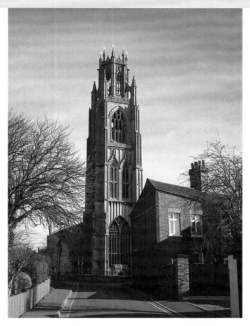

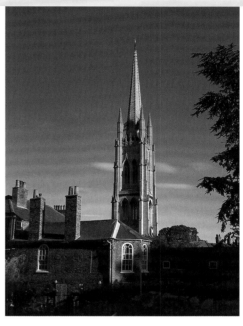

St Mary and All Saints, Fotheringhay
Northamptonshire

At this collegiate church, a rather ornate lantern sits on top of a much plainer tower, without even a parapet between them. The transition from square to octagon is not eased with flying buttresses, and the jump from one shape to another is rather abrupt. But one inspired detail pulls the design together – at each corner of the tower is a small octagonal corner turret topped with a statue, mirroring the shape of the lantern. Unusually, we know the name of this building's master mason: William Horwood contracted for the job in September 1434.

St Botolph, Boston
Lincolnshire

This tower, all 272 ft (83 m) of it, is known locally as the Boston Stump, because of a tradition that it was intended to have been topped with a spire. Yet the eight-sided lantern provides a fitting climax to this great structure, which is hardly stump-like to the unprejudiced eye. In fact it was built in three phases. The lower section, with its stone panelling, was followed by the storey with the broad unglazed openings before the filigree octagonal lantern was built. Perhaps this had a practical purpose, as a beacon to shipping in the Wash and North Sea as well as a welcoming landmark for those travelling on the Fens.

St James, Louth
Lincolnshire

Although the Perpendicular period is most famous for its towers, sometimes the masons added a spire, as they did at Louth, with breathtaking effect. Built at the beginning of the 16th century as an addition to a slightly earlier tower, the spire reaches a height of 295 ft (90 m). The design is artfully managed to emphasise this height and to lead the eye upwards. The openings in the tower, narrower at each higher stage, the upper ones topped with tapering ogee hood-moulds, all add to this effect. So do the flying buttresses, which make the visual transition from tower to slender spire. The people of Louth got good value for the £305 7s 5d that their spire cost.

The main use of a church tower is to house bells. As can be seen at Fotheringhay, each bell is mounted on a wheel in a wooden frame, allowing it to be turned when the ringer pulls the rope.

See also

Perpendicular parish churches, previous page
Perpendicular greater churches, 74
Early schools and colleges, 268

Gothic-survival parish churches

The Tudor era and the early 17th century, the period of the English Reformation and its turbulent aftermath, was a quiet time for church building. The few churches that were constructed were built in the Gothic style, but they were usually small buildings that did not aspire to the glories of Perpendicular. Church furnishing was a different matter, however. By the 17th century, English woodworkers were already feeling the influence of Classicism and their pulpits, panelling, and

St Lawrence, Diddington
Cambridgeshire

Gothic churches continued to be built into the Tudor period in the Perpendicular style, but such buildings are uncommon and they rarely aspire to the scale of the great Perpendicular churches with their large windows and prominent towers. But here is an exception. At Diddington the west tower was built, during the reign of Henry VIII, in striking red brick dressed with stone. Apart from the unusual material, this tower has most of the features of a tower of the 15th century, including a large west window, bell openings near the top, battlements, and diagonal corner buttresses, but no west door.

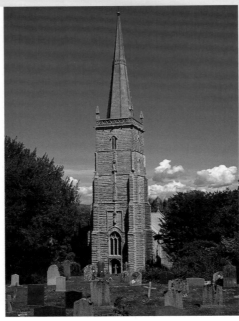

St Mary, East Brent
Somerset

The church at East Brent looks at first glance like a Perpendicular Gothic building, though it is unusual for a Somerset church in having a spire. But inside there are a number of Gothic details that were later added in the 17th century. Most notable is the nave ceiling, a surprising construction of 1637 in the form of a curving vault divided into panels. These panels are mostly of lozenge shape and there are also several plaster pendants of the kind often seen on Jacobean ceilings. But the detailing, made up of repeated cusps, is thoroughly Gothic.

St Michael, Arthuret
Cumbria

Begun in 1609, and built in one go when the previous church was in serious decay, the church at Arthuret is striking for its regular windows. Each light is topped with a flattened or four-centred arch of the kind that is common in late Perpendicular buildings of around a century before and the tower could also belong to a modest Perpendicular church, though its pyramidal roof is unusual. But the uniformity, together with the rigidly rectangular, domestic-looking windows, is more typical of the 17th century.

A late Perpendicular pulpit, with its panelling and crocketed pinnacles, is like a miniature building within a building – this example at St Mary and All Saints, Fotheringhay, Northamptonshire, even has a hinged opening door. It has been repainted, to remind one that medieval churches were originally full of colour. The canopy is a Jacobean addition.

other fittings often show the vigour of the period's grander domestic architecture. So 17th-century churches could be hybrid creatures – Gothic in masonry, Jacobean in furnishings.

Holy Trinity, Staunton Harold
Leicestershire

This is one of the best Gothic-survival churches and was built – unusually during the Commonwealth period – near the great house at Staunton Harold. Outside, the building is a mixture of Perpendicular and earlier Gothic. The overall outline of the building, with battlemented parapets, pinnacled buttresses, and rectangular clerestory windows, is Perpendicular in inspiration. The openwork battlements are a delicate late Gothic touch. But the lower windows, with their different tracery patterns, imitate an earlier kind of Gothic, while the west front is Classical, with swags, pilasters, and the heads of angels.

The interior has Gothic arcades, but the whole has a much more 17th-century feel, because of the woodwork – the screen, gallery, panelling, and box pews. The resulting layout, with the high-sided pews dividing up the nave, embodies the rigid organisation of churches – and indeed of society as a whole – in this period. Large pews, often made comfortable with cushions and draft-excluding curtains, would have been allocated to specific families (important people at the front, poorer people towards the back). Smaller pews were for the still lower classes, and men and women were segregated.

The pulpit and reading desk were large and prominent, and at Staunton Harold there is also a western gallery at the rear of the nave, which now accommodates the organ but would originally have housed a group of musicians. The whole is topped by a striking ceiling depicting light shining through greyish clouds to represent creation replacing chaos, which is described by the architectural writer Nikolaus Pevsner as 'pathetic'.

Stuart Classical parish churches

Inigo Jones transformed English architecture with his strict Classicism based on a study of the writings of Roman and Renaissance theorists and a knowledge of buildings in Italy. But as the 17th century progressed, church architecture became somewhat freer. The greatest exponent of this more flexible style was Sir Christopher Wren, whose work rebuilding London's churches after that city's Great Fire of 1666 gave him greater scope than virtually any other church architect. Above all, Wren's City

St Paul, Covent Garden
London

All Saints
Northampton

The serious Classicism of Inigo Jones must have come as a shock when he started work on this church for the Duke of Bedford (who was redeveloping Covent Garden in 1631). Jones's original idea was to have the entrance on the east front, facing the open space outside, but the clergy objected to this 'incorrect' arrangement so Jones built a conventional west doorway. But the eastern façade, on the public square, is still the main public face of the building. It is in the Tuscan order, the simplest and least adorned of all the Classical orders, so the capitals and bases have the briefest of mouldings and the pediment is so bare it looks almost unfinished.

This was building in an all-out Roman style and demanded that architects take notice. And they certainly did. Countless later Classical churches are fronted with a portico, although these later designs are rarely quite as plain as the one Jones provided here. We now take such buildings so much for granted that tourists hardly notice St Paul's church except as a backdrop for Covent Garden's regular street theatre performances.

All but the tower of the medieval church of All Saints was destroyed in a fire that devastated the centre of Northampton in 1675. For the rebuilding, Charles II donated 'a thousand tun' of timber; above the portico, a statue of the king, clad in Roman armour and luxuriant wig, commemorates this gift. The main rebuilding work was done in 1676–80 under surveyors Henry Bell and Edward Edwards, who gave the new church a dome. Further elaborations followed, including the cupola on the tower in the first years of the 18th century and the Ionic portico. The portico is famous to lovers of poetry as the place where Northamptonshire poet John Clare used to sit when he was allowed out of the asylum.

English monumental sculpture was strong in the Stuart era and many older churches have notable Stuart memorials. The large monument to Viscount Campden, who died in 1683, and his wife at St Peter and St Paul, Exton, Rutland, is thoroughly Classical. The luscious festoons of fruit and leaves were carved by Grinling Gibbons.

churches are known for their fine interiors – with plenty of accommodation for the congregation and an inventive use of space – and for his steeples, which transformed London's skyline.

St Stephen, Walbrook
London

The entrance porch at St Stephen, Walbrook, is at the west end, to the right of the tower. Its round arch is topped by an elliptical *oeil de boeuf,* and the two openings are linked by a curious section of masonry, along the edges of which are carved leaves that curve upwards and turn in baroque curls. Much richer swags of fruit and foliage hang heavily on either side of the ellipse. This portal is an interesting mix of bold, plain mouldings with intricate carving, and the combination seems to mediate between the plain exterior and the beautifully decorated interior of the church.

Of all Sir Christopher Wren's City churches, the interior of St Stephen, Walbrook, is the most successful. The focus of the whole design is the dome, its central lantern adorned with plaster decoration. Here in this church of 1672–9, Wren showed himself a master of dome design, years before his design for St Paul's Cathedral was completed. Wren's gift for the handling of space enabled him to use columns, ceilings, vaults, arches, and the dome, to define the spaces in the church. There is an overall rectangular plan; within this is a cross-shaped space, the eastern arm of which provides a chancel area.

Inside the cross is the circular space of the nave, roofed by the great dome. The details are just as assured. Where Jones used the Tuscan order, Wren's columns are the ornate Corinthian, with their capitals wrapped in carved stone acanthus leaves. Arches, circular windows, and the great circle of the dome set up a rhythm of curves. The panels in the dome and the bases of the columns answer with a counterpoint of squares. Generous upper windows flood the interior with light so that one can see Wren's work at its best.

See also

Wren steeples, 46
Classical greater churches, 78
Stuart Classical houses, 128

Wren steeples

Cramped sites and limited costs meant that the exterior walls of Wren's churches are usually rather plain. But the architect lavished great care over his steeples, which replaced the spires and towers that had punctuated London's skyline before the Great Fire. Wren could quickly see the effect that his buildings would have on the entire capital. So when money began to become available to build towers for his London churches, he seized the opportunity to give London the skyline it deserved.

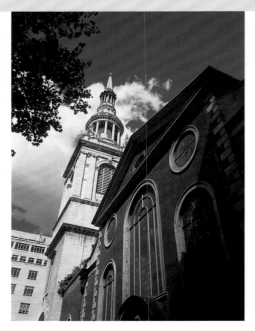

St Mary-le-Bow, Cheapside London

The first of Sir Christopher Wren's London church steeples to be completed, in 1680, was that of St Mary-le-Bow, and it typifies the way in which Wren reinterpreted the tapering Gothic spire in the Classical language of his time. The tower is restrained (though there is a grand doorway and the bell openings are framed with pilasters) but the steeple itself is a highly original composition of columns, stone brackets, and a tapering, obelisk-like spire.

St Nicholas Cole Abbey Queen Victoria Street, London

This is another early example of Wren's work in the City, begun in 1671. Like so many of his churches, it was badly damaged during the Second World War – the interior was burned out and the steeple decapitated – but it has been restored. The steeple is one of Wren's stumpier specimens, but it is full of character, with its slightly concave sides and extraordinary round windows, like a ship's portholes. Since the restoration, the nautical theme has been continued with the addition of a weathervane, a striking example in the form of a ship, which came from the destroyed church of St Michael Queenhythe.

St Augustine, Watling Street London

This church, close to St Paul's Cathedral, was built in the early 1680s, and its spire was added in 1695. Most of the building was destroyed during the Second World War, but the tower and lead spire, an especially delicate example of Wren's work, were rebuilt after the war as a fitting climax to the new St Paul's Cathedral Choir School. The gently bulbous gold-tipped spire, the open lead-lined lantern storey on which it rests, and the top of the tower with its pierced parapet and obelisk-shaped pinnacles, together form a structure of both grace and originality.

Although some fell in the Second World War and the remainder are overshadowed by office towers, these unique buildings still enliven the City.

This pre-war photograph shows the interior of St Bride, Fleet Street, before it was damaged in the Blitz. The church has now been restored, but without galleries and with different seating.

St Vedast, Foster Lane
London

This steeple, completed in 1697, is remarkable for the twisting lines of its sides, first concave, then convex. These contrasting curves have led some to call Wren a baroque designer, but the steeple lacks the weight and drama of the later English baroque. Wren aims for delicacy and refinement, as one can see from the subtle profiles of the mouldings and pilasters that he uses high up the steeple. Even the architraves that top each storey project much less forcefully than if they had been designed by a later baroque architect. Wren was seeking far gentler effects.

St Bride, Fleet Street
London

Like most of Sir Christopher Wren's steeples, that at St Bride's was built after the main body of the church, when extra funds were available. It was completed in 1703 and is made up of a series of octagons, ever smaller in size as they rise, with open round-headed arches on each face. Only the topmost octagon is different and more delicate in appearance, setting this steeple apart from Wren's other designs.

St Stephen, Walbrook
London

Arguably Wren's most beautiful parish church had to wait until 1717 to get its steeple, but it was worth the delay. In contrast to many of Wren's steeples, where a square tower is topped with a spire of a completely different shape, Wren continued the square shape at St Stephen, with a series of repeated square structures, smaller and smaller, leading the eye up to a gilded pinnacle. The lower levels of the steeple are enlivened with a trio of columns at each corner. The upper ones, too small to hold such additional details, are plain.

The skyline at Walbrook is enlivened by St Stephen's dome with its central lantern, a rare feature on a Wren church because there was usually not the budget for such an elaborate structure.

See also
Stuart Classical parish churches, 44
Classical greater churches, 78

Baroque parish churches

The best churches of the early 18th century have a solid, monumental quality characterised by heavy masses, unusual shapes and forms, and grandiose features such as tall Roman-style arches and deeply rusticated masonry. This style is seen most notably in the work of architects such as Nicholas Hawksmoor and Thomas Archer, who designed several new churches in London at this time. It is a way of building that has been called baroque, but whereas European baroque buildings

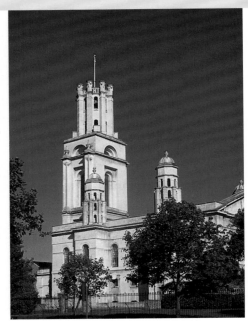

Christ Church, Spitalfields
London

This London landmark is perhaps the boldest of all architect Nicholas Hawksmoor's designs, with a rather medieval-looking spire sitting atop a solid Classical tower, the latter built on an odd oblong plan and designed to be viewed from the front. The portico's great arch between two flat-topped openings has been compared to the similar-shaped venetian window, a favourite Palladian motif. But at Christ Church it is vaster than any Palladian window – once again, Hawksmoor is adapting motifs from elsewhere and making them his own. Inside, the tall arch is echoed in the high arcades between nave and aisles and a true venetian window lights the altar.

St George-in-the-East
Cannon Street Road, London

Like Christ Church, Spitalfields, this is one of the 'Commissioners' churches', so-called after the Fifty New Churches Commission that arranged for their construction between 1711 and 1733. St George-in-the-East makes its impression by sheer size – a weighty mass that gets visual interest from additional weighty masses, the apse and side stair turrets. Above the roof line, though, the building takes off, with five towers challenging the skyline. The one at the west seems to get its shape from medieval lantern towers, but with added classical details such as urns and semicircular openings. The four pepper-pot turrets were an inspired afterthought.

St Alfege, Greenwich
London

St Alfege is a bold design, essentially a vast stone box with a portico at the east end, like St Paul, Covent Garden. But at Greenwich the portico is broken by a vast semicircular arch, the building's most obvious monumental feature. The tall Doric order continues around the sides of the building, leading the eye to a pair of projecting porches and to the steeple beyond, the work of John James. To confirm the monumental impression, the building is topped with a vast dentil course and monster urns.

The emphatic architecture of St Alfege, Greenwich, is enhanced by details such as the heavily rusticated surround to the opening and the recessed portico. Both these features are designed to catch the light and produce dramatic shadows.

seem constantly on the move with hyperactive
ornament or curving walls, the English baroque
churches of Hawksmoor are massive, uncompromising
– and quite original.

St Paul, Deptford
London

St Michael, Aynho
Northamptonshire

Thomas Archer's St Paul, Deptford, completed in 1730, is a more delicate composition than Nicholas Hawksmoor's churches. But much of the decoration – urns, rustication, tall window openings – shows the kinship of the two designers. Like Hawksmoor, Archer is notable for his handling of space. The semicircular portico is one example of this. Topped by a tower on a circular plan it brings the use of curves to the fore and ends with a steeple very much in the vein of Christopher Wren's City churches.

Another example of Archer's use of space is his almost square plan with heavily emphasised north and south doors in addition to the western portico. This was very different from the English norm, for most parishes still had medieval churches, which were usually planned with a long, narrow nave. The square plan produced an imposing space. It looked impressive and satisfied architects, but the clergy liked it for another reason: it kept everyone close to the pulpit so that they could hear the sermon.

Edward Wing rebuilt this church in 1723–5, leaving the medieval tower in position. Its long north and south façades look like a country house – and harmonise with Aynhoe Park next door, which had been partly remodelled by Thomas Archer a few years before. The massing, with projecting corners and window breaking the central pediment, is typical of the Hawksmoor-Archer style. But everything is plain and severe, with little decoration – it is like Hawksmoor on a tight budget.

See also

Baroque houses, 134
Garden pavilions, 354

Georgian Gothic parish churches

Although the Classical style remained popular throughout the Georgian period, many patrons and architects were enthusiasts of the Gothic. Men of taste such as Horace Walpole studied medieval buildings carefully. But Walpole and his followers used medieval Gothic as a starting point. In their hands it became something different – more delicate, more filigree, and more a style of decoration than a system of building in which structure and decoration were integrated. So 18th-century Gothic churches (sometimes called Gothick, to distinguish them from the real thing) are full of extravagant plaster fan vaults and curvaceous ogee arches – they are extravagant but very much of their time.

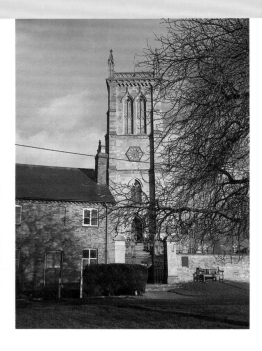

St John the Baptist, King's Norton
Leicestershire

This church was built by the Leicestershire architect John Wing the younger between 1757 and 1775 and stands out beautifully in its upland setting. Instead of the fantasy that was such a strong quality of most 18th-century Gothic, Wing went for a more serious approach, producing a form of authentic-looking Gothic that was more common in the 19th century than the 18th. The tower especially, could be mistaken for a 15th-century original, with beautiful detailing on the parapet, bell openings, and windows.

It looks superb across the fields, a structure in which fabric and setting combine to great visual effect, and shows that Wing must have made a careful study of medieval church architecture. It must have looked even more stunning with its spire, which was destroyed after a lightning strike in 1850. The proportions of the rest of the church, with its tall windows topped with ogee-shaped hoods and set in tall bays, are rather more typical of the 18th century – medieval windows would probably have been stockier in appearance.

The windows fill the interior with light so that one can appreciate the fine fittings, most of which date from when the church was built. There are box pews, a gallery, and a three-decker pulpit. Of the major fittings, only the font is later, because the 18th-century original was destroyed beneath the fallen spire.

A long flight of stone steps leads to a rather plain arch at King's Norton. But the door has been given special treatment with Y-tracery, a popular motif in Georgian Gothic buildings.

A remarkable Norman church was demolished when St John, Shobdon, was built. Arches from the old church were set up as a monument nearby.

Hartwell
Buckinghamshire

Gothic-revival decoration did not have to go with a traditional Gothic plan, with a long nave. At Hartwell, Henry Keene came up with a highly original plan – an octagonal church with towers at east and west. Not since Wren had there been such a daring use of space in a parish church. But, with tall 18th-century Gothic windows below and little quatrefoils above, the effect is quite unlike that achieved by Wren. Inside, the eight-sided form gave Keene the chance for a gesture on the grandest scale in this small church: a fan vault with eight small fans and a monster circular pendant in the centre.

St John, Shobdon
Herefordshire

Full of ogee curves and pale decoration like cake icing, Shobdon (1746–56) has been called rococo Gothic, all frills and furbeloes. Rococo is a style of interior decoration, especially favoured in 18th-century France, in which everything is light and delicate, and ornamentation such as swags of fruit and flowers is prevalent. In spite of the elaborate pulpit, the impression created by its designer, the Hon Richard Bateman, is of a building more suited to performing early Mozart symphonies than listening to ardent sermons. In contrast to medieval Gothic, the crafts of the plasterer and woodcarver are more important than that of the stonemason.

Saints Peter and Paul, Tickencote
Rutland

Tickencote is not Gothic – it is actually a Norman church (with stunning 12th-century work inside) clothed in a remarkable Romanesque revival exterior by S P Cockerell in the early 1790s. Cockerell pulled out all the stops by using the richest Norman motifs – blind arcading, heavy string-courses, a doorway of several orders. Zigzag surrounds many of the arches and openings, and there are twin, intersecting arcades at ground level, a feature normally only seen on prestige buildings. No true Norman small church exterior would have looked quite as dazzling as this – Tickencote is unmistakably the product of a revivalist architect, but is no less fun for that.

The bench ends are among the most unusual features of the interior at Shobdon. Pierced with quatrefoils with added scrolls, ogees, and moulded edges, their wasp-waisted shapes are like nothing in medieval Gothic – a Georgian delight.

See also

Gothic survival parish churches, 42
Victorian parish churches, 56
Revival greater churches, 80
Georgian houses, 138
Georgian Bath, 142

Georgian Classical parish churches

The Georgian period was one of decline in the English parish church. Congregations lost interest, the clergy often lived the life of leisured gentry, pews were rented like real estate, and many church buildings decayed. It is not inappropriate that the typical architectural response of the Georgians was in the urbane and rather worldly Classical style of the time. Churches of this period look from the outside like Classical temples with their columned porticoes. Inside, the nave is invariably the most

St Mary-le-Strand, Strand and Aldwych London

This church was designed by James Gibbs and built between 1714 and 1717. It was one of the 'Commissioners' churches', so-called after the Fifty New Churches Commission, but it is more delicate in its style than the churches built around this time by Nicholas Hawksmoor. Its entrance front is dominated by a semicircular porch supported on Ionic columns; above is a Corinthian order; higher still is the steeple. The interplay between the curving porch and the rectangular church produces a satisfying effect, the more so because the church is prominently sited on its island location in the middle of the street.

St Martin-in-the-Fields, Trafalgar Square London

James Gibbs's church of St Martin-in-the-Fields (1720–6), famous through engravings, became a template for the Georgian Classical church. There were three main elements: a generous portico to make a grand entrance at the west; a steeple that combined Classical details with a spire in the way that Wren's towers did; and a rectangular body with a prominent pulpit and good acoustics providing what has been called a preaching box. There were many variations, especially in the designs of steeples, but the rectangular nave and small chancel, filled with box pews and often with a two- or three-decker pulpit, were widespread.

St Botolph, Bishopsgate London

George Dance the elder and James Gould built this church on the site of a medieval one in 1727–9. Like most London church builders in the decades after Wren, they picked up his challenge when it came to the steeple. Their design tops quite a decorative square stone tower with a circular drum surrounded by a balustrade. On top of the drum is a bell-shaped cupola with round opening and higher still is an urn. As with many of Wren's churches, the ornate tower and steeple make a strong contrast with the rather plain main body of the church.

important space. Yet there are signs of spiritual renewal, for Georgian churches are also temples to the Word, well designed for preaching and for listening to sermons.

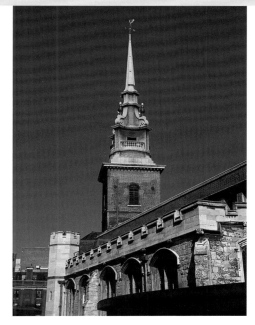

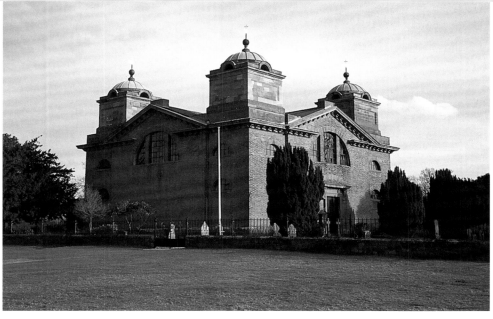

All Hallows, London Wall
London

Another jewel-box of an interior shows architect George Dance the younger turning towards a more grandiose antique revival style. Built in the 1760s, this church still follows the Georgian trend of a simple, large space – in fact there are not even aisles. Instead, the nave is punctuated with tall Ionic columns, attached to the walls and supporting a broad barrel-vault. Light comes from semicircular windows high up in the walls. Both vault and windows are details inspired by ancient Rome, where basilicas and bathhouses had similar features. But much of the decorative detail is derived from classical Greek style.

St James, Great Packington
Warwickshire

This is a Byzantine- and French-influenced Classical church by an Italian architect, lost among parkland in the English Midlands. It was designed by Joseph Bonomi for the fourth Earl of Aylesford of nearby Packington Hall to celebrate the return to sanity of George III in 1789–90. The earl was an enthusiast for Roman antiquity and employed Bonomi as both architect and architectural tutor. The result is as unusual as all this sounds: a wilfully plain box built of brick (very much a Roman material) with four corner towers, shallow cupolas, and semicircular three-light windows of the kind found in the Baths of Diocletian in Rome.

Inside there are beautiful Greek Doric columns at each corner, with a very correct section of entablature above each, but these columns support a very un-Greek, groined vault made of plaster but painted to look like stone. These combinations, the result of a close collaboration between a knowledgeable, well-travelled aristocrat and a highly original architect, ought to look crazy. But they work, the brickwork blending well with the greenery of the surrounding park. This is one of the most remarkable small churches of the 18th century.

This stone gateway, with its own miniature segmental roof, leads into the churchyard at All Hallows, London Wall. Like many churchyard gates, it is a tiny building in its own right.

See also

Stuart Classical parish churches, 44
Georgian houses, 138
Georgian Bath, 142

Regency parish churches

The popular image of the Regency is one of worldliness, and in architecture the period is famous for house building rather than churches. But in 1818 Parliament passed the Church Building Act, putting aside £1 million for the building of new churches. As a result, the Regency period saw the start of a boom in church building. The majority of these new churches were Classical and many were pleasant but unremarkable rectangles of brick with simple galleries inside, often supported on

St Pancras, Woburn Place
London

The Greek revival was rarely taken so literally as at St Pancras, built by W and H W Inwood in 1819–22. Casts made in Athens were sent over for some of the door architraves and the figures that hold up the roof of the portico are reproductions of those at the Erechtheion, the temple that stands near the Parthenon on the Acropolis. Here as in Athens, the figures stand in a wing that is set to one side of the building, forming a break with the usual Greek symmetry. At St Pancras, the draped bodies lend the building a warmth often lacking in Greek revival structures and still surprise newcomers to this London streetscape.

Holy Trinity, Marylebone Road
London

Sir John Soane, an architect known more for country houses and public buildings than for churches, designed several of the churches that were put up under the 1818 Church Building Act. Soane's churches include St Peter, Walworth, and St John, Bethnal Green, as well as Holy Trinity. Soane's London churches are simple, rather austere buildings that mostly lack the subtle details of his country houses. So Holy Trinity (1828) has a plain portico of the Ionic order, beyond which rises the tower, square at the bottom and round above, with a cupola. The Ionic order is also used for the half-columns on the sides of the tower.

If it is rather plain, and sometimes looked down on by architectural critics, it also provides welcome visual relief on the busy Marylebone Road. Inside, a galleried, flat-ceilinged nave has been converted to house offices for the Society for the Promotion of Christian Knowledge, a good example of the way in which the box-like interiors of Georgian churches often lend themselves to conversion to new uses.

Holy Trinity, Marylebone Road, has an unusual feature: an outdoor pulpit. This was added to the church as a memorial to Revd William Cadman, who died in 1891.

cast-iron columns. But a number were more striking designs. Some showed inventive planning, such as St Chad's, Shrewsbury, with its circular nave, built in 1790. Others were more conventionally Classical, like London's St Pancras, Woburn Place.

This shows St Matthew, Normanton, before it was flooded by the creation of Rutland Water.

All Souls, Langham Place
London

Since the early Georgian period, architects had wrestled with the problem of how to harmonise portico and tower. At All Souls, John Nash came up with a novel solution: a round portico with a round tower and spire directly above. The tall Corinthian columns of the portico are mirrored by the columns that surround the tower and at a glance the structure looks like a round, free-standing building rather than the entrance to a rectangular church. The unusual shape also provides a good focal point as Regent Street – also designed by Nash – curves its way round a double bend on its northward route towards Portland Place and Regent's Park.

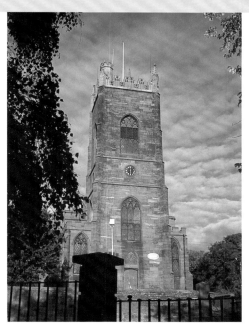

St George, Everton
Liverpool

This building is the result of a collaboration between architect Thomas Rickman, an expert on Gothic, and ironmaster John Cragg. Rickman designed the building so that its interior could be made from parts produced at Cragg's ironworks. This 'kit-of-parts' approach, plus perhaps the influence of an earlier architect, J M Gandy, on the design, gives the interior its quality of fantasy – it is quite unlike medieval Gothic, in spite of its use of tracery and pointed arches. The columns are much more delicate than medieval stone piers, for example, and the ceiling, made up of slate panels fitted into an iron framework, is like nothing from the Middle Ages.

St Matthew, Normanton
Rutland

With its circular lantern surrounded by free-standing Corinthian columns, heavy cornices, and occasional round openings, this tower looks like one of the London baroque inventions of Nicholas Hawksmoor or Thomas Archer. But it was actually constructed in the 1820s as part of a church built by the lord of the manor, who moved the villagers out to make his park more spacious and created a more fashionable church at the same time. In the 20th century the area was flooded by the vast lake that is Rutland Water and the lower part of the building is lost to view.

See also

Stuart Classical parish churches, 44
Regency town houses, 144

Victorian parish churches

The Victorians built more buildings, more quickly, than the people of any previous era, and they could manage virtually any style. As a result of forceful writers such as A W N Pugin, and of their love of the Middle Ages and its piety, they generally agreed that the best style for churches was Gothic. But for the Victorians, Gothic could mean many things, from a scholarly, correct imitation of the 14th century to the wildest fantasy in many-coloured bricks or painted stone. What is more, a few Victorian designers felt able to build churches in other styles, in neo-Norman, for example, or in modes that anticipate the Arts and Crafts movement of the late 19th century.

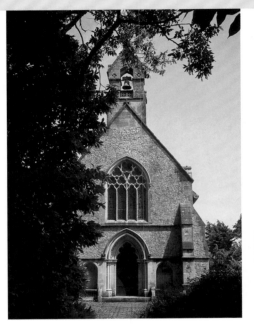

St Mary, Catherston Leweston Dorset

All Saints, Margaret Street London

This is a small, little known church that is easy to miss but, like many Victorian churches, it is a carefully designed work of art that repays a visit. It was the creation of J L Pearson, one of the most successful Victorian Gothic-revival architects. Pearson responded with sensitivity to several different forms of Gothic. Many of his churches are in his version of Early English, but here he chose the mode of around 1300, when window tracery was getting more elaborate and decorative carving more prolific. Pearson also worked well with different materials. He built some notable brick churches in London, such as the famous St Augustine, Kilburn. But here he worked in blue lias, laying it in crazy-paving fashion to produce walls with a lovely texture. The west wall is pierced by a fine window with narrow tracery bars making up six stone trefoils and a quatrefoil. The façade is topped by a chunky bellcote. The doorway is beautifully carved with foliage around the arch, along the capitals, and at the ends of the hood-moulds, and all this fine carving makes a subtle contrast with the jagged edges of the blue lias walls.

William Butterfield was a master of polychrome masonry – the use of different coloured bricks, tiles, and stones. Butterfield and his followers felt that by building in this way, the colour was an integral part of the structure – it was not an add-on, like, for instance, Pugin's murals. All Saints (1849–59) was Butterfield's first building to use full-blown polychromy and the effect is dazzling. The multi-coloured bricks dominate the exterior, but Butterfield shows that he could handle stone, too, as with the relief of the Annunciation on this buttress. Within, granite, various kinds of marble, coloured tiles, and coloured mastic inlay are all used to create a jewel-like interior.

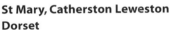

The Victorians used tiles widely in their churches, on floors and sometimes walls. These are behind the altar at St Peter, Barrowden, Rutland.

A W N Pugin was the most influential of all Victorian Gothic architects. His work was showcased in the Medieval Court at the Crystal Palace exhibition.

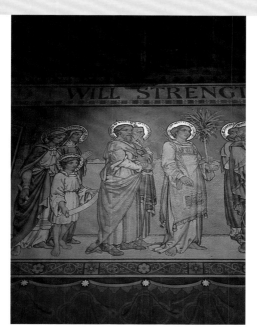

Holy Innocents, Highnam
Gloucestershire

Holy Innocents (1849–51) is a beautiful example of what has become known as Victorian Second Pointed, their version of Decorated Gothic. From ornate spire to lavishly painted interior, it is lovingly decorated – but the building still has a solid, well-balanced quality. Thomas Gambier Parry of nearby Highnam Court had the church built as a memorial to his wife Isabella and to their children, most of whom died as babies; Holy Innocents indeed. Parry was rich, artistically highly talented, and had strong views about architecture. He wanted a building in correct 14th-century style Gothic that was also beautifully decorated. So he

chose as his architect Henry Woodyer, a man influenced by Pugin, who designed the fittings, from screens to memorial tablets, as a whole. But Parry did the wall paintings himself, using his own technique, which he called 'spirit fresco'. He was no mean artist: the paintings are some of the best in a Victorian church. In the example from the north wall shown here, a procession of figures from the Gospels follows Christ as he enters Jerusalem. The haloes are picked out with gilding. There is just the right amount of gold to make the interior work in the dim lighting: everything is in the dark, but it gleams.

Holy Trinity, Prince Consort Road
London

This fine church in Kensington is a good example of a Perpendicular church of the Gothic revival. It was designed by prominent church architect G F Bodley, who began work on it in 1901, at the end of the Victorian period and at the end of his life. Inside and out the church is dominated by its large windows, with their Perpendicular tracery. The pattern of long mullions (uprights), a single transom (horizontal), and stylised tracery shapes in the head of the window is strong and distinctive. Many of the internal fittings were designed by Bodley, but the architect's own monument was designed in the Jacobean style by E P Warren, one of his pupils.

See also

Gothic survival parish churches, 42
Georgian Gothic parish churches, 50
Victorian parish churches, next page
Arts and Crafts parish churches, 60
Revival greater churches, 80
Village halls, 298

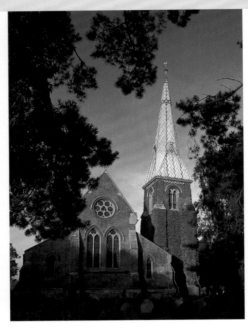

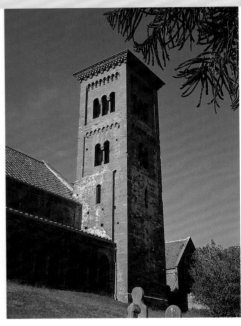

St Mary, Studley Royal
North Yorkshire

This is one of the masterpieces of William Burges, who was as inventive as any Victorian architect, while keeping within the bounds of acceptable Gothic. He designed Studley Royal in the Geometrical style (the transition between First and Second Pointed). Inside, the architecture is lavish. There is a double layer of tracery at each window, shafts in red, green, and black marble, and alabaster facing on the lower walls. Elsewhere the walls are covered with dazzling gilding and rows of images. The windows are full of contemporary stained glass. No medieval church was quite like this but it is how the Victorians imagined medieval architecture should be.

All Saints, Fosdyke
Lincolnshire

The church at Fosdyke, built in 1871–2 by E Browning, is an example of the strength of character a minor architect could bring to a small village church with the most basic materials. Using brick of the deepest, reddest red, Browning built in the First Pointed (Early English style), with a broach spire and simple plate tracery in the windows. Here and there, round and quatrefoil windows make the design less austere. Capitals carved with stiff leaf – again typical of the First Pointed style – enhance the interior. But the lasting impression is of the material, red brick set off by the churchyard's rich green foliage.

St Catherine, Hoarwithy
Herefordshire

J P Seddon's design for St Catherine, built in the 1880s, took its inspiration from the Romanesque style of the early Middle Ages in Europe with a large dose of influence from the Byzantine architecture of Constantinople and its empire. One of its most striking features is the tower. Pierced with round-headed openings and topped by a strong protruding cornice, it looks as if an Italian campanile has landed in the Herefordshire countryside. Other southern European features of the church are a cloister walk and an east end decorated with Byzantine capitals and a glittering gold mosaic of Christ as almighty ruler.

St Mary, Wreay
Cumbria

This is one of the most remarkable Victorian churches – for being the work of a woman, Sara Losh, and for being in a distinctive adaptation of the Romanesque style with roots in France and Germany rather than England or Italy. The focus of the 1842 interior is the apse, with its arcade of round-headed arches and its row of windows lined with metal grilles of fossilised ferns. Sara Losh, an amateur architect from a well-to-do family, designed all the fittings herself, with a dedication akin to that of the best Victorian professionals. The result is a far cry from traditional Romanesque – it is the creation of one individual mind, a designer who would have been at home in the Arts and Crafts movement 40 years later.

St Mary, Newton-by-the-Sea
Northumberland

An increase in population and number of parishes in the late 19th century led to a demand for more church buildings, but money was often scarce. One solution was the corrugated-iron church, which was cheap and very easy to erect – a small church for a congregation of 200 cost around £200 and the £1-per-parishioner formula continued up the size scale. Many of these buildings were produced by William Harbrow of South Bermondsey in London, who also built up a business supplying missionary churches in the empire. These buildings could even be ordered, in flat-pack form, from Harrods. They were made of iron sheeting that was galvanised (in other words given a coating of zinc) to protect them from rust.

A coat of often brightly coloured paint provided further protection and decoration. Although many examples were rather plain, some were elaborated with ornate details such as carved bargeboards. And they were often beautifully appointed inside, with walls covered in tongue-and-groove panelling. So although they were cheap buildings, intended as temporary accommodation, many won the affection of their congregations, who have looked after them well. With the occasional new roof and paint job, such churches could last well beyond their pray-by date.

Highlights of the exterior at St Mary, Wreay, are the carvings – ears of corn, all manner of flowers, vines, birds, beetles, and butterflies. Around the doorway are repeated motifs of water lilies and lily pads.

Railings made in the form of downward-pointing arrows are another original detail at St Mary, Wreay.

See also

Arts and Crafts parish churches

The Arts and Crafts movement produced some of the most beautiful churches of the late 19th and early 20th centuries. They are characterised by an interesting use of often local materials and originality of details such as window tracery.

A common motif is a nave divided into bays by huge arches, rising almost from the floor, rather like the wooden crucks of a medieval barn or cottage. In addition, these churches are full of the most wonderful decoration and furnishings, since many

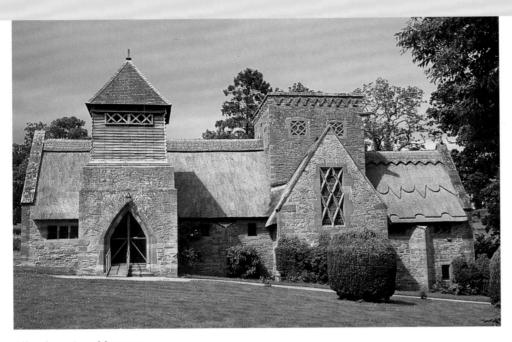

All Saints, Brockhampton
Herefordshire

St Mary, Great Warley
Essex

Constructed in 1901–2, this building came at the end of W R Lethaby's career as a working architect. From the outside it is an absorbing essay in local materials – sandstone, thatch, and timber – with strong massing provided by the two towers. The window tracery is highly original, with its cross-motifs and restrained Gothic cusping. Plenty of other telling details, such as the lead rainwater chutes and the patterned thatch on the chancel roof, show how much care Lethaby lavished on the design. But the thatch conceals a secret: beneath is a concrete roof resting on large stone arches that spring near the floor and rise to the ridge, making the nave interior nearly all roof space.

This interior houses many lovingly made Arts and Crafts furnishings. There is a font carved with a frieze of grapes and vines, wooden carvings of wild flowers, tapestries, elegant iron light fittings, and stained glass. None of this detracts from the white simplicity of the steep-roofed interior. Lethaby supervised the creation of this delightful church on-site, hiring labour directly like a building contractor. But the problems this and his demanding clients caused gave Lethaby endless headaches and he retired from practice to write and teach.

Charles Harrison Townsend designed this church of 1902–4. It looks plain outside, but is remarkable for the stunning decoration of its interior, on which he worked with designer William Reynolds-Stephens. The nave is impressive, its roof with ribs covered in aluminium leaf and garnished with roses and lilies. More roses, this time in bronze with angels emerging through them, adorn the rood screen. Beyond is the climax, the apse, its walls covered with marble and aluminium leaf, with decorations of pewter and mother-of-pearl. It is the closest English church architecture gets to Art Nouveau, but with none of the swirling curves of the French movement – everything is much more straight and disciplined.

A simple shallow segmental arch and a subtle contrast between rendered walls and stone dressings: details like this are typical of Charles Harrison Townsend's treatment of the church exterior at St Mary, Great Warley.

of their architects were also makers of furniture.
At their best, these churches can combine allusions
to medieval architecture with strikingly modern
features – like much 20th-century art they can
feel very old and very new at the same time.

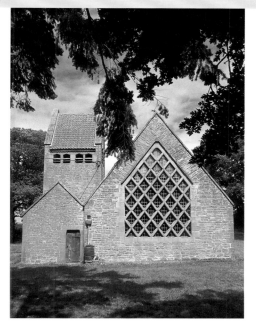

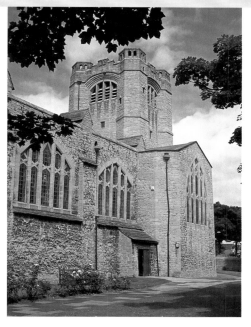

St Edward the Confessor, Kempley
Gloucestershire

Randall Wells (formerly clerk of works
for W R Lethaby at Brockhampton) used
local Forest of Dean stone for this church,
which was consecrated in 1904. Outside
the design is dominated by big gestures –
the imposing tower, sweeping roofs, and
large west window criss-crossed with
tracery. Inside, the low roof makes it more
intimate, with the crucifix and figures of
the rood standing on one of the horizontal
tie beams. Furniture includes pieces by
Ernest Gimson and Ernest Barnsley,
craftsmen-designers who lived in the
nearby Cotswolds, making the area a
centre for the arts and crafts.

St Andrew, Roker
County Durham

Arts and Crafts design is not all about
cosy country buildings. Architects such
as E S Prior used the idiom to create a
sense of grandeur as at this generously
proportioned grey stone church of 1906
near Sunderland. The large tower at the
east end makes a good landmark. Prior
took Gothic elements such as window
tracery but gave them a personal twist,
replacing curves with straight lines and
substituting plain masonry for moulded
stone. This simplified tracery and the
building's clean lines and plain stone walls
give the exterior a modern, unadorned
look. One can see how historians have
found some of the roots of modernism in
the work of the Arts and Crafts movement.

Inside this church, the most striking
feature is the painted decoration of the
chancel, dominated by a blue ceiling
dotted with gold stars and moon and
lit by a lamp surrounded by metal rays
like a sun. This glorious evocation of
the cosmos was actually added after
the church was built: it is the work of
Macdonald Gill and dates from 1927.
It follows a sketch that Prior himself
produced and is very much in the spirit
of the church and its exuberant architect.

Architect Randall Wells
and his brother Linley
carved the pattern of
grape vines in the
beams that support the
rood at St Edward the
Confessor, Kempley.
The carvings were then
picked out in black, red,
and green paint.

See also

Arts and Crafts houses, 156
Museums and libraries, 278

20th-century churches

The secular 20th century is not well known for its parish churches but a number were built, answering needs arising from war damage and urban expansion. There are 20th-century churches in virtually every style, from traditional Gothic to brutal modernism.

Some of the most interesting, for example those by H S Goodhart-Rendell, take Gothic in new directions, transforming both details and overall handling of space. Some of the modernist churches also push their architectural mode in new directions, adapting

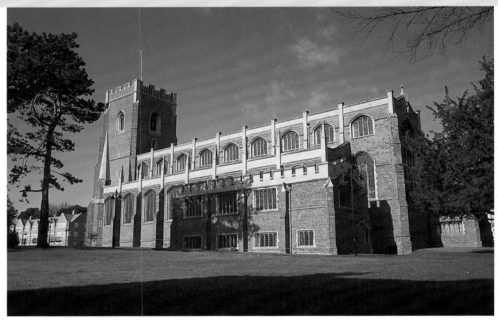

**St Mary, Wellingborough
Northamptonshire**

Sir Ninian Comper was the architect who created this Perpendicular church in 1908–30. Comper's career revolved around church building and restoration, but he was rarely if ever given such large scope as at Wellingborough, for here his task was to design a large town church and all the fixtures and fittings. It is impressive from the outside with its rows of clerestory windows and solid, four-square tower recalling the late medieval churches of East Anglia and, like so many of these forebears, was built in one long building campaign. It looks very much a worthy successor to the Perpendicular churches of the 15th century, and Comper obviously understood the style perfectly.

But it is even more impressive inside. Comper created virtually everything in the church, from the floral capitals to the three-arched, half-Classical half-Gothic rood screen, and seldom was a Perpendicular church of the Middle Ages so complete. Rarely too did a medieval church have a vaulted nave and chancel, especially one with such a ceiling as Comper designed, covering the huge open space of the church interior with its thousands of ribs and great drooping pendants, all executed in plaster. Under this vault, Comper drew together a range of his favourite designs and ideas, and these were amazingly diverse. The nave piers, for example, are octagonal with

concave faces, a design copied from some of the great Cotswold wool churches. The Christ in Majesty above the rood is influenced by a figure in Palermo. This figure, and the chancel screen, glitter with gilding. But other furnishings, such as the pulpit and pews, are rather plain. It is a building of contrasts, then, but the unifying hand and eye of Comper draw everything together.

Even details such as escutcheon plates show the hand of the master designer Sir Ninian Comper at St Mary, Wellingborough. Indeed, Comper thought of everything, as can be seen with the exquisitely lettered plate instructing visitors how to use the door handle.

an architecture refined in houses and factories to meet more spiritual needs – to provide not just 'machines for praying in' but buildings to make you think.

St James the Greater
Leicester

This church was completed in 1914 and is unusual for its time in being in an early Italian Renaissance style. It was designed by Leicester architect Henry Goddard, who had worked sporadically on it since 1895 – in fact its gestation went back even further to the architect's travels in Italy. The powerful west front makes its presence felt with a strong mixture of heavy masses of masonry and the occasional delicate carved detail, as if the very different architects Nicholas Hawksmoor and Robert Adam had been twin inspirations. Inside there is a long arcaded nave and short apsidal east end, as in an early Christian basilica.

American Military Cemetery Chapel
Madingley, Cambridgeshire

To commemorate the American servicemen and women who lost their lives in the Second World War, a highly serious development of church architecture was required. Architects Perry, Shaw, Hepburn and Kehoe used Portland stone, both for the 1950s chapel and for the long Memorial Wall in front of it. They built a monumental structure, rising sheer, its slab-like front recalling a cenotaph. Mirrored in water, the effect is multiplied. Looking more closely, the building is full of telling details, from the bronze reliefs of naval ships and military vehicles on the doors to the vast mosaic ceiling inside, commemorating the dead with ghostly aircraft and figures of angels.

Our Lady of the Rosary
Old Marylebone Road, London

A simple pattern of bricks, a very restrained version of the polychrome effect loved by some Victorian architects, dominates Goodhart-Rendell's church of Our Lady of the Rosary, built in 1959–63 after the architect's death. This rather plain frontage with its lone, round-headed window points to a simple, back-to-basics spirituality. This is reflected in the interior, which creates a space of chaste beauty through the interplay between pointed and round arches, between narrow lancets and broad windows, and between light and shadow.

See also

Modern cathedrals, 82

Stained glass, Coventry Cathedral, Warwickshire

GREATER CHURCHES

The cathedrals and larger churches of England are built on a more ambitious scale than the parish churches and this is not just a question of size. A greater church usually has a more complex plan and elevation than a parish church. And cathedral builders usually had more money at their disposal than people putting up parish churches, so a cathedral often makes a more lavish impression, with richer decoration, a fine west front, tall towers, and more use of expensive features such as stone vaults. What is more, these buildings were at the cutting edge of architecture. A new style of window tracery or ornament often appeared in a cathedral decades before it was taken up in smaller churches.

Cathedrals and large monastic churches follow the cruciform plan often seen in small churches, but with elaboration. The transepts that make up the 'arms' of the cross are often subdivided, to provide a number of small chapels. Larger cathedrals may also have two sets of transepts, offering more space for extra chapels. And greater churches are more complex, at the east end especially, with many chapels connected by a passage, called the ambulatory, that goes all the way around the back of the high altar. The easternmost chapel is generally the largest and is usually dedicated to the Virgin Mary. In addition, a cathedral has a chapter house for meetings of the clergy, and those cathedrals that began life as monastic churches may also preserve buildings such as cloisters.

In a parish church, the main entrance is usually through a door into the nave or aisle, in the building's south wall. Greater churches too may have south porches, but they usually also have one or more large ceremonial doorways in the west wall. This wall makes up the west front of the cathedral. English west fronts were originally highly decorative, filled with rows of niches containing statues. Most of these figures were destroyed during the 17th century, when some Puritans defaced or removed images in churches. But the higher statues often escaped destruction, and some have been replaced. Buildings such as Wells and Exeter still give a good idea of a medieval west front.

Another glory of the English cathedrals is their towers. Several cathedrals, such as York, Durham, Canterbury, and Lincoln, have three towers, two at the west end and one centrally placed. At Lichfield, all three towers are topped with graceful spires. Tall towers make these buildings stand out, dominating their cities and sometimes the surrounding landscape. Lincoln, for example, on its hilltop site, is visible for miles around.

Internally, the greater churches are set apart by their vaulted ceilings. A vault was the natural culmination of a Gothic space, and cathedral vaults range from the simple ribbed vault of Durham to the fantastic creations in the choir at Gloucester, where hundreds of stone ribs intersect to make the most intricate patterns.

These buildings were once still more ornate. As well as the removal of many statues, most have lost the bulk of their medieval stained glass, although most of the windows at York still have theirs. And the colourful paintwork that once covered much of the stonework has also largely gone: the beauty of these buildings is now more austere than lavish, more monochrome than polychrome.

This compelling architectural tradition, encompassing some two dozen major cathedrals and numerous monastic churches, has defined what we expect a place of worship to be like. This is so much the case that post-Reformation cathedrals, even fairly recent ones such as Coventry, have drawn heavily on the style created in the Middle Ages. We expect cathedrals to have columns, vaults, and large windows full of stained glass. We expect them to be tall buildings, with pointed arches, high ceilings, and spires reaching up towards heaven. We expect them to resound with the music of unaccompanied, mostly male, voices. The medieval bishops, and the master masons who designed their cathedrals, helped to define how we think about both buildings and religion in England.

Norman greater churches

One of the major projects of the Norman Conquest was the building of large churches – both cathedrals and abbey churches. Norman bishops and abbots were appointed at many, spreading the influence of the conquering power through one of the most important medieval institutions. These new churches were big, with long, often high naves. Inside, this height was achieved by several levels of arches – an arcade, below a gallery or triforium, below a row of arched windows or clerestory – and this

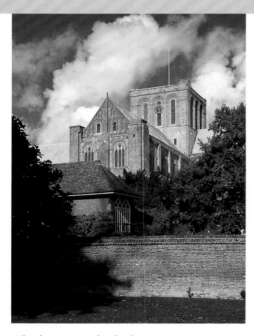

**Winchester Cathedral
Hampshire**

The transepts of this cathedral show what the original early Norman building of 1079–93 must have looked like. Much of the Norman detail has been altered, but the shallow blind arcading in the gable is very much as the Normans left it – six plain arches near the top and intersecting arches slightly lower down. Below this are two later windows with Gothic tracery, but they are set in round-headed arches of the Norman period. Along the side of the transept, one can just make out a series of shallow Norman buttresses. The tower, with its bold arches, is slightly later, but still Norman.

**St Albans Cathedral
Hertfordshire**

Originally an abbey church, St Albans was rebuilt between 1077 and 1115. Although the building has been altered over the years – changes culminating in a drastic Victorian restoration – there are still substantial remains of the early Norman church in the nave and tower. For their tower, the Normans reused bricks from the nearby Roman town of Verulamium. In an area with little building stone, they found the material well suited to their purpose. Roman bricks are much shallower than modern ones and are ideal for building semicircular arches and the other features of the Norman style, which derives from the Roman and is sometimes called Romanesque.

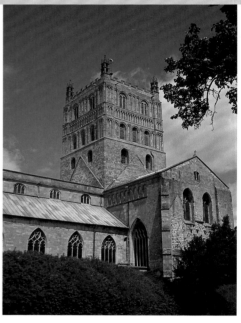

**Tewkesbury Abbey
Gloucestershire**

This was one of a number of great abbeys built during the Norman period in western England, by the powerful Benedictine order of monks. Nearby Gloucester Abbey, now the cathedral, is another example. Most were much altered and extended over the years, but still contain some of the original Norman features. One of the best survivals is Tewkesbury's 12th-century central tower. The upper stages, rising above the nave roof, are covered in blind arcading, with round-headed openings here and there to let out the sound of the bells. Some of the arches have chevron ornament, to add to the rich effect. Only the pinnacles and battlements were added later.

three-level pattern was used in large churches throughout the Middle Ages. Another enduring trend, in the most ambitious buildings, was the use of stone-vaulted roofs.

Durham Cathedral
County Durham

The city of Durham enjoys one of the best sites in England, on a meander of the River Wear. The Normans knew how to exploit this when they built their castle and cathedral, for the site is easy to defend. It also allowed the builders to make the most dramatic impression. By putting up the biggest building anyone was likely to have seen, and siting it in the most prominent position in the area, the conquerors made their presence felt in the most forceful way. The cathedral – a masterpiece of Norman architecture – was originally built between 1093 and around 1130 and so spans the early and late Norman periods. Originally it had no central tower and the western towers began life lower than they are now.

The most famous part of the building is the nave, with the varied incised patterns on its piers. There is nothing else quite like this in any other English cathedral, although the motifs were copied in one or two churches – for example Waltham Abbey, Essex. But the piers at Durham are much bigger and bolder than those at smaller churches such as Waltham, and the effect of these bold designs – flutes, spirals, and the repeated lattice-work shown here – is overwhelming, especially in contrast to the rather plain arches and windows beyond and above, where a more restrained effect is created with a succession of semicircular openings. The design of the nave piers represents the Normans at their boldest and is totally in

keeping with their desire to inspire awe in the conquered congregation. Durham's nave is also forward-looking, because the transverse arches in the vault are, for the first time in England, pointed. So this great Norman building was also the herald of the new Gothic pointed-arched style that was to dominate medieval architecture in the centuries to come.

Some of the piers in the cathedral at Durham are of this Composite type, clustered with attached shafts (far left).

Small round shafts, in a more modest Norman style, held up the cloister arches at Rievaulx Abbey, North Yorkshire (left).

See also

Early Norman parish churches, 28
Late Norman parish churches, 30
Norman greater churches, next page
Norman houses, 114
Great towers, 170

Norman greater churches (continued)

During the mid- to late 12th century, Norman buildings became more showy. Instead of the large expanses of plain, uncarved stone in buildings such as St Albans, walls were covered with decoration. Most commonly this took the form of blind arcading, repeated blank arches, meticulously treated with shafts and mouldings and sometimes arranged in two superimposed and overlapping layers. Doorways and arcades also became a focus for the stone-carvers, who employed a range of

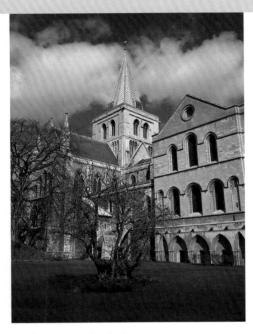

**Rochester Cathedral
Kent**

One of the most powerful bishops of the Norman period was Gundulf, who built the White Tower at the Tower of London and in around 1080 began to rebuild the cathedral at Rochester. Although Rochester, like most English cathedrals, has been much altered, Gundulf's work can still be seen in some of the nave arcades, the crypt, some of the aisle walls, and in the massive north tower. The west doorway is also Norman but is slightly later, in the most ornate style of around 1160, and the multiple orders of arches straight away signal that we are about to enter an important building.

Although much worn and defaced, they still evoke the magnificence of the original Norman building. The most important sculpture, however, is reserved for the tympanum, the semicircular panel above the door. This shows a central figure of Christ in Majesty flanked by a pair of angels and four animal figures that symbolise the four Evangelists. Just below, on the lintel above the door, sit the twelve Apostles. The sculpture is a reminder that medieval masons thought of their cathedrals as imitations in stone of the kingdom of heaven.

These buildings were also instruction manuals in theology, with images of Christ and the saints that priests could use as visual aids when they were explaining the Bible and the history of the church to illiterate congregations.

abstract designs such as the chevron or zigzag. This tendency towards surface elaboration in a much richer form than in Normandy began to take English architecture in a new direction, one that would be followed throughout the Middle Ages.

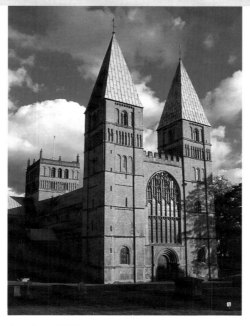

Peterborough Cathedral
Peterborough

The Norman nave at Peterborough is long and low, in the typical proportions of a cathedral in England, where, on the whole, masons did not aim to build as high as their colleagues in France. Outside, it seems to hug the ground, the Norman walls of the clerestory just visible above surrounding buildings and trees. But inside, the building is a lattice of round-headed arches, with arcades, triforia, and clerestories rising in decreasing size. These arches are rather plain by late Norman standards (the zigzag carving is very restrained) but their proportions have a beauty that makes this cathedral for many the best Norman example after Durham Cathedral.

Southwell Minster
Nottinghamshire

At Southwell Minster the west front, finished in 1140, is very plain – the showiest feature, the big west window, was inserted in the late Middle Ages. But looking closely, especially at the ornate doorway with its recessed orders and the small lower windows, one can see that this is in fact a late Norman façade. The rather flat wall surface, with only the shallowest of corner buttresses, is typical of more provincial Norman work, like a parish church on a very large scale. The crowning touches, the plain, bold spires, were added in the 19th century, but the cathedral may have had similar spires in Norman times.

Castle Acre Priory
Norfolk

The Cluniac order of monks built some outstanding churches in England, their quality still discernible through the ruins left after the monasteries were dissolved in the 16th century. Cluniac monasteries were always a reminder of English links with France, since the order's mother house was at Cluny in Burgundy. Castle Acre was founded by William de Warenne, a member of a family that came to England with William the Conqueror. But the richness of the 12th-century architecture here is very English. The repeated pattern of the blank arcading is relieved in some places by a sort of basket-weave pattern and above the door by a row of vigorously carved corbels.

The carving around the doorway at Castle Acre Priory is like a pattern book of late Norman ornament. There are examples of zigzag, pellet, rope or cable, and plain moulding.

See also

Early Norman parish churches, 28
Late Norman parish churches, 30
Norman greater churches, previous page
Norman houses, 114
Great towers, 170

Early English greater churches

The Gothic style developed in France and spread quickly to England. This new way of building was based on a theological precept. According to Abbot Suger, head of the first fully Gothic church at St Denis, France, churches should be flooded with inspirational light. So Gothic began as a way of dissolving the outside wall into a series of almost uninterrupted windows and supporting the high and heavy vaulted ceiling on flying buttresses. This formula – big windows, high vault, flying buttresses

Canterbury Cathedral
Kent

The choir at Canterbury, built in 1175 to 1184, is the earliest major Gothic structure in England. It was constructed after the previous choir was damaged in a fire, and its master mason, William of Sens, introduced many features from his native France. The tall round piers with their leafy capitals look very like those in cathedrals such as Reims and Notre-Dame, Paris, and the simple ribbed vault is after the French Gothic pattern. But other features, such as the clerestory set back behind arcading, are local in character – already, the French Gothic style is being adapted to suit English tastes.

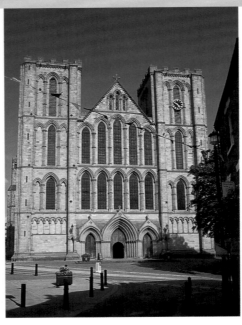

Ripon Cathedral
North Yorkshire

This west front of the 1250s is a perfect example of Early English Gothic, its rows of lancets the very image of early Gothic restraint. So unemphatic is the architecture, that even where there are groups of three windows, the central lancet is only slightly taller than the flanking ones. Clearly this was not ornate enough for the cathedral authorities of the 14th century, for in the 1370s these windows were provided with tracery to bring them up to date. But when the cathedral was restored in 1865 the tracery, by then in poor repair, was removed, returning the building to something like its 13th-century simplicity.

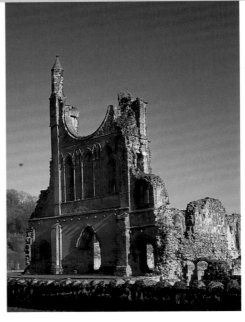

Byland Abbey
North Yorkshire

The large Cistercian abbey at Byland was begun in the late 1160s, when the Gothic style was young. It was traditional to start building with the east end, so by the time the masons got to the west front it was around 1195. The surviving ruins show that this was a grand front, with a rose window, three tall lancets, and three doorways, the central one with a beautiful trefoil shaped head. The Cistercian order was austere and shunned rich ornament, but at Byland they were slightly more liberal than at some of their other sites, as the elegant shape of this doorway shows.

Deeply cut mouldings around arches and doorways are a special feature of the kind of Early English Gothic found in cathedrals – such as this example at Ripon – and greater churches. The generous allowance of both stone and time to achieve this effect was only usually available on high-status buildings.

– was achieved with another major innovation, the pointed arch, which is both more adaptable than the Norman round arch and seems to have a symbolic role, pointing heavenwards.

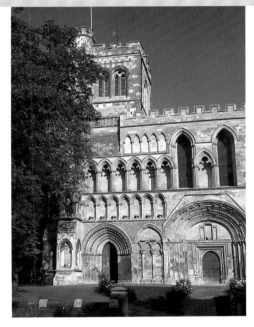

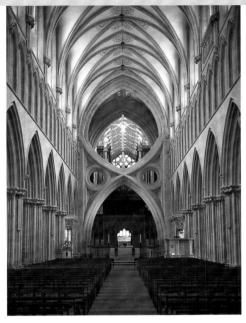

Dunstable Priory
Bedfordshire

This church has a complex building history, summed up in the larger of the two doorways, the one with a semicircular arch, which is Norman with a much later medieval doorway inserted in it. But much of the rest of this façade is in a rich Early English Gothic of the early to mid-13th century. The left-hand doorway, with its ornately carved receding orders, is of this period, and so are all the blank pointed arches above it. The arches immediately above the door were designed to contain statues, and the brackets for these remain. Higher still are more ornate, cusped arches, probably dating from about 1250.

Wells Cathedral
Somerset

This part of the nave at Wells Cathedral was completed by 1215. It shows the typical three-storey arrangement of a cathedral. At the lowest level are the arcades, the rows of arches that separate the nave and the aisles. Above each arcade is a row of arches called the triforium, which screens a gallery running over each aisle. Higher still is the clerestory, the row of windows providing top light, and above all is the vaulted ceiling. Everything here except the unusual strainer arch at the end (a later addition) is typical of the best quality Early English Gothic – clusters of shafts around the piers, deeply moulded arches, and a simple ribbed vault.

Rievaulx Abbey
North Yorkshire

Lancets are the dominant theme at Rievaulx, where the architecture of the church owes a lot to the austere beliefs and tastes of the Cistercians. Their order was founded as a reaction against the perceived luxury enjoyed by the Benedictines, and the monks found the perfect expression for this in the simplicity of the early Gothic style, which can achieve its effect with a minimum of ornament and carving. One compromise that they did make was to orient the church north–south, because of the sloping site. At the east end, the pale white stone shows off to perfection the simple elegance of the repeated windows.

The two small arches at Rievaulx Abbey are part of the triforium, the gallery running above the main arcade, which is a typical feature of larger medieval churches.

See also
Early English parish churches, 32

Decorated greater churches

English architecture in the mid-13th century began once more to diverge from the building styles used in France when the English love of elaborate surface decoration took hold and arches and window openings began to burgeon with carving. Large churches such as Lincoln Cathedral and Southwell Minster became showpieces of the carver's art with a mix of abstract patterns and increasingly naturalistic carvings of foliage, human heads and, famously at Lincoln, the heavenly host of angels. The Victorian name for this style of architecture, Decorated, was well earned.

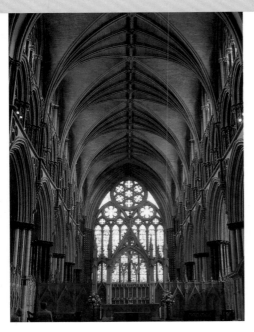

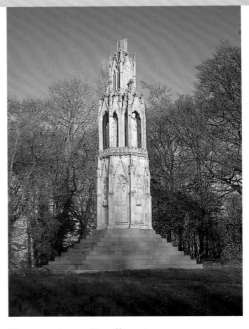

St Hugh's Choir, Lincoln Cathedral
Lincolnshire

The tracery at Lincoln shows the development of a range of geometrical patterns based on the circle, a shape that is satisfying visually as well as being an image of eternity. One of the best examples is the east window in St Hugh's Choir, where both sexfoils and quatrefoils are used. In large windows such as this there are circles within circles that make dazzling patterns of coloured glass and stone. But circles do not fit perfectly into pointed arches, so there are small spaces in between, shapes like curving elongated triangles filled with glass to add to the colour and light.

Angel Choir, Lincoln Cathedral
Lincolnshire

In 1256, the clergy at Lincoln began to extend their cathedral eastwards to provide space for pilgrims visiting the shrine of St Hugh. Just over 20 years later they had created the Angel Choir, one of the triumphs of the Decorated style. The Angel Choir is lit by admirable windows with geometrical tracery, but the glory of the choir is in its stonework, a harmonious mixture of pale limestone and dark Purbeck marble and a rich array of carving – dogtooth, foliage, heads, and the angels in the spandrels of the triforium arches that give the choir its name.

Eleanor Cross, Hardingstone
Northamptonshire

One of the ways in which the Decorated style was disseminated was in the series of 12 crosses built by Edward I to commemorate his queen, Eleanor of Castile, who died in 1290. These crosses marked the route of her funeral procession from Lincoln to London's Charing Cross. They are ornate, polygonal structures (this one has six sides) with statues of Eleanor, lots of niches, crockets, foliate carving, pinnacles, ogees, and other ornate details. These crosses are an example of how the most prominent patron in the land, the king, could spread a recent artistic style across the country.

The 'skeleton' of a Gothic vault was made up of stone ribs, like these examples that were found amongst the ruins of Hailes Abbey, Gloucestershire. These ribs are ornately moulded.

In the early 14th century this architecture became still more elaborate, and buildings were festooned with carved richness. Masons were discovering the interest that could be created with the use of complex curves – the double-curved ogee arch, the sinuous crocket, and new freer patterns in window tracery were the result. A new spatial freedom sometimes accompanied this decorative flair to produce striking, polygonal chapels.

Bristol Cathedral
Bristol

This cathedral, originally an Augustinian monastery church, was remodelled in the 50 years following 1298 and its east end is still a high point of the Decorated style. It is notable for the beauty of its vaulting and for the decorative scheme. The 14th-century reredos behind the altar in the eastern Lady Chapel gives a hint of the jewel-like beauty of Decorated church interiors. The colour was added by restorers but was based on surviving traces of the original paint. The niches, with cusps, ballflowers, and other motifs, are stunning, but even the slenderest pinnacle is given the same rich treatment.

Ely Cathedral
Cambridgeshire

In 1322 the central tower at Ely Cathedral collapsed. The decision was reached to rebuild the crossing in the shape of an octagon rather than the usual square and to roof it with a great eight-sided lantern, to fill the upper part of the crossing with light. This brilliant and original design was executed in wood – stone would have been too heavy for such a structure. But the carpenters succeeded in building their wooden walls, windows, and vaults in exactly the same form as if they had been made by stonemasons. Painted and gilded, they looked just like their medieval stone equivalents.

Tewkesbury Abbey
Gloucestershire

The Despenser family contributed their great wealth to upgrade the east end of Tewkesbury Abbey, beginning in the 1320s. This photograph shows the radiating chapels around the east end. The Despensers' legacy is seen to perfection in the choir, where they topped the ancient Norman piers with the very different filigree of Decorated tracery. Above the east window, with its 14th-century wheel-like pattern of glazing bars, is one of the most intricate vaults of the time. It is a lierne vault, in other words a vault with subsidiary ribs that link the ones passing from wall to ridge. There are dozens of these liernes, creating a dazzling network of patterns.

Carved heads adorn some of the tomb recesses and other details in Bristol Cathedral's richly decorated Lady Chapel. As with the reredos, the paint is modern, but based on medieval remains.

See also

Decorated parish churches, 36
Medieval great houses, 120

Perpendicular greater churches

The Perpendicular style was developed in the early 14th century, probably by masons working for the king. The earliest surviving example of the style is at Gloucester, where the abbey church (now the cathedral) was remodelled. Perpendicular remained fashionable through the 15th century. It is the last phase of English Gothic and has been called the first indigenous British artistic style. It is well named, because so much about Perpendicular architecture emphasises vertical lines. Window mullions stretch from the bottom of the window to the top, right into the tracery. Walls are covered with a kind of

**Gloucester Cathedral
Gloucestershire**

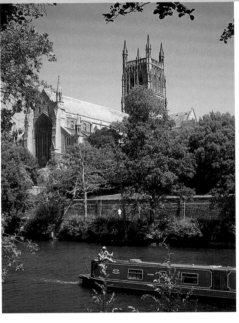

**Worcester Cathedral
Worcestershire**

The choir at Gloucester was remodelled in the second quarter of the 14th century in the Perpendicular style, with the aim of providing a fitting setting in the cathedral – originally an abbey of the Benedictine monks – for the tomb of Edward II, who had been murdered in nearby Berkeley Castle. The Perpendicular style had already been tried in Gloucester's south transept (and in the vanished St Stephen's Chapel, Westminster), but the choir is the most stunning surviving example. It soars. Endlessly repeated verticals lift the eye towards the vault. Patterns on walls and windows set up a gentle rhythm of repetition. Spreading ribs define a vault of great intricacy and beauty.

The repeated rhythms of lines and ribs unify the whole space and provide a framework for the stained glass. This choir influenced church builders all over England, and as the style spread, it became one of the great English contributions to the story of western architecture. At Gloucester the focal point of the architecture is the vast east window, the largest medieval window in Europe. It is canted, to fit on the foundations of the crypt below, and so has been compared to a triptych. Its mid-14th-century stained glass survives, portraying saints, bishops, kings, the Virgin Mary, and Christ.

The Norman central tower at Worcester fell down in 1175 and the cathedral had to wait almost 200 years for a replacement. When the new tower was built, in 1374, the resulting landmark above the River Severn was in the fashionable Perpendicular style and was the first of the Perpendicular cathedral towers. The lower stage, with its seven bays of stone panelling, is especially typical of the style, which would become widespread during the following century. The whole structure looks forward to other Perpendicular central towers in the west, notably Gloucester Cathedral and the abbey at Great Malvern.

blind stone panelling that imitates this effect.
In high-status buildings, fan vaulting takes
similar patterns into the ceiling, covering the
whole structure in an intricate network of tracery.

**Canterbury Cathedral
Kent**

**The Black Prince's Chantry
Canterbury Cathedral, Kent**

Work on the nave and aisles at Canterbury
began in around 1378 and lasted until
1405. The designer was probably Henry
Yevele, who was master mason to the
English royal family during the late 14th
century and is also listed as receiving
food and clothing from the prior of
Canterbury. At Canterbury Yevele used
the features of Perpendicular architecture
to emphasise the height of the building.
So the piers, surrounded by a multitude
of slender shafts, are designed to look
slender and they continue right up to the
vault, their line only interrupted by little
rings around the shafts – a feature that
Yevele used elsewhere and that is thought
to show his hand in the design of the
building – and by the smallest of capitals.

Tall windows flood the space with light.
At the east end of the nave, the stone choir
screen is also in the Perpendicular style.
As well as separating the nave and choir
it performs the structural function of
tying the massive crossing piers together,
to help them take the weight of the huge
tower above.

In 1363 this chantry chapel, now the church
of the Huguenots, was inserted into the
cathedral's South Transept by Edward the
Black Prince, son of Edward III, who built
it in return for the church's permission to
marry his kinswoman, Joan, Countess of
Kent. Its delicate late Gothic details were
added around the earlier Norman masonry.
The finest feature of the chapel, now used
for worship by the Huguenots, is the
vaulted ceiling with its beautiful bosses.
The central one shows the medieval
image of the pelican 'in her piety', feeding
her young from the blood of her own
breast – a medieval metaphor for Christ.

Edward the Black Prince, the medieval hero
who led the English army against the French at
the battles of Crecy and Poitiers, was buried in a
sacred spot in Canterbury Cathedral, next to the
martyr Thomas Becket. His effigy portrays him
in full armour and helmet, just as he requested
in his will.

The vault of the Black Prince's Chantry in
Canterbury Cathedral is a network with small
ribs called liernes.

See also

*Perpendicular parish churches, 38
Perpendicular greater churches, next page
Early schools and colleges, 268*

**King's College Chapel
Cambridge**

The large-scale chapels of the 15th and early 16th centuries are examples of Perpendicular architecture at its purest and of greater-church building at its grandest. These are the buildings in which the fan vault is used with greatest confidence, and in which the walls are virtually screens of glass. They display an intricate complexity of surface details – all tracery and stone panelling – but spatially they are quite simple. King's College Chapel is probably the most famous of all these buildings. Such structures are stunning because they can be taken in at a glance; they consist essentially of one great space and all the elements – windows, stonework, and vaulting – work together in harmony. The saintly Henry VI was the founder of King's, and his chapel was begun in 1446. But work came to a stop in 1461 when the king was defeated at the Battle of Towton and was not resumed until the reign of Henry VII. Henry VIII's glaziers put in the last window in 1547, and the sumptuous carvings of the royal arms and the high fan vault are the features that make the strongest impression inside. The vault in particular has a memorable combination of grace and power. The other principal chapel in this grand late Gothic vein is St George's Chapel, Windsor, home of the Order of the Garter. Both King's and St George's are complete, free-standing buildings. Henry VII's Chapel, Westminster Abbey, is a similar structure that forms part of a larger building; however, it is only attached to the rest of the abbey at one end and so gives the impression of a free-standing structure too.

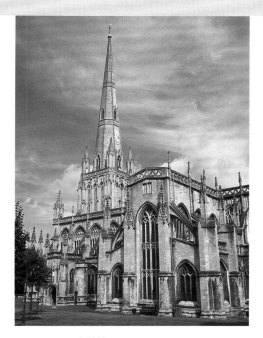

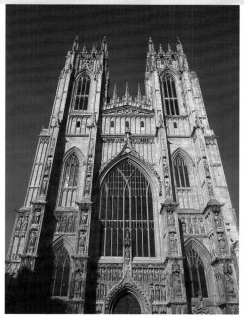

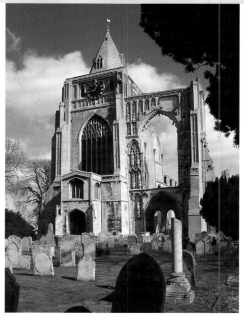

St Mary Redcliffe
Bristol

This is England's largest parish church, but it was built on the scale of a cathedral as a result of the benefactions of prosperous Bristol merchants and ship-owners, such as William Canynges. Canynges funded the work done on the nave in the second half of the 15th century, when the clerestory and vault were completed. The approach here is different to that at Canterbury – there is a much taller clerestory, no triforium, and rather shorter main arches. But the dominant impression is still one of soaring height. The uncluttered design, with a marked lack of statues or other ornate carving, adds to this effect.

Beverley Minster
East Yorkshire

This is one of the greatest examples of Perpendicular architecture, a west front of the first half of the 15th century with a pair of imposing towers. The minster is a former collegiate church constructed on a cathedral-like scale, and the front is worthy of such a vast building. Nearly all the architectural details – the stone panelling, window tracery, bell openings, doorway, buttresses, and niches – are original features that work together in a breathtaking composition. The main exceptions are the statues in the niches, all but one of which are Victorian replacements.

Croyland Abbey
Lincolnshire

This Benedictine abbey, where one aisle of the ruined church has been preserved to serve the local parish, is a good example of an early medieval building that was remodelled in the later medieval Perpendicular style. The tower on the left stands at the end of the aisle, with the ruined nave to the right. The remaining tower window, with its fine tracery, suggests the quality of what has gone, as do the rows of figures that stand in the niches. The main doorway to the abbey church was beneath the ruined window and dates from the 13th century. The small porch to the left is in the Perpendicular style.

The buttresses of Beverley Minster's west front have richly canopied niches for images. The statues are later replacements.

See also

Perpendicular parish churches, 38
Perpendicular greater churches,
previous page
Early schools and colleges, 268

Classical greater churches

Although many parish churches were built in the Classical style between the Reformation and the beginning of the 19th century, very few greater churches were constructed. The one major exception was St Paul's Cathedral which

Sir Christopher Wren designed in the late 17th century to replace Old St Paul's which had been irreparably damaged in the Great Fire of London in 1666. The challenges of building a Classical cathedral were considerable. A Classical parish

St Paul's Cathedral
London

After the Great Fire of London in 1666, the biggest rebuilding job was St Paul's Cathedral. Wren's design went through numerous versions, with building not finished until 1711, but at every stage the architect intended the dome to be a focal point both of the cathedral and of London's skyline. He could not have imagined the best modern view of the cathedral, across the recent Millennium Bridge over the River Thames. From this footbridge, the effort Wren made to build a tall structure that would make its mark on the skyline is clear. He raised the dome on a drum of columns, which almost double the height of the great hemisphere.

Then he added the finishing touch, the stone lantern topped with a ball and a cross that is 365 ft (111.25 m) above ground level. The wood-and-lead dome was not strong enough to support the lantern, so Wren built a hidden cone of brick inside – the structure is an engineering triumph as well as a visual one. Although the dome is the best known part of St Paul's, the cathedral also has outstanding elevations. The west front, with its twin towers and two storeys of Classical columns, forms a dramatic landmark on Ludgate Hill. To the sides, the transepts have fronts of their own.

The south transept front rises from a curving portico to a pediment decked with statuary. The spaces above the windows and niches are carved with reliefs by Cauis Gabriel Cibber featuring swags of foliage and heads of putti. Pride of place in the pediment is given to Cibber's relief of a phoenix rising from the ashes, an image of the cathedral itself rising again after the Great Fire – and a symbol of the Christian resurrection.

St Paul's has two western towers and their encircling columns, bell-shaped caps, and pineapple finials are triumphs of Wren's inventiveness. This is the south-western tower (far left), which was finished in 1708 by Wren's master mason William Kempster. Wren chose a two-level elevation for the side walls of St Paul's with a rhythm of windows and blind niches. The upper level (centre) is actually a stone screen, concealing flying buttresses above the hidden aisle roof. The eastern arm of St Paul's (left) ends in an apse. Its curves mirror those of the great dome above.

church could be planned simply – a rectangular space with good acoustics was the main requirement and the decoration could be basic if the budget was low. But a cathedral was a large, ceremonial space, and the entire British liturgical tradition had developed around the long-naved buildings of English Gothic. So Wren's St Paul's is a hybrid, a Classical building with a dome, built on a plan quite close to that of a Gothic cathedral – a very British compromise.

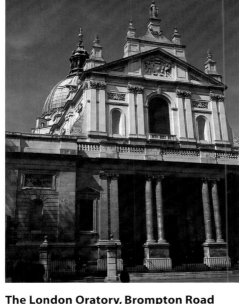

Birmingham Cathedral
Birmingham

St Philip in Birmingham was built as a commodious town church for expanding Birmingham between 1710 and 1715, and the tower was added subsequently and finished in 1725. It became a cathedral in 1905 when the Diocese of Birmingham was created. The architect was Thomas Archer and, with its large pilasters and horizontally banded masonry, his church belongs to the group of baroque buildings of the early 18th century, especially the churches of Nicholas Hawksmoor. Outside, the most striking part of the design is the tower, with its concave bell openings, leaded dome, and colonnaded lantern. Inside, the eye is drawn past the restrained arches of the nave, with their square, fluted piers, towards the chancel. This was an addition of 1883–4, by J A Chatwin. There is no chancel arch, giving an uninterrupted view of the six vast Corinthian columns, with big capitals and chunks of entablature above, that frame this grandiose space. The building only became a cathedral in 1905, but the architect, in creating this space, provided an appropriately imposing setting for the headquarters of the new diocese.

The London Oratory, Brompton Road
London

This building of 1880–93 marked a turning point. It was the first sizeable Roman Catholic church to be built in the capital of England since the Reformation – in other words, since England had ceased to be a predominantly Roman Catholic country. The architect was chosen in a competition, and the winner, Herbert Gribble, produced a design that was very Roman, with a series of domes roofing the nave and many statues imported from Rome itself. A façade of columns, pilasters, and Classical windows, topped by a triangular pediment, fronts the building on the Brompton Road.

Revival greater churches

Anglican cathedral architecture in the Victorian and Edwardian periods followed the fashion for the Gothic revival. As well as major projects such as Truro Cathedral, there were also important additions to existing buildings, such as the replacement nave at Southwark Cathedral, London, by Arthur Blomfield and the nave for Bristol Cathedral by G E Street. The trend continued into the 20th century, with even a mid-century building such as Guildford Cathedral rooted in Gothic tradition. But the other denominations sometimes looked in different stylistic directions.

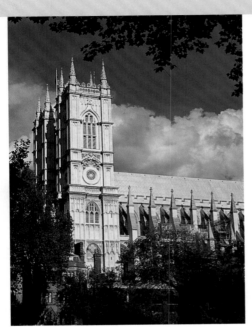

**Westminster Abbey
London**

The abbey at Westminster is London's most famous medieval church, but many visitors fail to realise that its two western towers are in fact post-medieval. They are the work of Nicholas Hawksmoor, who began work on them in 1734, and so are an early example of Gothic revival work on a prominent church. Looking closely, it is possible to see that some of the details such as the carvings above the clock, for example, are very different from what a medieval mason would have produced. But on the whole the towers are convincing, solid examples of medieval revival and a far cry from typical 18th-century 'Gothick'.

**Truro Cathedral
Cornwall**

At Truro the great Victorian church architect J L Pearson was given full scope to produce a Gothic church that would make a dramatic mark on the skyline. His response, begun in 1880, was to build a long, low nave and chancel in the English tradition, but to provide uplift with three spires and a multitude of pointed spirelets on the tops of turrets and pinnacles. Pearson used the early Gothic, or First Pointed style, borrowing the design for his spires from French sources but otherwise creating a very English cathedral exterior, with lancet windows and simple tracery.

**Liverpool Anglican Cathedral
Liverpool**

In 1903 a design by the 22-year-old Giles Gilbert Scott was chosen for Liverpool's new Anglican cathedral. Work on the building began in 1904 and continued until completion in 1978, with G F Bodley originally acting as joint architect with Scott. The cathedral is England's largest, 620 ft (189 m) in length with a central tower 328 ft (100 m) tall. The space beneath the tower alone, which widens into the vast double transepts, is 200 ft (61 m) in length. Scott's design, which he later modified after Bodley's death in 1907, is in an imposing version of Gothic in which the great masses and spaces are more impressive than the details.

The Greek Orthodox Cathedral in west London, built 1877–82, is a shallow-domed building with striped brick walls. This Byzantine style was also taken up by J F Bentley for the Roman Catholic Cathedral at Westminster.

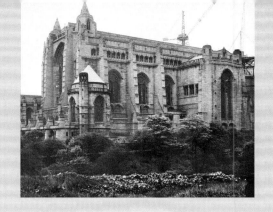

The builders of Liverpool's 20th-century Gothic cathedral used modern equipment such as tower cranes, but even these were dwarfed by the vast edifice.

Guildford Cathedral
Surrey

When the diocese of Winchester was divided in the 1930s, Sir Edward Maufe won the competition to design the new cathedral at Guildford, and his church was built between 1936 and 1961. The site was a challenge for the architect. The good news was that it is a very visible position, high on Stag Hill to the west of the city. The bad news was that the site was rather long and narrow, severely restricting the building's plan. Maufe responded well, planning a long, narrow cathedral, a shape that is very much in the English tradition, but with much slenderer transepts than in most English cathedrals.

For his main material he chose red brick, made from local clay. It looks well on the exterior, which is dominated by its tall, slender windows. It shares with Liverpool's Anglican Cathedral a similar flair for the arrangement of masses, but is rather less dramatic than Scott's vast building. The interior is much paler, combining white plaster with pale dressed limestone. Both inside and out, the building has a powerful simplicity.

Westminster Cathedral, Victoria
London

J F Bentley used a Byzantine style for this Roman Catholic cathedral, evoking images of early Christianity and reflecting the influence of churches in the Mediterranean and Turkey. If the stripes of brick and stone seem alien on an English church, they perhaps looked less unusual in London in 1895–1903 when the cathedral was built – London has plenty of houses and apartment blocks of this period built in brick with stone dressings. In contrast to the traditional materials – mosaic and marble inside as well as the brick and stone without – those who want to ascend the 284 ft (86.5 m)-high tower to admire the view – may do so in a lift.

From a distance, Guildford Cathedral looks rather lean and plain, but as one approaches the doorway in the south transept, a few sculptural details become apparent. The statue of St John the Baptist over the doorway is by Eric Gill, while the bronze doors were designed by Edward Maufe himself.

See also

Gothic survival parish churches, 42
Georgian Gothic parish churches, 50
Victorian parish churches, 56

Modern cathedrals

After the Second World War, two cathedral projects were begun using a modern architectural idiom. The Liverpool Roman Catholic Cathedral, round of plan and tapered of profile, seems to rethink the entire notion of a cathedral from the ground upwards. It is bold and admirable – but once one is used to the striking form of the building, rather disappointing. Coventry is more traditional – it even has a nave with an arcade. Some commentators have found the rich art collection (stained glass, tapestry,

**Coventry Cathedral
Warwickshire**

**Chapel of Christ the Servant
Coventry Cathedral, Warwickshire**

Coventry Cathedral, designed by Sir Basil Spence, was built between 1956 and 1962 next to the ruins of the city's medieval cathedral, destroyed by bombs in the Second World War. The two structures are linked by Spence's porch, with an engraved glass wall through which the ancient Gothic ruins are visible. The exterior is dominated by walls of warm red sandstone punctuated by angled, full-height windows. To the side is the contrasting shape and colour of the Chapel of Unity, a circular, almost free-standing structure connected to the nave by a low corridor. The chapel's radiating fins are clad in blue Westmorland slate and lit by wafer-thin windows. Inside, the eye is drawn inexorably towards

Graham Sutherland's vast tapestry, which occupies the place usually filled by the east window. The tapestry depicts an enormous Christ in Glory with a tiny human figure at his feet, surrounded by the four beasts mentioned in the Bible's Book of Revelation, Chapter 4. Up above is Spence's 20th-century interpretation of a vaulted ceiling, a network of slender concrete ribs infilled with timber slats and supported by tapering columns. The nave and choir are lit by tall, floor-to-ceiling stained-glass windows that are angled so that they cannot be seen from the entrance. When one walks to the choir and turns, the coloured glass is visible – an image of revelation.

This chapel is reached along a passageway from the cathedral's choir. It is a circular room, glazed all the way round with clear glass, in which healing oils are kept. The central altar stands on a plinth, on which are inscribed the words, 'I am among you as one that serves.' The clear glazing means that worshippers inside remain aware of the comings and goings in the street, and this awareness symbolises the unity of the cathedral and the outside world. The glass also allows those outside to look in and be reminded of the church's healing ministry.

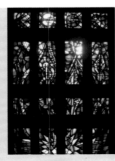

A number of artists, including John Piper, contributed windows to Coventry Cathedral. This example (far left) is by the Swedish artist, Einar Forseth.

The 70 ft (21 m)-tall nave windows of Coventry Cathedral were designed by Lawrence Lee, Geoffrey Clarke, and Keith New. Their effect is heightened because each window has its own dominant palette, so on a sunny day the panels of glass throw bands of colour on to the polished stone floors of nave and aisles.

carving, and so on) rather better than the architecture. But get to know the building, and one can see how the art and architecture work together in a happy marriage of novelty and tradition.

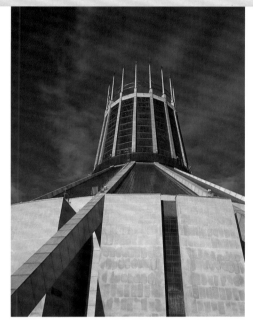

Liverpool Roman Catholic Cathedral
Liverpool

In the 19th century, Liverpool had a huge Roman Catholic population and a number of large Catholic churches, and in 1850 a diocese of Liverpool was created. However, there was still no purpose-built Catholic cathedral in 1928 when a new archbishop, Richard Downey, was appointed. Downey declared that the city needed a 'cathedral for our time' and soon Edwin Lutyens was chosen as architect. Lutyens produced a grand, Byzantine-style design on a massive scale, but only the crypt of this ambitious church was built. By the end of the Second World War it was realised that a smaller, less costly building was needed, and a competition was held to find a new design. The winner was

Frederick Gibberd and his cathedral seemed revolutionary when it was completed in 1967. Gibberd gave it a round shape, inspired by a movement to make the Mass more 'accessible'. The structure is held together by 16 radial ribs of concrete faced with stone and topped by a steel, concrete, and stained-glass lantern. Immediately below is the central altar, a single block of white marble with a crucifix of gilt bronze by Elizabeth Frink. The stained glass in the lantern, by John Piper and Patrick Reyntiens, suffuses the spacious interior with coloured light. The resulting form is rather angular, but certainly fulfils the brief of making the focus the altar.

The structure, which sits next to a piazza that conceals Lutyens' crypt, provoked the English trait for giving nicknames to unusual buildings: the architecturally and politically incorrect 'Paddy's wigwam' has stuck, 'Mersey funnel' has not.

See also
20th-century churches, 62

Union Chapel, Hallaton, Leicestershire

Religious nonconformity began outside the law. The puritans and separatists of the early 17th century wanted respectively to reform the Established Church – the Church of England – and to worship independently, but the law banned independent religious meetings. So dissent continued to be secret and illegal, yet by 1640 there were said to be around 80 regular 'conventicles' or meetings of dissenters, in London alone. This state of affairs carried on until the Toleration Act was passed in 1689, when there was an immediate boom in registering places of worship for use by Baptists, Independents, and other dissenting groups.

Religious dissent flourished throughout the 18th and 19th centuries. It was especially strong in the industrial towns that were growing during this period, towns that were targeted by inspiring preachers such as John Wesley, who could command outdoor congregations of thousands. But there were many Nonconformists in the countryside too. Small brick chapels became a familiar part of the landscape from Cornwall to Lincolnshire, with Methodists, Unitarians, Plymouth Brethren, and the Salvation Army joining the other denominations so that a large village might have several chapels, all with small but loyal congregations.

The background of secrecy and the dissenting suspicion of religious imagery made most of these buildings plain. But they are not drab. Honest use of simple materials such as brick and pine, together with the adoption of good proportions, make England's Nonconformist chapels and Quaker meeting houses real visual assets.

Like their faith, Nonconformists' architecture often relies on and serves the word of God, believed to be embodied in the Bible. Often there is an inscription on the entrance front, giving the name of the chapel and sometimes its date of building or foundation. Inside, texts painted on the walls may focus the mind on the Bible. The pulpit is generally the most prominent fitting and often the only item that is elaborately carved. Clear glass windows provide plenty of natural light so that worshippers can read their Bibles and hymn books.

Buildings such as Methodist chapels, Salvation Army 'citadels', and – often the plainest of them all – Quaker meeting houses, were long ignored by those interested in architecture. Plain and simple, they languished in the shadows of the showier and more ancient churches. So when congregations fell away in the secular 20th century, chapels were often demolished. But these buildings had their enthusiasts, such as the poet John Betjeman, and their scholars, such as those who surveyed and wrote about them for the Royal Commission on the Historical Monuments of England (now English Heritage). As a result, they are cherished more and more.

The non-Christian religions have their architectural heritage too, although their buildings are relatively few. Jewish communities have been building synagogues since the beginning of the 18th century and these are quite numerous because traditionally Jews need to live within walking distance of their place of worship. The first purpose-built mosque in England was built in 1889 and in the 20th century Hindu temples, Sikh gurdwaras, and other places of worship began to appear.

In most cases it is important to realise that for these faiths – although they may draw on all sorts of styles of building – elaborate architecture is less important than providing the necessary space and practical facilities for worship. A mosque, for example, does not have to have a minaret, and a gurdwara is not marked by exterior features but by the fact that it correctly houses a copy of the Sikh scriptures.

In this, these mosques and temples are not so unlike the dissenting Christian churches. They can take on a variety of exterior forms, so long as they provide the faithful with the needs prescribed by their faith. In creating the required religious form, building it, using it, and perhaps altering it over the years, religious communities of all kinds produce buildings that can inspire and absorb all, of whatever faith, who take the time to look at them.

Early chapels

The early dissenters turned their backs on the pomp, imagery, and magnificence of the Established Church. Simple, scarcely decorated buildings helped them to concentrate on the essence of their faith. Persecuted and traduced, they also favoured a low profile. So the earliest surviving Nonconformist chapels are unassuming, easy to miss or mistake for houses, and unremarkable as architecture. But their very simplicity makes them moving because it speaks of small, marginalised communities of Baptists and Presbyterians who had to struggle for their beliefs and for the right to celebrate the Lord's supper around a plain wooden table in a building that could truly be called the *house* of God.

Congregational Chapel, Walpole
Suffolk

From the outside, the old chapel at Walpole looks like a pair of cottages and is as unassuming as some of the early meeting houses in New England. It probably began life as a house or houses, since it was built in 1607 and converted to religious use in 1647. The building was enlarged at the end of the 17th century and remains very much as the early worshippers would have known it. Only the modern sign and the gravestones around it make it obvious that this is a religious building. The interior of this anonymous-looking building creates the kind of surprise that must once have been common in the dissenters' places of worship, because once you are inside a full array of pews and other furnishings make the chapel's function perfectly clear. Within the Walpole chapel everything is simple and light – the interior is well lit by windows in walls and roof, and many of the surfaces are painted white or cream. Numbered box pews stand on the plain brick floor. Oil lamps hang above. A large wooden column (reputed to have been the mast of a ship from Yarmouth) helps to hold up the roof. Smaller square pillars and charming, twisted-iron columns topped with spiral ornaments support galleries that run around three sides of the building, all facing towards a pulpit positioned in the middle of one of the long sides. No member of the congregation would be far away from the pulpit. Plain paintwork and pine boards afford little distraction from the sermon. The rest of the furnishings are simple and functional, apart from the early notice of a sermon and tea meeting, an item of printed ephemera that – like the building itself – brings to life in a vivid way the history of religious dissent.

When still in use for worship, the former Baptist chapel at Maltby-le-Marsh had a gallery, wooden panelling and plain white walls.

Old Baptist Chapel, Tewkesbury Gloucestershire

Tucked away up an alley in Tewkesbury, the Old Baptist Chapel is a timber-framed building that perhaps dates back to the early 16th century, when it would have been a house. It would have officially become a chapel in the late 17th century, although it may have been used for worship before. Unremarkable from the outside, apart from some picturesque timber framing, the chapel retains some of its 17th-century fittings inside, including the communion table. Sunk into the floor and hidden beneath a cover, a brick-lined baptistery for total immersion baptisms may be 18th century. The gallery is modern, but is in the style of a traditional chapel interior.

Former Baptist Chapel, Maltby-le-Marsh Lincolnshire

Chapels do not come much simpler than this early example at Maltby-le-Marsh. It is firmly in the vernacular tradition of this part of Lincolnshire, where nearly every house of any age is a box of red brick roofed with pantiles. The windows and door are similarly typical of the houses of north-east Lincolnshire, although here they are probably replacements. There was a Baptist chapel at Maltby as early as 1690 but this building was erected in 1776 with money given by local Baptist David Dent, who also bequeathed money to look after the chapel and graveyard.

Independent Chapel, Stoke Row Oxfordshire

By the early 19th century, the archetypal design of the small village chapel had emerged. The origins in the domestic-style buildings of the 17th and 18th centuries are clear: this building of 1815 is built of plain brick with a hipped roof, like the chapel at Maltby. But two additions make it look more like a religious building. The first is the small, round-headed window – much bigger ones, often in pairs, were favoured by chapel builders. The other detail is the porch, a place in which worshippers could wipe the mud from their shoes and generally prepare to enter the chapel proper.

A brick arch marked by a cast-iron sign leads to the burial ground next to the Old Baptist Chapel in Tewkesbury. Beyond is the river, which may well have been the scene of early baptisms.

See also

Rural chapels, 88
Urban chapels, 90
Quaker meeting houses, 92

Rural chapels

The great age of building for Nonconformism was in the 18th and 19th centuries when chapels were erected all over England. A pattern emerged, especially in the countryside, of a small chapel built of brick, often with a hipped roof. The windows were flat-topped or round-headed, usually with leaded lights, and the door was at the west end. Inside was a rectangular space dominated by the pulpit. All Nonconformist denominations – Baptists, Independents, Unitarians, Plymouth Brethren – built in this way, but in the 19th century the great expansion was in Methodism.

Methodist Church, Patrington
East Yorkshire

It is pleasing to come across a building that presents such a clean and bright face to the world as Patrington's Methodist Church of 1811. Like many such buildings, it is an interesting mixture of domestic simplicity and architectural pretension. The large Tuscan-looking pediment, the enormous quoins, and the scroll brackets on either side of the door point to grandeur – a rustic grandeur indeed – especially now that the details are picked out in green. But the windows are domestic in size and design and the sides are in patterned brickwork. It is a mixture of styles, but it works.

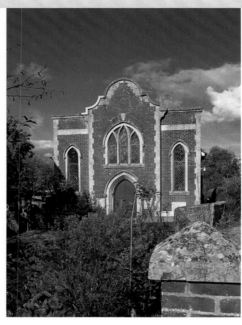

Memorial Baptist Chapel, Stockbridge
Hampshire

Many small chapels display a simple form of Gothic in brick, with windows and doorways in stone. The plainest Early English features were favoured – lancet windows and the most basic bar tracery, as here at Stockbridge. Such simplicity was fairly cheap to produce and appealed to Nonconformists who wanted to avoid what was seen as the frivolous – or even Popish – decoration of later Gothic. But the builders at Stockbridge did allow themselves a little more scope, framing their frontage with stone quoins and adding a rounded, almost Dutch, gable. The whole helps a little-noticed building make a serious but attractive impression.

Methodist Church, Misterton
Nottinghamshire

Another example of the Classical-Gothic mix in a Nonconformist building is found in the Methodist Church at Misterton. Here the level of grandeur is higher. There is a generous amount of pale brick, plaster, and painted decoration; the skyline is challenged with a row of finials; the central window has an ornate head with the date of the building; and the tall pilasters have rather lively Composite capitals that seem a world away from the simplicities of earlier chapels such as Stoke Row, Oxfordshire. The whole composition shows the Methodists could make their mark as boldly as any other denomination, old or new.

Because Methodism itself had a number of different divisions, this meant thousands of new buildings. Unregarded by conservationists until recently, many small chapels have been demolished or converted to other uses. Those that hang on deserve our support for their conservation.

Union Chapel, Hallaton
Leicestershire

The Union Chapel is one of those rural places of worship in which the formal style of the dissenting chapel seems to be emerging from the domestic form of the earliest Nonconformist churches. Here the main focus of interest is the middle of the frontage, with a clock, date stone, and doorway. Red brick, a common material in the Midlands, would have been the obvious material here in 1822 when the chapel was first built. It would soon be the usual material for hundreds of similar buildings, compact, unpretentious, and born of reverence for the word of God.

Meeting Room, Woodmancote
Worcestershire

We are used to thinking of buildings in a visual hierarchy, with stone cathedrals at the top of the aesthetic tree, followed by buildings in various kinds of brick lower down, and structures made of mud – timber-framed cottages and the like – near the bottom. Lower still come the buildings – usually farm sheds, warehouses, or factories and the like – made of corrugated iron. A tin church, of all things, is likely to get sneered at by passers-by because we expect churches to be built of 'high-status' materials such as stone – or at least of brick with decorative stone details. Yet metal churches had many advantages. They were inexpensive and practical. They were easy to erect by attaching the sheets of corrugated iron to a simple wooden frame, and they were straightforward to maintain. What is more, the corduroy lines of this building at Woodmancote, under their red iron roof with curvy bargeboards and finials, are rather attractive in this leafy setting. The church is functional and democratic too: 'All are welcome' says both the sign and the architecture.

The fanlight above the doorway of the Hallaton Union Chapel is enlivened with narrow glazing bars arranged in the form of Y-tracery, the front's one gesture towards the Gothic taste.

See also

Early chapels, 86
Urban chapels, 90
Quaker meeting houses, 92

Urban chapels

In the towns, Nonconformists were sometimes able to spend more money and produce chapels that were not only big enough for urban congregations but also more grandiose than their counterparts in the countryside. A Classical idiom was widely used, for the proportions of Classical architecture lent themselves to simple rectangular spaces with the good acoustics that were demanded in a sermon-based religious culture. In addition, Classical architecture could be effective without a lot of ornament. The style could also be adapted to provide internal galleries supported on columns, so that big town congregations could be accommodated without anyone having to sit too far away from the pulpit.

Octagon Chapel
Norwich

The Octagon Chapel in Norwich, with its unusual shape and details like round dormer windows that peep out of its roof, seems a surprisingly fanciful design for a Nonconformist place of worship. But Thomas Ivory, the resourceful builder, architect, timber merchant, and entrepreneur who designed this chapel of 1754–6 had an inspired idea. An octagonal plan made a good way of seating a sizeable congregation in a compact space within easy hearing distance of the pulpit, and the windows, including the little *oeils de boeuf* in the roof, make for a light and pleasant interior.

Independent Chapel, Market Harborough
Leicestershire

The Independent Chapel is an example of urban – and urbane – architecture. Its Classical façade of 1844 is impressive, but in a very restrained way. The light-coloured brickwork and even paler columns and cornices make a quietly elegant impression, the portico and centre bay do not stick out too far, most of the windows have very plain surrounds, and there is no pediment. Even the way in which the building stands back from the street is rather unassuming. This building seems to stand for a religious community that is confident enough to use the trappings of Classicism without trying to make a big show.

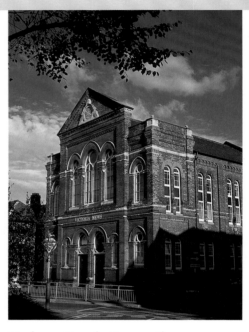

Wesleyan Temple, Tamworth
Staffordshire

This is quite a grandiose building, as the name 'Temple' suggests. The big pediment, large showy windows, and the side wings that make the front wider all seem to shout for our attention – the material may be humble red brick, yet the building is far from humble. But the builders could not seem to make up their minds what style they were building in. Although the pediment and pilasters are Classical features, the windows are topped with pointed Gothic dripstones and contain glazing bars that make patterns rather like medieval tracery.

Alcohol was frowned upon by most dissenters and chapels promoted tea drinking. As if to prove the point, The Tabernacle at Wellingborough in Northamptonshire emblazoned its name across its cups and saucers.

Surrey Chapel, Blackfriars Road, London, was an unusual round chapel built in 1782, later used for boxing matches, and finally destroyed in the Second World War. This picture shows it in the 1870s.

Bethesda Chapel, Stoke-on-Trent
Staffordshire

This corner of a large town chapel shows the variations a prosperous mid-19th-century urban community could play on the traditional Nonconformist interior. As in most chapels of this type, the main aim was to pack in plenty of box pews within comfortable distance of the pulpit. But here the box pews have panelling and mouldings in abundance and the galleries above, holding more pews, are supported by columns that are classically fluted. The most ingenious touch is the concave vaulted ceiling beneath the gallery. This allowed the builders to fit extra large windows, flooding the pews beneath with natural light so that everyone could read their hymn books.

Melbourne Hall
Leicester

Melbourne Hall was built in 1880–1 to the design of Goddard and Paget, a firm who had a long history of practice in the Leicester area and won this commission in a competition. The massive octagonal brick building is in an adapted early Gothic style, the huge interior space lit by lancets and wheel windows. With its towering roof it immediately became a landmark and some locals, perhaps put off by its unusual shape, compared it to a candle snuffer. But its admirers preferred Joseph Goddard's description of the church as a lantern – leading the faithful along the true path of righteousness, no doubt.

Fairhaven Congregational Church, Lytham
Lancashire

This extraordinary building has been surprising passers-by since it was completed in 1912. Clad in gleaming white faience slabs, and known locally simply as the White Church, it is built in a style which, with its little domes, round arches, and criss-crossing tracery, owes something to Byzantine architecture. As a contrast, and to remind worshippers they are in a Nonconformist church and not some place of worship by the Bosphorus, architects Briggs, Wolstenholme and Thornely of Blackburn commissioned stained-glass windows illustrating scenes from the lives of dissenting heroes such as Martin Luther, John Wyclif, and the American Pilgrims.

A terracotta gate pier contrasts with the pale walls of Lytham's White Church.

See also

Early chapels, 86
Rural chapels, 88
Quaker meeting houses, 92

Quaker meeting houses

There is no Quaker style of architecture. Quaker meetings take place in all sorts of buildings from ancient to modern. From the outside, meeting houses are nearly always very simple, because the Society of Friends, as the Quakers are formally known, has always been wary of showiness.

Inside, they have plain rooms simply furnished. The traditional arrangement was to have benches arranged around three sides of the room with the fourth side occupied by a dais or stand, where the elders sat. Today, many meeting houses still have their free-standing benches. Such movable seating

Jordans
Buckinghamshire

Hertford
Hertfordshire

This is one of the best known early Quaker meeting houses because of its connections with the Penn family (of Pennsylvania), many of whom are buried in the graveyard. Those who lie here include William Penn, the founder of Pennsylvania. Penn had intended to spend his last years in North America but, having come to England to oppose a bill to make Pennsylvania a crown colony, remained in the land of his birth until his death in 1718. Before the meeting house was constructed, members of the Society of Friends had to hold clandestine meetings in local houses, but in 1688 the Toleration Act permitted them to worship openly and the widow of local Quaker Isaac Pennington paid

for the meeting house to be built. It is a simple, hipped-roofed, brick structure incorporating a two-storey house for the caretaker next to the meeting house itself. Inside there is a gallery at one end, a slightly raised floor to form the stand at the other. The walls are panelled to dado level, and the panelling rises slightly at the elders' end. Everything is simple and the interior is filled with light from the rectangular windows.

Even in an important county town, the meeting house could be quite a modest building. This was not because the Quakers lacked wealth, rather because they did not believe that their meeting houses had any special claim to sanctity. Holiness was vested in beliefs and in the individual's relationship with God, not in fine buildings, and money was more likely to be spent on good works than on conspicuous architecture. The red-brick meeting house at Hertford goes back to 1670. Beneath its two gables there were originally mullioned windows and twin doors, in the traditional layout.

The white shutters and panelled double door lift the Jordans meeting house above the usual domestic-looking exterior. The shutters are also features that can provide extra privacy and warmth, two things no doubt valued by early worshippers.

is useful because the room accommodates a variety of functions: it is not a sanctified space like other Christian places of worship, although most meeting houses nevertheless have an atmosphere of devotion to God.

This old image of the furnishings at Nailsworth, Gloucestershire, shows a meeting-house interior at its simplest.

Mount Street
Manchester

Not all meeting houses are modest. This one, designed by Richard Lane and built in 1828–31, has a muted Classicism that owes a lot to the contemporary Greek revival and James Stuart and Nicholas Revett's book *The Antiquities of Athens*. The attached Ionic columns on this stone-clad front, however, have a seriousness that feels quite in keeping with the Friends' usual attitude to building. The interior has been much altered. Originally there were men's and women's rooms separated by screens that could be moved using a mechanism in the roof so that the two spaces could be made into one.

Gainsborough
Lincolnshire

Like many other meeting houses, this one is in the typical style of a local residential property, namely Lincolnshire brick. The main building is set modestly away from the street and a variety of sash and casement windows are testament to a history of basic repair and replacement, many no doubt dating from a number of changes made in the 1870s. Inside the traditional arrangements and fittings, including the stand (a dais) and the gallery, are preserved – once more, a fascinating history is housed in an apparently unassuming building.

Bournville
Warwickshire

The settlement of Bournville, near Birmingham, was founded by the Quaker Cadbury family for the workers in their Bournville chocolate factory. Its meeting house was designed by William Alexander Harvey in 1905 and enlarged some 15 years later. It is unusually ornate for a meeting house, a Y-shaped building with side rooms in the arms of the Y and the main meeting room in the centre. It is in the Arts and Crafts tradition, with its low, sweeping roofs, round-headed doorway, and quaint stair turret with conical roof. But although elaborate, it is not a showy building and fits well into the well-planted garden suburb ambience of Bournville.

See also

Early chapels, 86
Rural chapels, 88
Urban chapels, 90

Synagogues

In 1290, Edward I expelled the Jews from Britain and Jewish people were only legally readmitted and permitted to practise their religion during the 17th century, after a petition to Oliver Cromwell in 1655. The history of synagogue building in England is therefore only a little over 300 years old and early synagogues survive in the towns where Jews settled. Whatever the style synagogues may adopt, all share a number of common internal features. All have an Ark, or cabinet, in which the Torah scrolls are kept

Spanish and Portuguese Synagogue, Bevis Marks, London

Britain's oldest synagogue was built in 1700–1 for the local Sephardic Jews by Joseph Avis, a Quaker who refused payment for his work. Queen Anne donated one of the large timbers for the roof. It is a plain building, lit by round- and segmentally topped windows, but with beautiful fittings. As in all synagogues, the focus is the Ark, where the Torah scrolls are kept. Here it is beautifully made in wood, with a front of three sections, all panelled. The rest of the synagogue is also dominated by fine woodwork – twisted balusters, long benches, and a gallery with latticework front. Seven stunning brass chandeliers from Amsterdam provide candlelight.

Montefiore Synagogue, Ramsgate Kent

This synagogue is one of only a handful of pre-Victorian synagogues in Britain. Designed in elegant Classical style by the Anglo-Jewish architect David Mocatta, it was built in 1831–2. The founder of the synagogue was Sir Moses Montefiore (1784–1885), the most prominent member of Britain's Jewish community at the time and a generous philanthropist. The synagogue was originally in the grounds of Montefiore's house and his mausoleum of 1862 is next to it. The tomb is based on the one near Jerusalem which is said to belong to Rachel, the Old Testament character.

Middle Street Synagogue, Brighton East Sussex

One of the most ornate Victorian synagogues, Middle Street was built in 1874 when the local Jewish community moved from Devonshire Place in Brighton. Architect Thomas Lainson designed an imposing façade in a mixture of yellow brick and colourful dressings, colours that give the building a character different from anything else nearby. Inside, the building is still more ornate, with the colourful theme continued in bright stained glass that was fitted to the windows in the late 19th century. The synagogue's galleries are supported on columns that have capitals representing fruits mentioned in the Bible. Iron and brass railings enclose the Ark and frame the cantor's desk and the sanctuary.

and in front of which an Eternal Light burns. They have a bimah, or platform, from which the Torah is read. Orthodox synagogues have a separate area for the women of the congregation, although at other synagogues, men and women sit together.

Highfield Street Synagogue
Leicester

This impressive synagogue was built in 1898 for an expanding Jewish community in Leicester by Arthur Wakerley, a Leicester architect who produced many buildings for the growing city. Wakerley is one of the unsung local heroes of English architecture, a man who found fame in his own region but is little known outside it. He was a prominent Leicester citizen, a Methodist who was once mayor of his home town and who was appointed President of the Leicester Society of Architects. Like most local architects of the late 19th and early 20th centuries, Wakerley had to be versatile. For the

synagogue he adopted a vaguely eastern style, evoked by a prominent round-headed doorway, and, above all, by the tower. This has a pleasingly curvaceous parapet above which is a dome surmounted by a little lantern, topped in turn by an onion-shaped cupola. It is all very exotic, but the material, red brick, is reassuringly British.

Ryhope Road Synagogue, Sunderland
County Durham

Newcastle architect Marcus K Glass designed the Ryhope Road Synagogue, which has been described as Art Deco Ottoman in style and is certainly as exotic as many buildings put up in the 1920s, a decade that went in for exotic styles. The big, arched window, unusual pattern of tracery bars, polychrome brick, and bold massing combine to produce a building unlike anything from the Art Deco or Ottoman eras, a synagogue that stands out. The only similar building is another synagogue by Glass, which was built in Lea Bridge Road, east London, a few years later.

Chamfered brickwork and a neat Hebrew inscription surround the doorway of the Leicester synagogue.

See also

Mosques and temples

Of the faiths that have made an architectural mark on Britain during the last century or so, two stand out: Islam and Hinduism. There are now many Muslim communities in Britain and many mosques. Most are simple buildings, often in structures converted from other uses, but a few adopt the architectural style of the Arab states, Turkey, or Mughal India to create a stunning roofscape of domes and minarets. Such buildings may be quite complex, with rooms for education and the organisation of charitable works, but the essence of a mosque is that it provides a prayer hall

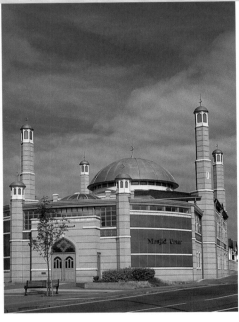

Shah Jehan Mosque, Woking
Surrey

Opened in 1889, this is the earliest purpose-built mosque in Britain. It was commissioned by Hungarian-born scholar Gottlieb Wilhelm Leitner, who had been professor of Arabic and Muslim Law at King's College London, and established a centre for oriental studies in Woking. The mosque was designed by W I Chambers, who based it on Indian buildings that he researched in the library of the Indian Office in London. The round dome, ogee arches, and window screens with their patterns of stars and hexagons all come from this source. Inside is a compact, square prayer hall adorned with verses from the Qur'an in beautiful calligraphy. On either side of this main building are apsed pavilions containing running water supplies for ritual washing.

Central Mosque, Regent's Park
London

London's main mosque was the result of years of planning throughout much of the 20th century. After a long campaign, an Islamic Centre was built in 1944 on a plot of land in Regent's Park given by King George VI. Plans for the mosque itself culminated in 1969 in a competition, won by architect Sir Frederick Gibberd. The finished mosque, with its large metal-clad dome, opened in 1977. Inside are large prayer halls, adorned in Islamic style with pierced screens and beautiful calligraphy, together with a library and other buildings. A new administrative and educational wing was opened in 1994.

Masjid Umar Mosque
Leicester

With no fewer than four minarets and a large dome, this mosque is on a grand scale, emulating the large mosques of cities such as Istanbul, as befits a city with a large Muslim population. As usual, the decoration is based on abstract patterns, for Islam forbids figurative art. So stripes in the brickwork and bands of stone give the walls interest, but not in a way that distracts from the overall form of the building, for the colours are subtle and the palette restricted.

Calligraphy is highly important in Islamic art, and an Arabic inscription crowns the entrance to Leicester's mosque.

containing a niche called a mihrab, which indicates the direction of Mecca. Hindu temples are a still more recent arrival. Again they may be simple buildings, but there are one or two stunning examples, drawing on the centuries old Hindu traditions of carving and decoration.

Central Oxford Mosque
Oxford

Designer Mohammed Ehsan used red brick for the recently built Central Oxford Mosque and Islamic Centre. It is an appropriate choice, since the mosque is not situated in the stone-built streets of the city centre, but in east Oxford, an area where there are streets of Victorian brick houses. Stone dressings are saved for details such as the minaret. So the building is very much of its community – as every mosque, which is a place of learning and a social centre as well as the home of prayer and worship, must be.

Shri Swaminarayan Mandir, Neasden
London

A place of prayer and worship for part of London's Hindu community, the Shri Swaminarayan Mandir was built according to ancient Hindu principles. In the early 1990s, thousands of tonnes of limestone and Carrara marble were shipped from Europe to India, where they were carved by more than 1,500 craft workers before being brought to London and fitted together, between 1993 and 1995, to make this extraordinary temple, the largest Hindu place of worship outside India.

Its domes are built along traditional Indian lines, without the use of steel or lead, and there are six of them, together with a number of pinnacles that are the outstanding landmark on the skyline of north-west London. The Mandir is not only a place of worship but also a centre for information and teaching about Hinduism, and the focus for a range of social welfare activities, from recycling aluminium cans to helping the poor in India.

The Central Oxford Mosque has red-brick perimeter walls in which flattened Islamic arches are picked out in paler bricks.

The crowning spires of the Neasden temple with their flags fluttering in the breeze are impossible to miss on the north London skyline.

See also
The Picturesque and exotic, 146

Buildwas Abbey, Shropshire

MONASTIC BUILDINGS

There were several hundred monastic houses in England throughout the Middle Ages until the monasteries were dissolved by Henry VIII in the 1530s. At this point many monasteries were left to become ruins, their stones partly removed and recycled elsewhere. In some cases, a group of monastic buildings was turned into a home by a Tudor lord, and some medieval monastic remains can still be found in later country houses. Sometimes the church continued in use by laypeople – several of our cathedrals, such as Durham and Gloucester, and some of our parish churches are former monastic churches. In this book, the monastic churches are included in the chapters on ecclesiastical architecture; the other buildings of the medieval monasteries – their domestic accommodation, cloisters, service buildings, and so on – are considered here.

In the early Middle Ages, England's monks and nuns mostly followed the rule of St Benedict and became known as Benedictines. They built numerous monasteries and many remain from the Norman period onwards. The Benedictines developed the standard monastic plan, with a church next to a covered passage round a quadrangle. This was called a cloister and gave access to a number of communal rooms for eating, sleeping, study, meetings, and other functions. The whole was contained within a precinct – an area containing all sorts of other buildings and protected by walls and gatehouses.

By the 10th century, many felt that the existing monasteries had moved away somewhat from the original monastic ideals. Monasteries had begun to interpret the rules of their monastic orders in a way that many people regarded as lax. Some monks wanted a return to a stricter regime, so a series of attempts at reform began, with the creation of new monastic orders. The Cluniac order was a reformed group stemming from Cluny in France, whose often ornate buildings can be seen at sites such as Much Wenlock, Shropshire.

The Cistercians, a yet more austere order, began in Cîteaux, France, in the 12th century. They built many abbeys in England, often in isolated rural settings, and usually in a particularly plain form of Gothic. Their number included lay brethren, whose duties included manual labour, and these men were accommodated separately from the other monks, meaning that Cistercian monasteries have a slightly different layout from those of other orders. The most striking Cistercian abbeys include Rievaulx and Fountains, both in North Yorkshire.

Other orders that appeared during the Middle Ages include the Carthusians, whose monasteries consisted of a number of separate cells next to a communal church; their most impressive English remains are at Mount Grace, North Yorkshire. There were also orders of friars, preaching monks who were usually based in friaries in towns, buildings that survive in mostly very fragmentary form. Another important group were the canons regular, monks whose duties involved a priestly ministry to their lay neighbours. Prominent among the orders of canons were the Augustinians, who were known for their provision of hospitals and who often settled in urban areas. Important remains of their buildings survive at Lacock, Wiltshire, and Haughmond, Shropshire. Another order of canons, the order of Premontré, also known as the White Canons, tended to prefer more rural settings and to value hard manual work. Easby, North Yorkshire, is one of their most notable houses. There were a number of other orders of monks and nuns, such as the Gilbertines, the only indigenous English order, but the remains they have left behind are mostly very fragmentary ruins.

This diversity of monastic order and lifestyle produced a rich architecture. How rich can be seen not just in vast ruined sites such as the Cistercian abbey at Fountains, but also in stunning individual buildings that have survived intact: the glorious chapter houses that remain in many formerly monastic cathedrals; elegant cloister walks; the abbot's kitchen at Glastonbury, Somerset; the fine dormitory and refectory at Cleeve, Somerset; the dozens of monastic gatehouses, often highly ornate, up and down the country – all these are examples of the glories of monastic architecture, preserved against the odds, to give us clues about the way of life of men and women who dedicated themselves to the service of God more than 500 years ago.

Cloisters

The cloister was a rectangular walkway that connected the main buildings of a monastery and also acted as a work space for the monks or nuns. Usually found to the south of the nave, the cloister walks had doorways on their outer walls, leading to such rooms as the chapter house and refectory. The inner sides of the walks were arcaded, and the arches of the arcade looked on to a rectangular courtyard or garden known as the garth. The cloister walk nearest the church was usually the place where the monks studied, and could contain carrels and book cupboards.

Rievaulx Abbey
North Yorkshire

Many cloisters have been in ruins since Henry VIII destroyed the monasteries in the 1530s, and visitors to sites such as Rievaulx have to use their imagination to piece them together. Most of those that survive are Gothic, but a few stone shafts and voussoirs survive from the Norman 12th-century cloister at the great ruined Cistercian abbey of Rievaulx. One corner of this cloister has been reconstructed so that its form can be seen. It has pairs of shafts supporting very plain arches with a cluster of four shafts at the corner itself. The simplicity of the arches was typical of the Cistercians, a strict order that did not approve of lavish architectural ornament.

Worcester Cathedral
Worcestershire

Cloister walks originally had open sides, but this must have made them uncomfortable for the monks or nuns who worked in the walkways in all seasons. So by the later Middle Ages, many were filled with tracery and glass like these at Worcester. These windows have tracery of the late Gothic Perpendicular style, but the glass is later and includes memorial panels to people connected with the cathedral who lost their lives in the First World War.

Cloister walk, Gloucester Cathedral
Gloucestershire

The cloister survived because the abbey became a cathedral under Henry VIII. The cloister walk is beautifully fan vaulted in the late Perpendicular manner, a style current in Gloucester by the 1350s, because the abbey was in the vanguard of architectural progress in the 14th century. Between each window and stone-panelled recess are the springings of the fan vault's swelling cones, each of which bears the tracery-like patterns that occur everywhere in Perpendicular architecture and give it such visual unity. In one of the other walks stone carrels, each with just enough space for a monk and a desk, provided spaces for study.

Cloisters in abbey churches that have become cathedrals sometimes house collections of items reclaimed from elsewhere in the medieval building. At Bristol there are many beautiful fragments of medieval stained glass let into the cloister windows, reminders of the colourful glory of the medieval church.

The western walk was commonly used for teaching the novices. Another walk, near the refectory, could contain the monks' washing place. With their elegant arches looking on to the garth and their vaulted ceilings, cloisters are among the most beautiful spaces in medieval buildings.

Although many are now ruined, there are good examples in monasteries that have survived as cathedrals.

Lavatorium, Gloucester Cathedral
Gloucestershire

Hailes Abbey
Gloucestershire

One of the most charming features of the cloister at Gloucester is also very practical – the washing-place or lavatorium. Washing was important in the Middle Ages to ensure the monk's physical cleanliness and to symbolise that he was ritually clean. So lavatoria were usually sited in or near the refectory so that the religious could wash their hands before meals. The one at Gloucester has a stone trough (originally lead-lined) which would have been filled with fresh water at one end and drained at the other. The lavatorium has a stone ceiling that is a miniature version of the cloister's fan vault.

At Hailes, only fragments remain of the cloister walks and much of this is not the original cloister because this part of the monastery was rebuilt in the late 15th century, more than 200 years after the abbey was founded. It appears that the first cloister was probably a simple lean-to construction of wood and that this was rebuilt with what was intended to be a more permanent structure. It is thought that building work was still going on almost up to the time when the abbey was dissolved in 1539. At Hailes, the cloister provided somewhere for the monks to store books. Books were central to the medieval monastic life.

In the centuries before printing, they had to be handmade, and many monks spent their working lives copying religious works. Produced slowly, carefully, and with great art, books were scarce, precious objects and a few dozen would comprise a large library. So monasteries did not need big rooms for book storage. Most had a cupboard or two in the cloister near where the monks read and worked. At Hailes, five large niches remain in the north wall of the cloister, three of which are still well preserved. These were probably book cupboards.

See also

Norman greater churches, 66
Early English greater churches, 70
Decorated greater churches, 72
Perpendicular greater churches, 74

Chapter houses

The daily business meeting of the inhabitants of a monastery was called the chapter (because a chapter of the order's rule was read there each day) and took place in the chapter house. This important room was usually located off the eastern walk of the cloister. It was a formal room, and was often beautifully decorated, or even grand. It was, after all, the place where important outsiders would meet with the monks or nuns to discuss business. Early chapter houses were rectangular, but during

Bristol Cathedral
Bristol

The decoration that the Augustinian monks of Bristol lavished on their chapter house indicates the significance of this room – after the church it was the most important space in the monastery. Covered with abstract patterns, it is in the most ornate manner of the 1150s or 1160s. At ground level the seats for the monks are ranged around the walls and above the seats the walls are decorated with intersecting arches. Look up still further and the eye is greeted with a profusion of lattice and zigzag decoration before the vault ribs, also covered with zigzag, take over.

Haughmond Abbey
Shropshire

An important room needed a grand entrance, and the doorways of some chapter houses were as imposing as those of major churches or cathedrals. At Haughmond, founded in around 1130 for the Augustinian order, the Normans built what at first glance looks like a triple portal in the most ornate style of the late 12th century. In fact the outer two arches were pierced with windows, each originally with two openings, which perhaps let a little light in on the deliberations within. The inner arch is the doorway proper, set off with three orders of arches resting on shafts. The decoration looks quite plain now, but the carved hood-mould shows that the doorway was once more ornate. The interior of this chapter house is also interesting because it has a carved timber ceiling. This is rather unusual, because chapter house ceilings were so often vaulted and where they did have wooden ceilings, these have not usually survived the ravages of time.

the Gothic period there was a fashion for many-sided chapter houses with beautiful vaulted ceilings and stone seats around the walls for all the monks or nuns.

**Wenlock Priory
Shropshire**

The remains of the chapter house at Much Wenlock show that the Cluniac order was just as resourceful with Norman decoration as their Augustinian counterparts at Bristol. Even in its ruined state, with only the springings to hint at the vault and many of the interlaced arches defaced or decayed, the magnificence is unmistakeable.

**Buildwas Abbey
Shropshire**

A monastery of the Cistercians, whose watchword was austerity, Buildwas was more plainly built than Augustinian or Cluniac houses such as Bristol and Wenlock. In the chapter house the big entrance doorway flanked by windows is retained, but the intricacies of interlace and zigzag are replaced by the simpler beauties of plain round and octagonal piers rising to a ribbed vault. Any decoration is provided by mouldings rather than bold patterning. This is still 12th-century work, but in spite of the rough surfaces one sees hints of the slender elegance of the Gothic style to come.

**Southwell Minster
Nottinghamshire**

In the later Middle Ages there was a fashion for polygonal chapter houses with seats all around the walls beneath large windows. One of the best, although it is not part of a monastic complex, is at Southwell Minster. It is eight-sided and is decorated with superb carving – mainly of foliage but also of birds, goats, hares and green men. The sculptures on the capitals of the shafts that separate the stalls around the walls are perfectly naturalistic and it is easy to recognise the leaves of the hop, oak, ivy, maple, and hawthorn, amongst other species.

Interlocking blind arches line the interior wall of Wenlock's chapter house. The arches rest on tiny attached shafts with 'cushion' capitals, a favourite motif of the Normans.

Exquisite carved foliage, remarkable amongst English work of the late 13th century for its detail and naturalism, adorns the chapter house at Southwell Minster.

See also

Norman greater churches, 66
Early English greater churches, 70
Decorated greater churches, 72
Perpendicular greater churches, 74

Domestic accommodation

The main living accommodation in a medieval monastery was in a number of large rooms leading off the cloister. In a common arrangement, the dormitory or dorter where the monks slept was an upper room on the eastern range of the cloister, and was connected to the church by a stairway, called the night stair. Below was often the parlour or warming room, the one room with a fire. The monks' dining room, the frater or refectory, was generally on the southern range while the western range contained storage and guest accommodation or, in Cistercian monasteries, accommodation for the lay brothers. Most monastic sites had separate accommodation for the abbot or abbess.

**Rievaulx Abbey
North Yorkshire**

**Hailes Abbey
Gloucestershire**

Amongst the extensive ruins of church and domestic buildings at the great Cistercian abbey of Rievaulx is the refectory. After the church, this was among the largest rooms in a medieval monastery. The refectory at Rievaulx Abbey is set at right-angles to the cloister, in the usual Cistercian fashion. This saved space on the southern cloister range so that the kitchen could be accommodated nearby, freeing the western range for the lay brothers' accommodation. The refectory is a large 125 ft (38 m)-long room constructed in around 1200. It is built over a vaulted undercroft that was probably used for storage. The generous single-opening windows let in lots of light. In the middle of the western wall a staircase marks the position of a pulpit used for readings while the monks ate their meals, for monastic mealtimes were intended for spiritual as well as physical nourishment.

This row of small niches is in the refectory at the Cistercian abbey at Hailes. They were probably storage spaces and, since they are near the door, perhaps were where cutlery was kept, so that each monk could pick up a spoon on entering the room at mealtimes. The neat trefoil heads that top these niches show the care with which even storage alcoves were designed.

Health, hygiene, and indeed survival depended on a good water supply and the medieval monks went to great lengths to ensure that their monasteries had clean water and proper drains. This drain at Kirkstall Abbey, West Yorkshire, shows the quality of the stonework.

Mount Grace Priory
North Yorkshire

This is the best preserved of the English Carthusian monasteries, or charterhouses. The Carthusians lived in a different way to the other orders. Instead of eating and sleeping communally, the monks lived separately in small cells around a cloister, meeting only in church to sing Vespers (the evening service), the night office, and Mass, and saying the other offices privately. The 15th-century charterhouse at Mount Grace has 15 cells, each with its own private garden. One of these two-storey cells has been reconstructed. It contains a living room, study, bedroom and oratory on the lower floor, and a workroom upstairs.

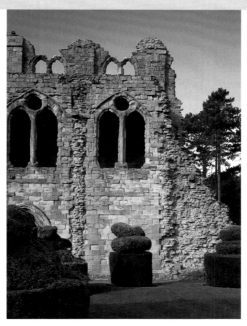

Wenlock Priory
Shropshire

This view of the church at Much Wenlock shows the prior's private chapel. It is on the first floor (there is a vaulted room beneath) and, as was common for a prior's chapel in this position, it was dedicated to St Michael. The original prior's lodging would have been adjacent, on the western range of the cloister, so that the prior could easily go to his chapel for private prayer and devotions. Later, priors built more spacious lodgings to the south-east. The chapel, like the rest of the ruined priory church, dates to the mid-13th century, a date borne out by the simple window tracery.

Castle Acre Priory
Norfolk

The Cluniac priory at Castle Acre has a large prior's house to the west of the cloister. The house grew over the centuries until, by the early 16th century, before the dissolution, the accommodation was much like that in a medieval manor house. The rooms included a large hall for the prior and his guests, plus a study or sitting room for the prior with a private chapel behind. These buildings were entered through this magnificent porch, with its striking panel of chequer work made up of dressed flint and ashlar masonry. There were originally pairs of canopied niches on either side of the doorway.

A mixture of flushwork, brickwork, and stone mouldings makes up this showy façade at Castle Acre Priory.

See also

Norman houses, 114
Medieval manor houses, 116
Medieval great houses, 120

Gatehouses

A monastery was an enclosed precinct. The admission of visitors and the exit of monks or nuns were both strictly controlled. So an abbey or priory had one or more gateways, through which visitors came and went. Monastic gatehouses were usually at least two storeys high with an arched entrance wide enough for horses or carts; there might also be a separate, smaller entrance for pedestrians. Inside was accommodation for the porter, who opened and closed the gate and oversaw all the comings

St James's Gate, Bury St Edmunds Abbey Suffolk

This is one of the oldest and most magnificent of all abbey gates. It is a dual purpose building, designed to be both the abbey gatehouse and the bell tower of the nearby church of St James, which was founded by Anselm, abbot of Bury between 1120 and 1148. This imposing structure, in a strong 12th-century Norman style, certainly gave early visitors the impression that they were entering an important precinct, as indeed they were. Bury was the shrine of St Edmund, the 9th-century king who was martyred by the Danes, and one of the six richest Benedictine houses in the country.

Cleeve Abbey Somerset

The gatehouse at Cleeve was built in the 13th century and was altered several times during the Middle Ages. This side of the gatehouse has a panel inscribed with the name of the last abbot, William Dovell, rebuilder of the upper floor. Above the window is a carving of the Crucifixion. The other side has a sculpture of the Virgin and Child and a Latin inscription, which translated, reads, 'Gate be open, shut to no honest person'. The inscription is a reminder that, although the entrance to the abbey was rigorously controlled, the monks would offer hospitality to all comers.

Great Gate, Bury St Edmunds Abbey Suffolk

The later of Bury's two surviving gates leads into the abbey's great court. Arriving here, one would have originally found oneself immediately opposite the abbot's great palace. Like St James's Gate, it is an impressive piece of work, dating from the first half of the 14th century. Beneath the sweeping, multiple-moulded archway above the gate are three niches made to contain images. These are three of around 20 on this face of the gatehouse alone. The statues have gone but their intricately carved settings, each niche with its own arched canopy and tiny ribbed vault, remain.

and goings. Many gatehouses have survived the dissolution of the monasteries, perhaps because they were compact, attractive structures with useful accommodation that were easy buildings to recycle.

Wetheral Priory
Cumbria

There is nothing left of Wetheral Priory except this gatehouse and some fragments of wall. The gatehouse survived the dissolution because it was used as the vicarage for the local parish church. It is 15th century, in a rather plain Perpendicular style with square-headed windows, battlements, and a tunnel-vaulted entrance. It looks more like part of a minor medieval manor house than a monastery, and is a reminder that many smaller houses were unassuming, working buildings that were often subsidiary to a larger house some distance away. Wetheral was just such a place, a dependent house of St Mary's Abbey, York.

Ramsey Abbey
Cambridgeshire

Little more than the gatehouse survives today, but Ramsey was once one of the largest abbeys in England. The building is a complete contrast to Wetheral, ornate and carved where Wetheral is plain and simple. Originally founded in the 10th century, Ramsey Abbey had had a long history as an independent house when the abbot decided it needed a new gatehouse in around 1500. The buttresses with their image niches, the remains of stone panelling, and the row of carved quatrefoils under the window and other decorations point to the cathedral-like quality of the Perpendicular style.

Christ Church Gate, Canterbury
Kent

This magnificent gate leads from the town to the monastic and cathedral precincts of Canterbury. It was built in 1517–20 and the heraldry indicates that it commemorates Prince Arthur, the elder brother of Henry VIII, who visited the cathedral two years before his death in 1502. The profusion of coats of arms, angels, late Gothic panelling, and pointed windows typifies the Perpendicular style in its richest form. But in the pilasters next to the entrance arch are some Renaissance-style decorative details, unusual in England as early as this, which look forward to the architecture of later in the century.

See also

House number, Roupell Street, London

HOUSES

Houses are our most numerous and varied buildings. There are houses in England dating from as far back as the Norman period; our houses vary in size from the tiniest cottage or back-to-back to the vast Palladian mansions of 18th-century grandees, and the buildings in which we live may be isolated in the countryside or packed into a crowded city.

Together, these houses make up an impressive body of buildings, a parade of apparently infinite variety. But what are the patterns that emerge? What makes the English house? First, and most enduring, is the long history of vernacular house building; in other words, the use of traditional materials by local builders (without the help of architects) to produce the typical cottages and farmhouses of our countryside. Such buildings are of their place like few others. The pargetted cottages of Essex, the brick-and-pantile farmhouses of Lincolnshire, and the cob buildings of Devon are all identified with their areas.

But there is another country scene, much more consciously designed, but just as typically English. This is the scene of the great country estate, which, employing scores of farm workers and servants, was the economic engine of the countryside until the First World War. At its heart was the country house, set amongst parkland, or perhaps in a landscaped garden. These houses, often vast, came to prominence in the Tudor period. For four centuries they set architectural trends as the nobility employed the most able architects to build or remodel their homes in the latest style.

Changes in agriculture, death duties, and the redrawing of the social and political maps of Britain in the 20th century led to the decline of the country house. Thousands were demolished after the Second World War as family after family, unable to maintain these costly buildings, retreated. But the nation – in the form of the richer or more tenacious landowners and organisations such as the National Trust – has clung on to a representative sample.

The story of the town house in England follows a different path. Although many fascinating early town houses survive from the medieval period to the 17th century, the story of our towns really takes off architecturally with the population rises and beginnings of modern industry in the 18th century. It is a story of rapid expansion, of sometimes almost frenzied building. But it is also a tale of the evolution of some distinctive building types and lifestyles which still affect the way millions of us live today.

One form of building, especially popular in England, bore the brunt of this urban expansion: the terraced house. After medieval beginnings, the terrace evolved in London in the late 17th century and became the typical house of the English city from the Georgian period onwards. Georgian Bath and London, Regency Brighton and Cheltenham, Victorian Manchester and Newcastle – all were transformed by terraces of houses, testimony to the willingness of the English to live close to their neighbours, provided that each household has its own front door onto the street. The terrace proved endlessly variable. It has provided tiny houses for workers and tall, palace-fronted London residences, large and imposing enough for the rich.

Other house forms have been given a very English twist. The villa was once a name for a substantial country house on the Palladian model, such as Lord Burlington's famous Chiswick House. But the term came to be applied to more modest detached houses and, especially from the Regency onwards, a detached villa became the house of choice for members of the middle classes who wanted more space around them than a terrace provided. There were many such houses around the leafy edges of Victorian towns and cities, and there were smaller ones, joined as semi-detached houses to make another famously English form of house.

The 'semi', usually described as the suburban semi, has had a bad press. Architects and critics alike deplored the inter-war semi with its false, Tudor-style beams and its tendency to sprawl through the suburbs creating a soulless no-man's land between country and city. But the British embraced the suburb, liking its spaciousness, its proximity to the countryside, and its transport links to the city. The suburban house was popular, and it still is.

Houses great and small, then, are among our most fascinating buildings. To look at their external decoration – from stucco columns to Tudoresque beams – is to imagine past aspirations. To walk through their rooms – the succession of chambers in a country house, each for a different stage in the entertaining process, or the cramped accommodation in the back-to-back houses of Victorian factory workers – is to relive past lives.

Vernacular houses

Vernacular architecture is local architecture – the work of local builders working in ways that have been handed down from one generation to the next and using materials available nearby. Vernacular buildings do not change much over time – the same shape of a window or roofline may be used from one century to the next.

However, they are geographically very diverse. This is because England has a variety of building materials, for example, sandstone in the Welsh borders, chalk and flint in the south-east and East Anglia, granite in Cornwall, limestone in a belt running from Dorset to Lincolnshire. And where good building stone is scarce, other materials –

Mapledurham
Oxfordshire

Hallaton
Leicestershire

This is chalk country, the area on the borders of Oxfordshire and Berkshire where the River Thames slices its way through the landscape on its way towards London. It is an area in which buildings of both stone and brick are common, but brick was especially popular where decent building stone was thin on the ground. Old brick houses look especially inviting in the leafy villages of the Thames valley. The lovely cottage in the foreground, once a smithy, is true to this vernacular tradition, being built of variegated brick walls with flint garden walls. The low eaves and substantial central chimney give it a cosy, inviting appearance among the foliage. Beyond, a grander house of about 1850 shows a more self-conscious use of red brick to produce a Jacobean style, with stone dressings and ranks of tall chimneys – hardly a vernacular building but one that draws on the local mix of colours and materials.

This Leicestershire village is a delightful mixture, with walls of brick or stone and roofs of tile or thatch. In this example, the mix of materials – stone, several kinds of brick, and tiles – comes together in one house, no doubt the result of a series of modifications over many generations. There is also a mix of construction techniques. The doors and upper window have the wooden lintels that are quite common in this area, but the lower window has a substantial stone surround. The resulting house is a glowing hotchpotch of the kind that makes many Midland villages satisfying and memorable.

The thatcher's art and craft are beautifully expressed in this roof at Hallaton, where the upper-floor windows are shielded and shaded by the encroaching reeds.

such as timber in the West Midlands or earth in Devon – have been pressed into service. So the English vernacular house is a key to local diversity; it is what makes many English towns, villages, and farmsteads what they are. Although threatened by modern developers, its popularity ensures its survival.

This thatcher was at work on a cottage in Hook Norton, Oxfordshire, in 1905. The skills he used are still in demand wherever thatch is a local roofing material.

Nettlecombe
Dorset

Dorset is at the far southern end of the belt of limestone that crosses England through Somerset, the Cotswolds, and the East Midlands to Lincolnshire. Limestone can have many colours, from the cream of the area around Bath to the orangey tones of Northamptonshire. Here it is a brownish-grey with tinges of buff. The stone makes attractive walls of coursed blocks and might have been carefully shaped and finished as ashlar if this had been a grander building. The roof is of thatch, a common feature in this area. Dorset and Wiltshire thatchers take pride in creating roofs with intricate features like the three neat dormers on this house.

Rievaulx
North Yorkshire

Rural Yorkshire still has many cottages with walls of warm grey stone that blend perfectly into untamed green landscape or colourful cottage gardens. Here on the edge of the North Yorkshire Moors the typical cottage is of yellowish or grey sandstone with, as here, a contrasting pantile roof and chimneys of brick. Two-storey farmhouses often have an adjoining barn of one storey, and this pattern is repeated here, with a lower building to one side that may have once been for agricultural use. The white-framed windows have wooden lintels.

The whole building makes a delightful picture in its charming garden setting, the epitome of the English rural house. But everything was built like this for a specific purpose, using local materials in an economic way to produce a building that worked for a farmer, his animals, and his equipment. We should enjoy such buildings for their practicality as well as for the way they conform to modern notions of rural beauty.

See also

Vernacular houses, next page
The early shop, 198
Watermills, 216
Farms, 246
Guildhalls, 254
Early schools and colleges, 268
Early inns, 308

**Lewes
East Sussex**

Mathematical tiles are clay tiles that are designed to imitate the appearance of bricks. They were widely used in the south-east from the mid-18th to the mid-19th centuries to clad the walls of timber-framed buildings to give the impression that they were made of more expensive bricks. They look so much like bricks that they often fool passers-by. Here, dark-coloured tiles have been laid around the bow and along the upper front wall. On the side elevation, where it was not quite so important to make a good impression, a range of different materials, including hung tiles and flint, have been used.

**Burnham-on-Crouch
Essex**

Weatherboarding can be seen all over the south-east, from Kent and Sussex to Hertfordshire and Essex. It was widely used to cover old timber-framed walls and give them a new lease of life. The technique was popular for all sorts of reasons – it required less skill to apply than plaster and it could be a way of avoiding taxes on bricks. The traditional approach was to waterproof the boards by covering them with tar, a finish still often found on farm buildings. But for houses, the usual approach today is to paint the boards white, as here, where they set off the red tiles and sage-green doors.

**Brasted
Kent**

Ruddy tile-hung walls are a particular feature of traditional houses in Kent. It is usually the upper floor that is tile-hung. This combination of a tile-hung upper floor and a white-painted lower one inspired the designers of houses in the garden suburbs, and there are now imitation Kentish cottages everywhere. By the 19th century, tile-makers were producing a range of fancy tiles in shapes like curving fish scales and diamond lozenges. These proved popular and give many Kentish walls a special texture – all the more characterful when the tiles warp and shift, to produce all sorts of pleasing variations.

Different-coloured tiles are sometimes used to produce patterns like this diaper effect on a building on the Kent–Sussex borders.

King's Norton
Leicestershire

There are many cottages like this in the East Midlands and eastern England. Here the brick was king even before railway transport made it possible to carry the material everywhere. In areas such as Lincolnshire and parts of Yorkshire, the traditional roofing material of the brick cottage is the pantile. But here the roof is made of slates. This is because Leicestershire has its own local source, and these Swithland slates were popular long before Welsh slates became widely available. So this is the original form of red-brick, slate-roofed house, with a plain wooden door and small casement windows, topped by relieving arches – of brick of course.

Old Warden
Bedfordshire

Bedfordshire is a county with a great variety of different building stones and materials, but in this example the plain rendered walls are eclipsed by a fine thatched roof. The thatch is expertly sculpted to accommodate the windows of the upper floor, throwing these windows heavily into shadow but creating a roof shape of great beauty. At the apex there is an ornate raised ridge with a criss-cross pattern and both semicircular scallops and triangular points. The finishing touch is a thatcher's signature, here in the form of a graceful bird.

Dedham
Essex

In Essex there are many colour-washed cottages, with a varied palette applied over plaster or rendered brickwork. Although the traditional colours are pale, from pinks to buffs, there are also examples of stronger colours like this glowing red in Dedham. The shade works well in an urban setting – a hint of sophistication is offered by the dentils above the sash window – and provides a rich backdrop for green foliage.

See also

Norman houses

Few houses remain from the Norman period. Most domestic buildings of the time were wooden and were replaced long ago and stone was usually reserved for high-status buildings such as churches and castles. The survivors are mostly much altered, but the round-headed doorways of rich merchants' and money-lenders' houses can be found in towns such as Lincoln and Southampton. They probably had business accommodation on the ground floor and a living room above. A similar

Norman House
Lincoln

This is one of two substantial Norman town houses in the centre of Lincoln. The city had a notable Jewish community in the Middle Ages and both of these houses have been linked to Jewish residents: this one was once known as Aaron's House, although it is now named for its antiquity not its owner. Its fine Norman doorway is flanked by stone shafts and topped with a chunky hood-mould which probably originally led the eye towards a chimney breast above, in the position occupied by the relatively recent sash window.

To the right upstairs is another more interesting window, in the two-light form that one would expect to see lighting a rich Norman's residence. The stonework in this window has been largely renewed, but with its shafts, capitals, and mouldings, it gives quite a good idea of the sort of window this house would have had in the late 12th century.

Jew's House
Lincoln

This sizeable town house was probably built in the 1170s. There would have been a ground-floor storage area where there are now shopfronts, but the doorway is the original one and two round-headed windows, which would have had two lights each, survive upstairs. The mouldings around the windows, and the added decoration of the horizontal string-courses that run along the wall at first-floor level, suggest that this was a high-status house owned by one of the richer members of Lincoln's medieval Jewish community.

Interlace carving surrounds the doorway of the Jew's House, Lincoln.

plan existed in manor houses where the living space was entered through an outside stair. In both cases the few round-headed windows were usually quite small – glass was an expensive rarity.

Manor House, Hemingford Grey Cambridgeshire

Sometimes it is only the presence of one or two small external features that suggests the long history of a building. At the Manor House at Hemingford Grey, for example, a simple two-light window with zigzag carving on the dripstone points to a Norman house, and so it proves. The building is constructed around the core of a late 12th-century Norman hall. The position of this window (others survive in other walls of the house) indicates that the main room was on the upper floor, with a storage undercroft beneath, a common layout for a Norman manor house.

Wolvesey Palace and Castle, Winchester Hampshire

The palace of the Norman bishops of Winchester was a major building within a few yards of the great cathedral. The keep and one range of buildings are as old as 1140, while the imposing great hall was built in around 1170. The enormous size of this hall gives an idea of the kind of accommodation that a king or senior cleric could expect in the 12th century. The complex also includes private apartments and the ruins of a keep and guard tower, indicating that in the early Middle Ages this was as much a castle as a palace.

Appropriately so, since the bishops of Winchester held great secular as well as spiritual power and some of these buildings were put up in times of civil strife. The earlier buildings, notably, date from the time of Henry of Blois, bishop from 1129, papal legate from 1139, supporter of King Stephen in his wars with the Empress Matilda, and one of the most powerful men in Europe.

Double rows of round-arched windows show the scale of the bishop's palace at Winchester, which was truly the grand residence of a great magnate.

See also

Medieval manor houses

At the heart of a medieval manor house was the hall, the large room in which the household ate, the lord conducted business, and the servants bedded down for the night. In addition there would usually be service rooms (such as pantry and buttery), the solar (a private room for the lord and his family), and perhaps a chapel. In the Middle Ages, a lord had military duties, and his house was often fortified – although not as heavily as a castle. Many manor houses had moats and gatehouses, and sometimes there was a tower to provide extra rooms and security in times of war.

**Stokesay Castle
Shropshire**

In spite of the tall battlemented tower, Stokesay does not have the full military defences of a castle – it is a fortified manor house, and with much 13th-century fabric, it is one of the best and earliest examples of its kind. It was built by Lawrence of Ludlow, a successful wool merchant who must have been one of the super-rich of the late 13th century. In building this very special combination of fortified stronghold and country house, Lawrence was no doubt mindful of the politics and geography of his time. Stokesay is near the Welsh border, an area where disputes and armed struggles were always likely, so a degree of protection was needed.

But Edward I had recently defeated the Welsh and brought peace to the region, so a certain amount of luxury, signalled by large windows and a big hall, was also possible. The result was one of England's most enchanting houses. The view to the right shows, from left to right: the north tower, originally a service block housing pantry and buttery, but in the later Middle Ages converted to provide living accommodation; the hall, with its tall windows, which formed the castle's main room; and the south tower which, with several self-contained apartments, might have been used to accommodate several branches of a large family. To the left is part of the north tower, with its overhanging timber-framed upper storey. This houses a large room that contains a late 13th-century stone fireplace. It must have been an impressive chamber in the Middle Ages, but it was made even more lavish in the 17th century when the present windows were added. Although we do not known how the medieval windows were laid out, they would have been far smaller than these.

Another outstanding feature of Stokesay Castle is the gatehouse, which dates to around 1640. It is glimpsed here from the main building. It is timber-framed in typical West of England style and, with its fine timbering and jettied upper floor, looks as if it were built more for show than for defence.

Old Soar Manor
Kent

This Kentish manor house preserves its solar block from the 1290s. The wing, built of local ragstone, contains the house's chapel and solar above a vaulted undercroft. The stone Y-tracery in the window has been renewed, but the stone of the walls is original. Inside there is a timber roof of the same period. Originally this wing would have joined onto a hall, also stone-built, but this was replaced when fashions changed and smaller, more luxurious rooms became the norm in manor houses. An 18th-century brick house now stands where the hall once was.

Ightham Mote
Kent

This beautiful moated manor house gets its character from the mix of building materials (stone, brick, timber, and tile) and from the way it has grown over the centuries with alterations and additions from the first buildings in about 1330 until the 20th century. The earliest parts are the hall, chapel, and two solars. Additions followed in Tudor times (including another chapel with a beautiful ceiling and a timber-framed cottage range) and the Jacobean period (another range of buildings and a drawing room). Recently, the house has been subject to a careful conservation programme.

Oxburgh Hall
Norfolk

Oxburgh is a courtyard house begun by Edward Bedingfield, who was given licence to build a house with defensive features in 1482. The main defences are the broad moat and the large gatehouse, with its pair of octagonal turrets, each seven storeys high. The stepped battlements and small window openings of these turrets (one of which is visible on the left of this picture) give a castle-like impression. But the rest of the building, with its larger windows, looks much more like a house. Although many of these openings come from a remodelling of 1835, the house probably always had windows rather than the tiny loopholes of a castle.

See also

Domestic accommodation, 104
Medieval town houses, 118
Medieval great houses, 120

Medieval town houses

English towns contain many houses that were originally built in the Middle Ages. Most of these were constructed in the local style of the time, using local materials and techniques. But there were also more 'planned' developments – the larger houses of rich merchants and groups of houses put up by local landowners to answer specific needs or to provide rental income. Most of these buildings have been altered over the centuries. Large living spaces have been subdivided into

Little Hall, Lavenham
Suffolk

This is one of Lavenham's clutch of beautiful medieval town houses, built in the 15th century. Such houses were built by the local cloth merchants and are testimony to the prosperity of the wool trade in the area in the late Middle Ages. They have been much modified inside, as demands for privacy and comfort increased and fashions changed. But their exterior appearance makes Lavenham one of the best places to come to appreciate the appearance and flavour of an English town of the period.

Old Wool Hall, Lavenham
Suffolk

Lavenham's Old Wool Hall is now part of the Swan Hotel but it was originally a hall house of the 15th century with a large, full-height room at its core. From the outside, the timber-framed structure is clear, dominated by ranks of uprights. There are so many of these that cross-bracing was only needed at the first-floor corners and in the gable. The upper floor overhangs the lower. This feature is called a jetty and is common in town houses of this date. Here, the jetty continues around both street sides of the corner property, a sign that this was a prestigious building with an owner who wanted to show off his wealth to one and all.

Nowadays the timbers of the house are jet-black and the infill brilliant white. This was probably not how it was in the Middle Ages, in spite of the fact that we think of black-and-white houses as typical of our old towns and villages. Originally, the oak timbers were more likely to have been allowed to go silvery grey and the infill might have been finished in a pastel shade or left a natural buff colour.

Carvings like this are another indication that the timber-framed houses in Lavenham were occupied by people of high status.

smaller rooms and windows have been enlarged or replaced, but in many cases there is enough of the medieval exterior left to show what these buildings were originally like.

Paycocke's, Coggeshall
Essex

Thomas Paycocke, clothier of Coggeshall, built this house in around 1500 and made it one of the most ornate of all town houses of this date. There are so many timbers, placed so closely, that there is little room left for the brick infill between them and many of the main timbers are beautifully carved. The bressummer, the horizontal beam that supports the jettied upper floor, has carvings of flowers, foliage, and other details on either side of a sinuously twisting stem, similar to decoration on many church screens. The doorposts have standing figures and the oriel windows are also carved.

Tewkesbury
Gloucestershire

One corner of a recently conserved town house in Tewkesbury shows how the traditional medieval construction has been retained. The oak beams and uprights are held together with pegs, also made of oak. When the timbers are prepared, holes are bored for the pegs, but they are offset very slightly so that when the peg is driven in, the two timbers are pulled tightly together. In this way, a heavy wooden frame can be held together without the use of nails or other fixings. The conservation work has been done without disguising the new timber by trying to make it look old, so that everyone can see straight away which pieces are ancient and which are modern.

Blagroves House, Barnard Castle
County Durham

By the beginning of the 16th century, glass was more widely available and more prosperous householders were beginning to build houses with larger windows. This coincided with a fashion for rectangular windows with many small panes of glass and also for bay windows, offering yet more scope for the glazier. Meanwhile, house plans were moving in the direction of a larger number of smaller rooms, each of which required at least one window. All these factors together added up to structures like the early Tudor Blagroves House, buildings that were much lighter and more dominated by glass than previous houses.

Carved stone figures of musicians stand on brackets protruding from the front wall of Blagroves House.

See also

Domestic accommodation, 104
Medieval manor houses, 116
The early shop, 198

Medieval great houses

The most important people of the Middle Ages – the royal family, nobles, and senior churchmen – lived in larger versions of the medieval manor, houses centred on a big, double-height hall. These halls were multi-purpose rooms, used alike for banqueting, court sessions, and royal ceremonies. Where they survive, at houses such as Penshurst Place and Eltham Palace, they are amongst the great English rooms, hierarchical spaces in which everyone, from the king to the lowliest servant, had their place.

Archbishop's Palace, Charing
Kent

The remains of the country palace of the archbishops of Canterbury, which was first built in the 13th century, are preserved at Charing. The original building had flint walls and the main section was a large hall where the archbishops entertained and conducted business, often stopping here on journeys between London and Canterbury. The flint walls of the old hall and some of the auxiliary buildings still stand, although they have been much altered – for much of the 20th century, the hall was used as a barn. But there are still a number of Gothic details, including several blocked windows and doorways. One of the most impressive remains is the wooden framework of the hall roof.

Building a structure such as this was a major undertaking, involving the selection and felling of dozens of trees. Whole mature trunks might be needed for the uprights and principal rafters, pieces of smaller section for the other components. A master carpenter would select these timbers and supervise their felling, shaping, and assembly into this intricate web of rafters, purlins, braces, and other parts. Today, the roof shows evidence of many repairs, but lots of the ancient timbers remain.

Westminster Hall
London

This vast hall was remodelled in the 1390s for Richard II by his master mason, Henry Yevele, and carpenter, Hugh Herland. Yevele increased the height of the existing building, which had been the site of royal banquets and courts since the time of William II, putting in large windows worthy of the building's status. Herland designed the great hammerbeam roof, a brilliant achievement of both engineering and aesthetics, to span the vast space without pillars or posts and create one huge room. This awesome hall has survived more than 600 years to remain the largest main extant portion of the medieval Palace of Westminster.

Their open timber roofs are masterpieces of carpentry, designed with networks of beams and braces to cover a broad span without any pillars or posts cluttering up the grand ceremonial space below.

**Penshurst Place
Kent**

**Eltham Palace, Greenwich
London**

Tall Gothic windows mark the double-height hall that was the main living room at Penshurst Place when the great house was first built in around 1341 by Sir John de Pulteney, who was Lord Mayor of London. Since de Pulteney's time, a cluster of extensions has grown around the hall, mostly dating from the 15th and 16th centuries. Together these buildings make up one of England's most beautiful houses, famous as the home of Elizabethan poet and hero Sir Philip Sidney. Inside the old hall there is still a central hearth, from which smoke rose towards louvres in the roof. At one end of the hall was the high table on its dais, with a long table where the lord and his family and guests ate.

Long tables for the rest of the household ran along the length of the hall. At the far end is a fine carved Gothic wooden screen concealing the entrance passage (known as the screens passage). The lord's private room, known as the solar, was reached from the hall via a staircase, and the solar at Penshurst, also dating from de Pulteney's time, is one of the oldest in England.

By the late Middle Ages, the main part of a great house was still the hall, and the most magnificent halls belonged to the royal family. This one was built for King Edward IV in 1475–80, probably by Thomas Jurdan, the royal mason. The large windows show that this is a high-status building, for even though glass was more widely available, you would have to be rich to afford so much. The biggest windows are reserved for the bay next to the high table, so that the king could dine in a well-lit space as he looked down at his household and up at his magnificent hammerbeam roof.

Four colossal stones – sill, lintel, and two uprights – were all that the builders needed to create this small opening at Penshurst Place, an example of economy of effort when good materials were available.

See also

Tudor and Jacobean houses

The Tudors loved bravura and display, as is clear from their great houses. Glass was still costly, but rather less so than in the Middle Ages, so big windows became a sign of status. Showiest of all are the timber-framed houses of the north-west, where woodwork and glazing combine in patterns that seem to prefigure 20th-century op art. Other regions built with more restraint, but the profusion of towers and bay windows still impresses, while the inclusion of rooms such as long galleries, built

Knole
Kent

Knole is enormous, more like a town than a house, with hundreds of rooms (there are said to be 365) built around several large courtyards between the 15th and 17th centuries. The house was originally built in the 1450s by Thomas Bourchier, Archbishop of Canterbury. Bourchier's house had a main courtyard with several smaller service courts. Many additions came in the 16th century, when the house became the property of the Sackville family. These changes took two main forms – new buildings and alterations to the interiors of Bourchier's buildings. The gate tower and Green Court in this picture, which form the entrance to the house today, were one such addition, built in 1540.

Apart from the gables, which were added when the court was re-roofed in 1605, the frontage presents a plain face to the world – this could almost be a medieval manor house. If you can afford a house as vast as Knole, you do not have to impress the world with elaborate exterior decoration. Inside, things are rather more showy, with a fine painted staircase and panelled rooms among the survivals from the Tudor and Jacobean periods.

Little Moreton Hall
Cheshire

One of the most striking timber-framed houses, Little Moreton Hall was begun in the late 15th century when the fashion for making patterns with struts and braces was at its height in Cheshire and Lancashire. When the first William Moreton's builders stopped with the first floor, they had already produced a showy house, with dramatic timber work and much glass. But Moreton's son, another William, made the house still more extravagant with the addition of a long gallery on top of his father's house. The gallery is clearly visible from the outside – its daring continuous strip of windows sits above what remains of the original roof.

so that the leisured classes could take a walk without going out into the rain and mud, speaks of people with time on their hands and money to spend.

Chastleton House
Oxfordshire

Tall and compact, Chastleton is a cluster of towers, chimneys and bays in warm ironstone around a tiny central courtyard. The designer is not known, and although the sophistication of the layout suggests an accomplished architect, the plainness of the detailing points to a local mason. The unknown designer was almost certainly at work between 1607 and 1612, building Chastleton for Walter Jones, a member of a family of wool merchants who had made it into the ranks of the gentry. His plain but well-built house has interiors with fine plaster ceilings, including a magnificent long gallery.

Blickling Hall
Norfolk

The south front of Blickling Hall is a perfect design of 1616 and the entrance front is still very much as its architect, Robert Lyminge, intended it. The red brick and fine stone dressings look inviting against the background of surrounding trees and grass and the composition is delightful. The exterior has virtually every feature that its first owner, Lord Chief Justice Sir Henry Hobart, could expect on a top-ranking house of the period – a well-carved entrance, lots of big windows, and ornamental strapwork.

But what really impresses is the skyline, with its corner towers topped with ogee roofs, its groups of chimneys, its Dutch gables, and its central stone clock tower. The interior of Blickling is more altered, but there are still glories from the 17th century, most notable of all the 127 ft (39 m)-long gallery, one of the great rooms of the period.

Heraldry and mythological beings crown the south entrance at Blickling Hall.

See also

Tudor and Jacobean houses, next page
Prodigy houses, 126
Stuart Classical houses, 128
Early schools and colleges, 268
Lodges, 358

Tudor and Jacobean houses (continued)

The 16th century saw something of a building boom. Rises in the price of food brought more wealth to farmers and the middle classes, who began to demand more comfort in their houses. Halls went out of fashion, replaced by smaller rooms offering greater privacy, while the open fire of the hall was replaced by enclosed hearths and chimney stacks. Builders still used local materials in the traditional manner, but the rich began to find visually exciting ways of expressing their wealth in the architecture of their homes. In areas where timber was plentiful, the art of the wood carver

Lyveden New Bield
Northamptonshire

The stark outline of Lyveden New Bield, an unfinished garden house in remote northern Northamptonshire, is almost as it was when the masons downed tools in 1605, never to return. It was the brainchild of Sir Thomas Tresham, and was designed to symbolise his Catholic faith, being planned in the form of a Greek cross and emblazoned with emblems of the Passion. Like Tresham's other great building, the Triangular Lodge at Rushton, Northamptonshire, the New Bield is full of number symbolism, including inscriptions of 81 letters (3 x 3 x 3 x 3, symbolising the Trinity), together with 5 ft (1.5 m)-long bay windows (Christ's five wounds), and a number of features in multiples of seven (Christ's seven wounds, his seven last words, Mary's seven sorrows). Tresham died in 1605 and work stopped on the building, leaving it quiet and isolated. It stands in the remains of Tresham's garden, which must have been an almost equally odd concoction, with its canals and earthen mounds.

Feathers Inn, Ludlow
Shropshire

The town of Ludlow was vitally important for the Welsh Marches in Tudor and Jacobean times, a prosperous centre of commerce and local administration. Its buildings reflect this wealth – they are ornate magpies of 16th- and 17th-century optical art, offering to the eye a feast of timber lozenges, barley-sugar columns, carved bargeboards, and grotesque heads. The Feathers Inn is one of the most extraordinary. It began life as a rich lawyer's house and it must have been as ornate as anything in London before the Great Fire of 1666. 'Hire me for my dazzling eloquence,' it seems to say, 'if you can afford the fees.'

Five-sided bay windows enliven the façade of Lyveden New Bield, creating small, light rooms inside.

These carved heads emerge from the woodwork beside the doorway at the Feathers. They are the kind of vigorous imaginings that were popular before the tide of Classicism swept across Britain, obliterating this sort of vernacular fun.

could be exercised on beams and posts; pargetting was practised extensively in some of the districts where plastered exteriors were popular. The middle classes had arrived, and were proud of their arrival.

Tewkesbury
Gloucestershire

Like Ludlow, Tewkesbury is another town to preserve many early timber-framed buildings. This corner house, with its later shop fronts, is a good example, less showy than the house in Ludlow but still dazzling. It is interesting how the building's two fronts are designed differently. The right-hand façade faces on to the main street. It is built with close-studded timbers and a pair of jetties – clearly, it is meant to impress passers-by. But the left-hand wall, which faces on to a side street, is more modest – the timbers are more widely spaced and there is no jetty.

Weobley
Herefordshire

Timber framing is the traditional house-building technique in the West Midlands, and in Herefordshire, still a remote and mainly rural county, a number of settlements still have their share of black-and-white houses. A profusion of such timber-framed houses, some more than 500 years old, lines the streets of Weobley. Some of these buildings have exposed crucks; some are built with rectangular frames; some are quite elaborate buildings with jettied upper floors overhanging the street; one even has carved wooden capitals and an ogee-framed door. But many of these buildings are humbler cottages, their square frameworks accommodating much wattle and daub between the timbers.

Chipping Campden
Gloucestershire

On the Cotswolds, builders used the local limestone to construct houses in a vernacular tradition that changed little over the years. The mullioned windows, big gables, and stone-tiled roofs with dormers in the town's streets could be of any century from the 16th to the 20th and they give Cotswold streets a unity and presence that is justly admired. Although there are also grander houses with Renaissance or Georgian details, much of the town retains its Tudor atmosphere, with houses begun in stone in the 16th century on the site of already ancient medieval timber-framed structures.

See also

Tudor and Jacobean houses, previous page
Prodigy houses, 126
Stuart Classical houses, 128
Early schools and colleges, 268
Lodges, 358

Prodigy houses

These are the houses of the Tudor and Jacobean super-rich, prodigious indeed in their size, luxury, and architectural inventiveness. These buildings are strokes of genius quite unlike anything that went before – Wollaton's towering central room, Burghley House's cupolas and spire, and Hardwick Hall's array of towers and windows are unforgettable. The decoration, a mixture of translated Classicism and English details like strapwork, is also distinctive. Much of this is due to the genius of one man,

Audley End
Essex

Wollaton Hall
Nottinghamshire

Audley End, designed by Bernart Janssen for the Earl of Suffolk in the early 17th century, looks large today and impresses with its ranks of big windows. But it was originally twice the size and the largest new house of its time. The principal room, the hall, is in the middle of this façade – its main window is the tall one in the centre. The hall is entered from one end, via a screens passage, as in a medieval house. However, Janssen wanted to make his frontage symmetrical, in the modern manner, so provided an extra porch to balance the first.

Master architect Robert Smythson designed Wollaton in the 1580s for Elizabethan grandee Sir Francis Willoughby, who was rich from the then rather new coal mining industry. Smythson was the greatest designer of his time – he also worked on Hardwick Hall in Derbyshire and at Longleat in Wiltshire. Wollaton is one of his masterpieces. It is an amazing house, a mixture of Classical details like Corinthian pilasters and busts with typical Elizabethan decorative touches, from strapwork to obelisk-shaped finials. But its most remarkable feature is its plan and the visual effect this creates. Instead of the central courtyard that one might expect in a house of this period,

there is a large hall, lit by clerestory windows that peep above the façade of the house. Set on top of this is another vast room, with still larger windows, making this central feature into a gigantic block, exploding on to the skyline. Ornate corner towers add still more to the effect. Wollaton Hall is a prodigy indeed.

Robert Smythson, designer of many of the greatest Elizabethan houses, who has claims to be called the first English architect.

**Kirby Hall
Northamptonshire**

This huge house was originally built in the 1570s and 1580s, and there was another phase of building in 1638–40. The result is a long, low rambling house, now largely ruined, containing a mix of traditional Jacobean and more revolutionary Classical architecture. Some of the Classicism is so strong that it has been attributed to Inigo Jones. There is no evidence for this, although Jones's associate, Nicholas Stone, produced some stone carvings at the house during the 17th-century building campaign. The long façade gives little hint of the palatial Classical splendours within. The north side of the courtyard, for example, dates from 1572 and shows a Classicism quite unlike that

of other contemporary houses. The bays are marked off by giant pilasters, some fluted with capitals resembling the Ionic, some richly carved. This is highly cultivated work, unusual at a time when many builders were still content with strapwork or linenfold panelling. The notion of giant pilasters has been traced to the influence of the books written by French Renaissance architect Philibert de l'Orme, while the decoration on the central pilasters derives from a book by English writer John Shute, *The First and Chief Groundes of Architecture* (1579–80).

**Bolsover Castle
Derbyshire**

The Star Chamber at Bolsover is one of the great Jacobean interiors. It has panelling and fireplaces inspired by the Italian theorist Serlio, whose *Five Books of Architecture* first appeared in England in 1611, but given an English twist. The grey-and-gilt decorative scheme, with the stars that give the room its name winking down from the ceiling, exudes a confident richness. But it is tempered in this room by the subject matter of the wall paintings, which are resolutely Christian. The panelling is filled with figures of the saints in austere monochrome – this example is Saint Katherine with the wheel on which she was martyred.

The tops of giant pilasters frame pedimented Classical windows on the north range at Kirby Hall.

Candelabra, musical putti, twists of foliage, and acanthus leaves adorn the carved pilasters at Kirby Hall.

See also

Tudor and Jacobean houses, 122
Stuart Classical houses, 128
Renaissance universities, 270

Stuart Classical houses

Unlike his Elizabethan predecessors, the architect Inigo Jones was a devoted Classicist. He travelled to Italy, studied the works of Italian architects and writers – especially Palladio and his follower Scamozzi – and read the great Roman writer on architecture, Vitruvius. Jones was employed by the royal family (he designed court masques as well as buildings) so his work was prominent and well known. Buildings such as the royal Banqueting House and the Queen's House at Greenwich were quite unlike anything else in London, with correctly used Classical orders, simple façades, and roofs hidden behind parapets. Soon colleagues such as Nicholas Stone were copying Jones's style and the new Classicism was spreading across town and country.

**Banqueting House, Whitehall
London**

Next to the timber-framed buildings of early 17th-century London, Inigo Jones's royal Banqueting House (1619–22) must have come as a total shock. For the first time in the capital here was the uncompromising Classicism of an Italian Renaissance palace, the whole language of pilasters and half-columns, pediments and cornices, and the ruthless symmetry accentuated by the way in which the middle three bays stand slightly forward of those on either side. It is a tight-lipped and regimented building compared to the houses of the previous generation, but is saved from being severe by the frieze of swags and masks. This small masterpiece was meant to be part of a much larger royal palace that remained unbuilt.

**Queen's House, Greenwich
London**

Inigo Jones's other major London domestic building was the Queen's House, begun in 1616 but only finished, after a delay and a redesign, in 1635. He used a simple Classicism, adding interest with a first-floor balcony with Ionic columns. This was an unusual feature that later designers did not copy, but one feature of this building that was imitated everywhere was the rusticated lower storey which, as well as giving extra texture to the walls, was used to indicate a difference in status between the floors – the main rooms were on the upper floor in the Italian manner on what the Italians called the *piano nobile*. Lesser apartments and service rooms were on the rusticated lower floor. In 1690, the royal family left the Queen's House (William and Mary preferred Hampton Court) and the building became the home of the Ranger of Greenwich Park and Governor of the Naval Hospital. A few years later, Sir Christopher Wren was brought in to design the expanded Naval Hospital and the house became its centrepiece. The two domed towers of Wren's vast building can be seen between the house and the river.

The interior of the Banqueting House, London, was once used as a museum. Now it is kept uncluttered so that visitors can appreciate the room's grandeur.

Wilton House
Wiltshire

This house of 1636 is another building associated with the circle of designers who gathered around Inigo Jones. Its original architect was probably Isaac de Caus, a member of Jones's team working in London's Covent Garden. De Caus produced a sober exterior typical of Jones, with only a central venetian window to relieve a very plain front. In the late 1640s, the house was severely damaged by fire and another Jones associate, his one-time pupil John Webb, restored the building, adding corner towers and some very lavish interiors. By the time of this rebuilding, Jones himself was an old man, but he seems to have advised his former pupil on the designs for the rebuilding. Webb's corner towers became a popular motif and were copied by 18th-century architects. Webb's other legacy was a series of luxurious state rooms, known for their gilded and panelled walls, their lavishly painted ceilings and coves, and their proportions – the most famous are called the double cube and single cube rooms.

Fonthill Gifford
Wiltshire

In the 17th century gateways and gatehouses also began to be designed in the Classical manner. There is a tradition that links this one at Fonthill Gifford with Inigo Jones although there is no documentary evidence that he was the designer. The building certainly looks as if it could be by Jones or one of his circle. The emphasised alternate blocks around the arch and up the sides of the gateway make a striking impression and are characteristic of the time. The effect on the emphasised blocks is known as vermiculation, suggesting that the stones look as if worms have burrowed through them.

Vermiculated stone blocks create a pattern of shadows on the entrance piers at Fonthill Gifford.

See also

Stuart Classical parish churches, 44
Classical greater churches, 78
Stuart Classical houses, next pages

Stuart Classical houses (continued)

In the later Stuart period, architects turned away from the uncompromising Classical style of Inigo Jones. Their typical house had a hipped roof with dormers, rows of windows on the main floors, pronounced quoins, and a few restrained Classical details such as a pediment above the door or attached columns on either side of it. Inside there were walls with wooden panelling and beautifully plastered ceilings. Houses like this, reproduced in varying forms from Yorkshire to Sussex and in various sizes to fit town and country settings, were so popular that their style is often seen as typically English.

Cobthorne, Oundle
Northamptonshire

This house of 1658 is a rare survival, a sizeable house from the Commonwealth period. It displays very few Classical details, except for the doorway, but is still Classical in its proportions and assured in the way features such as the deep roof overhang and double string-course draw the whole design together. Only the curious roof line – as if the builders could not decide between a hipped and a gabled roof – seems odd and slightly ungainly. At basement level, mullioned windows give an idea what the fenestration would have looked like before sash windows were installed, perhaps towards the end of the 17th century.

Uppark
West Sussex

Often a house is remarkable because of several phases in its history. Uppark was built in around 1685, the perfect late 17th-century house on the Sussex Downs. It was designed by William Talman and its symmetry, its hipped roof, and its dormer windows are typical of a style of house that was especially popular in England in this period. From the 1740s to the 1770s, the interiors were remodelled, after the house was bought by the Northumbrian baronet Sir Matthew Fetherstonehaugh. The interiors too, especially the plaster-ceilinged saloon, are outstanding examples of their period and style.

More interior alterations in the 19th century mean that the house has precious survivals from three periods. But in 1989 a fire almost destroyed the building. Courageously, the house's owners, the National Trust, decided to restore it to its condition immediately before the fire. This entailed a Herculean salvage operation, a vast team of skilled workers, and major research, sometimes leading to the virtual reinvention of forgotten craft techniques. So after six years of work Uppark became a tribute to the skills and efforts of workers, artists, and craftspeople of the 17th, 18th, 19th and 20th centuries.

A carved pediment surmounts the middle three bays of Uppark's main front. The projecting 'beams' recall the frugality of Inigo Jones, but the rich carving speaks of another, more worldly style.

Big stone quoins, with lovingly chamfered edges, frame Uppark's walls. Such details are typical of this style of house, but they are not always as beautifully finished as here.

Boughton House
Northamptonshire

The late 17th-century owner of Boughton House was Ralph Montagu, who had been English ambassador in France between 1669 and 1678 and had acquired a taste for French style. While he was in Paris, he began to collect French art and furnishings, and Louis XIV himself presented the ambassador with some prize items. Montagu's house of 1688 had a French look, with mansard roofs and banded rustication, as can be seen on the left-hand section of the building in this picture. To give the façades an uncluttered look, Montagu had the rainwater gutters and downpipes concealed inside the structure.

Inside, the house was planned in the continental manner with an enfilade – a suite of rooms with their connecting doors all lined up perfectly. Montagu commissioned a French artist, Louis Chéron, to do much of the decoration, creating a good setting to show off his collection of furniture from France. The house as Montagu conceived it was huge and ambitious, but the whole building was never completed: one wing is still an empty shell.

Waddon Manor, Portesham
Dorset

Originally much larger, Waddon Manor once extended farther westward – to the left of the picture. But it still retains all the signs of an important house of the late 17th century, from the dentil course beneath the hipped roof to the pair of ovals giving a little extra visual interest to the basement level. The adjoining lower wings form a service courtyard in a simpler, mid-17th-century version of the same style. The architecture and the fine stone make this house stand out. The site is also special, high on the downs with a sea view that makes this lovely, silvery-grey house a delight to look out from as well as to look at.

See also

Stuart Classical parish churches, 44
Classical greater churches, 78
Stuart Classical houses, previous and next pages

The 17th-century town house could take many forms. Occasionally, builders followed the Classical lead of Inigo Jones, but more often they looked to the work of Sir Christopher Wren for their model. By the late 17th century, sash windows had appeared and were being enthusiastically adopted, their narrow glazing bars ensuring that plenty of light found its way into the rooms inside. The variations on the Wren-style house were almost endless, but by the end of the century a new trend was just

Lindsey House, Lincoln's Inn Fields London

Buildings such as Inigo Jones's Banqueting House were soon influencing the way smaller houses were designed. One of the best surviving examples of this is a pair of houses in Lincoln's Inn Fields, which share many of the features of Jones's building – pilasters, rusticated lower floor, and pediments above the windows, for example. These houses were built in around 1640 and may have been designed by Jones's associate, Nicholas Stone. They show the notion, already popular in Europe but just emerging in England, of uniting two or more houses behind a unified façade – what would become known, with terraces of many houses, as the palace façade.

Sparrowe's House, Ipswich Suffolk

A smaller town house did not have to be quiet and retiring and did not have to be strictly Classical either. People such as the owners and builder of Sparrowe's House, who updated a building with 15th-century origins to provide a breathtaking visual feast, did not think in terms of Classicism. True, the exteriors of Sparrowe's House have pilasters and windows in the style of about 1670, when they were built. And there is a great brooding cornice that is influenced by the Classical tradition. But what dazzles is the plasterwork. The royal arms, figures such as shepherds and shepherdesses, mythological figures, and reliefs representing the continents are all featured. Africa sits on a crocodile,

America has a tobacco pipe, Asia has a domed building, and Europe is symbolised by a Gothic church. It is as if the tradition of pargetting, local to eastern England, has decided to take on the world. In the process this decorative technique has been taken to its logical conclusion – and beyond.

Close-ups of some of the figures in the plasterwork at Sparrowe's House show the depth and vigour of the moulding – no other building has such lively exterior plasterwork, or so much of it.

beginning. In parts of London such as Spitalfields, the first tall, narrow terraced houses were instigating a building type that would be popular in England for the next 300 years.

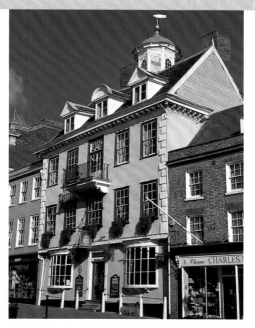

Catmos Street, Oakham
Rutland

The large Stuart house in the tradition of Uppark could be scaled down and simplified to create an elegant detached town house. Houses such as this one in Oakham are the result. This example keeps the shape of the large houses, with hipped roof and dormers, but the proportions are lower and less grandiose. Houses such as this show provincial builders adapting grander fashions to local taste. Details such as the ornate door head add a touch of individuality. Such houses provided light, comfortable accommodation for the middle classes of around 1690, and they still do.

Cupola House, Bury St Edmunds
Suffolk

In 1693 a Bury apothecary, Thomas Macro, built himself this house in the centre of the town. He had the money to build in features that were fashionable on larger houses, but not often seen on houses such as this. Most prominent is the little turret on the top of the house, roofed by the cupola that gives the building its name. From its windows, Macro had good views across the town. Other quality features are the Classical pediments above the dormer windows and the little balcony on its scroll-shaped brackets. A strong cornice and quoins frame the main part of the façade.

Fournier Street, Spitalfields
London

In the late 17th and early 18th centuries, thousands of Huguenots, French Protestants in flight from religious persecution, crossed the Channel and settled in this part of east London, where they created a successful silk-weaving industry. Many lived in the early 18th-century houses in Fournier Street. The brickwork, sash windows, and ornate door surrounds of these elegant houses provided a template for the countless Georgian terraces of the era to come. The weavers liked the light provided by the large windows, often fitting extra fenestration into the garrets, where they worked. From the beginning, the English terrace was an eminently practical form of housing.

Recent exterior shutters shade the Fournier Street windows.

See also

Stuart Classical parish churches, 44
Classical greater churches, 78
Stuart Classical houses, previous pages

Baroque houses

The late 17th century saw an important development in English building, when architects began to flirt with the baroque style. This is not the restless colossal baroque style of continental Europe, with its twisting façades and over-the-top decoration. It is something much more restrained. The English baroque is typified by massive forms, giant orders, the magnification of certain details such as keystones, features such as urns and statuary on parapets, and a freer use of curves. Grandeur is the keynote, even in relatively small buildings. Nicholas Hawksmoor and William Talman are perhaps the two most notable architects to work in this style. As the 17th century became the 18th, John Vanbrugh emerged

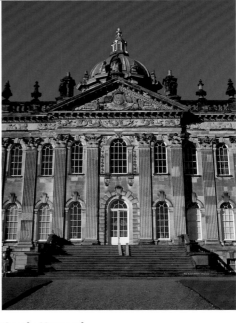

Chicheley Hall
Buckinghamshire

Castle Howard
North Yorkshire

An original way to treat the centre bays of a large house was to make them slightly taller than the flanking bays, with the parapet and cornice rising in a curve to accommodate the extra height. Without the thrusting upward curve, the strong horizontal line that divides the attic floor from the lower storeys would have made the house feel rather earthbound, but the rise in the cornice makes it soar. At Chicheley Hall, a house of the early 18th century, the architect combined this feature with an attic story above the cornice, the latter a common device in houses of this period. The two features together give this house quite a strong sense of height. The designer of Chicheley

Hall is unknown – Francis Smith and Thomas Archer have both been suggested. Whoever he was, he produced a strikingly original building, a strong design that was in a sense a clever English compromise between the more box-like houses of the earlier 17th century and the grander, more monumental buildings of Vanbrugh.

It is incredible that soldier and playwright John Vanbrugh had designed no buildings at all before taking on Castle Howard for the Earl of Carlisle in 1699. He could not have done the job without his assistant, Nicholas Hawksmoor, and Vanbrugh's bold style with its grand gestures and gigantic pilasters, owes a lot to the more experienced architect. But the details are telling, too. Both men knew how to use features such as flutes, dentils, and carved decoration to catch the sun and set up a play of light and shade. And the climax was a stroke of originality – Castle Howard was the first English house to have a dome as its central feature.

The curious crowning pediment above the doorway – its mouldings curving this way and that – is one of the baroque highlights of Chicheley's façade.

A close-up view shows the quality of Chicheley Hall's stonework, with the crisp flutes of the pilaster, the cornice carving, and other details catching the play of light and shade.

as a leading architect, with houses on a truly colossal scale. Hugely influenced by the baroque idiom of his assistant Hawksmoor, Vanbrugh had the opportunity to work on a still larger canvas and vast houses, such as Castle Howard, North Yorkshire, and Blenheim Palace, Oxfordshire, with their massive façades and vast courtyards, also seem to owe something to Vanbrugh's background in the theatre. Set in great parks and accessed via long drives, past vistas and temples strategically placed, these houses are meant to awe the visitor.

Seaton Delaval Hall
Northumberland

Seaton Delaval was built in 1718–28 for Admiral George Delaval. It was the last of architect John Vanbrugh's major houses and, although on a more compact scale than Castle Howard or Blenheim, the result was still powerful. The central block shows Vanbrugh's confident handling of the masses of a building. The polygonal corner towers, the central section that breaks forward, and the pairs of columns that break further forward still – all these features give power to the frontage. So do the shapes on the skyline, especially the two square towers and the central pediment.

All these features add up to a block that is both imposing and theatrical – and is one of Vanbrugh's most successful designs. Sadly, this great building was ravaged by fire in 1822 and was partially restored several times, most recently in 1999–2000. The more conventional west wing, visible on the edge of the picture, is still in use, while the great east wing contains large and noble stables.

Grimsthorpe Castle
Lincolnshire

This powerful house, designed by John Vanbrugh, has a strong north front with banded columns, statuary, and other delights – but Grimsthorpe also shows, in this pavilion, that Vanbrugh could build small. He could still cram in plenty of unusual or outlandish features into a little structure like this – the broadly splayed voussoirs above the blind window, the ornate surround to the window above, the bizarre drum-like finials at the very top – all give character to what could have been an unassuming building. Somehow Vanbrugh made all these oddities work as a group, pulled together by the heavy quoins and bulbous balustrade.

Vanbrugh liked to enliven his skylines, doing so at Grimsthorpe Castle with statuary, both heraldic and mythological.

See also

Palladian houses

A century after Inigo Jones began work, English building had come a long way from the Jacobean architect's strict, simple Classicism. But in the 1720s, a group of architects and patrons began to look again at the pure Classical style and at the works of Andrea Palladio which inspired it. Connoisseur Lord Burlington, designer-architect William Kent, and architect-publicist Colen Campbell all espoused Palladianism, going back to Classical basics. Their buildings usually had rather severe exteriors with Classical porticoes, and there was often a heavy stress on the first floor, which sat on a rusticated

Chiswick House
London

Holkham Hall
Norfolk

The most famous of all the early Palladian houses was Chiswick, built 1725–9 by Lord Burlington for his own use and to house his art collection. This building was based closely on Villa Capra near Vicenza, Italy, by the 16th-century Italian architect Palladio, but whereas Palladio had a portico on each front, Burlington included only one. Burlington also introduced some novel elements into the plan of the building, including a pair of circular rooms, another with apses at each end, and an octagonal space beneath the dome. From the outside, the pale, domed simplicity of the building with its single main floor must have amazed contemporaries.

Thomas Coke, Earl of Leicester, had been on the Grand Tour in Europe for five years and had collected many antiquities and works of art, including numerous Greek and Roman statues and old master paintings by the likes of Claude. On returning to England he needed a new house that was large enough to house his new possessions – and in a Classical style that would set them off to their best advantage. William Kent, who had been Burlington's protégé at Chiswick, obliged, designing one of the grandest of all Palladian houses. Begun in 1734, the house is vast but simple and built in a rather austere-looking pale brick.

Most of the detail is on the main floor, which sits on a rusticated base and is topped with towers, in a style similar to those at Wilton House. At each corner are wings, each the size of a Palladian villa, containing the chapel, kitchen, guest rooms, and everyday family rooms – but none of these compare with the state rooms in the central block, which are of imperial grandeur. There is a vast entrance hall with gigantic columns of pink Derbyshire marble, and this leads to a series of breathtaking rooms hung with paintings by Poussin and Claude, or with niches for statues.

This is a view of one of Holkham Hall's corner wings. The composition of squares topped with triangles shows how William Kent kept Wilton House, with its corner towers, in his subconscious.

ground floor. This first floor contained the main rooms of the house, which could be decorated in the grandest style, with marble columns, gilded details in the plaster ceilings, and rich wallcoverings.

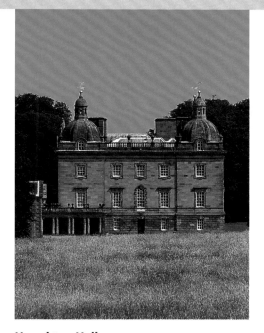

Houghton Hall
Norfolk

Wentworth Castle
South Yorkshire

At Houghton, architect Colen Campbell adapted the Palladian mode, keeping the portico and the rusticated base, but stretching the façade out and ending it with a pair of towers with venetian windows. In the original design, the towers were to rise above the parapet and terminate in triangular pediments, as at the earlier Wilton House. But the plans used when construction began in 1722 were modified by James Gibbs before the house was completed in 1735. It was Gibbs who devised the domes with their lanterns, their curves like a louder echo of the curving venetian windows on the main façade.

Wentworth is the vast house of one branch of the Wentworth family (another branch lived at nearby Wentworth Woodhouse). It is a house with work from several periods, notably when it was enlarged in two phases during the 18th century. The south range is Palladian in style, and the architect was Charles Ross, who signed a contract for the work in 1759 and made out his final receipt in 1764. Little is known about Ross, but he produced an impressive if somewhat sober design for this front of the house, its rows of windows enlivened by a venetian window at either end and a vigorously carved pediment. This frontage is in marked contrast to the north range of the house, which was designed a few decades earlier in the French taste by Jean de Bodt, and is much showier.

See also

Stuart Classical parish churches, 44
Stuart Classical houses, 128
Georgian houses, 138

Georgian houses

The builders of small Georgian houses, often speculators who were trying to maximise their profits, developed the most quintessentially English of all housing types – the terrace. Georgian terraces varied in size and elaboration, but had certain key features in common. Their uniformity was due in part to a series of laws, such as the 1774 Building Act, which laid down rules for the construction of different classes of houses, from First to Fourth Rate. The usual pattern was a basement with service rooms, an entrance floor rising to a first-floor *piano nobile*, with floors

**Castle Street, Bridgwater
Somerset**

Georgian brick terraces such as these give this Somerset town its special quality. Bridgwater's most impressive street was begun in 1723 for the Duke of Chandos. The designs look simple. Their material is mainly brick in this brick town, and each house is a regular five bays in width giving generous accommodation within. But the house fronts are full of quality touches, such as the gently curving segmental tops of the windows, the doorways discreetly emphasised with Classical columns, and the way the parapet breaks in a series of curves, to take the row of façades down the hill.

**High Street, Boston
Lincolnshire**

This doorway in a Boston town house has the simplest of surrounds, with just a plain keystone at the head of an arch of bricks. It seems to shelter rather shyly between the twin brick pilasters that stick out on either side. Although the fanlight has lost its glass, the pattern of glazing bars remains, as does the elegant, four-panelled door up the worn flight of stone steps. Even such simplicity can enhance the visual effect of an urban street.

**Barn Hill, Stamford
Lincolnshire**

Stamford is full of beautiful details such as this mid-18th-century doorway, executed in the limestone that gives the town its character. The heavy rusticated blocks and prominent keystone recall examples in pattern books by writers such as Batty Langley, whose *City and Country Workman's Remembrancer* came out in 1745. Langley was probably influenced both by earlier English designers and the work of the 16th-century Italian architectural theorist Sebastiano Serlio. But whatever the origins of the design, builders often made slight variations to mouldings and other details, so each example has features that make it special and unique.

of bedrooms above. Pitched roofs were hidden behind a parapet, so the house gave the impression of a vertical slice of masonry with the relative importance of the rooms indicated by window size. This is still one of the most common, and best-loved, of English house types.

Bedford Square
London

Begun in 1776 and still intact, Bedford Square is one of London's best-known Georgian developments. Originally it was a quiet enclave, gated off from the surrounding streets and served by mews where carriages were parked and horses stabled. It is noisier now, but one can still appreciate the work of the architect, perhaps Thomas Leverton, who accentuated the centre houses by coating them in stucco and adding a pediment. It is likely that the other houses were originally painted black, with the pointing picked out in white, which must have given them a rather jazzy appearance, a far cry from most people's idea of Georgian decorum.

The unified decorative scheme, together with the central pedimented feature would have given each side of the square a feeling of unity, but this is not a full-blown palace façade of the kind that came into fashion later. Today the whole has a very restrained look – with just the doorways given a note of showiness by their stripy bands of Coade Stone alternating with brick, a form of decoration that was soon to be copied in other London terraces and squares.

Peckover House, Wisbech
Cambridgeshire

Built in the mid-1720s, Peckover House shows how the Georgians could create an effect of grandeur with the most basic of materials. The façade is built mainly of brick – yellow brick highlighted with dressings of red. Most of the front is in one flat plane – the brick pilasters at either end and the shallow string-courses hardly stick out at all from the surface. All of this restraint allows the doorway to make its full effect. Here the builder pulled out all the stops, with an ornate fanlight and Tuscan half-columns that support a gigantic pediment, shaped in the form of a segment of a circle.

This ornate entrance at Peckover House reminds us how the way into a building was always one of the most important aspects for the Georgians.

See also

Stuart Classical parish churches, 44
Stuart Classical houses, 128
Palladian houses, 136
Georgian houses, next page
Georgian Bath, 142

Georgian houses (continued)

Palladianism was not for everyone. The mid-18th century saw a backward glance towards a different architectural idiom – the Gothic. Enthusiasts such as Horace Walpole collected pictures of Gothic churches and cathedrals, examples of medieval carving, and other architectural fragments. It was a short step to designing Gothic houses to display these curiosities. But medieval Gothic was essentially a way of building churches – 18th-century house builders had to adapt it to their needs and in doing

Strawberry Hill, Twickenham Middlesex

Horace Walpole, scholar, writer, and man of taste, remodelled his house at Strawberry Hill in a series of phases between 1747 and 1776, using the Gothic style. Walpole made his house thoroughly asymmetrical, adding features such as the round tower to give visual interest and create intriguing spaces within. As a result of Walpole's work – he was his own designer, relying on a hand-picked committee of friends for advice – Strawberry Hill became the first house since the Middle Ages to be completely in the Gothic idiom. Walpole's Gothic came from many sources. Some of the details, from vaults to niches, were copied from various English cathedrals and churches. Many other decorative motifs, such as the repeated *fleur-de-lys* on the staircase ceiling, came from heraldry. Walpole was fascinated by the connection heraldry gave him with the distant past and liked to make up false lineages for himself based on these evocative symbols. Another decorative source was old glass. Walpole was an avid collector of stained glass and built many panels, like this 17th-century example, into his house. Unlike many contemporaries, who collected Classical sculpture and oil paintings, Walpole cast his net much wider, constantly looking to medieval sources rather than to the Classical taste favoured by most contemporaries. The fantastic way in which Walpole used these Gothic sources – copying medieval originals but mixing them in new ways and using elements like vaulting as interior decoration rather than as structural features – made his version of the style immediately fashionable.

The metal floor inlay dates from a later remodelling of Strawberry Hill in the Gothic style.

so they chose the features of the style they liked best. So the Georgian Goths mixed and matched, combining plain 13th-century-style lancet windows with intricate 15th-century vaulting. The resulting houses were delicate, fanciful, and witty, like their owners. Soon after the fashion for Gothic began, however, Classicism reasserted itself with a revival of Greek architecture based on a study of the ruins of Athens. Serious-looking houses, demonstrating knowledge of the Classical orders, were the result.

Grange Park, Northington
Hampshire

Pitzhanger Manor, Ealing
London

In 1762 the first volume of *The Antiquities of Athens* by James Stuart and Nicholas Revett was published. This book contained beautiful engravings, based on careful surveys, of major monuments of ancient Greece. Further volumes appeared between 1789 and 1830 and became the reference books which architects in Britain used to create accurate copies of the Greek Doric, Ionic, and Corinthian orders. Antique revival country houses, with their porticoes, entablatures, and statuary, used this style on a large and triumphant scale. Perhaps the most severe of all buildings of the Classical revival movement is this house, built 1804–9, by William Wilkins.

This temple-like structure on its stone platform in Hampshire really does make one think that a bit of ancient Greece has crash-landed in southern England. This side elevation is inspired by the Thrasyllus Monument, a now vanished structure recorded in *The Antiquities of Athens*. The massive Doric portico, to the right in this picture, was copied from the Theseion, an Athenian temple. Many of the details are done in render over brickwork, but the effect is still monumental.

Architect Sir John Soane bought the old manor house at Pitzhanger in 1800. At the height of his career, he now wanted to build his own ideal country house, a building that he could pass on to his sons. After demolishing most of the existing house, Soane produced a souped-up Classical front with free-standing columns supporting statues, inset plaques, and a dramatic skyline. Inside, he created a rich interior, demonstrating his skill in the handling of space and his love of strong colours. Now restored, Pitzhanger is once more a worthy showcase for the talents of its creator.

See also

Stuart Classical parish churches, 44
Stuart Classical houses, 128
Palladian houses, 136
Georgian houses, previous page
Georgian Bath, 142

Georgian Bath

Bath is the greatest Georgian city, and still retains many of its 18th-century houses. A watering-place since Roman times, it became fashionable in the 1720s, when John Wood the elder began to build terrace after terrace of houses, faced in the golden local stone, for residents and visitors. Urban planning, with a succession of terraces, squares, and crescents, was developed here by Wood and his son, who redefined city form with magnificent effect. But it is not just the grand plan that impresses. One of the

General Wade's House
Abbey Church Yard

Bath was already up-and-coming before architect John Wood the elder began work. This beautiful frontage of about 1720 is an example of what local builders could do before the town became a bastion of sophistication. The whole façade is charming, meticulously decorated – and well restored. By strict metropolitan standards many of the details are 'wrong': there is not enough distinction in size between the first- and second-floor windows; an even number of bays leaves a pilaster in the centre of the front; the Ionic capitals are tiny; the attic storey looks like an afterthought. Yet from cornice to crisply carved swags, this house is a box of delights.

Gay Street

This street was begun by Georgian Bath's chief architect, John Wood the elder, in 1735 and continued by his son. The street connects two of Bath's most important developments, Queen Square and the Circus, forming a vital link in the layout of the city. Many of the details are of high quality, from the way in which the cornices step up the hill to the various doorway designs, some simply framed with mouldings, some with pilasters, some with luxurious half-columns supporting heavy cornices or pediments, and some with pediments resting on scroll-shaped stone brackets. The windows have changed, however. Most of the first-floor windows were enlarged in the 19th century, by

lowering the sills so that the windows break through the horizontal string-course. Plate glass also replaced smaller panes in this period.

Many of Bath's street names are incised directly into the stone walls of the houses. The small capitals are those of the Georgian period, and those that decay are recarved using the same letter forms.

joys of Bath's houses is the array of telling details, from carved Masonic symbols to cut lettering, meticulous cornices to elegant ironwork, most of it beautifully preserved.

Fine carved fireplace surrounds are a feature of many of Bath's houses.

The Circus

This circle of houses, begun in 1754 to the design of John Wood the elder, is one of the most imposing sights in Bath. The three main storeys are treated with the three main Classical orders, in their traditional hierarchy: the plain Doric at the bottom, then the Ionic, then the ornate Corinthian at the top. But behind this traditional Classicism lie Wood's more unusual ideas about ancient Britain, which he believed to have been a sophisticated civilisation led by the Druids. So the decoration on the Circus houses is full of Druidic (and Masonic) allusions – sickles, pyramids, squares and compasses abound. For Wood this great circle was like a new Stonehenge.

Royal Crescent

John Wood the younger designed the Royal Crescent, a sweeping half-ellipse of 30 houses looking out over what was open country in 1767. This notion of town houses with a country view is something new, but the choice of a half-ellipse for the form looks back again to Classical times – it is half a Roman Colosseum and also, as Michael Forsyth has pointed out in his Pevsner *Architectural Guide to Bath* (2003), a form that recalls the colonnade in the auditorium of the Teatro Olimpico, Palladio's Renaissance theatre in Vicenza, Italy. The grandeur of the design – with its 114 giant three-quarter Ionic columns on a plain ground floor – is Wood's own.

Ralph Allen House
Railway Place

Bath declined in popularity during the 1790s, and in the first half of the 19th century builders took to constructing villas on its outskirts, to attract residents who wanted Italianate architecture and views across the surrounding countryside. Some formal building continued closer to the city centre, however, with houses like this one, named for Ralph Allen, a businessman and promoter of Bath stone in the early Georgian period. Its banded rustication and symmetrical design, perhaps the work of the architect Underwood, fits well into the cityscape.

The ironwork surrounding the houses of Bath is almost as fascinating as the buildings themselves. Amongst the curvaceous array of gates and railings are details like this device for snuffing out flaming torches.

See also

Stuart Classical houses, 128
Palladian houses, 136
Georgian houses, 138
Spa buildings, 296

Regency town houses

The term Regency refers to the period 1811–20 when George III's illness forced the Prince Regent (the future George IV) to rule in his stead. Artistically, the trends that began at this time continued into the next reign, so Regency architecture lasts through the 1820s and into the 1840s when Victoria was on the throne. This was the period of the pleasure towns, when the Prince Regent gave Brighton its rakish reputation and when spas such as Cheltenham reached their peak. The buildings

Carlton House Terrace, The Mall London

This terrace was designed by John Nash in 1827–33 as part of his redevelopment of London. Like his terraces around London's Regent's Park it is the grandest Regency architecture, nominally drawing on Greek sources for its lower Doric and upper Corinthian columns, but in fact producing a vast stage set in which terraced houses combine to make huge palace-like fronts. The façade in fact is in a bewildering number of planes, with floors set back different amounts and with balconies protruding to different points behind bulbous balusters. It is a tribute to Nash's ability that he could pull such a complicated composition together.

Crooms Hill, Greenwich London

One of the most popular architectural forms of the Regency period was the bow window. It was especially common in Brighton but was also used on individual houses, as here. Architects and owners liked bow windows because they let in lots of sun, producing the light, airy interiors that were much favoured in the early 19th century. Bow windows also provide outside interest. Regency builders admired curves – like the Georgians, they built many crescents – as a way of breaking up façades and streetscapes and gently pushing the front of the house into the tree-lined street or garden.

Pittville Lawn, Cheltenham Gloucestershire

Cheltenham was an ancestor of garden city planning. The Pittville area, named after its developer, Joseph Pitt, and planned by John Forbes, groups terraces, squares, and villas around a central tree-planted greensward that culminates in the Pittville Pump Room. Among its glories are some notable detached villas, finely proportioned and large, the kind of houses that attracted many retired senior officials of the British Empire to settle here in the 19th century. This house of 1839–40 is one of the largest, and is full of high-status neo-Greek features – pediment, acanthus finials, fluted Ionic columns, stucco friezes, and all.

The thick Doric columns on the ground floor of Carlton House Terrace are its simplest and strongest feature. Surprisingly, they are made of cast iron.

drew on the vocabulary of terraces, squares, and crescents developed in Bath, but made them more theatrical than proper, more grand, tree-lined vista than urban enclave, more stucco than stone.

Lansdown Terrace, Cheltenham
Gloucestershire

Cheltenham became famous when George III spent a holiday there in 1788, after which it became fashionable as a summer resort to which one came, like the monarch, to take the health-giving waters at what became known as the Royal Well. Cheltenham's popularity increased further through the Regency period and immediately afterwards and the town was developed in a series of estates. One of Cheltenham's main estates was Lansdown, laid out by J B Papworth, a planner and architect who did a lot of work in the town, and completed by R W and C Jearrad. Its elegance found favour among retired army officers and officials of the British Empire.

This terrace is one of its most striking streets, the tall, pedimented and heavily corniced houses having a certain drama. The houses have very plain ground floors, but things get much livelier above with Ionic columns and pediments, big windows, and curious openwork balustrades. Copious cornicing separates each floor from the next. The overall effect is enhanced by the way the terrace snakes along, gently curving in an informal way that is a far cry from the geometrical precision usually favoured by earlier Georgian builders.

Regency Square, Brighton
East Sussex

Brighton, with its connections with the Prince Regent, was always more raffish than Cheltenham, and this quality is sometimes reflected in the buildings. A number of terraces use the bow window as a repeated motif, and sometimes rounded balconies protrude with broad, skirt-like canopies edged with ornate valances. This curvaceous architecture gives developments such as Regency Square (1818) a light-hearted feel, as if these are sun-houses in which the bows and balconies are designed to let in plenty of light and to let one look out at the view in every possible direction. It is a style that feels right for the seaside.

The name of this Brighton square is emblazoned across the parapet.

This detail of a Brighton porch sums up many of the features of Regency domestic architecture – stuccoed walls, rusticated with channelled joints, the base of a classical column, and iron railings. The white-painted stucco is typical of the Regency and later terraces and crescents of many seaside towns, such as Hastings and Brighton itself.

See also

Regency parish churches, 54
Georgian houses, 138
Spa buildings, 296
Hotels, 314

The Picturesque and exotic

One of the most fashionable artistic ideas of the Regency period was the notion of the Picturesque, which was popularised by Sir Uvedale Price in his *Essay on the Picturesque* (first published in 1794). Almost impossible to define concisely, the Picturesque involves pictorial values, variety, contrast, roughness, irregularity, and intricacy. Architecturally it is embodied in asymmetrical plans, theatrical effects, the adoption of styles such as that of the rustic cottage, and the blending of building and

Royal Pavilion, Brighton
East Sussex

Egyptian House, Penzance
Cornwall

In 1815–22, John Nash remodelled the Royal Pavilion – originally a Classical house by Henry Holland – for the Prince Regent in an outlandish quasi-Indian style that he called 'Hindoo'. This involved covering the existing Classical house in an immodest outfit of onion domes, minarets, pierced screens, octagonal columns, and scalloped arches. This decorative vocabulary derives mainly from Islamic not Hindu architecture – one can see curving domes and pierced screens at the Taj Mahal and many of Nash's motifs in Ottoman buildings. But the combination in which they are used at Brighton is quite individual – nowhere else are features more commonly seen on mosques and tombs used with such abandon. The interiors, by contrast, take their inspiration from China, their lacquer, dragons, and silks again mixed in a triumphantly inauthentic way. It is a politically incorrect pleasure palace, where the Prince could consort with his mistress, Mrs Fitzherbert, away from the prying eyes of London, and is quite unique.

Nelson's victory against Napoleon at the Battle of the Nile (1798), academic research into ancient Egypt, and furniture designs by Thomas Sheraton were among the factors that kept interest in Egyptian culture alive in England in the early 19th century. Plymouth architect John Foulston designed a number of Egyptian-style buildings, and this may be one of his. The proportions, with their sloping sides, are meant to recall the pylons, or gateways, of Egyptian temples. Other Egyptian motifs include the banded columns, the curious busts, and the giant cornice. The bizarre patterns of the glazing bars may owe something to the influence of the tile patterns in Islamic art.

The banded columns on the façade of the Egyptian House in Penzance are based on those that held up the roof of the Temple of Amenophis III at Luxor.

landscape. An asymmetrical Classical villa in a park can be Picturesque; so can a vista of crescents and trees in a town. So too can a building in an exotic style, such as the Royal Pavilion, breaking the regularity of the terraces in Regency Brighton.

Blaise Hamlet
Bristol

Today we are used to the idea that the humble cottage can be picturesque; we buy the postcards. But this was news at the beginning of the 19th century, when cottages were the dwellings of humble rural workers and many such buildings were poorly maintained, cramped, and insanitary. But then came the concept of the *cottage orné*, the rural dwelling that made an olde-worlde impression with an apparently random combination of thatch, stone, leaded lights, porches, chimneys, and gables. Rich landlords took to putting up a *cottage orné* here and there on their estates to house the workers and improve the view. But Blaise Hamlet is special because it is a whole village of *cottages ornés*, nine in all,

designed by John Nash as retirement homes for workers on the Blaise Castle estate in 1810–11. Nash took special trouble to provide verandas or sitting-places for the occupants of the cottages – who presumably had time to sit and gossip – and these are roofed over to provide shade and shelter. The result is that most of the cottages have two roof lines, one covering the house itself and one the sitting place, adding to the Picturesque quality of the buildings. Porches, chimneys, and some thatched roofs add to the effect. Each cottage has something special about its design – one has an integral dovecote, for example, another boasts a delightfully ornate set of chimneys – so that each occupant had something different to be

proud of in their dwelling while reflecting that the whole group was a far cry from the uniform row of almshouses that many pensioners felt lucky to occupy in the early 19th century. The sense of community is enhanced further by the way in which the houses are tastefully arranged around a green with a pillar that does double duty as sundial and pump.

This is part of the village pump on the central green at Blaise Hamlet. A carved stone lion disgorged the water.

Some of the cottages at Blaise Hamlet are thatched, with separate sections of roof for the main house, the dormers, and the verandas cascading down in a series of curving Picturesque forms.

See also

Mosques and temples, 96
Vernacular houses, 110
Garden pavilions, 354
Landscape towers, 356
Memorial buildings, 362

Victorian country houses

The upper classes of Victorian England, rich from empire, trade, and inherited wealth, built on an unprecedented scale. Their country houses were huge not because they had huge rooms but because there were so many rooms. Domestic offices multiplied to house armies of servants.

There could be dozens of bedrooms for legions of guests. Billiard rooms, saloons, drawing rooms, and libraries provided a social focus. And all this could be in any style, Classical, Gothic, or Jacobean. Houses were also changing technologically, too, with the arrival of electricity towards the end of the

Harlaxton Manor
Lincolnshire

With its forest of turrets and cupolas, its bay and oriel windows, and its constantly interesting façade of warm limestone, Harlaxton is the Victorian idea of an Elizabethan prodigy house and has been amazing passers-by for more than 150 years. The brainchild of its owner, Gregory Gregory, it took 12 years (1832–44) and the architectural skill of Anthony Salvin to create – not to mention an army of workers and even a private railway to bring materials to the site. Surprisingly, the house is also partly baroque: the gateway is as grand as anything by John Vanbrugh and the interior decoration includes many rich touches, including plaster ceilings more elaborate than in most Elizabethan houses.

The most lavish space in the house is probably the staircase, where there are plasterwork tassels that are said to sway slightly when touched. There is also a stunning drawing room with mirrors on opposite walls that reflect whatever is between them in an infinity of receding images. Much of this interior decoration was probably the work of another architect, William Burn, who took over the job from Salvin and who had a baroque specialist in his office.

Milton Ernest Hall
Bedfordshire

William Butterfield, the architect of Keble College, Oxford, and countless parish churches, schools, and rectories, loved the Gothic style, colourful masonry, and complex exteriors with lots of gables and protrusions. Milton Ernest Hall, built for the coal and candle merchant B H Starey, was one of Butterfield's few large houses, but with its profusion of Gothic windows and host of gables it is very assured. Butterfield used limestone with ashlar dressings, but also incorporated red brick in the relieving arches over the windows and in some polychrome stretches of wall. A variety of Gothic forms in the windows adds further interest.

century and the installation of bathrooms and other luxuries. It is the usual vibrant Victorian story of embracing new ideas while clinging for dear life to traditional values.

Brodsworth Hall
South Yorkshire

Charles Sabine Thellusson inherited Brodsworth Hall, a portfolio of property, and a coal mine in 1859. Two years later he embarked on a rebuilding programme at his ancestral home. He seems to have employed an Italian architect – an obscure man from Lucca called Chevaliere G M Casentini, whom he probably met in Italy. There is no evidence that Casentini ever came to England and the one recorded design that he made for the house has been lost. The work on the house, which took from 1861 to 1863, was supervised by a London architect, Philip Wilkinson. The result was a house built in local limestone but with a rather Italian feel. There are no Victorian fripperies like bell towers, just a very Classical pile with a service wing tucked neatly away at the back. Within are lavish marbled rooms that live up to the Italianate promise of the exterior. Thelluson filled them with rich silks and a sculpture collection that is Italian in its origin but Victorian in its sentimentality.

Cragside
Northumberland

William Armstrong was an inventor, arms manufacturer, and benefactor to his native Newcastle. A quiet man, his large, flamboyant house is surprising, but as so often, the tenacity and flair that made the Victorians great empire builders and business builders also made them remarkable house builders. Armstrong employed R Norman Shaw to build his fantasy house on a Northumberland crag. Holes had to be blasted in the hillside, a forest of trees was planted, and extra bits got added to the house as building went on and Armstrong's ambitions mounted. The house was also a technological marvel: it boasted flushing toilets and was the first private house in England to be lit by electricity.

Among the clusters of gables and dormers at Cragside is a variety of different wall materials. Rough infill, timbers in diagonal patterns, irregular stone blocks, ashlar, and stone mouldings – all add up to one of the most diverse collections of textures.

See also

Victorian parish churches, 56
Prodigy houses, 126
Baroque houses, 134
Georgian houses, 138
Lodges, 358

Industrial villages and other alternatives

Throughout the 19th century the factories brought big new populations to England's cities, and these workers needed housing. Like the owners of the country estates where these migrants once lived and laboured, factory proprietors often provided housing for their workers. For many, this was bleak accommodation, houses that were cramped, with no sanitation, and with beds continuously occupied by relays of the family's shift-workers. There were few chances for working people to provide their

Charterville, Minster Lovell
Oxfordshire

Chartism was a working-class movement of the 1830s and 1840s that sought political equality and social justice. One of the Chartist experiments was in reforming property ownership, with the setting up of what they called land colonies, where self-sufficient families could work land in common ownership. One such colony was Charterville, where 78 houses were built on 120 hectares of land in 1847. The colony collapsed, but many of the houses remain. Chartist houses were usually bungalows and many were solidly built and have worn well. They often included fittings such as bookshelves, to encourage the self-improvement that was one of the Chartist goals.

Port Sunlight
Cheshire

Soap magnate William Hesketh Lever (later to become the first Lord Leverhulme) turned Sunlight Soap into the nation's best-selling brand. He was from a Nonconformist background and had an acute sense of his responsibility towards his workers. So when he was expanding his factory he decided that his staff should be housed decently and comfortably, that their accommodation should be conveniently near his factory, with all the social facilities they needed, and that the distinction between sub-standard workers' housing and houses for the affluent should be abolished. Lever began work on Port Sunlight in 1888 to achieve this goal. He lived near the site,

supervised the construction, which included a little hospital and even an art gallery, and maintained a close interest in the village once it was built. Indeed many residents found the constant presence of this paternalistic employer too much to take, but the environment he created was pleasant. The low-cost housing he built is attractively planned and set within plenty of greenery – Lever wanted his workers to have more experience of the natural world than was allowed tenants in 'back-to-backs'. The architectural idiom used by William Owen and the other designers was a mix of half-timber and Dutch-gabled brick that set a pattern for other garden village developments.

A world of cleanliness, health, harmony, and elegance is evoked in the early publicity for Sunlight Soap. Lever hoped for a similar atmosphere at Port Sunlight itself.

own housing, although the Chartists of the 1830s and 1840s made an attempt here and there. But a few employers were more enlightened, whether or not they were aware that comfortable workers might be more productive or more genuinely concerned for the welfare of those they employed. It is their houses, better designed, more spacious, and in more salubrious settings, that have survived to attract eager residents today.

Bournville
Birmingham

The Quaker chocolate manufacturer George Cadbury saw his staff as a holistic community – he wanted to house both factory and office workers, and to provide all the facilities they needed, from shops to sports grounds. Cadbury won respect because he followed a traditional Quaker lifestyle that was more modest than usual for a man of his wealth. The homes were not 'tied'; Cadbury simply wanted to create homes which were affordable and he made them available to workers from other firms, keeping the population genuinely mixed. He also put green spaces to good use, not just growing roses next to his factory but planting fruit trees near the houses and encouraging tenants to cultivate their own vegetables. After a small development close to the factory with housing for Cadbury's foremen, full-scale planning began in 1895, with curving streets, spacious gardens, and plentiful trees forming a backdrop for the houses and a green with public buildings acting as a centrepiece. This layout was the responsibility of Quaker surveyor Alfred Pickard Walker, while the architect was William Alexander Harvey, a young man with little experience who blossomed under Cadbury's watchful eye. His streets of houses, on which he began work in the late 1890s, were designed under the influence of the Arts and Crafts movement, and were both attractive and practical. Dappled bricks, tall chimneys, and overhanging eaves give these houses their characteristic look, which is still widely admired today. They were also well planned, with Walker increasingly adopting rectangular plans (instead of the typical Victorian plan with rear kitchen 'extension') to let in lots of natural light. New building technology and mechanisation kept the costs down, so the place was a financial as well as an architectural success. Bournville was hugely influential, encouraging better housing elsewhere and inspiring the men and women behind the garden city movement who wanted to bring a better environment to all.

Cast-iron signs such as this show the effort made to keep design standards high at Bournville. The upright, with its pair of brackets with pierced quatrefoils, is a delightful touch.

See also

Vernacular houses, 110
The Picturesque and exotic, 146
Commercial housing, 152
The developing factory, 222
20th-century schools, 276
Sports pavilions, 302

Commercial housing

The range of housing stock in Victorian towns and cities was vast. Builders often developed houses in a range of sizes – tiny, two-up, two-down homes for the unskilled workers; slightly larger ones for the slightly better-off artisans and the legions of clerks who staffed the offices in commercial centres such as London; bigger ones still for the middle classes. Decoration varied too, with the most elaborate fireplaces and ceiling plasterwork for the biggest houses. All but the largest were terraced, and the most common materials were red-brick walls and Welsh slate roofs. A lot of this housing is still in

Theed Street, Waterloo
London

Egerton Crescent, Chelsea
London

These flat-fronted terraced houses near London's Waterloo Station look almost Georgian. Like many Georgian houses, they have a deep parapet that hides a pitched roof and they lack the bay window that became such a popular Victorian feature. The doorways with their fanlights have a Georgian look too. But these workers' houses are early 19th century and, as the street was originally called Palmer Street, were probably built in the 1820s or soon after by local developer and scrap-metal merchant Richard Palmer Roupell. There is a Roupell Street, built in a similar style but without the parapet, around the corner. Richard's father, John Roupell, also developed land in south London and the pair built up a fortune. Richard's son William became a Member of Parliament but was eventually investigated for corruption and was found to have embezzled the family fortune away. The houses built by the Roupells in this part of Waterloo represent the beginnings of the great expansion that took place as 19th-century London became the world's commercial capital.

This white crescent is one of a number of streets behind the Brompton Road that were being developed in the 1840s, so although they look Regency at first glance, they are probably much later. Architect George Basevi was working in the area and may have been responsible for these houses too. They are well set off by the greenery in the Crescent's central garden.

The round-arched doorways of Roupell Street are part of the same enclave of 19th-century domesticity as Theed Street, an unexpected oasis in the middle of London.

enthusiastic use, and if there are modern kitchens and bathrooms inside and sometimes new window frames and roofs outside, some of the exteriors are little changed from when they were new.

Hornsea
East Yorkshire

As the Victorian period advanced and the population grew, the red-brick terrace became the universal solution to the housing problem. Most houses had bay windows to let in plenty of light to the rooms at the front, and the mouldings above these windows and over the doors provided opportunities for ornament. These houses, from the mid-Victorian period, have only a single-storey bay. They are small, basic houses, originally intended for the less well-off, although the builder allowed some ornament on the cornices to the bays. Many later Victorian houses, especially the larger ones aimed at the middle classes, have two-storey bays.

Brocklesby
Lincolnshire

By the 19th century, country estates were often huge operations, employing scores of men and women. Some of these people worked in the country house and its garden, but many were farm workers on what could be a large-scale commercial enterprise. All had to be housed and many 19th-century landlords, such as Lord Yarborough of Brocklesby, built houses for their workers, often in a uniform style. This example is one of the grander ones, its Gothic door with wooden Y-tracery and fancy, white-painted bargeboards to the gables indicating that it is a cut above the usual Lincolnshire vernacular cottage. It has a slate roof, rather than one covered with the local

pantiles, for by the time this cottage was built in the 19th century, Welsh slates had long been widely available all over the country, delivered by the growing network of railways.

Houses of some pretension – from grander terraces to villas – were often given names. These in Birmingham were supplied when they were built, in outlandishly lettered terracotta. Many were 'improved' with a coat of paint in the 20th century, but one still glows in its original red.

See also

Georgian houses, 138
Regency town houses, 144
Industrial villages and other alternatives, 150
Commercial housing, next page
Arts and Crafts houses, 156

Birmingham back-to-backs

**Granby Street
Leicester**

In the 19th century, thousands of people in Britain's rapidly growing industrial towns lived in small houses built back-to-back to save space and materials. With no back gardens, the only outdoor space was in the 'court' in front of the houses. Inside, accommodation was cramped and facilities were few – six or more people might share a two-bedroomed house and there were shared outside toilets. Most of these houses have long been replaced, but the National Trust cares for this last surviving group in Birmingham, which are displayed as they would have been in different periods from the 1840s to 1970s.

This street was part of the rapid expansion of central Leicester during the late 19th and early 20th centuries. In this manufacturing and market town, this expansion provided both shops and accommodation, and this example illustrates the growing trend to combine the two, with extensive accommodation over rows of shops. The development was done with great style, as can be seen where the upper parts of the buildings retain their original features – timber dormers in two sizes, brickwork with stone dressings, and windows with upper sections divided by glazing bars or leading. These are design features strongly influenced by the Arts and Crafts movement and the designers of the Queen Anne school and they still enliven the local streetscape and offer visual delight to passers-by who are prepared to look up.

The Birmingham back-to-backs bring to life the domestic round of past generations. Here, the hard labour of the washhouse is evoked with starch, soap, and tongs.

The Pryors, Hampstead
London

This Edwardian mansion block is a good example of its type, which was designed to offer spacious, convenient, and well-serviced accommodation, especially in desirable areas, from Kensington to Hampstead, where land was scarce. The Pryors was built in two phases in 1904 and 1910. The architect was Paul Waterhouse, son of the more famous Alfred Waterhouse who designed London's Natural History Museum. The red-brick walls with white detailing are typical of the mansion-block style, as are the windows, with small panes in the upper sections. The restrained Renaissance details (columns, emphasised voussoirs, and strapwork) add a touch of distinction.

Mansion flats, Queensgate
London

These mansion flats in Kensington show some of the features, mostly influenced by the Queen Anne movement, that appear on the better blocks in the area. The white dressings to the brickwork catch the eye and lead it up past terracotta panels and Classical pilasters towards a particularly ornate gable. This is quite small but crams in a whole repertoire of decorative features – cornices, arches, scrolls, and the curved top. But still more outstanding is the octagonal corner tower. This not only helps the building turn the corner with great style but also enhances the interiors of the flats to provide light, interestingly shaped rooms.

Hyde Park Mansions
London

How red can bricks be? At Hyde Park Mansions off London's Edgware Road the bricks are actually *painted* red to produce continuous bands of colour uninterrupted by lines of paler mortar. It is a vibrant effect, presumably done because the walls are built of cheap yellow stock bricks that the builder wanted to disguise. A few of these yellow bricks can be seen amongst the chimneys. The deep red of the walls offsets the block's white window frames, which display a strong pattern of glazing bars – lots of subdivisions in the tops of the windows and sweeping curves in the centre.

Pale cut letters on a black sign stand out against the painted brickwork of Hyde Park Mansions.

See also

Arts and Crafts houses

From the 1880s onwards, a number of architects fell under the spell of William Morris, the writer, designer, and manufacturer who wanted to get away from the Victorian reliance on industrial production and back to the medieval ideal of the craft worker who produces beautiful objects by hand. This led to a new-found respect for buildings that used local materials and that blended well with the surrounding landscape. Arts and Crafts architects who espoused these values included

Wightwick Manor
Staffordshire

Built on the crest of the wave of the half-timber revival that spread through Cheshire and Staffordshire in the late 19th century, Wightwick is outstanding. It was built for Theodore Mander, a Wolverhampton paint manufacturer who had read his Ruskin and Morris and knew what it meant for a building to be true to its materials. The house was designed by local architect Edward Ould in 1887 and extended by the same architect in an even more confident, timber-framed style in 1893. The timber framing is a good example of a building of that period using a style that was local to the area – brightly striped timber-framed houses had been a feature of the Staffordshire and Cheshire countryside since the Middle Ages. Wightwick represents the coming together of a local fashion with a deeper interest in the arts and crafts. And looking more closely, one can see how craftsmanship has been lavished on the building. The bargeboards are carved with more delicacy, the timbers curve more sinuously, than on most genuine medieval timber-framed buildings. Even the timbers that make up the framework, with perfectly spaced uprights and horizontals, have been assembled with care and precision. This is traditional craftsmanship in which the craftsman was challenged to take his skills to the limit. Within, just as much care was taken. There is a stunning interior by Morris & Co, the company founded by William Morris, which supplied wallpaper, embroideries, lamps, and numerous other fittings to create a rich and harmonious whole. From carpets and tiles, through inlaid furniture, to ceiling decorations, Wightwick gives perhaps the most complete example of an interior by Morris's firm.

Ranks of terracotta putti look down from above a doorway at Wightwick Manor.

C F A Voysey and M H Baillie Scott, whose houses often had low rooflines, asymmetrical façades with a strong horizontal emphasis, roughcast-rendered walls, and wide doorways. These were houses for enlightened, middle-class clients who, like their architects, admired Morris. They were also carefully planned buildings, with flexible internal spaces merging into each other. This mix of qualities made these houses highly influential on both architects and developers in the early 20th century.

14 and 16 Hans Road
London

Working in town, Arts and Crafts architect C F A Voysey adopted the red-brick walls and tall elevations of the neighbouring buildings in Knightsbridge. But even with these constraints, there is still so much about these houses that shows the influence of the Arts and Crafts movement. The mouldings that top and tail the narrow oriel windows and the finely cut house numbers above each door, set within Voysey's favourite heart shape, are two examples. More surprising still is the way in which Voysey, by using long strips of windows and subtle bands of stone, has given a horizontal emphasis even to these tall town houses.

The Pastures, North Luffenham
Rutland

The client for The Pastures, a Miss G C Conant, wanted a typical C F A Voysey house, and that is what she got – down to the long, low lines, broad, welcoming doorway, and sloping buttresses. This 1901 house also has rendered walls. Voysey would have preferred to use local stone, which he felt was more in keeping with the exposed position of the house. But the client vetoed stone walls, and Voysey was allowed to use stone only for the roof and for the dressings around the windows. Behind this wing, which houses the owner's accommodation, are two further ranges containing service rooms and stables, forming a charming, three-sided courtyard. This complex house embraces great variety, with windows of different sizes placed at varying levels, and with elements such as dormers and doorways adding diversity. The architect clearly loved this variety – it is a feature of most of his houses – but he also saw the need to pull the design together. He achieved this by unifying the whole building under a broad, sweeping roof, a typical Voysey feature.

Edwin Lutyens

Educated in the late 19th century, Edwin Lutyens began in the Arts and Crafts tradition, an admirer of William Morris and his architect colleague Philip Webb, with a genius for designing picturesque houses in local materials that integrated perfectly with their gardens (the latter often created by the great garden designer Gertrude Jekyll). Later in life, Lutyens became fluent in other architectural idioms, designing superbly in the Classical and Queen Anne modes. But look closer at a Lutyens house and it is always developing its adopted style, adding a quirk here and a twist there. Corners with

Little Thakeham, Thakeham West Sussex

Drawing on Tudor architecture, Lutyens designed this warm stone house in 1902–3. The layout, with side wings and central porch, is much influenced by 16th-century houses – Lutyens especially liked the Elizabethan Mapledurham House in Oxfordshire. Little Thakeham gives the impression of a group of buildings clustered around the entrance with typical Tudor informality, although in fact the façades are symmetrical. Inside, things are much more Classical. For example, one wall of the hall has a pair of doors topped with pediments and surrounded by rusticated masonry that seems to hark back to the designs found in Georgian pattern books.

Flats, Page Street and Vincent Street London

Lutyens's one design for social housing was a group of apartment blocks with fronts dominated by an extraordinary chequer-board pattern of brick and white stucco. When they were built in 1929–30, these blocks certainly attracted attention – although the fronts used traditional London materials they were nothing like anything else in the area and they still stand out proudly if incongruously. Lutyens, ever the eclectic, could not resist using the Classical style for the entries and pavilions carrying street-level shops, while adopting a thoroughly modern material, reinforced concrete, for the balconies in the inner courtyards. He was always full of surprises.

Castle Drogo Devon

This romantic vision, designed in 1910 and completed in 1930, has been called the last of the castles. It owes its existence and form to the client, grocer Julius Drewe, who wanted the sort of building that a 13th-century ancestor, one Drogo de Teigne, might have lived in. Lutyens obliged with a granite masterpiece, lit with mullioned windows and incorporating details that are as much Classical as medieval. The best word to describe the style is probably monumental, which is appropriate since the drama and simplicity of the house's shapes and forms owe a lot to the architect's work on war memorials such as London's famous Cenotaph.

This cornucopia of flowers and foliage is one of the Classical details on Lutyens's otherwise severe Page Street flats.

no visible means of support, balconies emerging from chimney breasts, buttresses that do not really buttress anything – all are typical Lutyens touches of wit which both make one smile and yet look perfectly and inimitably right.

The Salutation, Sandwich
Kent

Edwin Lutyens could also handle the brick Wren or Georgian style, as in this 1911 house, The Salutation, which he built for Henry Farrer in brick with stone dressings. There is plenty of warmth in the red brick and tile here, but in fact the design of the house is rather austere. This is the gateway, which displays a few of Lutyens's more playful details – the little square half-dormer windows, the curving fascia board, and the delicate carved brackets. It all adds up to a warm welcome.

Ashby St Ledgers
Northamptonshire

Lutyens designed these low Northamptonshire cottages in 1909. They fit well into the village, with their thatched roofs and details picked out in rusty ironstone. Further along the row, Lutyens gave them his favourite sloping buttresses. Here, in the middle of the row, are more details that point to the work of an architect of distinction – the opening with its flattened arch and giant keystone and the carved initials in their moulded cartouche. But nothing is too grandiose or heavy-handed: Lutyens knew what scale to use on these small cottages with the same unerring instinct that he used on his big country houses.

As a result, casual visitors are likely to pass them by, admiring as they go their picturesque proportions and neatly thatched roofs and taking them for buildings that have graced the village for hundreds of years. Their creator, who was at home in both town and country, and who practised successfully in both London and New Delhi, would probably have smiled.

Queen Anne houses

In the 1870s, a group of architects, dissatisfied with the Gothic revival on the one hand and the rows of recently built stock brick houses on the other, turned to a new source of inspiration: the elegant Dutch-influenced houses of the late 17th century, with their dormer windows, tall chimneys, and occasional Classical details. Revived by architects such as W E Nesfield and R Norman Shaw, the style became known as Queen Anne. Victorian Queen Anne houses were less formal than their Stuart ancestors, more freely planned and with lively façades featuring bay windows, oriels, fancy

Lodge, Kew Gardens
London

This neat little building is one of the earliest examples of the Queen Anne style. It was built in 1866–7 to designs by William Eden Nesfield during the short period when the architect was in partnership with R Norman Shaw. The tall chimney, steeply pitched hipped roof, and dormer window were all to become hallmarks of the Queen Anne movement. The dormer's rounded roof and pediment are pleasant details that show how Nesfield wanted to give this small building all the quality touches that he could. Soon such details were being widely copied on much bigger buildings.

Swan House, Chelsea Embankment
London

This house of 1875–7 was designed by R Norman Shaw, one of the foremost architects to use the Queen Anne style. The picture shows the stunning front doors. Many of the other features of Swan House are lifted straight from the architectural language of the 17th century – the three large oriels with their emphatic mouldings and round-headed main lights are the most showy examples, but the dormer windows in the roof are also typical of the earlier period. Curiously, the building is also jettied, a feature that recalls a still earlier phase of English building. But the sash windows and slender oriels of the second floor add a touch of more Classical elegance.

Cheyne House, Chelsea Embankment
London

The neighbour of Swan House is Cheyne House, built immediately afterwards and another example of R Norman Shaw's work. Here the delight is provided by the patterns of the glazing bars in the upper portions of the windows. They form an ever-changing play of geometry, lovingly picked out in white against the background of brick. And from inside there are ample views for anyone who wants to watch the comings and goings on Chelsea Reach.

This rosette enlivens the side of the dormer of the Kew Gardens lodge. It is testimony to the care Nesfield took with his design – even in places that most people hardly notice.

gables, and bits of ornamental terracotta here and there. This flexibility helped free up late Victorian architecture and began to take it in exciting new directions.

Clock House, Chelsea Embankment
London

This house by R Norman Shaw dates from 1879 and is typical of his versatile way with curves. Many builders would have been pleased to follow fashion by topping off their houses with a few curvy Dutch gables like the three on Clock House. But Shaw added more curves on virtually every floor – the segmental tops to the ground-floor windows, the great semicircular opening on the first floor, above the front door, the half-round lights on the main second-floor windows, and the curved balcony openings on the third floor. All these curves combine to make one of the liveliest façades on the embankment.

170 Queen's Gate
London

West London is full of pale stucco terraced houses, tall buildings – now mostly converted to flats or commercial use – that are rather severe and a far cry from the light-hearted Regency terraces in towns such as Brighton. But now and then there is an outstanding exception to the stucco rule. This large west London house was designed by R Norman Shaw and built in 1888–9. Shaw's client, F A White, specifically asked for a house that reflected the architecture of the early 18th century, and the versatile Shaw obliged, including more Classical detailing (for example around the doorway) than he would have done otherwise. In other ways, the red-brick façade sets the tone for its period, disturbing like a large interloper the stucco of earlier decades. The house is also an interloper in Shaw's career. Early in his working life, Shaw preferred a free style, although later he turned more and more towards the baroque. This building, with its elongated windows and Classical door case, is a bit of both, and all the more interesting as a result.

See also

Stuart Classical houses, 128
Arts and Crafts houses, 156
Edwin Lutyens, 158

Garden cities and suburbs

In the last quarter of the 19th century, a movement began to bring pleasanter, more village-like residential areas to some towns and cities. The resulting garden suburbs and garden cities have many influences, from an interest in the Picturesque movement to progressive social ideas. However, they all show two parallel trends. First, there is the wish to produce better living environments with pleasant, well-appointed, vernacular-looking houses, in a green setting. Secondly, there is the element of social reform, specifically the desire to provide good facilities, from shops and schools

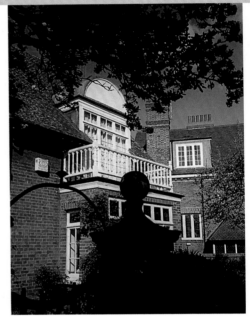

Bedford Park
London

This west London suburb was the first development to be built in the village-like mode. Constructed between 1875 and 1883, it began as a speculative venture by Jonathan Carr, who employed the architect E W Godwin to produce a number of initial house designs. Later many other architects were involved, most importantly R Norman Shaw. Shaw designed several pivotal buildings – a church, a bank, and a public house – on the estate, as well as a large number of houses. Most of these are in the Queen Anne style and have the red-brick and tile-hung walls and the dramatic rooflines and tall chimneys of the time. Decorative interest is provided with terracotta panels and by the variety of window shapes, usually with small panes and white-painted frames. Many houses also have balconies with wooden railings, and it is the interplay between red brick and white railings that creates much of the visual impact of the estate. Bedford Park is also full of greenery, which adds to the effect and ensures that the pleasant environment is as attractive now as it was in the late 19th century. Bedford Park was always especially appealing to those working in the arts and allied areas, and the area acquired a reputation as an enclave of the artistic and the enlightened. This, together with the involvement of influential figures such as R Norman Shaw and C F A Voysey, brought the estate to the attention of architects and planners, and Bedford Park became hugely influential – both on future garden cities and, in turn, on more modest developments that still sought to emulate its green environment.

The combination of brickwork, terracotta, and white-painted iron and woodwork enhances gardens in Bedford Park.

to institutes and laundries, and to create the right social mix, with rich and poor living nearby. Although the social mix never quite worked, from Hampstead to Letchworth, the garden cities and suburbs are still home to some of our best designed and most inviting townscapes.

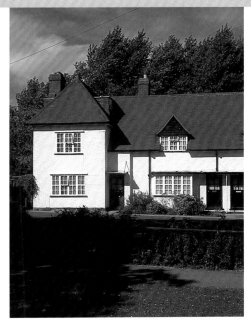

Letchworth
Hertfordshire

The first garden city was Letchworth. In 1903 Barry Parker and Raymond Unwin began to plan curving streets with plenty of trees, including some that existed before they started work. The houses, detached, semi-detached, and in terraces of four, are mostly rendered and have small windows. There are large, sweeping gables and tall chimneys. The whole package – both the building style and the street layout – became a template for the future. It was adopted in countless developments all over the country, many of them run by local authorities that did not have the funds to be quite so generous with land, planting, and design quality.

Welwyn Garden City
Hertfordshire

Louis de Soissons and A W Kenyon took on the job of planning Welwyn, the second garden city, after the end of the First World War. Many industries found the place an attractive place to relocate and the town soon found itself a success, combining a flourishing economy with a pleasant environment – with Parker and Unwin influenced curving streets, generous gardens and the best playing-field provision in Britain. Residential areas were kept away from the main traffic routes so that people could enjoy their mostly neo-Georgian houses in peace. Welwyn has retained its strong sense of place and still keeps the words 'Garden City' as part of its name.

Hampstead Garden Suburb
London

Philanthropist Dame Henrietta Barnett was the driving force behind Hampstead Garden Suburb. Her vision was one of an integrated community, in which all classes would live side by side, although this was not realised in practice. The main planners were Parker and Unwin, natural choices since they had already planned Rowntree's model factory village at New Earswick, York. As one would expect, the main theme was cottage groups of brick houses in a neo-Tudor style. Steeply pitched roofs and clusters of gables predominate. Other architects made important contributions, including Edwin Lutyens (the church of St Jude), Baillie Scott, and Guy Dawber.

The pleasant environment of the garden suburbs encouraged people to take a pride in their houses and gardens. Such pride encouraged the beginnings of the fashion for 'doing-it-yourself', and residents still keep the garden gates glowing like these in Hampsted Garden Suburb.

Modernist houses

In the 1920s and 1930s a few houses in the modernist tradition of Swiss architect Le Corbusier were built in Britain. These buildings mostly have white walls, metal-framed windows, and flat roofs or parapets; balconies and terraces were also common. Such houses look rather stark and rectilinear after the low-pitched roofs and natural materials of the Arts and Crafts movement. They were an indication that English architects were looking to continental Europe for their inspiration – indeed a number of

New Ways, Wellingborough Road Northampton

In 1925 the model railway manufacturer W J Bassett-Lowke employed the then little-known German modernist Peter Behrens to design his new house. The rear of the building looks forward to the pared-down modernism for which Behrens would later be famous. But the entrance front is rather different, notwithstanding the expanse of white wall and the flat parapet. The triangular bay window, cantilevered porch with its fins above the door, the group of little pinnacles, and the splash of colour on the door itself, are all part of the vocabulary of the architecture of the 1920s and 1930s.

Bata houses, East Tilbury Essex

Some of the most uncompromising early modern houses were built in a 670-acre (271 hectares) estate by the Czech industrialist Thomas Bata to house workers in his Essex shoe factory. This was one of a series of factories built by Bata around Europe, and the industrialist and his architects developed a modernist house style that was both distinctive and simple to build. The planning of the 1930s East Tilbury estate was based on a similar Bata development in Moravia, with a community house for young unmarried staff, these flat-roofed semi-detached houses for married workers, and larger houses for managers. Czech architects Vladimir Karfik and Frantisek Gahura were responsible for the design and planning, and all the components and fittings – everything except bricks, mortar, and concrete – were brought in from Czechoslovakia. The result looks ruthlessly efficient – Bata wanted to control his workforce, keep them close to the factory, and make sure they arrived for work on time. But, like the garden city planners, Bata catered well for the residents' welfare, and facilities on the site ranged from a ballroom and cinema to sports pitches and a pool. His constructivist houses, however, are quite unlike the architecture of the garden cities.

the architects, such as Serge Chermayeff and Peter Behrens, were themselves Europeans – to produce houses that were, sometimes literally with all those roof balconies, a breath of fresh air.

Isokon Flats, Lawn Road
London

Wells Coates, famous as the creator of bakelite radio sets and similar icons of early 20th-century design, was the architect of this 1934 block of flats in Hampstead. He was working for Jack Pritchard, a furniture manufacturer whose company was called Isokon, and the pair had a vision of compact, minimalist flats let on short leases to a highly mobile middle class. The minimalism was reflected in the exteriors, which consist of the simple access stairs and walkways protruding from equally plain walls patterned only with regularly spaced doors and windows – the image of rationalism amongst the trees of London NW3.

Highpoint One, Highgate
London

Berthold Lubetkin was a different kind of architect: a Russian émigré with strong ideas about society and design who worked in a cooperative practice called Tecton. He built two blocks called Highpoint. Highpoint One dates from 1933 to 1935. It is planned like two linked crosses, white, with strip windows and balconies with concrete sides that curve in a surprising way in this modernist building. The way these elements are arranged, especially the balance between white walls and strips of windows, produces a very satisfying effect. Careful planning concentrates the services in the crossings of the cruciform layout, and the apartments themselves in the arms.

Highpoint Two, Highgate
London

In 1936–8 came Highpoint Two, more squat and less graceful than its next-door neighbour Highpoint One. In architectural circles this was a highly controversial building because Lubetkin chose to support the entrance canopy with Classical caryatids. By introducing these decorative figures, not seen in British architecture since the 19th century, Lubetkin was provoking the architectural establishment. Architects who espoused what was becoming known as modernism believed that form should follow function and that embellishing buildings with extraneous ornament was little short of criminal. Lubetkin was suggesting a new direction for English architecture, but he was some 50 years too early.

Every book on modernist architecture refers to these famous flats as Highpoint, but this admirably plain sans-serif lettering standing proud on the parapet tells a different, two-word story. The great modernist architect Le Corbusier liked to raise his buildings off the ground on plain pillars that he called 'pilotis'. These pillars at Highpoint do the same job, separating the cream-clad flats from the darker entrance floor below.

The suburbs and beyond

The increasing population and the growing cities of the early 20th century posed a challenge to architects: how to build enough housing that catered for modern needs. Modernism offered one route, and some estates of flat-roofed, white-walled houses were built. Prefabrication offered another possible solution. Art Deco, with its use of Egyptian motifs and bright colours, provided modernism with a heretical decorative twist, and the vernacular tradition, popularised by the garden cities, spawned thousands of houses based on those of Hampstead or Letchworth. Most popular of all between the wars, however, was the mock-Tudor style that spread through countless suburbs.

Kenton
London

For most developers in the 1930s, modernism was too risky and, with a nod to the vernacular and to folk-memories of merrie England, Tudoresque, with fake beams, prominent gables, and persistent bay windows, spread through England's suburbs. One place where it was especially popular was Metroland, the area north-west of London served by the Metropolitan railway line. Wooden beams on the first floor, a prominent gable, a little tile hanging, and some stained glass in the door – these were the characteristic features that meant home to thousands of London workers. And for many they still do.

Thorpeness
Suffolk

This house, with its green-framed windows, one extending right to the corner, also shows the influence of the Moderne style, an elegant way of building that combined the white walls and metal-framed windows of modernism with decorative details such as curves and occasional porthole-like windows. The pantiles, white walls, and dormer windows are all traditional features, but the proportions, from tall roof to strip windows, are very much of the 20th century. The building is one small example of how a local builder can pick up influences and run with them.

Catford
London

Prefabricated bungalows were developed as one solution to the intensive house building programme that was needed after the Second World War. The idea was to build houses of steel or aluminium, using factories that had been making metal products for the war effort, although actual construction arrangements varied. The bungalows were supplied with fixtures such as fitted kitchens already installed and by 1948 some 156,000 prefabs had been built. These homes were designed to be temporary, but many lasted 40 years and a few survive today, proudly maintained by owners who value these compact, convenient detached homes, each in its own plot of land.

Stained glass was a common feature of suburban front doors in the early 20th century. From Art Nouveau-inspired curves and hearts like these to the sunbursts of the 1930s, it added a touch of colour and light to lift the heart of the homecoming commuter.

Such houses remain popular, but builders took a new turn after the Second World War when once more there was a need for new houses. Much social housing was built in large estates, often in mixtures of houses and flats. The tall point block was evolved to accommodate many flats on a small footprint. Many of these estates lost favour with residents who experienced problems such as the distance from amenities and workplaces combined with poor maintenance standards. But a few developers, such as Span, managed to produce well designed and affordable houses, tempering the hard lines of modernism with interesting textures and imaginative planting.

West Camel
Somerset

The Nissen hut was a First World War solution to the problem of housing troops in temporary buildings that were quick to erect. The structure of the hut was based on corrugated-iron sheeting bent to form a semicircle and anchored in a concrete curb. After the First World War the idea was adapted for house building, and a number of 'Nissen-Petren' houses of 1925 survive at West Camel. They have a framework of semicircular ribs, over which is laid a corrugated-steel roof. This structure sits on a low brick wall. The design provides generous ground-floor accommodation but a small upper floor that only allows windows in the end walls. The simple structure must have made the houses inexpensive to build and easy to live in, but they did not catch on. Perhaps they look a little too like refugees from the periphery of an aerodrome to be embraced by the British, who usually like their houses to be conservatively 'house-shaped'.

New Ash Green
Kent

Developer Span and architect Eric Lyons built some of the better housing of the 1960s. High-quality materials, an appropriate balance of houses and services, and good design set their urban village at New Ash Green apart from many of the estates that were built to supply housing needs in the post-war period. In these examples, a mixture of slate-hanging, timber cladding, and brickwork gives an interesting texture. But the key is the planting. As with the garden cities and suburbs of half a century before, the profusion of trees and shrubs softens the straight lines and brings the residents closer to nature.

Affordable houses built for an ever-increasing inter-war population fuelled the enthusiasm for DIY and gave owners the chance to customise their own property. Paint manufacturers responded with new colours and helpful publications like this *Colour in the Home* paint booklet.

See also

Commercial housing, 152
Garden cities and suburbs, 162
Modernist houses, 164
Airports and allied buildings, 348

CASTLES

The castle was a specialised form of structure built in the Middle Ages as the fortified residence of a lord and his household. A castle combined military and domestic functions in a unique way that lasted only as long as the feudal system was the main driver of government, land holding, and military service in England – roughly, the period between the Norman Conquest (1066) and the early 16th century. Later buildings that are known as castles may be either palatial houses or military forts, but do not have this unique dual role.

The Normans brought the castle with them when they conquered England. One of William of Normandy's first actions in England, recorded in the Bayeux Tapestry, was to build a castle. This first English castle was a structure of wood and earth. It consisted of a timber tower atop an artificial mound (the motte) next to a courtyard (the bailey) protected by a wooden fence. Motte and bailey castles such as this were built widely by the Normans. Their wooden structures have long since disappeared, but their earthworks can often be found, either forming part of later stone castles or as isolated remains in fields.

Motte and bailey castles could be built very quickly. It used to be said that this kind of structure could be built in a matter of days, but a recent study shows that a few weeks is a more likely estimate. But these rapidly built structures were vulnerable to attack. So the Normans were soon putting up castles of stone, and these buildings survive in large numbers. Many were built by the king himself, others were the work of important nobles, who had to get royal permission to erect these formidable buildings. Like other ancient English buildings, most were altered over the centuries as fashions in architecture – and warfare – changed. There were a number of different designs. Some have massive square keeps, some are circular, others get their strength from one or more circuits of curtain walls,

some concentrate their strength in the gatehouse – and many combine several of these features. Today, the majority are in ruins from damage sustained during warfare, while some evolved into luxurious country houses when they became redundant for military use.

Castles were sustained by the feudal system, under which lords held land in return for military service. A lord would agree to provide a certain number of knights or men-at-arms in return for the right to occupy a tract of land. Many lords held several manors and had a home in each, but usually only one of these homes would be a castle because castles were expensive buildings. A lord would be constantly on the move from one manor to another and he would be absent from his castle for much of the year. So he appointed an official called a constable to run the castle in his absence.

For much of the time, a medieval castle would be a quiet, peaceful place, but it would erupt into activity on the arrival of the lord and his household. Buildings that had been empty, such as the hall and the lord's private chambers, would rapidly be transformed with tapestries on the walls and rushes on the floor, into comfortable apartments bustling with knights, ladies, servants, children, and dogs.

A castle was even more frenetic during a war. At such times, all sorts of special features designed into castles to make them effective fighting machines were put into use. The drawbridge would be pulled up, wooden hoardings would be built on to the walls to act as firing platforms, and archers would stand ready by the arrow loops. Even in the early years of artillery, castles still provided the best defensive bases, and many survived until the 17th century, when they were slighted or put beyond use during the English Civil War, when Oliver Cromwell and his troops blew holes in the walls of many castles with gunpowder, producing in the process some of our most evocative ruins.

Great towers

The great towers, often known as keeps, built by the kings of the 11th and 12th centuries and their most powerful lords, are some of the most impressive medieval buildings. They are tall and their thick walls (up to 12 ft [3.6 m] thick in some keeps), small windows, and strong doors made them easy to defend. A keep originally stood in a courtyard or bailey protected by an outer wall. The bailey contained a number of other buildings, such as a great hall and stables, but these lesser structures have often disappeared, leaving the great tower isolated. Historians are unsure exactly how these towers were used. Since castles usually had a separate great hall, the tower was clearly not the principal residence of the lord – but its

The White Tower, Tower of London
London

William the Conqueror began the Tower of London in 1087. The White Tower was completed by his son, William Rufus, in the 1090s. For his main London base, William the Conqueror wanted a grand structure and its sheer size (it is 90 ft [27.4 m] high), its rows of buttresses, and its corner turrets certainly look powerful. But inside, it was quite a simple building, with most of the space being devoted to the three main requirements of the king – a main double-height room, a private chamber, and a chapel. Similar rooms would always be the main components of a medieval great tower.

Rochester
Kent

This tower was begun in 1127 by the archbishop of Canterbury. By this time, the more powerful builders were starting to make their castles slightly more complex. The archbishop's massive tower still had a main room and chapel on the second floor. But the first and third floors each had two large chambers, while the third floor also had several smaller rooms in the thickness of the walls. Pairs of chambers such as this, perhaps one for the daytime, one for the night, would soon appear in other castles, as would smaller rooms to provide extra accommodation for members of the household or guests.

Richmond
North Yorkshire

The great tower at Richmond is built against the curtain wall because it formed the extension of an 11th-century gate tower. The arch of the gate is still visible on the ground floor of the tower. In its present form, the structure dates to about 1170 and is very impressive. It was originally very well built of squared stone blocks, although in some places these have been removed and replaced with rubble. The walls themselves are very thick (up to 12 ft [3.6 m] in places) and contain small rooms and garderobes within their thickness. The openings are very small – this is the classic Norman defensive structure.

main rooms were large and impressive. Perhaps they were used as presence chambers where the lord held meetings or received important visitors. Additional rooms may have provided accommodation for the constable, who ran the castle on the lord's behalf. Finally, as the strongest building in the castle, the tower provided a secure refuge for all in times of war.

Castle Rising
Norfolk

The Earl of Sussex, William d'Albini, built this tower in about 1138, after he married the widow of Henry I. It is a simply planned building, with a hall and single chamber providing the main accommodation. Unusually, there is also a kitchen, suggesting that the tower provided William's main living accommodation. William showed his status not by the number of rooms but by lavish decoration – the use of zigzag carving and blind arcading indicates that this tower was the home of someone who wanted to emphasise his status. The other notable feature of this tower is that the entrance section, known as the forebuilding, also survives.

Orford
Suffolk

Henry II built this unique castle in 1165–73. It is a polygonal structure with three massive buttressing towers, one of which abuts on to a substantial forebuilding. Inside there are large circular rooms and smaller chambers in the turrets. This striking building looks as if it was planned by a man who wanted to make a point – it is a tall, powerful looking, even bizarre structure built at a time when the king was especially keen to assert his power over the barons. It also overlooks the harbour and in the 12th century Orford was an important port.

Conisborough
North Yorkshire

The corners were the most vulnerable parts of a Norman great tower, being prone to damage from attackers' undermining. A solution to this problem was to do away with the corners altogether and make the tower round. At Conisborough the round tower, built in the 1170s or 1180s, was strengthened by six massive, wedge-shaped buttresses. It is an ingenious design, but lacks a forebuilding to protect the door. Some of the buttresses do double duty – one contains a hexagonal chapel, two others accommodate water cisterns, which would have been invaluable if the castle had ever been besieged, but it was not.

One of the most impressive things about an early castle is the sheer bulk of the masonry. These arched recesses show the solidity of the construction at Castle Rising.

See also

Curtain walls

The outer or curtain wall was a castle's front line of defence. It had to be well built, with thick masonry; a wall walk from which defenders could shoot at attackers; and protruding wall towers, which as well as containing useful rooms gave the defenders different lines of fire. Soon curtain walls became so strong that many castle builders decided that they would do away with the keep altogether to create courtyard castles, structures consisting of a curtain wall that formed a courtyard containing the usual

Framlingham
Suffolk

Goodrich
Herefordshire

The castle of Roger Bigod, Earl of Norfolk, is a good example of how a well-defended structure could be built without a great tower. There is little to the castle now except for the curtain wall with its towers. The walls are very strong – they are around 8 ft (2.4 m) thick and rise to 44 ft (13.4 m), about half the height of many great towers. The flanking towers are higher still. The earl provided arrow slits at various levels – they are visible here towards the top of the wall and still higher in the towers. There are a dozen towers around the walls. Each of these supported a fighting platform, from which archers could shoot at attackers. Lower levels could be used for storage or extra accommodation.

In the Tudor period, most of these towers were provided with chimneys, but few of these connect to fireplaces – most of them were just for show, to convince anyone passing by that this was a well-appointed Tudor mansion. Most of the accommodation was in courtyard buildings, including a large great hall, which have since been demolished. The hall was built against the wall on the western side of the courtyard and it did have fireplaces for which real chimneys survive.

The castle at Goodrich began life as a fairly small Norman tower which may have been protected by a timber palisade. In the 13th century the castle was strengthened substantially, with the addition of a quadrangle of massive curtain walls with big cylindrical corner towers. The builders made use of a rocky outcrop to provide firm foundations, shored up the round towers with great battered buttresses, and surrounded the entire structure with a moat. These defensive works produced one of the strongest medium-sized castles of the Middle Ages. Its walls stood unbreached until it was slighted during the Civil War of the 1640s.

The Norman stone walls of Framlingham Castle were repaired and altered in later centuries. Many of the Tudor alterations were made in brick.

The castle at Framlingham was held by the Howard family in the early 16th century, and their coat of arms is above the entrance.

castle accommodation, from hall to stables. The shape of the courtyard could be adapted to local conditions. Some of the most powerful castles are based on this kind of layout, a cluster of large wall towers providing just as much security as a single tall keep.

Barnwell
Northamptonshire

Castles were not all vast complexes like the Tower of London. There were also smaller courtyard castles, such as Barnwell, which was begun in around 1265 near the site of an earlier motte and bailey castle. It was the home of a lord called Berengar Le Moyne, and according to a document of 1276, he built it illegally, in other words without being granted a licence by the king. The castle has a simple rectangular plan with a rounded tower at each corner and a gatehouse with twin, D-shaped towers.

Two of these towers were made up of a cluster of turrets, one containing a spiral staircase and another containing garderobes, simple medieval latrines which usually discharged straight into a ditch or moat. Originally there would have been buildings such as a hall inside the courtyard. Although compact, the castle was strongly built – the walls are about 12 ft (3.6 m) thick and offered powerful resistance to any kind of attack, from catapulting to mining, that 13th-century military technology could throw at it.

Rochester
Kent

Parts of the curtain wall that protects Rochester Castle, are still standing, including this corner bastion, which was probably built in the 1220s during a campaign of repairs and improvements that took place after a damaging siege in King John's reign. As well as restoring the damaged keep, the builders upgraded this outer curtain wall. It enclosed a large yard, with a keep in one corner and plenty of space for other buildings, including a great hall, which have long since vanished. Beyond the curtain wall there was a wide defensive ditch.

See also

Great towers, 170
Later medieval castles, 174
Town defences, 182

Later medieval castles

In the 14th and 15th centuries, castle architecture became even more varied. Builders adopted whatever form suited their purpose – often with an eye on creating the right kind of image. A knight who had fought in France might choose a design influenced by French castles, while a traditionalist might build a large square tower reminiscent of a Norman keep. Most of these structures were built not by kings or high-ranking nobles, whose families had built castles for themselves in the early Middle Ages, but by 'new' men, knights and lesser aristocrats who had done well and wanted a building to symbolise

Warkworth
Northumberland

The castle at Warkworth was originally built in the 12th century, and was expanded and altered over the years until it passed to Henry Percy, Earl of Northumberland, who was granted it by Edward III in around 1390. Percy extended the castle further by adding this extraordinary great tower. It is a sort of castle within a castle, containing a suite of rooms for Lord Percy together with public rooms in which the day-to-day business of the castle was conducted. The tower is built on a plan that resembles a cross superimposed on a square – but each arm of the cross and each corner of the square is canted, to give a unique multi-angled design.

At the centre is a turret where rainwater was collected. From a basement tank the water could be taken to the garderobes and basins in the private apartments. The whole structure stands on a splayed plinth of stone and originally had small windows – the larger openings were inserted later. In the meantime Warkworth had been attacked when Percy rebelled against Henry IV in 1403–5, when the king's armies eventually forced the garrison to surrender. The castle also saw action during the Civil War.

Bodiam
East Sussex

Perhaps Bodiam (1385), with its cluster of towers and broad moat, is the most beautiful of all English castles. It was built by a war veteran, Edward Dalyngrigge, and it looks strong. The great moat is just one of a host of defensive features, from portcullises to gun loops. But, like a number of later medieval castles, it was probably built mainly for show. Dalyngrigge had recently been humiliated in a court battle with John of Gaunt, one of the sons of Edward III, and he may have built Bodiam to show that he was still a person of substance. With some 33 fireplaces and 28 garderobes he could live there in comfort too.

At Bodiam Castle a gun loop, a slit with a round opening at the bottom, enabled an artilleryman to aim and fire at the enemy.

their status. It is no accident that these are some of the most attractive of castles, and those in which a visible degree of domestic comfort can be detected among the stone towers and battlements.

Bodiam
East Sussex

Inside the courtyard at Bodiam are the foundations of a number of rooms that were built against the castle's outside walls. This view, looking towards the gatehouse, shows the site of the household apartments and chapel to the right. The building to the left, convenient for the entrance, may have been the stables. Directly opposite these rooms on the other side of the courtyard were the great hall and kitchen. Between these two ranges were suites of rooms for other residents. There were also rooms in the corner towers, one of which contained a well.

Tattershall
Lincolnshire

Ralph, Lord Cromwell, built Tattershall in the mid-15th century, soon after he was appointed to the high office of Treasurer of England. This grand castle is a great tower with corner turrets that rise to around 100 ft (30 m) built of locally made red bricks that glow in the sun. But this is not a castle in the Norman sense. Instead of narrow arrow slits, Cromwell installed large windows. In spite of the moat, this place would not have been easy to defend against a determined attacker. Once more, the building was a status symbol – and a comfortable home for Cromwell and his large household.

Kirby Muxloe
Leicestershire

An early example of brickwork, Kirby Muxloe Castle was begun in 1480 by William, Lord Hastings, but remained unfinished because its builder was executed by Richard III. The castle was to have been a rectangular structure built around a courtyard with square corner towers (one of which survives to its battlements) and a large gatehouse. In the surviving portions there are gun loops, and records show that the gatehouse should have had machicolations. The broad moat remains. In spite of these military features, as with the other late medieval castles, there was probably also a large element of show in the design.

See also

Medieval manor houses, 116
Medieval great houses, 120
Curtain walls, 172
Gatehouses, 176

Gatehouses

Every legitimate visitor to a castle had to pass through the gatehouse – and attackers would try to force their way in here too. So the gatehouse had to be one of the strongest parts of a castle, and when the fashion for keeps had passed, it was usually the most substantial part of the whole castle complex. A gate protected by at least one portcullis, a drawbridge over the ditch or moat, and a pair of flanking towers was the basic minimum. More security-conscious lords added further portcullises and other defensive devices. The flanking towers, frequently large, each contained several rooms.

**Byward Tower, Tower of London
London**

The main entrance to the Tower of London is through this gatehouse, the Byward Tower, in the outer ring of walls. This structure was originally built in the late 13th century and forms part of a system of defences that block the way to any attacker. First, there is a ditch (originally filled with water to form a moat), which an enemy would have to cross before reaching the Byward Tower itself. If he managed to get through the tower, he would then be faced with a further circuit of walls. Only if he breached the latter could he reach the central stronghold, the White Tower.

**Warkworth
Northumberland**

In 1173 Warkworth Castle, at the time a stronghold of the English crown, was taken by William the Lion, King of Scotland. It then passed to the Clavering family, who proceeded to strengthen it with a stronger curtain wall, flanking towers, and this gatehouse, which was later strengthened still further. Although ruined, several of the gatehouse's defensive features can still be seen. There are cross-shaped arrow slits and above the entrance between the towers are machicolations, which consist of a protruding gallery with holes through which missiles or boiling liquids could be dropped on enemies below. There would also have been a drawbridge over the ditch.

**Cooling
Kent**

The castle at Cooling was constructed in 1381 when John de Cobham received permission to fortify his house there. He wanted especially to protect the River Thames nearby, which had proved vulnerable to French raiders shortly before. The most striking part of the building's remains is the gatehouse, which has a pair of flanking towers with bold overhanging machicolations and crenellations above. These defensive details, together with the narrow arrow slits, make the entrance look as if it means business. Around the back, however, one can see that these are not fully cylindrical towers, but semicircular bastions, open on the inside.

Gatehouses, such as this at Bodiam Castle, were designed with a pair of portcullises, so that an enemy could be trapped inside. Small openings in the ceiling, often known as murder holes, enabled defenders to fire on the trapped attackers from above.

Portcullis winding gear is concealed in the Bloody Tower at the Tower of London.

Donnington
Berkshire

All that remains of the late 15th-century Donnington Castle is the large gatehouse with its tall towers. Originally this structure gave access to a courtyard, with numerous other towers and buildings. The gatehouse was always the main military feature of the castle, a building that was designed to be easy to defend and to provide many rooms for accommodation – in other words to play the same role as the great tower did for the Normans. It was so successful in its role here that it helped its Royalist garrison sit out a siege of almost two years during the Civil War.

Kirby Muxloe
Leicestershire

This late medieval castle has a big brick gatehouse looking out over a broad, lake-like moat measuring 360 x 300 ft (110 x 91 m). Although the brickwork goes beneath the level of the moat, other parts of the building are clearly raised on an older stone plinth, showing that there was a castle here before this one was built in the 1480s. When it was at its full height, this gatehouse must have been an imposing structure, a serious piece of military architecture for a building on the cusp between castle and fortified manor house. The ground floor of the gatehouse is brick vaulted, making this a very substantial structure. The staircases are also made of brick, with brick vaults spiralling their way to the upper floors. The whole castle is too fragmentary to tell how the rooms inside the gatehouse would have been used, but again this is a large building that provided much space, whether for people or goods. At the top of the walls would have been machicolations (these are specified in surviving accounts for the building of the castle) and the building is equipped with a number of gun loops.

See also

Gatehouses, 106
Medieval manor houses, 116
Later medieval castles, 174
Town defences, 182

Tower houses

In the Middle Ages the far north of England was often a place of danger or insecurity. Wars between England and Scotland were only part of the problem – there was regular cross-border raiding, and both sides had to protect their families and their animals. Few people had the resources to build a full-blown castle, but many could manage a compact tower house, a Scottish form of fortification also used south of the border. These were simple, dour buildings, with a room on each floor, thick stone walls, a few tiny windows, and a roof that

Vicar's Pele, Corbridge
Northumberland

The medieval vicarage at Corbridge is in the form of a tower and is known as the Vicar's Pele, 'pele' being a northern word for a tower house. It was built in around 1300 using recycled stones from the nearby Roman military base and supply depot south of Hadrian's Wall. The tiny windows and projecting turrets give the house a military air, and the tunnel-vaulted ground-floor room is similarly spartan. This evocative building dates to a time when settlements near the Scottish border were often vulnerable from fighting between England and Scotland and from the frequent opportunistic raids that took place.

Halton
Northumberland

Like the Vicar's Pele at Corbridge, this border stronghold was built during the 14th century with stone from the nearby Roman military base. The corner turrets project only slightly from the walls, but are in better condition, so that one can see the overall shape of the building and appreciate its similarity to Scottish tower houses. The sash window is a later addition, as are the surrounding lower buildings, which turned the tower into a comfortable house in the 16th century. In medieval times the tower was surrounded by a stone precinct wall (known locally as a barmkin wall), parts of which still survive.

Caister
Norfolk

This is a different kind of tower, part of a larger castle consisting of a quadrangle surrounded by water, but it is included here because it shows another variation on the theme of the late medieval fortified tower. The slender tower, some 89 ft (27 m) tall, had five floors of living accommodation and was topped by a machicolated parapet, parts of which remain. Begun in 1432 for the knight and adventurer Sir John Fastolf, the building is of local red brick but, unlike structures such as Tattershall Castle, is seriously defended with gun loops. The walls are well over a metre thick.

could act as an observation post. A later response to the need for a strong house in the borders was the bastle, a kind of horizontal version of the tower house, which was favoured by farmers in Northumberland.

Brackenhill, Longtown
Cumbria

The way in which the battlements are slightly overhanging, supported on corbels, gives Brackenhill the appearance of a medieval Scottish tower house, yet it was built in the 1580s in England (albeit near the border). The tower was the home of the Graham family, notorious reivers (the regional word for raiders, usually in search of cattle) who needed a strong base for their cross-border raids. Solid stone walls about 5 ft (1.5 m) thick at the base, a stout wooden door, and minimal windows kept the place secure – and helped keep the inhabitants warm in this chilly northern country. There was also a vaulted basement to keep possessions and booty secure.

But the reivers' way of life had not long to last when Brackenhill was built. When James VI of Scotland came to the throne as James I of England in 1603, he decided to enforce law and order on the border, and sent many reivers, including some of the Grahams, into exile. But some of the family returned to Brackenhill and the tower became a more peaceful home. By the Victorian period it had passed to another family, who made it more comfortable and installed bigger windows, some of which remain round the back of the tower.

Bastle, Doddington
Northumberland

A 16th- and 17th-century solution to trouble in the border country was the bastle, a defensible farm house with room for livestock on the ground floor and accommodation for the farmer and his family above. Originally, the family entered their room via the ground floor, first barring the outer door to protect the animals. They then climbed a ladder to a trapdoor and pulled the ladder up with them. In later, more peaceful times, a first-floor doorway and outside stone steps were usually added. This ruined bastle was built in 1584. Like most, it has thick walls and small windows.

There is very little decoration on Brackenhill Tower. A coat of arms, reminding us of the presence of the feared Graham family, is one of the few ornamental touches.

A close-up shows Brackenhill's massive quoins. The rougher stones would originally have been made smooth with a covering of render, known in the north as harling.

See also

Great towers, 170
Later medieval castles, 174

Tilbury Fort, Essex

FORTIFICATIONS

Since the time of the Romans at least, Britain has had a long tradition of fortifying itself against invasion. The medieval habit of castle building played its part in this, for among the roles of the castle was to defend its local area from attackers and to house men-at-arms who could swiftly join a defending army when a threat arose. But castles had a domestic function as well as a military one. There were in addition numerous purely military structures bolstering the national, island-bound independence.

For centuries, fortification meant first and foremost walls, and the thickest, toughest walls were the best. In addition, it meant lines of fire – in other words, giving the defender the greatest number of possible angles from which to aim arrows, and later guns, at an attacker. Fortification might also mean devices to keep an enemy at a distance, such as moats, lakes, and earthworks.

From the Middle Ages onwards, military engineers combined these elements. So a medieval city would be surrounded by a wall, which would also be punctuated with towers, to provide shooting platforms for archers. Later, fire power would be concentrated on bastions, protruding round or triangular platforms that could accommodate several guns pointing in different directions. Both Tudor gun forts, which survive intact in several places, and 17th-century town defences, which have largely disappeared, were designed in this way.

As guns got bigger and more deadly, walls had to get thicker and the endless struggle between the competing technologies of attack and defence was under way. Some of Henry VIII's gun forts had such thick walls that they could not be blown apart with gunpowder. But in the following centuries enemies devised ever more formidable weapons. England's defenders have had successively to be prepared for ironclad battleships, rifled guns, bombs dropped from the air, tanks, incendiary devices, and nuclear weapons. They have responded in turn with complex forts with big guns housed in casemates, radar stations, tank traps, concrete blockhouses and pillboxes, and virtually invisible bunkers sunk deep under the ground.

All of these structures, from forts to city walls, were designed first and foremost to be functional. Many castles, formidable as they are, betray signs – bits of decoration, fireplaces, small private chambers – that they were also loved and comfortable homes. Fortifications are different. They are there above all to be strong and efficient. But this very single-mindedness makes for impressive architecture. The brick vaults that roof the casemates in Victorian forts are built with skill and craftsmanship, and the granite outer walls of such buildings are often made of beautifully cut blocks. The masons and engineers responsible for these structures were proud of their work.

Military technology, which is often at the cutting edge because of the large investment it can command, is brought dramatically before our eyes in these buildings. Sometimes, in a fort such as Coalhouse, Essex, originally built in 1870 to guard the Thames and the approach to London, the advances can be seen in a single building, as adaptations made for Victorian conflicts and the two 20th-century World Wars remain largely intact. One building can provide a long and absorbing history lesson.

Indeed the main importance of England's fortifications is their role in our national story. They mark not so much the succession of great battles that punctuate the nation's history, as the tensions and threats, the invasions that might have been. And in doing so they reveal an especially English trait of self-defence, of keeping the fortress-island intact and undamaged, that has characterised our history for centuries.

Town defences

It was usual for medieval towns to be protected by walls, which defined the boundaries of the settlement and provided wartime protection for the inhabitants. These walls were built of stone, pierced by gates at the main entrances to the town, and could also have towers at strategic points along their length. Their architecture was similar to that of medieval castles, with the gates forming the most imposing features. Expansion and development have destroyed most of the walls around England's

Bootham Bar
York

York, one of the most important English cities in the Middle Ages, has the longest and best medieval city walls in England – they even incorporate a stretch of the city's Roman fortifications. Most notable are the gateways, known here as bars, which were built between the 12th and 14th centuries. This one was partially rebuilt in the 18th and 19th centuries, but is still very much the medieval town gate. Typical features of York gateways are the bartizans, or protruding towers, at each corner, and the cross-shaped slits through which city guards could fire. The heraldry and stone figures are replacements, but in keeping with the originals.

City walls
York

Looking along the top of York's city walls from one gateway to the next one can get an impression of the extent of these fortifications. Altogether there are some 2 miles (3.2 km) of walls and they contain much medieval masonry, although it has been patched, especially in the 19th century. This is the walk that runs along the top of them. Along the outside edge of the walk are stone battlements, also known as crenellations, which consist of short upstanding sections called merlons and gaps called crenels. The crenel gave the defending archer a space through which to shoot, while the merlon gave him protection.

Town walls, Newcastle upon Tyne
Northumberland

Newcastle has some 2 miles (3.2 km) of medieval walls. Most of the walls were probably built during the 13th century and the standard of the masonry is very consistent – for the most part large ashlar blocks arranged neatly in courses and supported by a chamfered plinth. Some stretches also have regularly spaced watch turrets, corbelled out from the wall. The chambers in these turrets are so small that there was scarcely room to draw a bow, so a recess at the rear provided extra elbow room. This view shows some of the masonry around one of the corbelled-out portions.

Walmgate Bar is another of York's ancient gates. It is important to historians of fortification because it still has its barbican, an additional level of defence on the out-of-city side. But this is the city side, interesting because the gate was extended with a timber-framed structure in the late 16th century to convert it into a dwelling.

towns, but a few stretches remain and a number of gatehouses, valued for the accommodation they provided, have survived intact.

**Wall tower, Newcastle upon Tyne
Northumberland**

**Hotspur Gate, Alnwick
Northumberland**

The town walls of Newcastle were begun by Henry III in the 13th century and strengthened under Edward III in the 14th. By this time they were very strong, their solid masonry punctuated by seven main gates (all of which have been demolished) and a total of 19 towers, of which eight remain. The impressive masonry is seen at its best in the towers. This one still has a series of stone brackets which presumably originally supported a hoarding that could act as a firing and observation platform. In spite of the continuous warring between England and Scotland during the Middle Ages, the walls remained unbreached until the Civil War, allowing Newcastle to flourish inside. After the Civil War the walls were repaired, so that the city could be defended during the Jacobite risings of 1715 and 1745. In 1803 they were again refurbished, ready to defend Newcastle in the event of a much-feared French invasion. But Napoleon did not arrive and 20 years later the remaining gates, together with many stretches of wall, were demolished. The remaining towers and lengths of wall were restored in the 20th century.

This gate, also known as the Bondgate, was probably built during the 15th century, some time after a grant of money for wall building in the town in 1434. The most likely date is 1450, when a mason called Matthew from Alnwick Abbey was paid to carve a stone lion over the archway. The gate itself is a plain ashlar structure without battlements, though some corbels above the arch suggest that the building was once higher and had crenellations. The gate presents a plain surface to the town but has twin polygonal towers, lit by tiny slits, on the outer face.

See also

Tudor gun forts

In 1539, the Tudor historian John Lambarde described how Henry VIII, having provoked the enmity of both France and the Holy Roman Empire, felt the need to defend the English coastline and, 'builded Castles, platfourmes and blockhouses, in all needfull places of the Realme'. Most prominent of these buildings was a string of gun forts between Kent and Cornwall, low stone structures with thick walls to repel enemy fire and with rounded platforms on which large

Camber Castle
East Sussex

Deal Castle
Kent

The round tower of Camber Castle was built in 1511–14. In about 1540, Henry VIII and his Austrian designer, Stefan von Haschenperg, extended it in the standard Tudor pattern. By the time of the English Civil War, the castle had lost its importance – the river that it guarded had shifted course and it was isolated. It would have been destroyed with gunpowder, like many medieval castles, in the 1640s, but its thick walls were built to resist explosives. So what could be removed from the structure was taken away and the impressive stone shell remains.

Perhaps the most perfect of the forts built by Henry VIII is Deal Castle. It consists of a low, round central tower surrounded by six slightly lower semicircular bastions surrounded in turn by a further six bastions, themselves lower again and larger. Set within a deep ditch that follows the curving outline of the bastions, the building looks from above like a large flower. But this beauty was achieved for purely functional reasons, to give many possible lines of fire. There are plenty of gun ports in all the bastions, and holes in the vaulted roofs for the smoke from the artillery to escape.

The building also contains living quarters. Henry's forts were not, like medieval castles, fortified residences for a lord or king. But they did have a garrison to man the guns, and these men had to be housed. Here their rooms are mostly segments of the round bastions. They and their guns were well protected from any invader who tried to get inside – thick, iron-studded doors, murder holes, and a cannon aimed at the entrance greeted the intruder.

A close-up of the rugged walls at Camber Castle shows the solidity of the masonry, so strong that it could withstand Tudor guns and even 17th-century gunpowder.

guns were mounted. Eventually the chain of forts was extended further, with defences as far north as Hull in Yorkshire. The most complex buildings had bastions facing inland as well as out to sea, so that they could be defended against land-based as well as water-borne attackers. These buildings, primarily firing platforms, mark a radical turn in English fortifications from the castle, in which lordly domestic accommodation was a vital element.

Portland Castle
Dorset

This fort, built by Henry VIII in 1540, is exceptionally well preserved. It is a low, ground-hugging structure, with a fan-shaped plan, the curved edge of which gives plenty of lines of fire across Weymouth Bay. In contrast to Deal and Camber, Portland retains its curving battlements, which are quite unlike those of a medieval castle. There are also numerous splayed gun ports, together with a few arrow slits around the back of the fort. Inside there are rooms with fireplaces for the garrison as well as firing chambers for the guns.

St Mawes Castle
Cornwall

Cornwall was one of the last parts of the south coast to be fortified. The castle at St Mawes was built by Henry VIII in 1542 to a four-lobed, ace of clubs plan and retains its curving battlements. The building is surrounded by a moat and this is crossed by a bridge on the landward side to form the stalk of the multi-lobed plan. Inside, the barrel of each gun nestled in its own recess and each recess has a smoke vent in the ceiling and a shelf for ammunition. It is very impressive and Henry's confidence is perhaps reflected in the fact that this is one of the more showy of his forts. By the mid-16th century, when St Mawes was built, the royal ego found expression in heraldry and wall inscriptions. This showiness is confirmed by the way the castle sits proud of the surrounding land, with its high central tower and stair turret, giving a less low-slung impression than Henry's forts in Kent and Sussex.

See also

Later medieval castles, 174
Early modern fortifications, 186

Early modern fortifications

During the English Civil War extraordinary chains of bastions were erected around key towns such as Newark and Oxford. These vast, star-like structures are known from paintings showing the military campaigns that went on around them and have mostly disappeared beneath the expanding towns they once protected, though some earthworks, and some alterations to older fortifications, survive. But the man who designed Oxford's fortifications, Sir Bernard de Gomme, was called in once again when Britain was at war with the Dutch during the 1660s. His lasting legacy is the fort on the River Thames at Tilbury, Essex, an enormous structure still largely intact. There were two main waves

Gatehouse, Tilbury Fort
Essex

The fort at Tilbury was begun in 1672 on the site of a blockhouse built by Henry VIII and near the place where Elizabeth I's troops had gathered almost a century before to defend England from the Spanish Armada. The fort was built to protect England from invaders sailing up the Thames Estuary. Its gatehouse announces the building in correctly Classical style, with Ionic columns below, Corinthian above, and carvings of the cannon on either side. As the decoration indicates, this was an artillery fort, housing a powerful supply of gunpowder, plus the troops and guns to stop attackers arriving on both land and water.

Artillery store, Tilbury Fort
Essex

Apart from the stone-faced gatehouse, much of the fort is of plain brick construction, with solid walls and earth bastions, which are angular polygonal ramparts that give a range of lines of fire for heavy artillery. In addition to the 17th-century fortifications, which are the best preserved of their type in the country, Tilbury has 19th-century remains, such as this artillery store, and structures dating from 1902, when the fort was modified to take larger and larger guns. There were still more changes during the First World War, when the fort was a supply base and anti-aircraft defence (its gunners shot down a German Zeppelin in 1916).

Landguard Fort, Felixstowe
Suffolk

This was one of many forts built in the 18th and 19th centuries to protect Britain from potential sea invaders. It was built to guard the harbour of Harwich and much of it, such as a massive gateway with its enormous stone voussoirs and the shallow brick vault beyond, is Victorian, as the date stone proudly proclaims. But there have been invasion threats since Tudor times, when Landguard was first built, and further scares precipitated rebuilds, including one in the early 18th century, when the fort got its current plan, with angle bastions of brick from which to fire on incoming ships.

of fortification during the 19th century, both to protect the coast against invaders who never arrived. First came the Martello towers, built 1803–14 to defend England against the threat of invasion by France's Napoleon. Later, from the 1850s onwards, a variety of forts were put up to counter threats posed by French ironclad ships and rifled guns. In the latter case, the buildings needed to stand up to the formidable new military technology and were so large, strong, and expensive that they could only be built on carefully selected sites. They were concentrated around the main naval bases, particularly Chatham in Kent, Plymouth, Devon, and Portsmouth, Hampshire.

Martello Tower, Aldeburgh
Suffolk

Fort Clarence, Rochester
Kent

Between 1803 and 1814 the Board of Ordinance built 164 Martello towers around the south and east coasts to protect the country from a possible Napoleonic invasion. Most are simple brick towers in the shape of an inverted flowerpot, but the one at Aldeburgh, the most northerly of the chain, is atypical. It is the largest of the Martello towers and is built on a quatrefoil plan, which makes it a rather decorative structure on the windy coast. It is a massive building, made of around a million bricks – this statistic alone is testimony to the huge amount of effort that must have gone into building the Napoleonic defences. The tower's layout is quite simple. There is a stone-paved battery for four guns – one in each section of the quatrefoil – on the top. The vaulted interior, originally for storage, is now used for holiday accommodation.

Another part of the defences against Napoleon was Fort Clarence, a vast brick pile of 1812 built to defend the naval dockyard at Chatham. It is the central part of a 656 yard (600 m)-long defensible line consisting of a revetted ditch punctuated with guard towers and casemates, some connected by tunnels. The tower itself, with its corner turrets and machicolations, was built to resemble nearby Rochester Castle. But it was used in a very different way, to house large guns on three levels. A post-war wooden floor has recently been removed to reveal three gun positions, with the sockets for timber gun pivots.

The splayed insides of the openings and the large relieving arches above them show the precision of the brickwork at Fort Clarence in Rochester.

See also

Town defences, 182
Early modern fortifications, next page

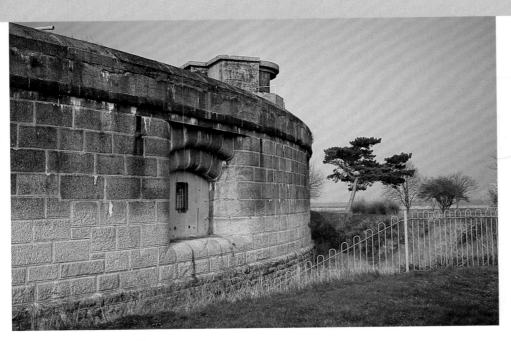

Coalhouse Fort, East Tilbury
Essex

Coalhouse Fort was built near the Thames estuary as one of a group of strongholds designed to protect London from invasion by sea. Begun in 1870, its massive curving granite walls were intended to repel enemy ammunition while at the same time offering multiple firing platforms from which its garrison could attack hostile shipping on the river. Within were large vaulted chambers called casemates, from which big guns could be fired. The size of the artillery was important as there was an increased threat from ironclad ships. The fort also had places from which soldiers could fire handguns. The guns and gunners were well protected. The outsides of the fort's walls, shown here, were faced in granite, the toughest of British rocks, while further in, bricks and concrete were used in the construction. Altogether the walls of the gun casemates were some 20 ft (6 m) thick and, had they been tested in action, would have withstood attack from the largest enemy artillery. This solid construction would also have been proof against later weapons and this fact, combined with Coalhouse Fort's strategic site, meant that it continued in use during the First World War and was an anti-aircraft position in the Second World War.

Coalhouse Fort, East Tilbury
Essex

A big artillery fort needed a sizeable garrison, and there would have been a number of specialists from engineers to doctors on the site, as well as the ordinary soldiers and their commanders. So the interior of Coalhouse Fort is full of barracks, service rooms, and even a hospital. This accommodation is built mainly of London stock bricks. Walkways run around the upper floors of some of these buildings, supported on slender iron columns. Brick was also an ideal material for arches and for the fort's large, gun-accommodating casemates.

Fire buckets are still hung on the inner walls of Coalhouse Fort at East Tilbury.

Hurst Castle
Hampshire

Hurst Castle
Hampshire

The threat of invasion during the 19th century also led to the construction of a number of defences at other places along the coast. The huge investment needed to build forts that could withstand ironclad battleships and the latest artillery meant that it was impossible to fortify vast lengths of the coastline in the way that had been achieved by Henry VIII's gun forts or by the Martello towers. So it was decided to concentrate on the most likely targets – the Royal Navy's main bases in the south, especially Chatham, Portsmouth, Plymouth, (and, in Wales, Milford Haven). Hurst Castle, standing guard on the western entrance to the Solent to protect Portsmouth, is one of the most prominent and best

preserved of these fortifications. The structures visible today were built in the 19th century as extensions to an existing fort constructed by Henry VIII. The adaptation consisted of adding two long mid-19th-century wings to Henry's castle. Both of these wings were built of brick with heavy grey stone facing to make them strong enough to withstand a bombardment from the sea. They were equipped with powerful guns designed to defeat the swift, iron-hulled ships that had recently come into service.

A view towards the northern bastion at Hurst Castle shows how much of the interior is built of red brick. This was an ideal material for constructing the great arching casemates, which were simply brick barrel vaults of the kind that had been used since the time of the Romans to roof large buildings. Some of their openings, useful for storage or creating into workplaces, have been walled in with more modern brickwork.

See also

Town defences, 182
Early modern fortifications, previous page

World War to Cold War

The 20th century brought entirely new approaches to fortifying Britain. During the Second World War the first threat came from aerial bombardment, so the priority was to provide anti-aircraft emplacements and, when the technology was developed, radar stations to detect bombers on their way to their targets. But in May 1940, France was invaded by Germany and a German invasion of Britain seemed suddenly imminent. Britain was quickly fortified, with lines of tank-traps, machine-gun posts, and, above all, countless pillboxes. This rapid building programme was made possible with

Bawdsey Radar Station
Suffolk

Radar was developed at Bawdsey, and the base became the first of a chain of radar stations lining the east and south coasts of England during the Second World War and warning the British of the arrival of Hitler's bombers. Although the 250 ft (76 m)-tall transmitter and receiver towers have long gone, many of the buildings remain. Some of the structures were sheltered by banks of earth, some were underground, reached through thick concrete trapdoors. The development and use of radar was secret work, a part of the war effort in which the British were technologically ahead of Nazi Germany. So underground and earth-sheltered buildings helped keep radar out of the public eye as well as out of the sights of the bombers.

Whittlesey
Cambridgeshire

During the Second World War thousands of concrete pillboxes were built as artillery emplacements to defend the country against invasion. Some pillboxes were cunningly disguised, taking the form of piles of logs or coastal shops. This one is clad in brick, but up close its concrete structure can be seen. Many pillboxes were on the coast, but there were also thousands of examples at strategic positions inland. There was a line of boxes running southwards from the River Tees through Yorkshire, Lincolnshire, and Cambridgeshire and down to London. Between the pillboxes were concrete defences designed to stop invading tanks. This pillbox is part of that line of defence, designed to shield key targets such as the factories of the Midlands.

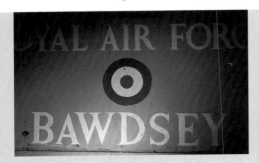

An RAF sign at Bawdsey Radar Station remains as a reminder that radar was a vital protection for British aircraft.

the use of quick-setting concrete, which enabled numerous, thick-walled buildings to be erected at speed. After the Second World War, a new defensive architecture evolved to cope with the conditions of what was known as the Cold War – the 40 years of tension between the Soviet Union and the West, an alliance which included the United States and Britain. This architecture of bunkers and concealed bases has only been widely publicised in the last few years and although the structures are big and very widespread, they are largely underground and still hidden from view.

Pillbox, Audley End
Essex

This pillbox is undisguised, its concrete construction clear to the eye. A slot for shooting and sighting is the only opening on this side of its solid walls. There was a time when these gaunt, unadorned structures were frowned on as ugly intrusions on our countryside – and harsh reminders of the bad times of the Second World War. A pillbox in a beautiful country park, such as this one at Audley End, was especially likely to come in for criticism. But now pillboxes are valued precisely because they are reminders of their era. They are a key part of the story of how this island was defended.

Kelvedon nuclear bunker
Essex

Most people are only beginning to become aware of Britain's Cold War architecture, especially the hundreds of underground shelters or bunkers that were intended to protect key members of society in the event of a nuclear war. But now that many of the buildings have been decommissioned and scholars are chronicling their history and structure, it is possible to appreciate the enormous efforts that went into creating these extraordinary underground structures, the late 20th-century equivalents of castles and forts. One place where it is possible to visit an example is Kelvedon, where one of the most important bunkers has been preserved and opened.

The statistics are amazing – the structure stretches down to 100 ft (30 m) underground, is protected by 10 ft (3 m)-thick concrete walls, and was designed to accommodate up to 600 people, from the Prime Minister to key civil servants and military personnel. Air-cleaning equipment and chemical toilets, food and water storage kept life going. Operations rooms, offices, and a radio studio were supposed to enable the inhabitants to keep the country running. And everything is accessed from an unassuming 1950s bungalow leading to a 350 ft (107 m) tunnel. Built in the early 1950s and decommissioned in 1992, the Kelvedon nuclear bunker is a salutary reminder of our recent history.

Some surviving nuclear bunkers still contain the remains of the equipment that the authorities intended to use to run the country in the event of a nuclear attack. The complex at Hack Green, Nantwich, Cheshire – a former Second World War radar station converted for Cold War use – contains banks of telephones and other communications kit, together with a studio to broadcast to the nation.

See also
Early modern fortifications, 186

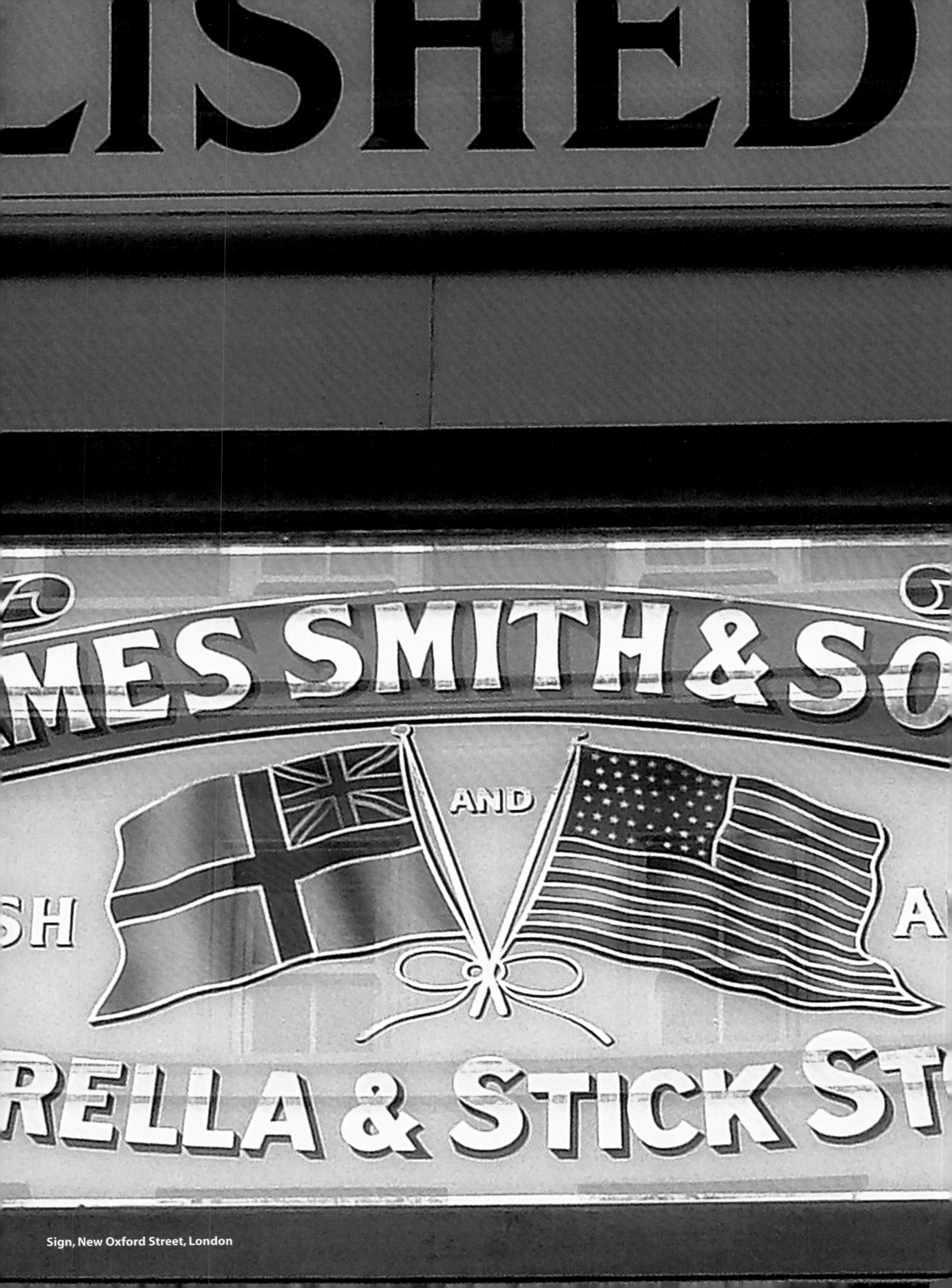

Sign, New Oxford Street, London

BUILDINGS FOR COMMERCE

For thousands of years, shops were simple and similar. Nikolaus Pevsner, in his pioneering book *A History of Building Types*, says that there is 'no essential difference' between the shops of ancient Rome and those of Renaissance Italy. Changing fashions and patterns of trade have meant that few of these early shops survive in anything like their original form. The most interesting retail buildings from the Middle Ages are the market halls that still form centrepieces to many small towns.

Shops began to change dramatically in the 18th century, when the rise of industry combined with the buying power of the middle classes opened up huge new markets for everything from tallboys to teapots, and suddenly shops became diverse and different. Retailers reflected changing fashions in their shopfronts and these mirrored the changing development of architectural styles.

Even in the 18th and 19th centuries, however, shop exteriors did not offer too many opportunities to the architect. They were straightforward buildings offering working spaces for storage and selling, fronted by a façade that displayed the goods to their best advantage and attracted customers through the door. The shopfront was the most interesting part of the building, but very often major architects, who liked to concern themselves with the creation of spaces and structures, wanted little to do with shopfronts. These were often lifted or adapted from books, such as Nathaniel Whittock's *On the Construction and Decoration of the Shop Fronts of London* (1840), or based on drawings by designers such as the Victorian scholar of ornament, Owen Jones.

Indeed fashion and ornament often provided the keynote. In the mid-18th century there was a flush of Chinese-style shopfronts in London. A few decades later Gothic was the craze. There were frequent flirtations with Classicism, from delicacy inspired by the work of Robert Adam to heavier Greek revival, though the Classical orders had to be adapted to accommodate increasing areas of window. There is no point being hidebound by architectural rules when you want to make a sale, and areas of glass certainly did get bigger, especially after 1825, when plate glass became cheaper and more widely available.

Given the fickle nature of design fashions, it is gratifying that many good early shopfronts survive in our towns and cities (not in our villages, for the rural shop has been for much of its life a more discreet and cottagey phenomenon). The small shops of cities such as London and Birmingham include excellent examples of 18th-century elegance, Victorian swagger, Art Nouveau fantasy, Moderne angularity, and more.

Meanwhile, more architectural opportunities were offered by large covered markets, buildings that flourished in the 19th century and still offer delightful retail spaces in great Victorian cities such as Leeds. These iron structures put to another use the technology developed in 19th-century railway stations. They may be smaller than the train sheds of the great railway stations such as St Pancras, but they are often more complex and filigree, and have a charm of their own.

Several developments in the early 20th century disrupted this confident design history. One was the evolution of retail chains, each with its own corporate style of design. Another was the emergence of the department stores. Small shopkeepers felt threatened by the new American-style monster emporia that began to appear in late Victorian times, and who can blame them? William Whiteley, west London's store magnate, had his effigy burned by local butchers on 5 November 1876, and Whiteley himself was murdered in 1907 after a number of arson attacks on his store. But the arsonists could not defeat the department stores, and a new, large architectural form became established on the high street.

Similar shocks to the retail system have been delivered more recently with the rise of the supermarket and the out-of-town mall, both, like so many other retail developments, heavily influenced by innovations in the United States. As yet these forms have to come of age architecturally. One hopes that proprietors will soon begin to learn the lessons of their forebears, and put good design at the front of their priorities and their buildings.

Markets

For centuries people have been buying and selling goods in markets. Today, we are most familiar with open-air markets in streets and squares, but there is a long history of covered market buildings. In the late Middle Ages, these were open-sided structures that lured the customers in with glimpses of the stalls, while keeping the stallholders and their goods under cover. Many towns have buildings such as this at their heart, and they often have an upper room that could be put to many different uses.

**Market Hall, Chipping Campden
Gloucestershire**

The market hall in Chipping Campden was built by local magnate Sir Baptist Hicks in 1627. It was one of a number of buildings provided by this generous local lord to enhance the town where he lived. The market hall is essentially a series of Cotswold-stone arches and piers supporting a roof. In a sense, then, it is the bare minimum of a market hall – there is no upper room and the building provides a covering and little else. But this is exactly what the stallholders of the local market would have wanted – the right combination of shelter and visibility, so that they could attract customers inside.

The task of providing this facility is managed with considerable charm, marrying, as in many Cotswold buildings of this period, traditional elements such as the stone-tiled roof with typical Jacobean ones, such as the round arches with their keystones. Slightly elevated on its plinth, the building provides a fitting focal point for the main street of this distinguished Cotswold town.

**Piece Hall, Halifax
West Yorkshire**

This vast Classical courtyard is a market like no other. It was built in 1775 for the cloth merchants of Halifax (the term 'Piece' refers to pieces of cloth) to a design by local architect Thomas Bradley. Its Classicism is austere and businesslike – rusticated piers below and columns of the plainest of the Roman orders – Tuscan – above. This framework of columns contains more than 300 rooms for the cloth sellers and the stark simplicity of the design must have been enlivened by frantic activity when Halifax was one of the biggest textile centres in the world.

The lamb and flag is one of the motifs in the ornate gates of Halifax Piece Hall. It is both a Christian symbol and a reminder that textiles were the source of the city's wealth.

This variety of functions means that you will find further examples of market houses in the sections of this book dealing with schools and guildhalls. Another great age of market building came with the development of iron-and-glass structures in the second half of the 19th century. This technology produced light, spacious structures like miniature Crystal Palaces – though they usually hide their high-tech skeletons behind a brick or stone skin.

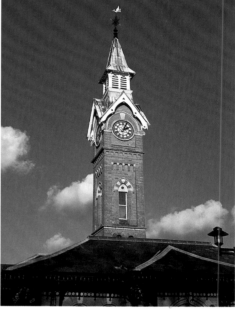

Cloisters, Kirkby Stephen
Cumbria

This colourful piece of early 19th-century market architecture links the market place and churchyard in the centre of this Cumbria town. Its Tuscan splendour was the work of George Gibson, funded by a bequest from local seaman John Waller. The strong brown paint scheme, together with the cross and bell, makes an eye-catching focal point. It is a good example of the way in which an old market structure still provides a visual asset. Retailing may have changed, but the architectural benefits remain.

Borough Market, Southwark
London

There has been a market in London's Borough of Southwark since the Middle Ages and on this site since 1756. Until recently it was a wholesale fruit and vegetable market, but the 19th-century market hall form is adaptable and the site, its paintwork spruced up, is now host to a variety of high-quality retail food stalls selling directly to the public. They shelter under glass-and-iron roofs first put up to designs by H Rose in 1851, the year of Joseph Paxton's Crystal Palace. The structure, which has been adapted and extended over the years, uses both barrel-vault and pointed roof forms, in each case glazed to let in plenty of light.

Cattle Market
Leicester

Leicester expanded hugely during the 19th century, mainly because of its successful hosiery industry and allied businesses such as boot and shoe manufacturing. But the city was also a marketing centre for local farmers and when part of the South Fields area of the city was earmarked by the local authority for development, one priority was a new cattle market. J B Everard was the architect of this building of 1871. Using red brick with stone dressings (some of them finely carved), he achieved a balance of practicality and civic pride with a slender clock tower, topped with a spire-like roof for extra height.

Keystones and gate piers bear the heads of some of the beasts traded in Leicester's cattle market, two of a number of details that recall the Victorian love of glorifying the sources of their wealth and success.

Arcades

Covered passages lined with shops began to be popular in the early 19th century, a time when travellers to Cairo and Constantinople were bringing back tales of eastern bazaars. But they reached their definitive form slightly later in the century when builders applied iron technology to give arcades glass roofs, providing the top lighting that has been popular in arcades and malls ever since. At the same time, industrial booms, overproduction, and the Victorian passion for knick-knacks combined to make the development of small shops selling luxury goods attractive to retailer and shopper alike.

Royal Opera Arcade, Haymarket
London

The earliest, and still one of the most elegant, shopping arcades is the Royal Opera Arcade of 1817. Designed by John Nash – better known for his work on Regent Street and the Brighton Pavilion – and G S Repton, it originally ran along one side of the Royal Opera House on Haymarket. The theatre burnt down in 1867 but the shops survived. Within the Classical portal is a passageway with shops along one side – the other side was the flank wall of the theatre. The vaulted ceiling is punctured all the way along with round glass domes, sending light down onto the bow-fronted shops, their dark glazing bars contrasting with the surrounding pale paintwork.

Burlington Arcade, Piccadilly
London

The most famous of all arcades, the Burlington Arcade was highly ambitious – it was both very long, at 585 ft (178 m), and in a good position near the prestigious Old Bond Street. It was built by Lord George Cavendish, who employed Samuel Ware as his architect. It opened in 1818 and became a notable success. The design was elegant in a restrained sort of way and traders were carefully picked to occupy the flattened-bow-fronted shops. And the atmosphere was kept exclusive. There was even a special private police force of beadles, who patrolled the arcade making sure that shoppers did not do anything unseemly, a category of behaviour that included whistling, carrying parcels, and pushing prams.

The formula worked, the best and richest of Regency society came to the arcade to shop, and the place became a sought-after address for retailers. News of the Burlington Arcade spread quickly, and soon arcades were being built in other towns and cities offering a chic and secure way to shop. The blend of elegance and exclusivity continues to this day and the beadles are still on patrol.

This lion is one of many that look down on shoppers in the Lower Arcade in Bristol.

An arcade was somewhere where people could shop in a protected environment, away from the mud and hurly-burly of the street, in an atmosphere of elegance or luxury. It was the first 'retail experience'.

Lower Arcade
Bristol

Shoppers liked the seclusion of arcades, away from the dust and dirt of the street. London's Royal Opera and Burlington Arcades were followed by one of the most beautiful of the Regency bazaars, Bristol's Lower Arcade of 1824–5. Its street frontage was designed in the latest Greek revival style by James and Thomas Foster. The tall front, with Ionic columns leading the eye up to a delicate anthemion moulding, gives access to two-storey shops, the walkway lit from above by a glass and cast-iron roof. Lion masks look down from the spandrels of the roof arches.

Leadenhall Market, Gracechurch Street
London

The origins of Leadenhall Market go back to the Middle Ages – Richard (Dick) Whittington secured market rights for the City of London here in 1411 and the City still controls the market. But the buildings are much more recent. They were put up in 1881 and the architect was Sir Horace Jones, who was surveyor to the City and designer of Tower Bridge as well as Smithfield and old Billingsgate markets. With its top-lit aisles and rows of compact shops, Leadenhall preserves some of the atmosphere of the earlier shopping arcades, but with the red, cream, and gold decorative scheme the place feels, if anything, still more opulent.

Royal Arcade
Norwich

Just like today's builders of shopping malls, the arcade builders of the late 19th century liked to reflect the latest fashions in design and presentation. On the whole, they did so with more flair. The Royal Arcade of 1899 is covered with tiles in the Art Nouveau mode that was then the latest thing in Britain. W J Neatby's tile designs, with their foliage, repeated hearts, and over-the-top curvaceous lettering, show a subtle use of colour that has worn well. It is an extraordinary mixture of elements, but they have been blended with thought and true craftsmanship.

The relief panels between the upper windows are just one kind of detail that sets London's Leadenhall Market apart. Similar touches include stencilled borders and gilding on some of the capitals.

See also

Regency town houses, 144
Markets, 194
The great termini, 332

The early shop

The shop as we know it evolved in the Middle Ages, in part from temporary stalls that evolved into permanent buildings, in part from the workspaces of home-working tradesmen such as carpenters and metalworkers. Retailing, ever fashion-conscious and with an eye for the main chance, has developed so much that most early shops are much altered. Even the attractive shopfronts in cities such as York have to be modern compromises that allow shopkeepers to trade in today's market. But with a little imagination,

Guildhall, Lavenham
Suffolk

In the Middle Ages, most goods were sold at market stalls or booths, but there were a few permanent shops. These could take the form of the lower room of a merchant's house or a simple lock-up. Goods were displayed through an opening at the front of the shop that was protected by wooden shutters such as this one at the early 16th-century Guildhall at Lavenham – not a shop as we know it, but a rare example of a surviving shop shutter. There was often also a lower shutter that folded downwards to form a stall to display more goods, bringing the trading area out into the street.

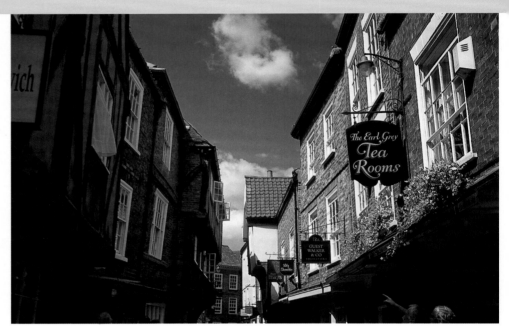

The Shambles
York

'Shambles' were originally wooden stalls built by butchers or fishmongers who, in the way of medieval traders, often congregated in the same street. As time went by, the medieval equivalent of the city council gave traders permission to turn their flimsy stalls into proper shops and many such structures were extended and strengthened to become permanent buildings. They continued to evolve through the Middle Ages into streets of substantial shops. The Shambles in York is the most famous surviving example, and its buildings display generous jettied (overhanging) upper storeys that indicate that their owners were people of substance.

Although many of the shops have been over-restored and are now dedicated to the tourist trade, they still give one an idea of what a medieval street would have been like – narrow, winding, and higgledy-piggledy. Other cities have streets called Shambles, or use a different name such as Butchers' or Fleshmongers' Row.

and some knowledge of preserved or restored medieval shops, one can grasp something of the way medieval people bought and sold.

Church Street, Tewkesbury
Gloucestershire

This row of 15th-century timber-framed houses was built by the monks of the adjacent abbey and let to tenants. Most of the occupiers were probably shopkeepers, who used the ground-floor front room for trading. In the Middle Ages the window openings would have been protected by shutters that would have been opened to reveal the goods during trading hours. The room behind would have been a compact hall, two storeys high, while a stair rose to a private room above the shop. One house in the row has been restored to reflect this arrangement of rooms. Few such examples of medieval speculative building survive.

The Rows, Chester
Cheshire

Think of colonnaded streets, and you probably think of a town in Italy with rows of stone arches. But there were a few such shopping streets in medieval England, built in timber with posts supporting an overhanging upper floor or, as at Chester, with a colonnaded first floor over a semi-basement. The resulting 'Rows', which were probably begun in the 13th century, have been much altered by the incursions of Georgian additions and the inevitable modern shopfronts. But there are still a large number of timber-framed shops in the most dazzling Cheshire style, and many keep their arcaded upper floors with their carved woodwork and their promise of a sheltered window-

shopping environment, like arcades in the making. The upper levels often reveal high-quality details. As so often in early market and shop buildings, wooden posts are carved like columns and the ornate carved brackets are outstanding.

A view from the other side of the street shows how the Rows in Chester present a brilliant black-and-white frontage to the world. Lots of diagonal struts make patterns between the big windows, themselves a sign of high status when glass was a costly luxury.

See also

Vernacular houses, 110
Medieval town houses, 118
Markets, 194

The art of display

There was a boom in consumer goods from the mid-18th century onwards, the period during which the middle classes discovered how to define themselves with the 'stuff' that they owned. Retailers fuelled this boom with shops that prioritised display: bow windows showed off the goods; Classical architecture was adapted to fit retailing, with the entablature pressed into service to hold the signboard; carved brackets and cornices added to the ornate effect; wooden shutters protected the window at night, until the introduction of steel-roller shutters in the 1830s. By this time, fashionable shopfronts were still more Classical, with architects such as J B Papworth using the orders and pilasters in plaster or wood.

Oundle
Northamptonshire

One of the most attractive and popular shop designs of the 18th century consisted of a pair of bow windows flanking a central doorway. Shopkeepers liked bow windows because they extended the selling area into the street, colonising 'free' space and attracting passers-by. Their shape let in lots of light and gave good opportunities for displaying goods – the items for sale could be seen from some way away, not just from directly in front of the window. But some cities resisted too much encroachment into the street. Projections in London were limited to 10 inches (25 cm) on wide streets, 5 inches (12.5 cm) in narrower ones.

Woburn Walk
London

London builder Thomas Cubitt developed this street, then known as Woburn Buildings, in 1822, and it preserves many of the features of an exclusive development of small Regency shops, purposely built out of sight of the well-heeled residents of the adjacent Bedford Estate. The flat-fronted bow windows of the shops were very much the fashion of the time, popularised by developments such as the Royal Opera House Arcade.

They did the same job as the curved bows of the previous century, giving good display space and pushing the shop out into the street, but perhaps the straight lines made them easier and cheaper to build, as well as being very much in keeping with the elegant image that Regency shopkeepers liked to present. The Woburn Walk shops have dwellings above and doors on either side of the window – one to the living accommodation, one to the shop itself.

Woburn Walk traders still like to use the street as a display area.

But by the Victorian period, stucco and veined marble were joined by more modern materials, such as iron, sheet brass, plate glass, and painted glass, to animate shopfronts in many towns, bringing increased colour and pizzazz to the High Street.

A grocer occupied this shop in Stamford, Lincolnshire, in 1944 when this picture was taken. It shows how the medieval building was adapted with the addition of a fashionable bow-windowed early 19th-century shopfront.

Berry Bros & Rudd, St James's Street London

London wine merchants Berry Bros & Rudd trace their origins back to 1698, and their shop was last rebuilt in the 1730s. This was a period when many fashionable shops were established in what was then the western part of the capital. St James's has been an exclusive shopping area ever since, but few retailers can boast a shop not only with its 18th-century frontage, projecting slightly into the street in the 18th-century manner, but also with so many original features. Glazing bars, fanlights, and pilasters are all intact – even the shutters, still put up at weekends. The panelled, wooden-floored interior is just as delightful.

Adnam's Wine Shop, Southwold Suffolk

A huge curving bow like this was the ultimate display window in the early 19th century. This example is one of the most outstanding of all, its beautifully hand-made appearance far superior to the usual offerings of today's shop-fitting industry. The window originally displayed the urns and carboys of a pharmacist when it was built in 1825. Now it is an off-licence, highlighted still further by very strong gilt lettering on the fascia.

Montpellier Walk, Cheltenham Gloucestershire

Nineteenth-century developers sometimes had the opportunity to create an impression of elegance along an entire street. Cheltenham's Montpellier Walk is one of the most delightful of all, with its rows of caryatids separating the shops. It was designed in 1843 by local architects R W and C Jearrad and the caryatids themselves were carved in stone, except for two in painted terracotta on which the stone ones were based. The gorgeous dipping cornice and the slightly later glass window complement the caryatid's curves – who said Regency Cheltenham was always prim and proper?

See also

Regency town houses, 144
The art of display, next page
The pub comes of age, 312

James Smith & Sons, New Oxford Street London

Martin Wilkinson, Newark Nottinghamshire

Glass became a favourite Victorian material, and was even used for signs, many of which survive on Smith's umbrella shop, which dates from about 1870. The lettering was painted on the back of the glass, which then presented a perfectly smooth and vibrantly colourful surface to the viewer in the street. The flamboyant Victorian imagination let itself go with the letter forms. Here ornate initials are combined with quite plain lettering, to give the required combination of ornament and readability. The catalogue of stock, from ladies' umbrellas to swordsticks, extends across the whole vast double front.

A glittering glass sign was just right for a jeweller and silversmith, and this late Victorian one still draws the eye with its gold scrolls and slightly outré Art Nouveau lettering with its I's like exclamation marks. There were several ways of producing such sparkling signs. Here, the signwriter painted on to the back of the glass. Another technique was to carve letters into a fascia, gild them, and cover the whole thing with a sheet of glass. Simpler still was to buy ready-made letters that could be of gilded wood or, for added dazzle, polished metal, and make them up into a sign. An engraved and polished metal plate was another possibility.

Of course, many Victorian shop owners stuck to simple signage painted by the local sign writer, but a fashionable Victorian shopping street in a big city centre could be a riot of gilded, polished metal and regularly cleaned glass.

The umbrella shop on New Oxford Street displays the whole repertoire of Victorian signwriting: curly capital letters, gilding, monograms, a scroll, and flags linked with a golden bow of transatlantic unity.

Walker's, Whitchurch
Shropshire

Many Victorian shopkeepers liked to take full advantage of big sheets of plate glass to produce a full display. In this case, narrow corner columns were the order of the day, and these could be in cast iron or, as here, wood. For extra decoration, there could be a separate stained-glass panel in the upper part of the window, the area known as the transom light. This was higher than most shoppers would normally look for goods, so the aim here was to produce a rich and colourful effect, one that would be enhanced still further when the window was lit up at night.

Allen's Butchers, Mount Street
London

Terracotta gave almost endless scope for showy display, exploited here to the full by architects George and Peto in their design of 1886. The range of columns, cartouches, swags, scrolls, and sprigs of foliage could be repeated and varied to provide a visual feast that was even at risk of distracting from the culinary feast within. But here in fashionable Mayfair, the need was to provide an image of assured richness – if you look away from the windows, the place could almost be a bank, and the decoration suggests that you can bank on the quality of the beef on sale.

Shipston-on-Stour
Warwickshire

Pilasters – narrow, decorative features in the style of Classical columns – often run up the edges of shopfronts, framing the window and door and visually tying the sides to the top of the frontage. Sometimes the notion of a column was abandoned but the pilaster remained, to become a home for various kinds of Victorian ornament. This example, made of painted wood, includes amongst its decorative motifs flutes, stylised leaves, a design such as a shell or fan, and a pointed finial.

Above the rich coloured glass of the transom light, Walker's shop in Whitchurch has a bright gilded number.

See also

Regency town houses, 144
The art of display, previous page
The pub comes of age, 312

Small shops of the 20th century

With the late 19th-century vogue for architecture of the Queen Anne style, many shop designers went back to the pre-Victorian style of small glass panes and lots of woodwork. But this did not last. The early years of the 20th century saw a return to the priority of display, with shopfronts showing large areas of plate glass, deep entrances glazed with further tempting windows, a lighter hygienic look for food shops, widespread use of decorative tiles, and sometimes the adoption of sinuous Art Nouveau

Chemist's, High Street
Leicester

Chemists' shops once had some of the most fascinating of all retail displays. Jars and bottles of chemicals filled windows and rows of drawers lined the interior walls. Nowadays, chemists' displays are more likely to be full of modern packaging. A shop in Leicester preserves a reminder of a beautiful pharmacy. Tiled panels of 1903 include a whole repertoire of symbols – flasks, mortars, pestles, opium poppy seed heads – before we even reach the delights of 'Sea Breeze', which promises to blow away our headaches with typical Edwardian confidence.

Johnson's, Oundle
Northamptonshire

Tiling, at once hygienic and decorative, became a popular way of decorating shop interiors and exteriors in the Victorian period. Companies such as Minton and Doulton supplied pictorial tiles with scenes appropriate for any trade where a bright, wipe-down surface was useful. Fishmongers and butchers were especially keen customers and the tile-makers produced ranges showing scenes with sheep and cattle or selections of fish and seafood. The fashion for such tiles, which were valued for both their beauty and their practicality, did not die in the 20th century and these tiles date from 1911. Many butchers in the post-war period were still decorated with tiles like these, which seemed to speak of the traditional values upheld by an old-fashioned butcher who knew how to hang his meat.

Traditional three-dimensional shop signs sometimes survived into the 20th century. This example in Cheltenham, Gloucestershire, marked a chemist's premises with a gilded mortar and pestle.

curves. A common feature was a glazed clerestory above the main windows and door, which could have smaller panes and some decorative woodwork.

Outfitter's, Aldeburgh
Suffolk

Shops with so-called arcade displays, in which there was a deep entrance lobby with lots of windows and island display cases, were popular among drapers, outfitters, and shoe-sellers in the first few decades of the 20th century. Shopkeepers liked these displays because they dramatically increased the window area, luring customers deeper and deeper into the lobby and then into the shop itself. In this example the minimal architecture, with large plate-glass panels and thin glazing bars, is relieved by the Art Deco stained glass in the upper portion of the window, the part known as the transom light.

The Bag Stores
Leicester

Look up above the shop windows in the high street, and you can sometimes have a pleasant surprise. Today's shopfitters are concerned mainly with the ground-floor windows – the part that the potential customer usually looks at – so first-floor bits of retail architecture and decoration from earlier periods can get left behind. This frontage retains some lovely period details from before the Second World War: large panes of glass with narrow glazing bars and, above, a black fascia displaying a luggage logo that speaks of an earlier age of long-distance travel to the orient. The clock, with hands that seem to turn magically without any mechanism, is a clever touch.

Post Office, Helpringham
Lincolnshire

The village post office and stores, often in a converted house, sometimes barely noticeable as a shop at all, sometimes decked out, as here, with traditional signs, is a cherished part of the rural scene. The rise of town and out-of-town shopping has brought the end for many of these village stores, to the chagrin of those with no transport. But some have bounced back, offering distinctive regional produce or diversifying in response to local markets. The result, as here, can be a visual delight as well as a source of essential supplies, from stamps to string, pensions to potatoes.

The most interesting thing about small shops is often the signage. Many used tin signs or boards with raised lettering to advertise products sold. One of the most familiar and enduring are the raised letters advertising the golden-brown bread produced by Hovis – a classic style for a much-loved loaf.

See also

Chain stores

Chain stores emerged in the late 19th century. Thomas Lipton, a Glasgow grocer, opened his first store in 1872. Marks and Spencer began in 1884 in Leeds. Soon after Woolworth started in the United States, before coming to Britain in 1909. Sainsbury's began with market stalls and W H Smith was king of the station bookstalls – both hit the high street in the early years of the 20th century. We recognise these stores instantly because they developed distinctive design styles, embracing everything from shopfronts to paper bags – it was corporate identity, before the term had been invented.

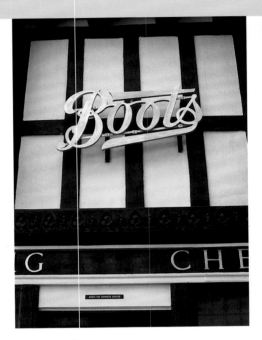

Boots, Ludlow
Shropshire

In the first two decades of the 20th century Boots the chemist expanded rapidly, with new stores in many towns. A number of these were stylish 'black-and-white' shops, with half-timbering, carved bargeboards, and elaborate windows with leaded lights. Such a style was often used in old town centres. The familiar Boots logo was always a dominant feature. In creating these shops Boots were in the frontline of developing a corporate identity that would make their premises easy to recognise wherever you were in the country. Other chain retailers were soon following suit.

Marks & Spencer, Gallowtree Gate
Leicester

In the 1920s and 1930s, Marks & Spencer embarked on an ambitious programme of large-store building, creating more than 200 large stores, mostly designed by one of three firms of architects. At ground-floor level these so-called superstores had big windows and a new green-and-gold fascia. Above, the usual pattern was a Portland-stone façade, divided vertically (often by Classical attached columns) with plenty of windows typically including diamond patterned glazing bars. The result was a clearly recognisable house style and a chain of stores that could take on the challenge posed by Woolworth, then its main rival.

Woolworth, Ludlow
Shropshire

The American-founded F W Woolworth chain underwent a big expansion between the wars, when every item of stock cost sixpence or less. Woolworth's stores of the 1920s and 1930s followed a standard design. One of the usual features was pairs of double doors set in lobbies in which a weighing machine was often installed for the use of customers and passers-by. The wooden-framed doors had prominent brass push plates and kick plates. The lobby floors were usually covered in mosaic tiles with a W in a diamond in the centre.

An old Smith's newsboy sign from Hull's Paragon Station evokes the chain's bookstall origins. Few of these signs survive now.

Though today this is achieved with plastic, neon, and stainless steel, some of the retail chains also value their design history and preserve early examples of their styles.

Co-operative store, Saxilby
Lincolnshire

The Co-operative movement began in the mid-19th century. The roots of the movement were in Rochdale, Lancashire, where the Rochdale Society of Equitable Pioneers was set up in 1844 to buy and sell groceries, apportioning the profits between members according to how much they spent. Many Co-operative societies were founded in the following decades, each locally based. They usually began with one shop before expanding into a number of smaller branches. So by the late Victorian period, Co-op stores had spread from the towns into rural areas. The Lincoln Co-operative Society had several rural stores by the early 1900s, by which time a building department was putting up new premises. Most of these were in brick, and a speciality was ceramic lettering spelling out the name of the local society and here the branch number and date. A manager's house was incorporated into the block and the store has retained its identity even though it is no longer a branch of the Co-op.

W H Smith, Stratford-upon-Avon
Warwickshire

W H Smith's began in the 18th century and dominated the newspaper distribution business in the 19th. They opened hundreds of station bookstalls in the Victorian period, but really only became a big presence on the high street in the early 20th century. They became known for stylish shops with polished woodwork and masonry stallrisers. Stratford's branch, opened in 1922, has timber framing and a panel with a quotation 'come and take choice of all my library…' from Shakespeare. Branches occasionally also used delightful tiled panels illustrating themes connected with their wares.

W H Smith's sometimes added pictorial tiles to their shopfronts. These examples, in Great Malvern, Worcestershire, are rare survivors on either side of a façade that has otherwise been revamped, an evocative way of advertising the stationer's stock-in-trade.

See also

Vernacular houses, 110
Tudor and Jacobean houses, 122
The art of display, 200
Small shops of the 20th century, 204

Larger shops

According to London store-keeper William Whiteley, the department store should sell everything 'from pins to elephants'. Such stores transformed British high streets in the early 20th century, offering a shopping experience in a more integrated and sophisticated form than the old arcades and bazaars.

Such stores began in Paris, with the Bon Marché of 1852. From there the concept spread and by 1900 there were department stores in England. Some, such as Harrods, Whiteleys, and a number of stores in major cities such as Birmingham and Leeds, expanded from established smaller shops.

Harrods, Brompton Road
London

West London's most famous store grew from an 1880s core, soon becoming the envy of rivals. By 1898 it had London's first escalator, in 1905 the long Brompton Road frontage was complete, and this Hans Road façade followed in 1906–12. The shop's curving window tracery, designed by the practice of Stephens and Munt, is very much in the Art Nouveau fashion of the time and inside were luxurious sales areas fitted out by prominent carpenters and shopfitters Frederick Sage & Co. The interior layout revealed the store's steady development – it was actually a series of interconnecting shops. But the variety of goods on offer justified the store's motto, *Omnia omnibus ubique* (Everything for everyone everywhere).

Selfridges, Oxford Street
London

Begun in 1906, Selfridges was extended to its present form in the 1920s. It looks traditional, with its heavy Portland stone columns supporting an entablature so vast that it houses the store's fourth floor. But in the spaces between the columns are panels of cast iron and glass and behind these is a steel frame that supports the floors. This frame is based on a 22 x 24 ft grid (6.7 x 7.3 m), which was to become the standard for large-store construction. Selfridges was not the first store to be built in this way, but it was large, high-profile, and packed with interest, from the rooftop tea garden and the restaurants, smokers' rooms, gallery, and other facilities on the upper levels, to the sales floors below. Selfridges showed the way forward.

Liberty's, Great Marlborough Street
London

The Tudor block at Liberty's was an architectural statement if ever there was one. Built in 1922–4, it turned its back on Classicism and steel frames, and went for an Arts and Crafts-style building, constructed in part from timbers re-used from HMS *Impregnable* and HMS *Hindustan*. Inside, customers could look up through spacious wells to floors above held up on wooden posts and fenced around with linenfold panelling in the Jacobean style. It was the department store as a cross between country house and medieval coaching inn, and was designed to create an image of luxurious goods and high-class service.

Pale terracotta cladding unifies the long façade of Harrods. The richness of the decoration began a reputation for the ornate that continues today.

Others, such as Selfridges, burst onto the scene new and perfectly formed. Architecturally, they were usually steel-frame structures with ornate Classical or baroque façades, divided by internal partition walls into a multiplicity of departments.

**Simpson's, Piccadilly
London**

Joseph Emberton's Simpson's is a statement of a different kind, up-to-the-minute 1935–6 modernism in an environment of Edwardian baroque. The landlords had insisted on a stone frontage, but if they had done so with the hope that this would fit in, they were in for a shock. Emberton obliged with strips of glass and Portland stone topped with a canopy of 'glasscrete' and enhanced with unmistakeable lettering. The Jermyn Street façade was equally uncompromising. Buildings such as this opened the way for a wave of modern stores using concrete, glass, and steel in new ways to catch the eye and project a fashionable image.

**Granby Corner
Leicester**

The 1930s were times of optimism for many retailers, with chains and larger specialist shops alike expanding and creating a new modern image. Art Deco and Moderne were popular styles for shop-owners who wanted their stores to look up-to-the-minute and, if they were lucky, they got a distinguished frontage such as Granby Corner in Leicester, designed by the firm of Symington, Prince and Dyke. Most of the effect comes from the gentle curve as the building turns the corner, together with the strips of green, metal-framed windows and the green tiles.

The ornament is relatively restrained, consisting of motifs such as the pleated stone cladding, artfully reproduced on the brackets for the flagpoles.

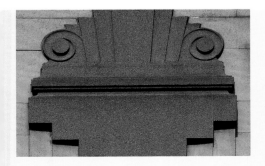

An Art Deco detail from the 1930s – all steps, pleats, and curves in low relief – adds a touch of elegance to the Granby Corner store in Leicester.

See also

Chain stores, 206
Modernist houses, 164

Transforming retail

Change or die: fashion, competition, and moves out of town continually force the retail sector to reinvent itself, and this is reflected in the design of shops everywhere. Many shopfronts only last a few years and from a design point of view this is often just as well. The appearance of most malls and out-of-town supermarkets is not much more inspiring. But here and there a company takes a longer view, keeping faith with the tradition that uses good design to attract custom or that links innovative shopfronts with upmarket goods inside. From boutique to supermarket, retail design can still be inspiring.

Harvey Nichols
Leeds

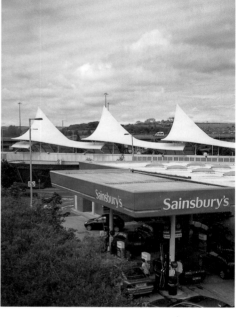

Sainsbury's, Marsh Mills, Plymouth
Devon

Faced with designing a new shopfront in a row of distinguished older façades, there is a stark choice. Does the designer go for some sort of imitation of or homage to the old, or turn in a radically new direction? Sometimes planning restrictions dictate a traditional design, but here there was more freedom – the shop was replacing a former theatre and linking Harvey Nichols's premises on either side. In this 1995 scheme architects Brooker Flynn went for an uncompromising design, totally unlike the store's Edwardian shops on either side. The solution acknowledges that shops benefit from daylight – and from big windows that project light out on to the street at night. The glass front and curving segmental canopy still allow the brick, terracotta, and curves of the neighbouring buildings to make their effect. The glazed upper floors allow a view into the store, inviting the pedestrian in. And this dramatic shopfront also gives the store an image of modernity that no doubt helps their sales.

The out-of-town supermarket is more often than not a low point of recent architecture, a warehouse or barn whose exterior ugliness is only effective in making the shopper think that things must, surely, be better inside. But there have been some more impressive efforts, and this Sainsbury's is one. It is the work of Dixon Jones, whose 1994 design combines a rather elegant steel-fronted box of a building with a series of upward-sweeping sail-like structures that shelter arriving shoppers while also alluding to Plymouth's maritime history. This is one of a number of stores for which Sainsbury's has appointed well-known architects to pleasing effect.

BUILDINGS FOR INDUSTRY

The industrial revolution came to Britain first and this country was in the forefront when it came to the development of the buildings that went with it – the factories, warehouses, and the host of specialised structures built to house machines such as steam engines and processes such as smelting. It is a rich legacy, one that shaped major cities such as Birmingham and Manchester, and which left its mark on the countryside too, from the mines of Cornwall to the mills of Yorkshire.

Bottle kilns, engine houses, furnaces, lime kilns – the sheer variety of industrial structures is amazing. But the building type that was most widespread and most influential was the factory. Factories began as simple and rather dour buildings. Many early factory owners cared little for their workers and everything for cramming in the maximum number of machines to increase profits. There was little natural light, not much space, and a great deal of noise. The exteriors of these buildings reflect this grim purposefulness. One can understand why Blake's epithet, satanic mills, has got stuck to them, even if their brickwork and proportions are admirable.

But the factory did not stand still. It developed in all sorts of directions. For one thing, the abandonment of wooden floors and posts in favour of more fire-resistant structures made it safer; better lighting improved working conditions too. In addition, the factory form influenced other building types, such as the warehouse and office block, which transformed mercantile cities such as Manchester and Bristol. And in the hands of master engineers such as Jesse Hartley, designer of Liverpool's Albert Dock, the factory and warehouse could become a laboratory for exciting new construction techniques.

But if it was a laboratory, the factory was also a generous playground for the imagination of architects. The Victorians needed this. Their prescriptive attitude to architectural style meant that most of the time a church architect, say, was confined to working in Gothic. A designer of public buildings was most likely to adopt a Classical idiom, although Gothic civic buildings became more acceptable after the construction of the Houses of Parliament and Manchester Town Hall. With factories and warehouses, though, there were no such restrictions and some builders seized their stylistic licence. Sometimes it was simply a case of making a factory more 'architectural' by adding a feature such as a cupola or an ornate chimney. Sometimes it was a case of picking up an established style – Gothic, say, or Egyptian – and adapting it with abandon and exuberance to the factory form. And 20th-century factory designers could be almost as adventurous, embracing modes of building from pared down modernism to over-the-top Art Deco.

At the same time, builders and architects had to grasp new ideas about efficiency and understand the processes that went on in their buildings. The advent of mass production, the technique whereby items are manufactured on an assembly line using standardised components, put fresh demands on this understanding. And as technology advanced, so buildings had to be more adaptable. Planning a factory could be just as demanding as designing a cathedral or a town hall.

For a long time, the sophistication of much factory architecture was misunderstood and our industrial heritage was largely ignored. As technology changed, many redundant factories were demolished. But two things above others have changed this state of affairs, so that we now value our industrial buildings as never before. The first is the effort made by archaeologists to investigate the industrial past and its buildings. The second is the realisation, amongst conservationists, developers, and clients alike, that industrial buildings are some of the most adaptable ever built. The uncluttered spaces inside a former factory can make superb apartments, shops, offices, museums, or restaurants. Sensitive conversions of these buildings are now common, and have played a part, not only in regenerating run-down areas of cities, but also in helping us to see the importance of our past.

Watermills

Watermills work by using a wheel to harness the power of running water to drive machinery – traditionally, the machinery was used to grind corn. Watermills are traditional buildings made with local materials. They were designed and built not by architects but by millwrights, who combined design ability with an understanding of mill machinery, often the practical understanding of the craftworker who could himself operate the spinning millstones. It did not take long for people to realise that water

Baylham Mill
Suffolk

The brick and weatherboarded mill is a particular feature of East Anglia. This mill stands next to a hump-backed bridge on the River Gipping, a river with several mills. Baylham is one of the most attractive and well preserved of these East Anglian mills – its neighbouring house has medieval remains at its heart. Apart from the sheer beauty of its white-painted walls, the mill's most notable feature is the extra-large, two-storey lucam above the entrance. With this simple piece of machinery, sacks of grain could be hoisted directly off a cart in the street and hauled up to the bin floor. No sacks needed to be unloaded and carted into the mill, as was the case with a mill with an internal sack hoist.

Lower Slaughter
Gloucestershire

Lower Slaughter is one of the prettiest of Cotswold villages, with a 17th-century manor house and a group of small stone cottages, mostly built along the north bank of a brook. Stone bridges, a green, and the presence of water all add vital ingredients to a scene that attracts tourists throughout the season and finds a place in many a souvenir calendar. In such a picturesque setting, the brick-built watermill comes as something of a surprise. But there was always plenty of industry in the Cotswolds, taking advantage of the power that could be harnessed from swiftly flowing local streams. At the Lower Slaughter mill there is enough stone in the building, and the brick has weathered gracefully enough since it was built in the early 19th century, for it to fit into the village scene. What is more, the mill is still a working building, reminding the visitor that Cotswold villages were built for real people with real work to do, not to provide scenic delights for the tourist. The metal wheel still turns to grind flour for the bakery next door which explains the presence of the tall chimney.

power could also be used for fulling (one of the processes used in the manufacture of cloth), sawing timber, and mashing rags for paper-making. With the industrial revolution came a range of water-powered cloth-working machinery too.

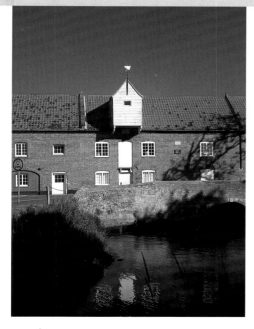

Burnham Overy
Suffolk

This solid and attractive mill near Overy Staithe in Suffolk was built around 1795. Like many mills it is in fact a complex of buildings – a barn, maltings, miller's house, and cottages for workers are all grouped together next to the mill itself. The mill is built mainly in the brick typical of the area, with a pantiled roof. Above the bin floor is a white weatherboarded lucam, with which sacks could be taken directly off a cart outside and hoisted to the bin floor.

Wadenhoe
Northamptonshire

A stone-built mill in this stone county, Wadenhoe sits beautiful and businesslike next to its stream. There was a mill here at the time of the Domesday Book and for some time in the Middle Ages we know that the rent was paid in eels. But it was not always the backwater that this implies. When it was working, the mill supplied flour as far afield as Leicester, and for a while it was also the scene of remarkable innovations. This was in the 19th century, when George Ward Hunt, MP for North Northamptonshire, who served as Chancellor of the Exchequer and First Lord of the Admiralty, lived at Wadenhoe House.

Ward Hunt was a remarkable innovator who was famous for having the first telegraph line outside London laid to Wadenhoe for his use. At the mill, he introduced a very early hydroelectric power scheme. But now the technological breakthroughs seem far away – the mill is a pleasant and picturesque private house.

Windmills

These distinctive buildings first appeared in Britain during the Middle Ages. Windmills were always tall structures, to catch the wind and provide several working floors. Most had at least three working levels: on the top a bin floor where the grain was poured into hoppers to trickle down to a stone floor where it was ground before the flour dropped to a meal floor where it was collected and bagged. The earliest mills were wooden post mills, in which the whole working structure of the mill could be turned into the wind on its supporting post. Later came tower and smock mills, which have a turning cap to hold the sails.

Saxtead Green
Suffolk

At the heart of a post mill such as this one at Saxtead Green is a stout, vertical wooden post that supports the entire upper part of the mill, the section known in East Anglia as the buck. The buck at Saxtead Green, with weatherboarded walls and curving roof, dates to a rebuild of 1854, though there was a mill on this site in 1706 and probably long before. It contains all the working parts of the mill, from the shaft that holds the sails to the millstones themselves. Below the buck is a brick roundhouse and a ladder with a fantail.

Sutton
Norfolk

Tower mills, such as the mid-19th-century one at Sutton, Norfolk, are meticulous displays of brickwork, the courses laid in ever-decreasing, inward-leaning circles by bricklayers working from inside. The result is plenty of space and a solid base for the sails and cap. The whole structure at Sutton is topped with an elegant boat-shaped roof, with a fantail at the stern to turn the sails into the wind. With nine floors, it is one of England's tallest mills, its great height helping the mill to catch every breath of wind that blows across the Norfolk Broads. This it did until 1940, when lightning hit its sails.

Shipley
West Sussex

A smock mill has three main sections – a stone or brick base, a tapering wooden body, and a turning cap for the sails. The resulting shape (often on a polygonal plan) is said to resemble a peasant in his smock, hence the name. The smock mill at Shipley has a two-storey brick base for storage below a three-floor wooden section that contains the machinery and millstones. Its fine condition, with well-kept weatherboarding and a full set of machinery, owes much to the author Hilaire Belloc, who, from 1906 to 1953, lived at the mill and kept the sails turning.

Windmills have such striking silhouettes that pictures of them are widely used in all sorts of graphics, where they seem to symbolise the happy marriage of industry and the environment. These examples are a 1940s book jacket from publisher Batsford designed by Brian Cook; the colophon of publisher William Heinemann; and the symbol of the eastern-England brewery Bateman's.

Thurne
Norfolk

Windmills played a major part in the drainage of the Fens from the 17th century on. A few were dual-purpose machines, grinding corn and pumping water. But most drainage mills, which are usually short tower mills, are quite straightforward in operation – the sails drive a paddle wheel that scoops up water and discharges it at a higher level. The one at Thurne Dyke has an attractive white tower, although many drainage mills were tarred black. It began pumping water in 1820 and survived through until early in the 20th century, when most drainage mills were abandoned in favour of steam or diesel pumps.

Chesterton
Warwickshire

There are relatively few windmills in western England, and this example on a Warwickshire hilltop is unusual in more than location. It is a rare example of a windmill with architectural pretensions, its classical arches supporting a date of 1632. The building, probably designed by Sir Edward Peyto, is rather impractical – there is no staircase to the upper floor and the open ground floor is far from ideal for storage. Some historians have suggested that the building may have started life as an observatory or gazebo, but there was a windmill at Chesterton in 1674 – presumably manned by an agile miller who did not mind using a ladder.

South Luffenham
Rutland

Steam milling machinery – soon followed by diesel and electricity – killed off the windmill and there were few working mills left by the early 20th century. Many wooden post mills quickly rotted away when they were abandoned, but brick tower mills remained. They can still be found. Some have been converted into houses, others remain as shells, punctuating the landscape of the eastern lowlands. This example in Rutland is one such, its brick outline a reminder of the centuries of milling activity that put these buildings at the heart of the rural economy.

Old mills are often veritable museums of the craft and business of the miller. Their contents range from machinery to evocative smaller items, such as this flour sack from Moulton Windmill, Lincolnshire.

See also

Watermills, 216
Water and gas, 232

The industrial revolution

The factory developed during the 18th century to bring together in one building a large number of workers tending machines supplied by a central power source, such as a waterwheel or steam engine. Because factories usually contained many similar machines, their design was generally based on repeated units, with rows of windows mirroring rows of columns holding up walls and ceilings. This kind of layout is seen clearly in Richard Arkwright's first mill at Cromford (1771), although some earlier buildings, such as John Lombe's silk mill at Derby, (1717 but later largely rebuilt), have claims to be

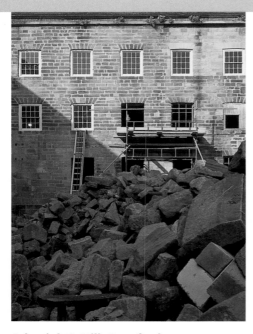

Arkwright's Mill, Cromford
Derbyshire

Richard Arkwright's original 1771 mill at Cromford is the building that signalled the true start of the industrial revolution, a factory in which ranks of water frames (water-powered spinning machines) produced yarn at many times the speed possible by hand. The architecture set the style for the period too. The large open floors provided big flexible spaces for the machinery, which was driven by an adjacent waterwheel. Soon Arkwright's enterprise was paying off, and he was building more mill structures at Cromford. The mill is now part of a complex paying tribute to this industrial pioneer.

Gayle Mill, Hawes
North Yorkshire

Arkwright had dozens of followers, men eager to build mills and make money from the expanding textile industry. Some of these mills were even named Cromford after the great pioneering factory. Gayle Mill was another pioneer, built less than a decade after Arkwright began Cromford. The owners were the local Routh family, who installed water frames for cotton spinning, making considerable effort to bring in water power from a mill pond at some distance from the mill itself. But Gayle Mill did not pay. One problem was its rural setting. Although it was near transport links, it was still some distance from customers and transporting goods was an additional cost.

More problematic still were mechanical breakdowns, together with the relatively small scale of the operation. The future lay with the big urban factories, where economy of scale could combine with a readily available workforce. So Gayle was one mill that did not prosper. Its owners tried different businesses, including saw milling, but none of these lasted long. Its solid stone structure has survived better than many, however, to the benefit of industrial archaeologists and conservationists.

An old sign can sum up the atmosphere of an entire industry. This one is from the Lion Salt Works at Northwich, Cheshire. Steam and corrosive salt particles were a way of life in the late 19th-century works where brine was boiled down to produce salt.

called the first factory. Early factories were conventional structures, with load-bearing brick walls and wooden floors. Later factories were often framework structures in which the weight of the building was borne largely on a network of columns, pointing the way forward to the skyscrapers of the 20th century.

The earliest iron-framed building was the mill of Marshall, Benyon, and Bage, at Ditherington, Shrewsbury, designed in 1796 by Charles Bage. Its slim cast-iron columns hold up iron beams that support the brick ceilings.

East Mill, Belper
Derbyshire

This is one part of a mill complex that dated back to the industrial revolution and expanded through the 19th century and into the 20th. It was begun in 1797 by Arkwright with his partner Jedediah Strutt and when the pair parted company, Arkwright kept Cromford while Strutt remained at Belper. The Strutt family expanded the site, William Strutt adding the North Mill in 1803–4, using cast-iron columns and beams to help prevent the fire that had destroyed an earlier building on the site. Just over a century later, in 1912, came the East Mill, a vast structure that dwarfs its predecessors.

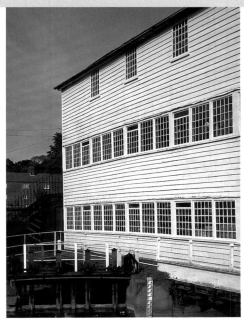

Courtauld's Mill, Halstead
Essex

Built in the late 18th century, this mill became the centre of another complex of factory buildings, this time belonging to the renowned family of industrialists, the Courtaulds. A traditional vernacular style was used for this mill, with its weatherboarded walls stretching over the stream. But the strips of windows point towards the fact that this is also a building of the industrial revolution, built of wood but using this material to produce large internal spaces. It demonstrates another distinctive way in which an early factory building can be attractive from the outside – even if it housed a noisy and unpleasant working environment.

Stanley Mill, Kings Stanley
Gloucestershire

Millers George Harris, Donald Maclean, and Charles Stephens built this superb structure in 1813. Their architect is unknown but they seem to have had a penchant for good design, for their mill is more than usually ornate. Brick walls sit on a stone ground floor and there are venetian windows and ornate fanlights. The beauty is more than skin-deep because the mill is a fireproof structure with brick vaults supported on iron columns. Even here there is elegance, with delightful ironwork arches. Iron circles in the spandrels of the arches accommodated the line shafting for the machines. Benjamin Gibbons, a Dudley ironmaster, produced the metal fittings.

See also

Watermills, 216
The developing factory, 222
The rise of the warehouse, 224
Specialised structures, 234

The developing factory

Fuelled by the British empire, which provided both raw materials and a captive market for manufactured goods, industry expanded rapidly in the Victorian period. The Victorians built countless factories using the fireproof construction methods developed in the previous century. Many of these were simple, utilitarian structures, but many bigger, high-profile factories erupted in every imaginable style, creating large, exuberant buildings that seemed to embody the national confidence. It was as if the British, founding their manufacturing on a world empire, could use any source in the world for their industrial architecture.

Ancoats Mills
Manchester

The Ancoats district of Manchester is full of cotton mills, mostly large, brick-built with fireproof construction, and dating from the 19th century. These two blocks built on the banks of the Rochdale Canal belonged to two of the most successful companies, both begun by Scottish incomers in the 1790s, that expanded throughout the 19th century. The block on the left is part of McConnel & Kennedy's Mills, the largest employers in Manchester in 1836, when they had more than 1,500 workers. They began as manufacturers of textile-making machinery and their in-depth knowledge of spinning mules and similar devices gave them the edge when they branched out into textile-production themselves.

They always tried to be ahead of the game technologically and were the first to use steam power successfully for spinning and one of the first to have their mills lit by gas. Next door are Murray's Mills, the factory of another successful spinning family. At the beginning of the 19th century their mills were Manchester's largest. Behind this building is a courtyard that was surrounded by more of their mill buildings and originally contained the firm's own canal basin.

Wallis and Linnell, Brigstock
Northamptonshire

This surprising factory was constructed on a long, shallow site in 1873–4. It was built as a clothing factory in stone, appropriately enough in this sizeable stone village. The works is beautifully built, very much in the early 19th century style, with round-headed windows and a Classical pediment, and with high-quality masonry including big ashlar quoins and window surrounds. There is a niche in the pediment to take a bell. The real surprise comes with the proportions, for this building is 13 bays long but only two bays deep.

Fogarty's blanket factory in Boston, Lincolnshire, proudly displays its swan symbol high on the building's parapet.

Sheep once grazed on the grass-covered roof of Temple Mill in Leeds.

Saltaire Mill, Saltaire
West Yorkshire

Industrial Italianate was the style chosen for Sir Titus Salt's mill in his model town of Saltaire. Some 4,000 people worked in this vast edifice, at almost 600 ft (183 m) the longest building in Yorkshire when it opened in the 1850s, and perhaps Salt thought that the Italian style was the one that gave the required sense of importance. This is achieved quite simply with the rusticated central entrance and the pair of lantern towers, one on either side. Most of the rest of the frontage is made up of rows of standard windows. Elsewhere on the site there is a tower like a campanile and a chimney disguised as an obelisk.

Bliss Mill, Chipping Norton
Oxfordshire

By the late 19th century many mill owners were demanding grander architecture than was usual in the traditional factory. Instead of plain rows of windows and brick walls, mill architects were introducing details from the Classical world or even ancient Egypt. Bliss Mill is one of the grandest. Details such as the corner parapets studded with urns saw architect George Woodhouse of Bolton raiding the vocabulary of country-house design for this tweed mill in a valley in the Cotswolds.

The chimney of the 1870s building is an even more extraordinary feature of the skyline, a Tuscan column resting on a dome, set on a masonry drum, above a rounded bulge that houses a grand staircase. It is all very improbable, and is still a surprise to travellers approaching Chipping Norton because it is bigger, more imposing, and simply more bizarre than the few large industrial buildings in the area. Like many other mill buildings, when its industrial life came to an end it was far too good to demolish. Bliss Mill found another life as an apartment block, giving its occupants delightful views and palatial surroundings.

See also

The industrial revolution, 220
The rise of the warehouse, 224

The rise of the warehouse

The warehouse developed as a dockside building type in the late Middle Ages. So by the time of the industrial revolution, a number of ports had warehouses and some of these buildings, such as those by the River Witham at Boston, were several storeys high. But in the industrial era, warehouses came to be built still bigger and higher – more like factories, in fact, but often with deeper plans because light was not such a priority. Like factories they were very practical buildings, with uncluttered interiors to give a maximum of usable space and goods' hoists for rapid loading and unloading.

Albert Dock
Liverpool

Jesse Hartley and Philip Hardwick built one of the world's great dock and warehouse complexes in the 1840s in Liverpool. It consists of a large dock, almost 8 acres (3.24 ha) in area, surrounded by a group of magnificent iron-framed, brick-clad warehouses that stand on almost 5,300 piles of beechwood. The engineers used thick cast-iron Doric columns to hold up the structure of their warehouses, brick arches for the floors, and wrought-iron plates for the roofs. This adds up to a fireproof structure that was ideal for the bonded goods kept here – and, as we can appreciate now, the buildings are restored and put to modern use – a series of noble structures whose brick walls and red columns, standing above heavy granite dock walls, delight the eye. The fronts come right up to those dock walls, so that goods could be unloaded on the quayside while extra storage space was provided on the overhanging upper floors. Everything is very simple in pinkish brick, with a touch of elegance added by the elliptical crane arches and extra strength provided by granite reinforcements on corners, where passing carts might damage brickwork. Inside, brick-arched ceilings are supported on cast-iron columns and beams.

Alexandra Warehouse
Gloucester

The docks at Gloucester opened in 1812, making the city a major inland port on the River Severn and the Gloucester–Berkeley Canal. The Alexandra Warehouse, flanked by a maltings and a harbour office, is one of more than a dozen Victorian grain warehouses with brick walls, slate roofs, and wooden floors. This one dates from the 1870s and has six storeys, like most of the others on the site. After the port declined in the mid-20th century, these fine buildings fell into disrepair. But the vast, flexible spaces inside them are now valued for a variety of uses, from a museum to offices.

As well as harbours and warehouses, docks need a whole infrastructure for transporting goods along the quays to the main railways and roads. At Gloucester there is still plenty of evidence of this in the form of railway tracks and rolling stock, some of it with the old lettering brightly repainted.

But, again like factories, warehouses could also be symbols of pride. By the 19th century, cities suchas Manchester and Bristol boasted warehouses that were severely Classical, expressively Italianate, or even fantasies in the Scottish baronial style. And these delightful façades increasingly hid steel-frame structures, which could support more floors, making best use of the owner's investment in the site.

Faversham
Kent

This small town in Kent, barely a mile inland from the River Swale with its direct route to the North Sea, has had a notable industrial and mercantile history. Flour milling, brick-making, the production of gunpowder, food canning, and processing various fruit and vegetables grown round about have all employed many in Faversham. The town was also a port, and a larger one than visitors today would imagine. This 19th-century warehouse overlooking the water is a reminder of Faversham's once-flourishing trade. The painted signs of this structure, known locally as 'the big building' pick out two trades. Fertiliser was obviously always important in this region, adjacent to the 'garden of England'.

Oysters were a lucrative business too. If nearby Whitstable is more famous for this exclusive seafood, Faversham also contributed its share to the well-to-do tables of London and beyond. The river is much quieter now, but even so, boats from Rotterdam and London were moored here when this photograph was taken.

Welsh Back Granary
Bristol

The mercantile pride of Bristol in 1869 is eloquently expressed in the Welsh Back Granary by architects Ponton and Gough. It is in a variety of styles, bringing to mind prosperous empires of the past – Byzantine, Islamic, and Venetian Gothic – yet produces a unified impression because the building is composed so well, with the relations between groups of openings, arches, and cornices beautifully managed. Polychrome brick is used for the striking arches and patterned ventilation openings and for the round features above the ground-floor arches, which were originally openings through which grain chutes poured the contents of the granary into waiting carts below.

The joy of the brickwork of the Welsh Back Granary is not just its varied palette but also the way in which the bricks are used to form sinuous curves.

See also

The industrial revolution, 220
The developing factory, 222
Offices, 238

The 20th-century factory

Although many factories built in the industrial expansion of the early 20th century were unremarkable in appearance, a number of pioneer factories were both innovative and striking. There were several chapters to this story. One emerges from the turn of the century to produce factories combining Arts and Crafts details with modern features such as big windows with grids of glazing bars. Another looks to Art Deco to produce white, bright factories with splashes of coloured Classical or Egyptian detailing.

Spirella factory, Letchworth
Hertfordshire

The main employer in Britain's first garden city, the corset manufacturers Spirella, chose a factory design that was worthy of the town's architectural inheritance. The building grew between 1912 and 1920 in two different styles. The corner pavilions of the factory, one of which is shown here, are in an Arts and Crafts style with steep roofs and grid-like windows. The architecture is beautifully detailed. There is a tiny gablet at the apex of the hipped roof and the roof line on the long side is broken in the middle to accommodate larger windows and let more light into the interior.

The central block looks more modern, with concrete walls and still more glass – but also rather Queen Anne-style round windows. The whole embodies architect Cecil Hignett's vision of a building with lots of light and air in which the workers would be happy and comfortable – a worthy companion to the Arts and Crafts influenced houses in which most of the workers lived in the garden city.

Bournville
Birmingham

Cadbury's Bournville is another industrial complex where there is a combination of styles – here made all the more diverse by being a site that expanded through the 20th century as the chocolate-making empire grew. Work began here in 1899, when Herbert Ellis and Clarke designed the first buildings, which are in a mixture of half-timber and brick. These offices, at the front of the complex, are ornate, with prominent bargeboards, louvres with finials, a semi-dome, and other details providing the uplifting environment that Cadbury aimed for. Later, more utilitarian, but still impressive, brick factory buildings were put up in the 1920s and 1930s.

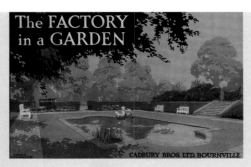

Early Cadbury's promotional booklets contained evocative images of the Bournville factory.

There were many of these factories along the western approaches to London, where firms such as Hoover, Firestone and Coty saw the potential for using their buildings as advertisements.

Ovaltine factory, Kings Langley Hertfordshire

The Ovaltine factory is a rare survival from the 1930s of an outstanding factory in the white, large-windowed style of the times. Designed by Sir Harry Hague, the frontage flirts with the Moderne style – the long lines emphasised by cornices and string courses, together with the metal-framed windows, come from that tradition, while the roundels and drop ornaments between the windows take their cue from Art Deco's liking for motifs that look vaguely historical. Above all the factory's pale walls look clean and hygienic, perfect for a food product.

Horlicks factory, Slough Buckinghamshire

During the 20th century, Slough became home to many famous firms, from Aspro to Chappie dog food, Mars to Berlei corsets. Many of these arrived to occupy parts of Slough's pioneering industrial estate, created in 1920, but Horlicks was ahead of the crowd with its factory of 1908. A cup of Horlicks at bedtime seems a very British indulgence, especially Horlicks made in a Victorian-looking, red-brick factory with a bulky, castellated tower, the tall black chimney looking rather like an afterthought.

In fact this Buckinghamshire landmark was based on the company's American factory in Racine, Wisconsin. It is a surprising building that gives the lie to the idea that the early 20th century marked the point in history when factories all began to look the same and when one industrial estate was very much like any other.

Throughout the 20th century the Ovaltine company was proud of the wholesome origins of its product and often featured pictures of dairy produce and dairymaids on its packaging.

The 20th-century factory (continued)

The thoughtful marriage of form and function, the development of a logical arrangement of machinery and processes, the highlighting of modern design – influences such as these produced factories at the cutting-edge of modern architecture in the early 20th century. Some of these buildings wear their modernism on their sleeves, with an abundance of white walls, flat roofs, and ridge-and-furrow roofs, partly glazed to let in lots of natural light. Some of this architecture was strongly influenced by developments in Europe such as Peter Behrens's famous A E G Turbine Factory in Berlin, built in 1909.

Shredded Wheat factory, Welwyn Garden City
Hertfordshire

Bata factory, East Tilbury
Essex

The very name of Welgar Shredded Wheat has always boasted of the product's origins in Welwyn Garden City and its 1925 factory was designed by Welwyn's master-planner, Louis de Soissons. In contrast to Slough's Horlicks factory, the Welgar works is uncompromisingly modernist – it is all straight lines, flat roofs, window grids, and metal railings, and functional-looking elements such as chimneys poke out of it here and there. It is in fact very much what we imagine a factory to be like nowadays, a building in which the shapes of each part have been dictated largely by the processes going on inside – a place, in other words, where the modernist doctrine of 'form follows function' is made real before our eyes. But in the hands of a master-architect it is immensely satisfying visually, this careful arrangement of cuboids and cylinders. It was supposed to be pleasant to be an employee here, too – in keeping with the advanced planning of the garden city, the factory originally had its own leisure and welfare facilities, including a football pitch that was subsequently built over.

Czech shoe manufacturer Thomas Bata opened his British factory in East Tilbury in 1933. The factory is in the modernist style that was well established in Czechoslovakia by this time and the design was based on Bata's factory in Zlin, Moravia. It was built by Bata's in-house building department under the direction of Czech architects Vladimir Karfik and Frantisek Gahura, who also designed the workers' housing. Standardised components were used for speedy construction – a steel frame was built and infilled with concrete, brick, or glass. The result was a confident modernism rare in Britain at this time.

The Welgar company were so proud of their factory that they frequently used images of it on their packaging. Here it is surrounded by the green of Welwyn, the garden city.

But there were also home-grown structural innovations, seen for example in the ground-breaking work of Sir Owen Williams in his Nottingham factory for the pharmaceutical firm, Boots.

**Baltic, Gateshead
County Durham**

The Baltic flour mills were built for J Arthur Rank's flour milling firm, Rank Hovis, and opened in 1950. There were five buildings in the complex, the most impressive of which was the vast silo, where wheat was both stored and cleaned before milling. It remains a huge concrete form with a tower at each corner and almost blank walls in between. Falling sales and a fire led to a decline in the business and the mills closed in 1982: only the silo escaped demolition. It has enjoyed a triumphant renaissance, converted by Ellis Williams Architects into a high-profile centre for the arts and an engine for the regeneration of Gateshead.

**Corby flour mills
Northamptonshire**

Still plainer than the Baltic silo, these flour mills are about as simple as one can get – abstract forms that look as if they have been left in the countryside by some giant playing with building blocks. They hardly blend into the scenery – how ironic, one might think, that the products of rural agriculture end up in such alien buildings. Yet they combine a certain elegance of form with an absolute response to modernism's creed that this form should follow closely in the footsteps of function. These uncompromising buildings have been treated with thought and care. The arrangement of the openings in their tall walls, positioned no doubt for functional reasons, still manages to achieve the elegance of a composition by a Russian abstract painter. And even the paintwork has just enough variation to give the buildings a feeling of warmth. One can learn to admire them, as their pale sides catch the light and their careful arrangements of dark openings are picked out against walls of cream and buff.

The logo of the Bata company, in its bulbous red lettering, forms a dramatic silhouette against the sky. Both the name and the typography were once familiar on many British high streets.

Electricity

Electricity has been generated on a commercial scale since the late 19th century and since then the industry has produced two unmistakeable building forms – the traditional coal-fired power station with its vast turbine hall and chimneys, and the cooling tower.

Although these buildings are not beautiful in the conventional sense, they are an unmissable part of the English landscape. Cooling towers dot the countryside of the East Midlands and South Yorkshire. London's great Bankside power station became an

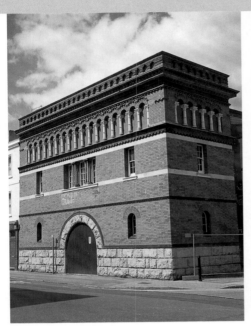

Central electricity lighting station
Cheltenham, Gloucestershire

This stunning little building was the work of Cheltenham's borough surveyor, Joseph Hall. The main structure was built in 1894–5 and the top floor was added in 1900. The lighting station's style is clearly heavily influenced by Italian palazzi, although the row of blind arches on the top storey, with their ceramic columns and round heads of brick, looks more Romanesque than Roman. The whole thing is like nothing else in the centre of this Regency town of stucco and stone, sticking out with all the confidence of a structure that contains a brave new technology.

Tramways generating station
Bristol

This building dates from 1899 and was designed by W Curtis Green. This was the period when power stations were symbols of power indeed. A blend of Classical details with big baroque gestures – such as vast semicircular windows and heavy masses – creates an image of strength and importance. Electricity was modern, the latest technology, but most architects had not yet found the visual language with which to symbolise this. The building is more to do with civic pride than with the whirring turbines inside.

Brown Hart Gardens substation
London

In 1905, C S Peach faced a similar question of style. He had the guts, and the budget, to go for the full Edwardian baroque, with four rusticated, shallow-domed pavilions on an arched and balustraded terrace. These are small pavilions, but the details are on the biggest scale, with the rusticated masonry above the doors and windows taking up so much space that there is no room for the base of the pediment. A 'broken pediment' normally has a gap in the middle of the base to accommodate a window or niche, but these pediments have no bases at all. The effect is one of grandeur: 'It's important, this electricity,' the building seems to say.

This ornate keystone tops one of the grand baroque archways at Brown Hart Gardens.

asset when it was decommissioned and now has
a new life as the popular art gallery, Tate Modern,
where visitors can appreciate it in a new light.

**Cooling towers, Ferrybridge C
Power Station, West Yorkshire**

Much of Britain's power is still generated
by burning fossil fuels to produce steam,
which is used to drive turbines that turn
alternators which produce electric current.
This process generates enormous heat
which is often lost to the atmosphere
through cooling towers. Cooling towers
are for now an inescapable part of the
scene wherever there are inland power
stations, their curved forms in their own
way as emblematic of our era as bottle
kilns were of the towns of Staffordshire
during the industrial revolution. From
the top of Lincoln Cathedral dozens of
cooling towers can be seen and they do
have a certain formal beauty.

**Sutton Bridge power station
Lincolnshire**

This is one of the latest generation of
power stations, completed in 1999. It uses
combined cycle gas turbine generation. It
is fuelled by natural gas which is burned
to heat water to make steam; the steam
then drives a pair of turbines which
generate electricity. In addition, exhaust
gases from the turbines are used to feed
another device, a heat recovery steam
generator, to produce more electricity.

Altogether, this plant can produce up
to 2 per cent of the electricity needs
of England and Wales. The architecture
in which these processes are housed
is functional with its plain sheds and
chimneys. But tactful use of colour, from
vibrant red to earthy shades, lifts the
building beyond the mundane and sets
it off against the greenery beside the
River Nene.

See also

The industrial revolution, 220
Water and gas, 232

Water and gas

Three public utilities transformed the quality of British life in the 19th century – the supply of water and gas and the provision of proper drainage. While the gas industry has left little of architectural interest save the occasional gasworks and gas holder and the sewers are underground, the business of moving and supplying water has created many buildings of lasting note. There are some remarkable pumping stations, in which the quality of the engineering that created the engines and pumps

Guyhirn and Wisbech pumping stations
Cambridgeshire

On the fens and marshes of East Anglia, draining away excess water has been a challenge for centuries. Major drains were famously excavated in the 17th century under the auspices of the Earl of Bedford, but water management on the Fens went back far earlier, and continues to be an issue today. Pumping stations are a sight. They are usually easy to spot because of their chimneys, which need to be tall to provide adequate draft and act as stark landmarks in the flat fen country. Nearby are clustered the other buildings – the engine house (tall enough to accommodate both the engine and the lifting gear needed for maintenance), the boiler house, together with stores for fuel and, often, a workshop, since deep in the countryside it was usually a long way to the nearest engineer. This pumping station has two major phases. In the centre is the 19th-century pumping station, with its chimney to one side, a traditional brick-and-slate structure. To the right is the 20th-century flat-roofed equivalent. The house of the manager is on the left.

Mappleton water tower
East Yorkshire

By the 1920s, concrete was a common material for water towers and one popular design supported the tower on a ring of arches, often with a central shaft containing a ladder to give access to the tank and its roof. This kind of design was chosen by Hornsea Council in 1928 when they abandoned their old supply (with a borehole near the sea, it tended to get salty) and decided to take their water from Hull. There are still many water towers such as this one in service up and down the country, but few are quite as distinctive as this, with its slightly splayed base and neatly panelled tank sides.

A waterworks supplying a large city with fresh, clean water was a source of great civic pride. Manchester reflected this fact with a colourful coat of arms on the Manchester Waterworks at Thirlmere, Cumbria.

is matched by the beauty of the ornamentation. And water towers, built as reservoirs-in-the-air to bring water mainly to flat areas, come in a variety of ingenious shapes and sizes.

**Clevedon waterworks
Somerset**

For much of human history we have relied on local springs and wells for our water – and in isolated areas some people still do. But most of us now get our water from the local water company, a situation which developed as cities expanded and the need for piped water became increasingly acute. Pumping domestic water began in London as far back as the 17th century, but the great age of waterworks was the Victorian period, when many water companies were founded and countless waterworks built. This one, part Arts and Crafts, part neo-Jacobean, brought water to its part of the world from the late 19th century onwards.

**Gas holder, Bedford
Bedfordshire**

Great cylinders such as this one in Bedford, for the storage of gas, spread across the country with the development of gas supply and were once a feature of virtually every town. Now, in the era of natural gas, they are much rarer. This one is a veritable symphony in rust. The widespread production of coal gas brought with it street lighting, better domestic lighting, and all sorts of possibilities for cooking and heating from the early 19th century onwards. Gas was made by burning coal, collecting the resulting gas, and removing the various impurities.

The purified coal gas – known as town gas – was stored in gas holders. These huge containers expanded and contracted as gas was put in or taken out. The first were installed in the early 19th century and a rule of 1813 insisted that they should be housed in masonry buildings until someone pointed out that if they exploded, passers-by would be felled by dangerous flying stones. So instead, they were often caged inside an open framework of metal.

See also

The industrial revolution, 220
Electricity, 230

Specialised structures

Industry generates buildings adapted precisely to particular processes. This tendency has produced a richness of structural types, often looking like nothing else in the built environment. Shot towers were shaped exactly around the process of making lead shot for guns which they house; engine houses were built to accommodate large stationary steam engines; a whole suite of buildings was evolved for the brewing process, and so on. The processes come and go but, if we are lucky, some of the buildings

Oast houses, Stonepitts
Kent

With their cowl-topped conical roofs, circular oast houses for drying hops have been a familiar sight in Herefordshire, Kent, and Sussex since they were first designed by the gardener John Reade in 1815. The lower chamber of the round building contained a kiln, heat from which rose through a slatted floor to the upper chamber, where the hops were dried. Good air movement was vital, hence the cowl, which turned downwind, improving the flow of air. After about 12 hours drying, the hops were raked out of the drying chamber and put on the floor of the adjoining building to cool.

Maltings, Snape
Suffolk

A key stage in the brewing process is the conversion of barley into malt by allowing the grain to germinate under the influence of warm air from a kiln. Malthouses could form part of a farm complex so that the process could be carried out where the barley was grown. But increasingly malt processing became a specialist process and large maltings were built in many country towns. Traditional malt kilns have pyramid-shaped roofs topped with louvred vents; the adjacent maltings usually have rows of small windows with shallow buttresses between them.

The maltings at Snape, converted in the 1960s to provide the now famous concert hall for the Aldeburgh Festival, were built in several phases, mainly during the late 19th century. Above the brickwork are several weatherboarded features, including the lucam, originally containing hoisting tackle to haul sacks of grain to the upper floors. This attractive combination of materials is typical both of the small-scale industrial architecture of East Anglia, and especially of buildings connected with the brewing industry.

This detail of an oast house ventilator, with its vane for moving the cowl with the wind, comes from the Hop Farm Country Park at Beltring, Kent.

remain to tell the story of our manufacturing industries. Sometimes it is hard to imagine how many of these structures have disappeared, how buildings that now seem exotic were once commonplace. They are windows on a past world.

**Hook Norton brewery
Oxfordshire**

**Harvey's brewery, Lewes
East Sussex**

Done on a large scale, brewing is a gravity-driven business, demanding buildings several storeys tall. In the Victorian period these specialised buildings had their specialist architect, William Bradford, who designed many breweries, but few as ornate as this one, an astounding structure to discover as one walks down a narrow lane in the village of Hook Norton. As well as the local ironstone, Bradford used a range of materials – timber framing, weatherboarding, brick, slate, and iron – to create a phantasmagorical structure of bays, gables, and projecting wings. Triumphantly, it is still producing beer, the last remaining steam-driven brewery in England.

Lewes's fine brewery was founded in 1790 and still has some Georgian buildings. But there was a big rebuild in 1880 under brewery architect William Bradford, designer of Hook Norton brewery in Oxfordshire, together with Shipstone's brewery in Nottingham and Ipswich's Tolly Cobold. It was Bradford's work that gave the Lewes complex its striking appearance. Bradford's tall tower and brewhouse, in his strong factory Gothic style, stands in front of the Georgian fermenting room, cellars, and vat house. The result is a typical cluster of buildings, built where they are because that is where the brewing business needed them to be.

It is a sort of Victorian version of 'form follows function' – but with added joyous ornament. The tower is topped by a weather vane and some fancy finials – a favourite touch of Bradford's – and is proudly lettered with the company name. The brewery still functions, although there is modern equipment inside the old buildings, some of which have changed their functions. It is a tribute both to the durability and adaptability of Bradford's buildings and to the care of the owners that this fine structure is still used for its original purpose.

Souvenir jugs display the name of a beer much admired by connoisseurs of real ale – and the brewery where the precious fluid is produced.

See also

The industrial revolution, 220
Electricity, 230
Water and gas, 232
Specialised structures, next page

Specialised structures (continued)

Calcine kilns, Wakerley
Northamptonshire

These are surprising buildings to come across among rolling Midlands sheep pastures, industrial-looking brick-and-concrete cylinders (each 70 ft [21 m] high and 33 ft [10 m] across) that baffle most people who come across them. They are calcine or lime kilns, in which the local limestone was burned to produce the lime that is used in mortar, limewash, and other products. The kilns are part of a vanished landscape of transport and industry that never took off. The upper section of each kiln is built of orangey-red brick, while the bases are concrete, a strikingly modern-looking material in this rural setting. In fact, the kilns were constructed during the First World War, but building work halted before the planned group of four was finished, and the two completed kilns were never used. Nearby are more traces of this fugitive industry – the remains of a dismantled railway track, a tramway embankment, traces of a trackside tipping dock, and bases for two more kilns that were never built.

Blast furnace, Moira
Leicestershire

The blast furnace was introduced to Britain at the very end of the Middle Ages for the production of cast iron. The principle is that the iron ore and coke are put in at the top of the furnace and a powerful blast of air, provided by a pair of bellows, is injected at the bottom. As the ore and coke fall, the coke ignites due to the hot gas ascending from below. The burning coke produces carbon monoxide and the iron oxide is reduced to relatively pure iron. Blast furnaces were key drivers of the industrial revolution and they had to be solid, heat-proof buildings. This fine example of about 1804 was built to smelt local ore. It is at the heart of the Moira ironworks, with its engine house, canal bridge for loading the furnace, lime kilns, and other remains.

FARM BUILDINGS

Agriculture and architecture, it has been said, have changed the face of the earth as much as any human activities, and they come together on the farm. Farmers need buildings for storing and processing crops, for accommodating livestock, for keeping implements and machinery, and for fodder. A large farm can have a diverse collection of buildings, from barns to pigsties and hen houses, of all shapes and sizes but all unified in appearance because, on a traditional farm at least, they were all built in the local style, using materials obtained nearby.

Such buildings traditionally congregated near the farmhouse, but the actual layout could vary a great deal. On small upland farms, for example, buildings such as the cowhouse could be attached to the farmhouse itself, making a lengthy, linear building derived from the ancient longhouse. Larger farms could be collections of separate buildings arranged either in a loose group or around a yard.

There are still countless traditional farm buildings like this, all typical of their regions. Big weatherboarded barns with sweeping roofs in Oxfordshire; Cotswold granaries perched on mushroom-shaped staddle-stones to keep vermin out; small rubble-stone barns in the Lake District; linhays (open-fronted cattle shelters) in Devon; laithhouses, with farmhouse and cattle buildings under one continuous roof in Yorkshire – all are typical elements in their local scene, well adapted to the traditional local agriculture. There are also sometimes neighbouring buildings that play vital local roles – cider houses in Somerset or Herefordshire, oast houses in Kent, dairies in which local cheeses were produced, and so on. Agricultural buildings and their allied structures are rich indicators of regional distinctiveness and diversity.

But in the 18th and 19th centuries, developments took place that began to change the course of this ancient vernacular tradition. These changes were known as agricultural 'improvements'. They arose as the result of fluctuating food prices and increasing demand as the result of a rising population, and

they were connected with the movement in many parts of the country to enclose the old open fields (not to mention commons and marginal or waste lands) and bring them into a more efficient kind of production. The improvements involved selective breeding to create heavier livestock that yielded more meat, different crop rotations to get more out of the soil, and new fodder crops.

Among those who spearheaded these new agricultural methods were prominent aristocrats and members of the landed gentry – the kind of people, in other words, who expressed themselves by building country houses. It is not surprising, then, that along with these changes in farming methods there often came new farm buildings. Big landowners (who often benefited from enclosures at the expense of small farmers), built what they called model farms, often employing architects to design them – something that would have seemed bizarre to most earlier farmers. The aim was to provide a more efficient environment for the agricultural processes – and also to advertise the fact that, on this estate, the latest improvements were in place.

Ancillary buildings such as dairies, built along modern, hygienic lines, were also part of some of the more elaborate farms. Such complexes, often near their owners' country houses and frequently ornamented with the important-looking trappings of Classical architecture, transformed parts of the landscape. In their scientific, businesslike, even ruthless approach, they point the way towards modern agriculture.

Farming is a business and has to move with the times. The model farms of the 18th century assert this just as forcefully as the industrial-style buildings that accommodate modern farming techniques and today's super-size machinery. As a result, many traditional farm buildings have been demolished or converted for housing or other uses. Paradoxically, though, the need for agriculture to change and adapt, and to get involved in activities such as retailing and tourism, may save some of the old buildings too.

Great barns

The barn was usually the biggest building in the farmyard, with doors large enough to admit farm carts and plenty of space to store the annual harvest of corn. In the middle of the barn was generally a threshing floor, where the corn was beaten to detach the grain from the stalks. This was then separated from the dust and chaff by winnowing, a process involving blowing air across the corn, often by opening two sets of barn doors to create a cross-draught. Barns needed to be well ventilated, so most

**Barley barn, Cressing Temple
Essex**

**Wheat barn, Cressing Temple
Essex**

Cressing Temple was the first place where the Knights Templar settled in England. The Templars were a curious combination, who took the vows of the medieval monk but were also charged with the duty of taking up arms for the Christian cause, which they did by going to fight in the Crusades. But when they were not fighting, they farmed large estates, and were especially known for growing crops. They arrived in Essex in 1135 and their manor passed to the other main military order, the Hospitallers, in 1312 after the Templars were suppressed. The Templars' lands were large and productive and in the 13th century they constructed the first of the two great barns that survive here.

The barley barn is timber-framed and weatherboarded, in the traditional style of farm buildings in the counties around London. Dendrochronology (tree-ring dating) confirms that the timbers of its frame were felled between 1205 and 1235. Such early timber structures are very rare indeed and, as a result, the barn has been a key building for the study of medieval carpentry.

The beautiful brick and timber wheat barn was probably built by the Knights Templar a few decades after the neighbouring barley barn at Cressing Temple. Dendrochronology reveals that its timbers were felled between 1259 and 1280. Like the barley barn, it is an aisled structure, but its lower walls are of brick and its upper walls have a timber frame infilled with brickwork. A vast hipped roof with gablets at each end covers the entire length of the 140 ft (43 m) building. This is supported on a complex timber structure, this time with straight-braced tie-beams and collar-beams.

The web of posts, tie-beams, and braces in the roof of the barley barn, Cressing Temple, is a wonder of medieval woodwork.

have holes or slits in the walls; sometimes there are also holes high up to let in owls, welcome predators of rats and mice. Although many traditional barns share these features, they can differ considerably, because they are usually built of local materials.

Some of the most impressive are the great medieval barns built by abbots and bishops to house the harvests from the extensive church lands or the tithes paid to the church by lay landholders.

Great Coxwell
Oxfordshire

The Cistercians were another monastic order who held large estates and became successful farmers. They built scores of barns to house produce from their farms as well as corn given to them under the tithe system. Great Coxwell, built in around 1300, is one of no fewer than 27 that were owned by Beaulieu Abbey, Hampshire, and it is one of the greatest of all medieval barns. It is 152.5 ft (46.5 m) long, 44 ft (13.5 m) wide, and 51 ft (15.5 m) high, much of this height being accounted for by the sweeping roof of Cotswold stone slates. The beautiful limestone walls are pierced with ventilation slits and with holes to encourage owls to roost inside and keep down vermin. Within, the barn is

aisled, the aisle posts branching out with diagonal braces to give added strength to the roof structure above. The resulting succession of posts, braces, and beams gives the interior a great nobility, an effect coming from the combination of a regular, ordered structure that yet retains much of the organic quality that comes from the timbers. William Morris lived quite near to Great Coxwell in the last decades of the 19th century and loved this barn. He compared it to a cathedral.

Bredon
Worcestershire

The 124 ft (38 m)-long Bredon barn was part of a farm built for the bishops of Worcester in the 14th century. The barn's transepts provide a pair of entrances to the aisled interior, their doors tall, rectangular, and businesslike. One of the transepts boasts stairs running up the outside, because the room over the entrance was the chamber of the granger, or farm manager. Agricultural decline in the 15th century meant that the barn was no longer required by the bishop and in 1410, like many other large church-owned barns, it was leased to a tenant.

As usual in a large barn, the central doorway at Great Coxwell is big enough for a cart to be pulled right in.

Barns

Wherever corn is grown there are barns, and like most agricultural buildings, they followed the vernacular tradition until the 20th century, and so were timber-framed in some regions, brick or stone in others. Many are large buildings built in or near the main farmyard. Like the great medieval barns, they were originally designed for threshing and storing crops, so have a large central entrance through which a cart could be driven. In areas where less corn was grown there are still barns, but these are usually smaller and used for storing animal fodder. Large barns became less common with the

**Helpston
Cambridgeshire**

In addition to large threshing barns, many places also have field barns. These are smaller structures, isolated in the countryside and are dual-purpose buildings: they may be used to store fodder for cattle, and also to act as livestock shelters when required. They are common in upland areas such as the Yorkshire Dales and the Peak District, where they are often subdivided. A byre for cattle takes up one end, with lofts above for hay that could be pulled down quickly and easily to feed the animals beneath. More fodder can be stored at the other end of the barn.

This field barn is a lowland version, on the Fens. Stone walls and a tiled roof are the materials, neatly symbolising the building's location, within shouting distance of the limestone belt that stretches from the south-west to Lincolnshire, but on the flat lands where clay tiles are a common roofing material.

**Grizebeck
Cumbria**

In the Lake District there are many field barns dotted around the countryside. They are timeless buildings that can be difficult to date, but some go back to the 17th century. This one is probably later, but is very much in the local style with its rubble masonry and large quoins. The openings suggest a hay loft with room for cattle below.

This barn in Lenham, Kent, has boarded walls and a wooden door, darkened with years of protective treatment. Wooden farm buildings like this are common in the counties around London.

agricultural changes of the 18th century, when greater and greater emphasis was laid on cattle breeding and dairying, especially in the north and west. Today, barns are still built, and these modern barns are often metal-framed structures.

Mapledurham
Oxfordshire

Aydon
Northumberland

There are many timber-framed and weatherboarded barns in southern England. They were practical buildings because timber framing was easy and quick to make and assemble, often from trees available on the farm itself. Such barns usually stand on a stone or brick base to keep the wooden superstructure above the damp ground. The base here is quite large and is made of flint and brick. Above are the weatherboards, traditionally treated with pitch or creosote to keep out the moisture and to make them a sooty black. A half-hipped roof of tiles completes the structure. Originally many barns like this were thatched, and there are still thatched barns in some areas, notably in Essex.

Buildings like this were eminently practical. You could make them in a range of sizes, the dimensions only limited by the size of the timbers needed to hold up the roof, and for all sorts of functions, from compact equipment sheds to large barns. And if the damp did get into the weatherboarding, it was easy enough to repair by taking out the damaged timbers and replacing them.

The 20th-century equivalent of the timber-framed structure was the steel-framed barn, which could either be left open as a Dutch barn or clad as here in corrugated iron. This material was even easier to assemble than weatherboarding. But it was not normally a local product. Many farm buildings of corrugated iron display the name of their maker. This one was made by A J Main and Co of Glasgow and London, who supplied iron buildings to customers far and wide and whose diamond-shaped sign is easy to recognise.

See also

Farms

Traditional farms vary from region to region. In some areas (especially the north and west), linear farmsteads, with byre and other buildings attached to the end of the house, are common. In others (especially in the south and east) it is more usual to see buildings forming the sides of a courtyard. The agricultural improvements that took place from the 17th to the 19th centuries led to the building of many completely new, planned farms to accommodate the latest techniques and ideas

Holkham Hall
Norfolk

Thomas Coke, Earl of Leicester, built the lavish Palladian mansion, Holkham Hall. His fortune was founded on farming, and he was a prime advocate of the new scientific approach to agriculture, introducing large-scale wheat growing to north Norfolk, promoting a new breed of sheep, and breeding his own strain of pig. He staged annual sheep-shearing shows to publicise his views and commissioned Samuel Wyatt, a versatile architect who designed everything from country houses to factories, but who came from a farming family, to design impressive farm buildings. The Classical pavilions and round arches are in keeping with the Palladian swagger of Coke's house, but many of his estate farms were built along more traditional lines. The usual layout consisted of a central large barn surrounded by cow houses, and Wyatt was innovative in his use of materials, for example making the lower sections of stall fences out of slate. Because of their design, and Coke's flair for publicising his improvements, the Holkham farms attracted many visitors, and inspired other farmers to build along similar lines, sometimes employing Wyatt as their architect too.

Gallow Lodge, Great Bowden
Leicestershire

This is a more traditional cowhouse, with walls and piers of Midlands brick supporting a pitched timber-framed roof. There are still plenty of shelters like this, built in local materials, in small farms where cattle are raised. Similar structures were also built to house wagons. A yard with a cowhouse such as this was used for rearing young stock. Straw was provided for litter and the animals trod this and their dung together to form manure. The yard needed regular mucking out, but the ready source of manure was an advantage – 'Muck is the mother of money', as an old farming proverb ran.

This plaque enlivens a Northamptonshire farm wall and its material is as much a part of the local landscape as the creature it illustrates.

about farm design. These so-called model farms were usually built around a courtyard. Many were designed as one-offs by specialist architects; still more were copied from textbooks such as C Waistell's *Designs for Agricultural Buildings* (1827).

Such farms might include, as well as the usual granary and barn, accommodation for fattening cattle, facilities for the efficient manufacture of manure, and wheelhouses (and later steam engines) to power threshing machines.

**Withcote
Leicestershire**

This is part of a farmyard in an area of Leicestershire where stone is used for building, although even here part of the structure is in brick. A brick stair leads to a loft above animal sheds – once such lofts were the sleeping places of farmhands, who simply had to roll out of bed to get to work. Nearby there are plenty of covered stores for fodder and machinery.

**Normanton
Rutland**

Normanton was a village that was obliterated in the 18th century when Sir Gilbert Heathcote built himself a large house surrounded by a park. Since farming brought in some of the income that allowed him to do this, the family's own farm was retained, and this mid-19th-century one was also built nearby. It is very much of its time, with stone yard and barn, together with workshops. The tall, square chimney indicates that there would have been a steam engine, for by this period writers and farm-builders were advocating stationary steam engines to power large threshing machines. A family such as the Heathcotes would expect to have the latest technology on

their new farm and by this time a 12-horsepower steam engine could thresh around 15 tons a day compared to less than a quarter of a ton that could be threshed by hand using a flail. So on a big farm, investment in this kind of machinery was worthwhile, but most smaller farmers made do with a movable engine that was cheaper and less powerful, and could be used on different sites.

See also

Vernacular houses, 110
Palladian houses, 136
The 20th-century factory, 226
Great barns, 242
Barns, 244

Stables

The horse was central to life on the farm and to the life of the country house. So stables evolved as a distinctive building type and examples ranged from utilitarian buildings to house farm horses to grand ranges that accommodated the mounts of the rich. They reached their most developed form in the stable yards that were built next to great houses, blocks that were sometimes almost as grand as the houses themselves. Divided into separate boxes with often exquisite carpentry, they could be an interesting blend of working building and impressive design.

Audley End
Essex

Brockhall Hall
Northamptonshire

With its gables, dormers, and finials, the stable block at Audley End looks like a house in its own right, an appropriate setting in which a nobleman could show off his finest mounts to his friends. It certainly looks inviting, its rich, deep brickwork reflected in the lake, and it is a worthy companion to one of the finest houses of the period. But dating from the beginning of the 17th century, the stables seem old-fashioned compared to the nearby house, which has fashionable flat roofs and larger windows. Giles Worsley, in *The English Stable* (2004), suggests that this difference is because the large-windowed Jacobean style was simply unsuitable for stables, in which the provision of views was the opposite of what was wanted – and the sloping roofs provided useful accommodation for both grooms and hay.

Stables may be little regarded, and they certainly do not have to be grand. But even such practical corners of a country house are often designed with a quiet flair. Here, in stables built at the very end of the 18th century around three sides of a courtyard, the combination of the curving arch above the door, the simple windows, and the horizontal division between floors, all produce an effect of quiet elegance. England is full of such careful examples of design where just enough effort has been made to lift a simple structure above the mundane.

With the rise of the motor car, many country house stable blocks were converted to accommodate garages. Occasionally a petrol pump was added too, like this early one at Brockhall.

Ravensworth Castle
County Durham

The vast Ravensworth Castle was a 19th-century house designed by John Nash in a mixture of Tudor and baronial styles. It is a ruin now, but the stable yard is one of the best-preserved parts. There are two ranges of single-storey stables in the rectangular courtyard, together with some cottages, and the yard is entered through a large three-storey gatehouse. Nash incorporated some of the castle's medieval ruins into the courtyard, allowing the owner, Thomas Liddell, to point to part of the ancestral home with the assurance that his wealth (from coal mining) was not all new.

Wightwick Manor
Staffordshire

Wightwick Manor is famous as a timber-framed Arts and Crafts house of the 19th century. Its stables are built in tougher, more utilitarian brick – but with occasional blocks of stone to give added visual texture. Evidence of the building's Arts and Crafts heritage appears in the handmade metalwork – for example, the hinges and bars of the upper part of the stable door. Such specially made details are usual in country houses from before the era of mass production and it is good to see them preserved in the often ignored service areas of the house. By the time these stables were built, architects were aware that well-designed stables could help preserve the health and well-being of the precious animals which they housed. So stables such as these were designed with stalls that were easily cleaned and drained, and were well ventilated – here, broad doors and louvres ensure good air circulation. Stalls were positioned so that they could be readily replenished. And there were adequate harness and tack rooms that were dry and well supplied with the various hooks and brackets needed for hanging equipment, and the presses needed for items such as rugs and saddlecloths.

Some of the woodwork of the stables at Ravensworth Castle remains; finials such as this were common in stable interiors.

See also

Dovecotes

For centuries pigeons were highly valued for the table, especially in times when other meat was in short supply, so dovecotes or pigeon houses were built on many farms and next to manor houses. Pigeons were easy to keep – they needed little feeding except in the frostiest days of the winter, and the main job was to clean out the dovecote periodically. Today few dovecotes are used for their original purpose. Most stand empty, but they are often picturesque buildings and so have been frequently preserved. They come in all sorts of shapes from plain round or square buildings to

Sibthorpe
Nottinghamshire

Perhaps the earliest and most common form of dovecote is the cylindrical type. Windowless, this medieval one is beautifully built with small blocks of stone. It has a door at the base and an entrance for the doves, which would originally have been protected by a lantern, at the top of the conical roof. It is almost 60 ft (18 m) high and contains nest holes for 1,260 birds. The main interior fitting would have been a device called a potence, consisting of a central pole with lateral arms to which a ladder was attached. The ladder could rotate, giving access to all the nest compartments.

Newton-in-the-Willows
Northamptonshire

Many dovecotes were rectangular, and they could come in all sorts of different designs. Some have showy, stepped gables, others have ornate lanterns in the roof through which the birds can come and go. They also come in a range of materials, usually following the vernacular traditions of their locality, with timber-framed examples in counties such as Hereford and Worcester, and limestone ones from Somerset to Lincolnshire. Often these stone examples are simple rectangular structures, little different from other farm buildings. This one is Elizabethan and belonged to a vanished house of a branch of the local Tresham family. It is mainly notable for its size – it is nearly 65 ft (19.8 m) long and is divided into two sections, each with its own doorway and lantern. There are said to be some 3,000 nest holes inside. This puts it into the category of extra-large dovecotes.

A sundial complements the dovecote at Milton Ernest Hall, Bedfordshire.

among their membership, they frequently played a key role in local government, and a guildhall often became the town hall too.

Guildhall, King's Lynn
Norfolk

The original guildhall at King's Lynn was built for the Guild of Holy Trinity in 1421 – part of its gable is just visible on the right-hand side of this picture. The dramatic chequerboard masonry was extended in the Elizabethan period when the building was enlarged with the central doorway section. It is built in a lively Tudor-Classical style, with columns on either side of the door, but the masonry preserves the building's unified appearance. Still further to the left is the town hall of 1895, again in flint and stone chequer pattern and this time mixing Gothic and Renaissance details to complete the picture.

Moot Hall, Aldeburgh
Suffolk

The Moot Hall was built in the first half of the 16th century as a dual-purpose building. The ground floor was originally an open space for market stalls and the upper room, reached by the outside stair, has been used for centuries for meetings of the town council. It seems to sum up what Suffolk vernacular architecture is all about. There is not much good stone available locally, so Suffolk builders became skilled in three techniques. First, they made good use of East Anglian flint often making chequerboard patterns with large, square stones. Second, they were expert carpenters, and their timber frames were often finely carved. Third, they used brick well, as in the Moot Hall's chimneys and the brick nogging between the timbers.

Guildhall, Thaxted
Essex

Jettying, the practice of building out an upper storey so that it overhangs the one below, is a sign of a high-status structure. The 15th-century Guildhall at Thaxted, therefore, with its two jetties on each of its three free-standing sides, is about as high-status as can be. The ground-floor posts that hold up the rest of the building terminate in graceful arches, another sign that special trouble was taken with this building. And during the 20th century, when the Guildhall was restored, the arch motif was imitated in the timber framing of the first floor. If not authentic, this was quite in keeping with the building.

The combination of herringbone brick and old oak makes a rich texture at the Moot Hall, Aldeburgh.

See also

Town halls

Some towns, even in the Georgian period, built medieval 'guildhall-style' halls, with an open ground floor. But 17th- and 18th-century halls could be kitted out with a full array of Classical details. As with domestic architecture, the type of Classicism varied enormously. Some towns hit upon an architect who was completely absorbed in the Classical style, sometimes a local builder simply assembled Classical motifs from pattern books and memories of other buildings. Later, civic architects developed other styles, such as neo-Jacobean or exuberant Edwardian baroque, for their town halls. What they all have in common is that they make bold statements of civic importance and pride.

Town hall, Faversham
Kent

This building in the heart of Faversham shows how a guildhall could develop over the centuries and combine different functions. Through the ground-floor opening one can see the octagonal timber columns of the market hall, which was how this structure began life in 1574. In 1604 it became a guildhall and there was a rebuild in the early 19th century, when the upper floor was refurbished. This is when the building got its round-headed windows and cupola-topped tower. So it is market, guildhall, and clock tower rolled into one – and a reminder that sometimes buildings are multi-purpose and do not fall into the neat categories imposed by scholars.

Old Guildhall
Peterborough

The Old Guildhall at Peterborough was built in 1671. Like many others, its upper rooms are built over an open market area, here supported on columns in the Tuscan style. One of the delights of the building is the painted heraldry, especially this royal arms with its characterful lion and unicorn supporters. As prominent public buildings, guildhalls often have clocks, and this one is no exception. Its face is an interesting compromise – Roman numbers for the hours and Arabic for the minutes.

Town hall, Abingdon
Oxfordshire

One of the noblest of all town halls dominates the centre of Abingdon. A large building made to seem all the larger by giant pilasters, huge first-floor windows and a monumental cornice, it was designed and built in 1670–80 by Christopher Kempster, an Oxfordshire master mason who had worked for Sir Christopher Wren and won the great architect's praise. Perhaps he sought Wren's advice and guidance for this building. It follows the same overall layout as the medieval guildhalls, with an open ground floor with rooms above. But the Classical details, from cupola to bases, are typical of the age of Wren.

The giant pilasters between Abingdon's large windows have crisply carved Composite capitals.

A close-up of the cupola at Abingdon reveals details such as the ornate pediments in two different alternating shapes – triangular and segmental.

A curving ceiling and Jacobean-style windows dominate the interior of the town hall at Thame, Oxfordshire, new in 1888.

Town hall, Shaftesbury
Dorset

One style that was popular around the 1820s was a rather plain corporation Tudor revival, the idiom used for Shaftesbury town hall, which dates from this period. Hood-moulds, battlements, and flattened arches are the keynotes. Two details on this entrance front look slightly different and are the result of alterations. In 1879 the porch was extended to form a modest clock tower, with a pediment and keystone above the clock face. At some point the ground-floor arcade was filled in with Gothic glazing. So the façade now boasts an exotic mixture of Gothic, Tudor, and Classical details, reflecting changing civic fashions.

Town hall, Penrith
Cumbria

There are many town halls such as this, designed by little-known architects and built in the late Victorian and Edwardian periods to reflect civic aspirations up and down the country. They are not exceptional buildings and they are often little noticed. This one, designed by local architect J J Knewstubb and built in 1905–6, is in an Italianate style that Nikolaus Pevsner described as 'out-of-date by a whole generation after 1900'. An Italianate building may seem odd as the symbol of an English town, and the little broken pediment high above the entrance, with a tiny urn in the middle, might make the more pedantic architectural critic smile.

But older fashions lingered in the provinces, and here they produced a building that played the role required of it, with features such as urns and columns denoting civic pride and rows of windows letting in plenty of natural light.

See also

Stuart Classical houses, 128
Guildhalls, 254
Town halls, next page

Town halls (continued)

Cities and the larger towns needed bigger halls to accommodate all the offices, committee rooms, public spaces, and other facilities that were required as local government became more sophisticated in the later 19th century. Until the mid-19th century, most cities still favoured Classicism, but often in an antique-revival style, with rows of columns recalling ancient temples – both the democratic heritage of ancient Greece and the might of ancient Rome had something to do with this. Leeds and Birmingham produced outstanding examples. But a turning point came

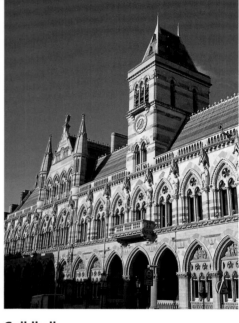

**Town hall
Liverpool**

**Guildhall
Northampton**

When the city of Liverpool needed a new town hall in the mid-18th century, the great architect of Bath, John Wood the elder, was brought in to design it. Today the building shows the results of several alterations – the portico, dome, and other elements were added in the early 19th century by James Wyatt – while retaining much of Wood's work. Wood went for the classic Georgian solution – a *piano nobile*, or first floor containing the main rooms, enlivened with Corinthian pilasters above a rusticated base. Above the windows of the *piano nobile* he installed carved reliefs depicting the kinds of trade – including those based on slavery – that had made Liverpool rich. When in 1785

the demolition of adjoining buildings allowed the town hall to be given a west front, more of these panels were added, this time without allusion to the slave trade. The town hall's interior contains rooms of a variety of dates. The council chamber is in the addition designed by Wyatt but was enlarged in 1899–1900. The first floor has a suite of sumptuous entertaining rooms (reception rooms, ballrooms, and a dining room) in which Wyatt's decorative schemes, with plaster ceilings and artificial marble pilasters, survive.

Architect Edward Godwin had just read John Ruskin's *Stones of Venice* when he did the design for Northampton Guildhall (1861–4), and the Gothic style he chose, with its jutting balcony and two-tone stone, shows a strong European influence. But the building is also a clear expression of local pride, with reliefs showing local industries and statues of local heroes. In the late 1880s the building was extended in the same style – the gable and the bays to the left are from this date. Crisp carving and meticulously cut inlay (the latter reminiscent of some of Ruskin's drawings) are also characteristic of the interior.

Details highlight the meticulous craftsmanship and Ruskinian detail of Northampton's Guildhall.

after 1837, when the new Gothic Houses of Parliament were begun. Manchester's vast town hall was also influential here, showing that Gothic was more than acceptable as a symbol of a city's importance, and more than flexible enough to produce a complex Victorian city headquarters.

Town hall
Leicester

Local architect F J Hames designed Leicester town hall, which was built in the 1870s (the arms were added later). It is one of the many late Victorian public buildings that show how versions of the Classical style refused to die throughout the period, even with the rise and rise of Gothic that is shown by such halls as Manchester. At Leicester, Hames went for quite a free interpretation of Classicism, and quite a lot of the features – the big sash windows, the curvy Dutch gables, and the interplay of red brick and stone detailing – are shared with the houses of the Queen Anne or Wren revival that were by now fashionable in London.

Town hall
Manchester

Alfred Waterhouse's town hall for Manchester (1868–77) is one of the great Victorian buildings – skilfully planned on a difficult triangular site and dramatic enough to give the city the civic symbol that it needed. The public rooms are on the Albert Square front, offices line the other two sides and corridors run around the inside of the triangle for good circulation. A big public hall occupies most of the space in the middle. A lively rhythm of bays and recesses animates the building's façade, as do countless pinnacles, turrets, and dormer windows.

Above it all rise the great tower and spire in an ornate early Gothic style, with tall windows deeply recessed in orders of arches. The big windows in the spire make it seem almost to turn into a lantern. These effects created a sort of picturesque Gothic, a style that became highly influential on many public buildings of the later 19th century. Waterhouse took trouble with the details. Rows of repeated floral decorations around doorways and arches, thousands of shafts with tiny foliate capitals, trefoils, finials, heraldry, statues, and gargoyles – the productivity of Waterhouse's carvers reflected that of Manchester's burgeoning trade and industry.

See also

Guildhalls, 254
Town halls, previous page
National government, 260

National government

National government began in royal palaces, especially the Palace of Westminster where, from the Middle Ages, the king's council and parliament met in Westminster Hall. In 1834 the medieval palace was destroyed in a fire and only Westminster Hall itself and a few other portions remained.

This was the opportunity for the Houses of Lords and Commons, which had worked for centuries in an assortment of rooms in the palace, to be given purpose-built accommodation. The current Houses of Parliament, designed by Charles Barry with major input on the interiors

Clock Tower, Houses of Parliament
London

This tower, known as Big Ben after the great bell it contains, is the most famous part of the Houses of Parliament building, an icon so familiar that Londoners usually pass it by without giving it a second look. A more careful examination reveals the range of architect Charles Barry's Perpendicular style. Below the great clock face it is serious, covered all over by blank stone panelling with strong verticals to emphasise the tower's height. But the top, above the clock faces in their gilded surrounds, is more delicate and feminine, the pointed roof encrusted with crockets, lucarnes (the little openings in the sloping roof), finials, and an openwork lantern.

Houses of Parliament
London

The view from across the river shows the sheer size of the building that was designed by Charles Barry and A W N Pugin to replace the old Palace of Westminster after a fire in 1834 destroyed practically all the old medieval building. The river front contains the libraries and committee rooms that are the unsung engines of the business of government. In the heart of the building is the central lobby, from which corridors lead to further lobbies and to the Houses of Lords and Commons. Visual interest is provided by the clock tower (with Big Ben) and, at the other end, the still larger Victoria tower, beneath which is the monarch's ceremonial entrance to the building.

Famous as the clock tower is, the Victoria tower is taller – at 337 ft (103 m) high it was the country's tallest non-religious building when it was completed. Inside, A W N Pugin's hand is visible in the decoration, where the wallpapers, carvings, and other details are kept in good condition. Pugin's grandest conception was the House of Lords, decorated in rich red and gold. The Commons' chamber suffered bomb damage during the Second World War and as restored is much plainer. But all over the building is evidence of the master Goth's meticulous care. Sadly, he died before the building was completed.

From a distance the Houses of Parliament look like a rather regimented building, with its regular lines of windows. But up close, the surfaces of the walls are a riot of rich decoration, with crocketed canopies, fancy finials, open-work flying buttresses, ornate carvings, and the whole panoply of late Gothic detail.

from A W N Pugin, is the result. It is still the centre of parliamentary government, but there are in addition dozens of buildings housing the offices of civil servants – a few of which, like those in Whitehall, have become almost as iconic as the Houses of Parliament themselves.

Somerset House
London

This enormous building was built on the site of the 16th-century house of the Protector Somerset between 1776 and 1801, as the country's first purpose-built office block for government, the ancestor of all the government offices in Westminster and Whitehall. It was designed by Sir William Chambers to house offices and the headquarters of learned societies. Everything is on a vast scale, but Chambers could have a light touch and the serious Classical architecture is here and there relieved with delicate effects such as round windows and carvings. The vast courtyard, now adorned with rows of fountains spraying straight up from the stone paving, is one of London's most remarkable urban spaces, 350 x 310 ft (107 x 94.5 m). Spaces such as the vestibule are full of delightful Classical details, from plaster ceilings to column bases. One of the institutions that originally occupied Somerset House was the Royal Academy of Arts, which moved in after the building was completed and stayed until 1836. It is fitting, therefore, that its rooms now house the Courtauld collection, one of the finest of all art collections, amassed mainly by the industrialist Samuel Courtauld and left, between 1923 and 1947, to the Courtauld Institute which he had founded.

Portcullis House, Bridge Street
London

This striking building was designed by Michael Hopkins and Partners to provide additional office space for the Houses of Parliament nearby. Some 200 MPs and their staff occupy the building, where they have access to facilities such as a covered courtyard with cafés. The exterior is dominated by 14 blackened bronze chimneys that convey stale air out of the building. Some people think they make an unpleasant-looking building look still uglier; others admire their strong lines.

See also

Victorian parish churches, 56
Georgian houses, 138
Victorian country houses, 148

Legal buildings

Law courts had been held for hundreds of years in palaces, castles, and churches before they began to have their own purpose-built homes in the 17th and 18th centuries. When they came, these buildings tended to be Classical, with all the air of authority that such a style can evoke, and accommodated cells as well as a courtroom. There is a good example at York. Buildings such as this were usually called either assize courts (after the assizes, presided over by judges from Westminster who toured the country on circuit) or sessions houses (after the quarter sessions, held four times a year

Sessions House
Northampton

This is one of the buildings that Northampton acquired after a fire in 1675. A document says that it was laid out by Sir Roger Norwich, but he was head of the Committee of justices of the peace, so may merely have advised on the layout of the courts. Though quite small, the building announces its importance with numerous Corinthian columns and pilasters, together with plenty of deeply cut sculpture. Inside it is just as rich, with plaster ceilings created in the 1680s by the skilled artist Edward Goudge – fruit, foliage, and flowers abound, and there are also heads (a devil and angel) and a figure of Justice.

Old Court House, Ripon
North Yorkshire

This is the archetypal Georgian court house, with its restrained Tuscan attached columns and pediment above the door. This sobriety is compounded by the Classical window openings, although they do have some rather un-Classical Y-traceried glazing bars. Otherwise, propriety is the order of the day in this compact, clean-lined building which Nikolaus Pevsner compared to a Nonconformist chapel.

Royal Courts of Justice, Strand
London

George Edmund Street produced one of the great Victorian façades for the law courts, a stylish composition of towers and turrets, windows and niches, spires and roofs. In Portland stone throughout, it has a rather serious aspect, but this quality is hardly out of keeping with its purpose. It was one of the great Victorian projects, designed in 1866 and under construction from 1874 to 1882, and in the process it exhausted its architect, who died in 1881. Inside the most spectacular space is the huge central hall, cathedral-like in its proportions, off which lead stairways and corridors to the courtrooms.

The animal supporters on either side of the coat of arms on the Northampton Sessions House are a world away from the stylised beasts often seen in heraldry. The lion is a real character, with a rather human nose and slimmed-down body, while the unicorn is a horse with a horn.

by local justices of the peace). Court buildings developed during the 19th century in a similar way to city halls, with a trend towards more complex Gothic structures in the high Victorian period followed by a dose of Edwardian baroque.

Central Criminal Courts, Old Bailey
London

Edward Mountford's design for the Old Bailey (1900–6) was criticised by *The Architectural Review* of the time: it did not look like a sessions house and its plan was not adequately reflected in the exterior. But it is hard to imagine the Edwardian critics wanting this nationally important building to resemble anything like the Court House at Ripon, or even imagining that they would get such a thing from Mountford, one of the most successful baroque architects of the period. Moreover, the Old Bailey's site was difficult and cramped – with more space Mountford could have overcome many of the complaints.

As it was, he produced a serious baroque building with a dome which, with its statue of Justice, has become a landmark. There is also a sumptuously decorated interior – the great hall drips with marble, carved reliefs, paintings, and uplifting inscriptions. This and the other public spaces are vast and over-the-top, but in a major public building with lots of coming and going this is better than them being mean. Today, if the building reeks of the Edwardian period, it has also worn well.

King's Bench Walk, Temple
London

This row of buildings was designed by Sir Christopher Wren and built in 1677–8. Like many similar terraces of buildings in the area of London known as Temple, it houses barristers' chambers, the offices from which members of one of the four Inns of Court conduct their practices. Inside, those who need to consult lawyers will find panelled rooms, pilastered fireplaces, and stairs with wooden, turned balusters. These simple but well-proportioned buildings are similar in outward appearance to the London terraced houses that were evolving at about the same time, although their arrangement, with rooms accessed off staircases, also owes something to the design of the colleges of Oxford and Cambridge.

See also

Stuart Classical houses, 128
Georgian houses, 138
Town halls, 256

Police and fire stations

These are relatively modern building types, for policing was patchy and parochial until the Metropolitan Police Act of 1829 and did not become mandatory until 1856. As for the fire service, this was a matter for insurance companies, whose engine would only turn up if you paid the premium, until the end of the 19th century. So police and fire stations date from the late 19th century onwards. Many police stations are utilitarian buildings little different from houses or office blocks, while fire stations often look like garages. But with care and attention, any building type can blossom and some of London's early 20th-century fire stations, fine examples of the adaptability of Edwardian architecture, are visual assets.

Police station, Ashby de la Zouch
Leicestershire

Many 19th-century police stations were built in a style similar to that of the smaller Victorian railway stations – an idiom ideal for hard-working buildings that were expected to look both tough and respectable. The round-arched door and windows could almost come from a Midlands station. So could the walls, in which the red bricks are relieved with a few paler ones around the windows and with dirt-disguising grey engineering bricks near the ground. But the crisp Victorian block-lettered sign leaves no doubt as to the identity of the building, which has worn as well as its tough, matter-of-fact architecture might suggest.

Police station
Leicester

G Noel Hill chose a neo-Georgian style for this police station of 1933. A Classical style no doubt seemed appropriate for a building of such serious purpose, and the large expanse of pale stone facing seems to tie in with this. It is a far cry, at any rate, from the more modish Art Deco that was being used for countless shops and cinemas at this time. And yet there is something oddly decorative about the curious little balcony beneath the central window and the swag motif above that feels not entirely serious. Perhaps it was features such as these that led Nikolaus Pevsner to remark, 'The mood is not specifically adapted to the job.' But why should the police not have the swag?

Bishopsgate police station
London

Built in 1938 to designs by Vine & Vine, Bishopsgate police station is very much of its time. The strips of windows and pale upper walls recall modernist buildings of the time and the three-dimensional lettering above the door, the 'round' letters all acute angles, is very much a period piece. But the grey granite facing lower down the wall gives the building a hard edge – it looks like a police station that means business. So much so, indeed, that the traditional blue lamps look like something from another era, as if Dixon of Dock Green had paid a call on the Sweeney.

As here at Ashby de la Zouch, the blue lamp is still the universally recognised symbol of the small police station.

A 1905 photograph of the town centre at Faringdon, Oxfordshire, shows how the town hall incorporated the fire station. With the arrival of motorised fire engines, a new fire station was provided.

Euston Road fire station
London

The turn of the 20th century was in many ways a good time for London building. Even little-known names, such as London County Council architect W E Riley, had learned to develop the revivalist styles of period High Victorian into something more flexible. Free Tudor style was one result, a mode that could be adapted to suit all sorts of new building types. For the remarkable fire station in Euston Road, Riley took the style further, adding elements of Arts and Crafts and a dash of Art Nouveau, softening the red brick with pale stone, breaking up the wall with interesting windows, and including discreet but elegant mouldings to some of the window surrounds. A working building became a landmark.

Holt fire station
Norfolk

A small local fire station can be the simplest of buildings, pared-down flat-roofed mid-20th-century modernism providing a garage just big enough for the fire engine and accommodation for the fire crew. It is just the sort of building that it is easy to pass by without a second glance. That would be a pity, because thought went into this unassuming little structure. Look at the care that lies behind the simplicity. The garage has been built with pleasant-coloured bricks in a header-and-stretcher bond. The tasteful lettering has been spaced with precision so that it fits exactly above the doorway. There is

no clutter. Everything is ready for the crew to hurtle off in their gleaming red fire engine and do whatever job is required of them, whether fighting a fire or rescuing a cat up a tree. And if they are out during an emergency, the tiny white-framed door to the left of the window bears the useful legend, 'In case of fire, open door and use telephone.'

The gables of the fire station in Bishopsgate, London, are alive with carved stone, chimneys, and pepperpot turrets in a skyline of 1885 that harks back to London a few decades before the Great Fire of 1666.

See also

Georgian houses, 138
Arts and Crafts houses, 156
Modernist houses, 164
Small stations, 326
Town stations, 328

BUILDINGS FOR EDUCATION

This chapter looks at some of the most architecturally interesting schools, colleges, and universities, and also at those storehouses of culture and education: libraries, museums, and art galleries. This is a diverse heritage, encompassing village schools and great universities, local libraries and the British Museum.

Its story, however, has a certain unity, not just because all these buildings aim to inform and educate but also because their history is bound up with the change from charitable provision to public funding.

All had their beginnings in buildings that were part of something else. The library was first of all the book cupboard of the monastery or the aristocrat's study. The museum was the cabinet of curiosities in the home of the specialist collector. Schools were adjuncts to monasteries or held in a room above the local church porch. There were separate schools and Oxford and Cambridge colleges in the Middle Ages (University, Merton, and Balliol Colleges in Oxford and Peterhouse in Cambridge claim the greatest antiquity), but even these owed their foundation to prominent churchmen or nobles.

And so it continued. Before the 19th century, provision of schools, museums, and libraries relied almost completely on charitable bodies such as the livery companies and on philanthropic individuals. Coverage was patchy and varied – and, for the lover of old buildings this is a bonus, since these early educational buildings have a lack of uniformity and a character that makes them a joy to seek out. The early examples follow their local vernacular tradition, drawing on domestic architecture – a school was, after all, often simply the master's house with a schoolroom attached. So there are timber-framed schools in the West Midlands, stone ones on the limestone belt that stretches from Dorset to Lincolnshire, and so on.

In addition to this domestic tradition, there is also the collegiate. The colleges of Oxford and Cambridge, together with the older public schools such as Winchester, came from an architectural line begun by the monasteries. So they arrange their buildings – students' and teachers' rooms, chapel, library, hall – around a courtyard or two, a picturesque but inward-looking way of building that has helped perhaps to foster the image of academe as cut off from the rest of the world.

And yet the older universities were architectural trendsetters in the Georgian and Victorian periods. Oxford and Cambridge are full of pioneering examples of Palladian, baroque, Greek-revival, and Gothic-revival architecture. Victorian public schools, providing education for Christian gentlemen, remained architecturally more conservative, mostly favouring the Gothic style.

When in the Victorian period the serious business began of filling in the educational gaps, of providing schooling for the millions, designers looked back to the humbler domestic schools of the past. Building of the schools coincided with the widespread availability of brick and slate, which could be transported nationally by canal, so for the first time schools were instantly recognisable all over the country, whether they were tiny village schools with one or two rooms or vast London board schools with dozens of classrooms, they belonged visually to the same type.

These buildings changed with their function, too. While medieval grammar schools taught mainly Latin, Victorian and 20th-century schools took on the task of preparing their pupils for a variety of jobs and ways of life. Schools acquired laboratories and libraries, together with rooms for teaching art, music, and physical education. In the process plans got more complex, and buildings were constantly being extended and altered. Schools have to be adaptable, like those who teach in them.

Museums, galleries, and libraries have had to change too. Holdings have increased; standards of curating and librarianship have improved; new technologies have arrived. And the people who work in these buildings have thought more, and more deeply about the purpose and role of what they do. Museums now routinely employ education officers and get closely involved with local schools and communities. Modern museum architects have to acknowledge this and to accommodate such activities in their buildings, as the apparently distinct building types of school and museum get ever closer.

Early schools and colleges

In the Middle Ages, education was for the few – mostly younger sons of the rich who were destined for a career in the church. The early colleges of Oxford and Cambridge and the public schools were often founded by high-ranking churchmen to fulfil this purpose and their large-scale collegiate architecture of stone quadrangles still impresses. But there were also smaller schools, many of which were founded in the 16th and 17th centuries by local grandees to educate boys from less well-off families. These grammar schools, as they were known, concentrated on teaching Latin, the

Old Grammar School, King's Norton Birmingham

King's Norton's Old Grammar School was originally built in the mid-15th century as a timber-framed structure of a kind typical of the West Midlands. During the Elizabethan period the lower floor was faced in brick with stone dressings. The school was recorded as working during the reign of Edward VI and had won a good reputation by the 17th century, its large, open-plan rooms the scene of a solid, Latin-based education. Schools such as this were simply planned buildings – there was no need for specialist facilities or even separate classrooms, just a teaching room and accommodation for the master.

Wainfleet School, Wainfleet All Saints Lincolnshire

William of Waynflete was Bishop of Winchester between 1447 and 1486 and founded Magdalen College, Oxford. The school in this his native village was a sister foundation begun in 1484, with this imposing twin-towered brick building in the tradition of that other Lincolnshire masterpiece of late medieval brick, Tattershall Castle. The front has little decoration apart from the string-courses and the diaper-work in the walls. The grand Perpendicular Gothic window suggests that inside there is a large first-floor schoolroom, and this is the case. The room is further lit by a row of windows on the north side.

Old Grammar School, Market Harborough Leicestershire

The Old Grammar School is a dual-purpose building that stands as a symbol, for once, of the unity of town and gown. On the ground floor, beneath the first-floor schoolroom, is an open market area. The whole is a good example of a restored 17th-century timber-framed building (the school was founded in 1614 and restored in 1868). An extra decorative touch, unusual in the Midlands, is provided by the pargetted lozenges in each panel of plaster. These lozenges, and the octagonal posts that hold the structure up, have a Jacobean character. The more intricate details, such as the pierced bargeboards, may be later.

A close-up shows how darker bricks are used to make a diaper pattern that stands out against the alternating header and stretcher bond of the Wainfleet School's walls.

Post, capital, and base are carved out of one large piece of oak; dense, heavy wood that offers good support for the large room at the Old Grammar School, originally full of Market Harborough's schoolboys. More big timbers were needed for the braces, which are almost equally massive.

language of church and scholarship, though many also provided a basic elementary education for younger boys. Such schools often began in the parish church but when they acquired their own buildings, these were usually vernacular structures, simply planned.

Peacock's School, Rye
East Sussex

Of the variety of materials used in the wonderfully varied town of Rye, from tiles to weatherboarding, the builders of Peacock's School in 1636 turned to brick and showed what they could do. They produced a design that was strikingly modern for a provincial building of the time and rather elaborate for a school. The giant pilasters were a very new feature and Dutch gables were relatively recent too. True, the relationship between the pilasters and the windows seems rather odd – the lower windows sit half-way up the bases – but this is typical of a builder finding his way with a new style.

New College
Oxford

William of Wykeham, Bishop of Winchester between 1367 and 1404, was one of the greatest architectural and artistic patrons of his day. He founded Winchester College, now the famous public school, in 1382 and his innovation was to make it part of an integrated education system in which scholars could progress to his other foundation, New College, Oxford. At New College the gate and great quadrangle of the 1380s (the first Oxford quad to be planned as a whole) are still impressive. The third storey and battlements on the residential ranges to the east, south, and west are additions of the 17th and 18th centuries, but the lower storeys are the work of Wykeham's mason, William Wynford.

The north side contains Wynford's magnificent chapel, with its huge Perpendicular windows, and his hall, with its rather smaller ones; a symbolic indication, perhaps, that the feeding of the spirit came before that of the body in Wykeham's list of priorities. Wykeham was setting a trend at New College. As the Middle Ages waned and the Tudor period began, a number of powerful clergymen stamped their mark on the university, founding colleges, strengthening Oxford's links with the church, and creating the city's pattern of narrow streets leading past stone quadrangles.

This feathery angel adorns one of the walls of the front quad at New College, Oxford. It is a reminder that the college was founded by a bishop and, like all early colleges, was first and foremost a Christian institution.

See also

Perpendicular parish churches, 38
Vernacular houses, 110
Markets, 194
Guildhalls, 254
Town halls, 256
Renaissance universities, 270

Renaissance universities

The late medieval and Tudor periods saw a flowering of learning in Britain. The work of international scholars and humanists such as Erasmus of Rotterdam, together with the wide availability of printed books, stimulated European scholarship and England's two universities expanded with the foundation of new colleges and libraries. The new colleges stuck to the medieval quadrangular plan, but the buildings gradually became more ambitious, with taller gate towers, heraldic memorials to founders and, as time

Divinity School
Oxford

Jesus College
Cambridge

The Divinity School is a magnificent building, expanded as donations came in through the 15th century. The lower room, the Divinity School proper, was designed by Richard Winchcombe and begun in 1424 with broad Perpendicular windows. The upper storey was added after 1453 to house the library donated by Humphrey, Duke of Gloucester. The lower room was given its vault, the work of William Orchard, by 1483. This is a daring composition of sweeping four-centred arches and dipping pendants, linked by a spider's web of ribs and studded with bosses showing the arms and monograms of benefactors.

Jesus College was founded in 1496 by John Alcock, Bishop of Ely, who suppressed and took over the site of a medieval nunnery, adapting its buildings for the college and taking advantage of its spacious grounds slightly away from the centre of the town. The gate tower was built soon after the foundation in a rather grander, higher, and swankier manner – with its diapered brickwork and stepped battlements – than most of the equivalent buildings in Oxford. It is typical of English Renaissance university building of the early Tudor period – an essentially medieval structure emblazoned with statues and heraldic symbols, including Bishop Alcock's ubiquitous cock, which appear above the

central niche and in other places in the college. If all these details could plausibly come from the Middle Ages, the flattened arches and rectangular windows point clearly to the Tudor period. The college also took over an existing medieval chapel on its site and this was restored in the Victorian period so it is now a treasure house of 19th-century church art with an altar frontal by A W N Pugin, windows by Sir Edward Burne-Jones, and paintings by Morris and Company.

A painted carving of a book is placed over the door of Oxford's Divinity School. The rays of the sun – suggesting illuminating scholarship – edge the cover, while the pages with their Greek inscription remind us that students in the Renaissance were expected to master the Hellenic tongue as well as Latin.

went on, Classical imagery to remind students and visitors alike of the scholarly interest in the works of the Greeks and Romans.

Corpus Christi College
Oxford

Bishop Richard Foxe of Winchester, Lord Privy Seal to Henry VII, founded Corpus in 1517. His academic expectations were high – there was to be tuition in Greek, Latin, and Hebrew – but his college was small, compact of site and low of elevation. There have been some additions to the front quad: the battlements were added in 1625 and the founder's statue in 1817. But Corpus remains the archetypal small Oxbridge college, with hall, students' rooms, and library (praised by Erasmus) all on the front quad. In keeping with its size, the architecture eschews Classical magnificence – four-centred arches and simple domestic windows are the order of the day.

St John's College
Cambridge

One of Cambridge's largest colleges, St John's was founded by Lady Margaret Beaufort, mother of Henry VII, in 1511. Lady Margaret's foundation was made a reality by John Fisher, Bishop of Rochester, who built the college on the grounds of a former hospital, retaining the chapel of the old building. Fisher was a scholarly man who ensured that Greek was taught in the new college, and the place soon got a good reputation for its academic standards. The imposing gate tower leads into First Court, part of the original college (though much altered), and there is a succession of further, later courts beyond.

Gonville and Caius College
Cambridge

Scholar and doctor John Caius refounded the old Gonville Hall in the 1550s, since when it has been known popularly as Caius. Of its early buildings, the Gate of Virtue is one of the most interesting. It is one of a sequence of gates, enabling the student to enter via Humility, walk a straight path through Virtue and leave the college with Honour. The Gate of Virtue is a medieval-style gate tower adorned with Classical pilasters (plus figures of Fame and Fortune in the spandrels), a transitional design that sums up the backward- and forward-looking stance of the English Renaissance.

The Gate of Honour is another of the splendid symbolic gateways at Caius College.

The Enlightenment

The 17th and 18th centuries were a time of change in education. Many grammar schools were in financial crisis, but the successful schools took in boarders to increase their incomes. Some new schools were founded, including a number that began to plug the gap in elementary education and to give pupils practical skills, such as book-keeping, that would be useful in a career outside the church. Meanwhile, the universities were still expanding, with the colleges putting up new buildings in a

Clare College
Cambridge

Trinity College
Cambridge

Clare is an old college, originally founded in the 14th century as University Hall. But the college was substantially rebuilt during the 17th and early 18th centuries, and so looks much more recent. Work started on the west front at Clare in 1669. The building's Classical details, such as the tall Ionic pilasters, show the influence of Christopher Wren, who had designed Pembroke College Chapel in the early 1660s. Clare is an assured building, with a long façade that sets up a rhythm of sash windows and of dormers with a mixture of triangular and segmental pediments. Robert Grumbold, the master mason, was clearly an accomplished craftsman – there are some lovely details, such as the stepped window surrounds and the small, characterful spirals on the Ionic capitals at the top of each pilaster. The chapel, an impressive piece of neo-Classical architecture with fine plaster ceilings and contemporary fittings, is slightly later, dating from 1763–9. Clare is complemented by its gardens, some of the best in Cambridge, and its bridge, another 17th-century structure, is the university's oldest.

Christopher Wren designed Trinity College's library in 1690, raising the main room on to the first floor 'according to the manner of the ancients, who made double walks…around the forum' as Wren put it. There is something restful about the double row of windows, even though the library is rather too large for the court it occupies. Statues representing Divinity, Law, Physic, and Mathematics patrol the parapet. Inside is more sculpture – with lime-wood carvings by Grinling Gibbons and busts of great Trinity men. Treasures on the shelves included the personal books of the greatest of them all, Isaac Newton, who spent most of his life working at Cambridge.

confident-looking Classical style. Christopher Wren worked at both Oxford and at Cambridge in the 17th century. As both a scientist and an architect, he seemed the typical Enlightenment figure.

Senate House
Cambridge

In 1722, James Gibbs drew up plans for a new group of structures for Cambridge University. The plans were partly a response to the lavish gift of 30,000 books to the university from George I and there was to be a library, a printing house, and other buildings, as well as a senate house for ceremonies and gatherings. The whole would have made an impressive academic and ceremonial centre for the university but only the Senate House was built, between 1722 and 1730. It is the scene of Congregations, the thrice-yearly ceremonies at which degrees are confirmed, and General Admissions, the more prestigious annual ceremony in which honorary degrees are awarded.

The strong Classicism of Gibbs makes an appropriately formal backdrop to these grand occasions and Senate House still makes a bold impression, with its giant Corinthian pilasters and columns and its rows of Palladian windows. Most magnificent of all is the centre section like a Roman temple – Gibbs copied its capitals from a Classical temple on his visit to Rome, a fittingly scholarly source for a major university building. Inside there is one long room with galleries and a ceiling by master plaster artists Artari and Bagutti.

Christ's Hospital School
Hertford

In 1552, Edward VI founded Christ's Hospital for homeless children from London. The school taught reading, writing, and arithmetic and accepted both boys and girls. It moved to its present site in 1682 and statues of blue-coated boys were donated in 1721. The girls' school was built in 1778 during a period of expansion and reorganisation. In the 20th century both boys and girls moved to Horsham, West Sussex, and the surviving buildings at Hertford are now used for offices and sheltered housing.

A statue in a niche reminds visitors that this was the Christ's Hospital girls' school.

See also

The spread of learning

The 19th century was the period when education became universal. In the first part of the century, education was provided by voluntary bodies, which offered schooling in simple, barn-like buildings. It was a very basic system, but it brought schooling to many who would before have fallen through the educational net. The year 1870 saw the passing of the Education Act, which brought in secular elementary schools, supported by the rates and administered by local school boards. This development marked the beginning of education for all. There was also a broadening of university education, with the

Peasenhall Sibton School
Suffolk

Medbourne School
Leicestershire

Expansion in primary education in the 19th century saw the building of thousands of elementary schools in towns and villages. Most of those begun before 1870 were built by voluntary school societies or local benefactors, generally with the backing of the Anglican or Nonconformist churches. In towns, these could be huge, barn-like buildings in which a big class of pupils received lessons from a single teacher with the help of a team of pupil-monitors. In villages, schools were smaller, and individual attention from the teacher was much more likely. This is such a village school. It was originally founded in 1719 by Dorothea Scrivener and this building was put up by other members of the same family in 1840.

Even a modest village school like this has Gothic features such as pointed windows, which suggest the religious values of the founders and original teachers. Many such schools are solid buildings that survive in some form of educational use: this one is now the local nursery school.

On a rather larger scale and from slightly later in the 19th century, Medbourne School was built on the eve of the 1870 Education Act to provide improved accommodation for a school that, like so many in England, had been held in the parish church since about 1650. Instead of a converted church transept, the teacher had a spacious, high schoolroom, well lit with tall windows, in which there would have been plenty of room on either side of the rows of wooden desks for children to divide into groups to work under the supervision of monitors.

universities opening up to students who did not belong to the Church of England and, in the 1870s, to women. Brick-and-terracotta buildings – often called 'redbrick universities' – were the result.

Roade School
Northamptonshire

A large town or London borough might provide separate infant and elementary schools, but in the villages there were usually only pupils and money enough for a single school. At its simplest, this might consist of a single room with a partition to separate two classes, but here there were separate rooms and entrances for boys, girls, and infants, each signposted outside with clear lettered tiles. Construction on a budget meant most of the decoration was done with different coloured bricks. Here, darker red bricks form the arches over the windows, while other details are picked out in grey engineering bricks.

Marlborough Primary School
Sloane Avenue, London

After 1870, the London School Board was charged with the huge task of providing schools for the children of the capital with funds from the rates. The Board's first architect, Edward R Robson, began an ambitious programme of school building, with dozens of medium-sized schools and a textbook, *School Architecture* (1874). His work was continued by T J Bailey, who built many of the larger 1880s and 1890s schools which, like this one, still serve London well. Both men used the Queen Anne style widely, putting in plenty of large windows to light the schoolrooms and using occasional stone dressings amongst the brickwork.

Girton College
Cambridge

In 1869 Girton College was founded by Emily Davies. It was the first residential college to provide a university education for women. By 1873 the college had its first buildings designed in glowing red brick by Alfred Waterhouse. These formed part of Emily Davies Court and featured rooms accessed by corridors rather than the traditional Cambridge staircases. The college expanded into more buildings by Waterhouse's son Paul between 1884 and 1902, as the Cloisters Court, hall, chapel, and this gate tower were completed. Other women's colleges, such as Newnham (1871), followed and women's colleges were soon being founded in Oxford too.

Girton College has many Gothic details, such as arches, shafts, and hood-moulds in brick.

See also

Victorian parish churches, 56
Arts and Crafts houses, 156
Queen Anne houses, 160

20th-century schools

A rising population of children who were required to stay longer at school, greater subject diversity, more sophisticated equipment, higher standards of comfort and safety, and new theories of education – all these factors influenced school building during the 20th century. Population movements and a building backlog added to the problems of the education system after the Second World War. Meeting all these requirements was a big challenge for local-authority architects often having to work to tight budgets. Although some outstanding one-off schools were built, most education authorities went

Day Continuation Schools, Bournville Birmingham

Cadbury's, ever keen on the welfare of their staff, wanted employees to continue their education into their working lives. In 1911 the company made classes compulsory for workers between 14 and 18 years old, and up to the age of 19 for apprentices and 21 for clerks. Staff were given classes in the sciences, English, crafts, and physical training and in 1925 the continuation schools were built to provide a proper venue for this activity. Soon other companies were sending workers to the schools, with up to 3,000 attending each week. The schools now form part of the University of Central England.

Carillon, Bournville Birmingham

George Cadbury built the carillon, with its lantern filled with bells, atop the tower of Bournville's junior school after he saw a similar instrument during a trip to Bruges. Tunes are played on a keyboard, which is linked to hammers that strike the bells. Today the carillon is famous as one of only two working examples in England. It is an example of the care that Cadbury took over the environment of workers and children alike in Bournville. The building that houses it is now a visitor centre and the carillon itself has become the symbol of the Bournville Village Trust.

Impington Village College Cambridgeshire

The village college was a 1930s concept, designed to combine the educational needs of a group of villages with facilities, such as a library and sports hall, for the local adults. The one at Impington (1938) has become famous because its distinguished modernist architects, German refugee Walter Gropius and his British colleague Maxwell Fry, created here a modern idiom – with flat roofs, large windows, and a variety of materials including different-coloured bricks – that was used for schools everywhere in the following decades. But rarely as successfully as here, where features such as the canopy and sweeping roofs, not to mention the surrounding trees, break up the straight lines.

George Cadbury founded the Bournville Village Trust in 1900 to administer the village and its amenities. The Trust is still active, developing and managing good-quality social housing in Birmingham and beyond. This brochure from the Trust bears a cover, painted by Michael Reilly, showing one of Bournville's schools, together with Arts and Crafts inspired houses in the background.

for standardised forms of construction. Probably the most successful was Hertfordshire, where prefabricated buildings were built with architects and education officers working closely together. The resulting schools were light, well-planned, and provided with inspiring murals and sculptures.

Hunstanton School
Norfolk

This school was designed by Peter and Alison Smithson in the uncompromising New Brutalist style of the 1950s and 1960s. All glass walls, steel I-beams, and flat roofs, this 1954 building shows the decisive influence of the German high priest of modernism, Ludwig Mies van der Rohe. It looked stunning and its pared-down finesse won it lots of friends in the architectural community when it was new. Many architects were excited by the developments in modernism pioneered by Mies van der Rohe and his followers, in which materials such as steel and glass were used to create a new architectural language.

They saw buildings like this school as models of how the Brutalist style could be used in Britain, and used, what was more, in buildings that served a useful social purpose. But there were also doubts. Was a glass-walled building right for cold, windy eastern England? And did the idiom of modernism provide a nurturing environment? Staff and pupils confirmed the doubts, telling of a structure whose glass panels failed to keep out Norfolk's east winds and sometimes even fell out of their frames. They must have felt like architectural fashion victims.

Hampden Gurney School, Nutford Place
Westminster, London

Some Victorian schools, built on constricted sites, had roof-top playgrounds, and in 2002 architects BDP gave this idea a novel twist in this school, where the brief was to build a school and a block of flats on the site of an old school and playground. Each upper level of the school carries a play area, open to the fresh air but protected by the glass balustrading that gives the building its distinctive elevation. Behind is a light well and beyond this are the classrooms. The hall, library, offices, and other 'service' rooms are tucked away on the lower ground floor.

One of the entrances at Hunstanton School shows the Smithsons' powerful combination of black framework and bright red door.

Metal-and-glass balustrades front low walls of pale brick at Hampden Gurney School.

Museums and libraries

Although art collecting began during the Renaissance, the first dedicated museum opened in 1683 and the first gallery in 1814. By the early 19th century, a rash of collections, most originating in private hands, began to be put on public display. Early museums varied greatly in size but most were in the Classical style, which provided a neutral backdrop for displays. By 1850, Britain had 59 museums, and by 1914 a further 295 had been built and these later ones showed a high-Victorian eclecticism of style – they could be Classical, Gothic, or Romanesque – together with a similar variety of content – science, natural history, and ethnography were covered as well as history and the fine arts.

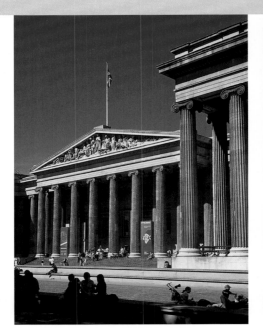  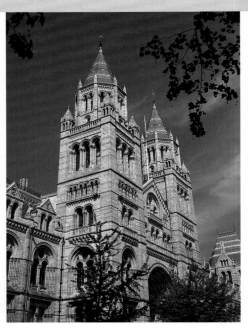

British Museum
London

The British Museum began life in 1823 when Robert Smirke started work on the Classical buildings that still provide much of its display space, a vast complex around a central courtyard, with a colonnaded frontage of the 1840s that is still a landmark on Great Russell Street. The Classical façade was in keeping with the collection of Parthenon sculptures that had been purchased from Lord Elgin in 1816. But the building also housed other collections, including the 65,000 books in the King's Library, one of London's finest interiors. The Museum has been altered much since Smirke's time, notable additions including the 1850s reading room and Norman Foster's 21st-century remodelling of the Great Court in which it stands.

Scarborough Museum
North Yorkshire

York architect Richard Sharp was working with William Wilkins on the museum in York when he was commissioned to design the Scarborough Museum in 1828. At the suggestion of engineer and geologist William Smith, the man who produced the first map of English rock strata, Sharp built it in the form of a rotunda, the circular form exactly fitting the planned chronological display. Although the building was extended with the addition of wings in 1860, the interior keeps much of its 18th-century character, with a spiral staircase that leads to the centre of the domed exhibition room. Original 18th-century display cases line the walls.

Natural History Museum
London

After the closure of the 1851 Great Exhibition, the profits were invested in land in South Kensington, and a series of buildings, including the Royal Albert Hall, the Royal College of Music, the Science Museum, and the Natural History Museum, was begun. This 'cultural quarter' was built under the aegis of Prince Albert and became known as Albertopolis. The Natural History Museum, constructed between 1873 and 1891 to designs by Alfred Waterhouse, is one of the quarter's most striking buildings. Waterhouse chose a round-arched Romanesque style and built on a huge scale – the towers are 192 ft (58.5 m) high, the façade is 675 ft (206 m) in length, and the galleries within are vast.

The Natural History Museum's walls are clad in buff and blue terracotta. Capitals and other surfaces are covered with images of animals and plants, living species on the east wing, extinct ones on the west.

The idea of public libraries began with the 18th-century circulating libraries, where readers paid to borrow books. But the movement to give the public free access to books for loan and reference began during the 19th century, and was another aspect of the powerful Victorian drive to provide education for all. It began in 1850, when an act of Parliament permitted local authorities to fund libraries from the rates, and was given huge stimulus after 1900 with funding from the charitable trust of the Scottish-born philanthropist Andrew Carnegie, who had made his fortune in the United States.

University Museum
Oxford

This museum of 1855–60 was set up at the encouragement of Henry Acland, anatomist and later Professor of Medicine, who had campaigned for natural sciences to be taught at Oxford University and saw the need for a place where geological and natural history specimens could be displayed. Benjamin Woodward was the designer of the museum, and he worked under the influence of Acland's friend John Ruskin. The exterior is enlivened with masonry of different colours, in the style that Ruskin had admired in Venice. Acland and Ruskin insisted that all the art in the museum should be instructive, so the windows feature an array of different capitals carved with natural subjects, some reputedly designed by Ruskin himself, which fit the building's role as a natural history museum. Woodward employed two sculptors, James and John O'Shea, who had worked with him on the museum at Trinity College, Dublin, and the results were more than worthy of Oxford's heritage of medieval carving. Inside, Woodward brilliantly adapted Gothic to suit modern materials, with a large central hall with a glazed roof, supported on Gothic ironwork produced by Skidmore of Coventry. The surrounding cloisters have columns in different British stones, all labelled like exhibits.

Victoria and Albert Museum
London

The Victoria and Albert Museum was a major element of Albertopolis, the cultural quarter, with museums and concert halls, built in South Kensington after the Great Exhibition. It was begun in 1859 to designs by the engineer Captain Francis Fowke, but Fowke died in 1865 and was succeeded by another engineer, Lieutenant-Colonel H Y D Scott. Many designers and decorators, including William Morris, were also employed on the interiors. Later still, Aston Webb designed the façade on the Brompton Road, which was completed in 1909. As a result of this long and varied history, the V & A, as it is known, is a mixture of Italian Renaissance, Arts and Crafts, and baroque designs, an architecture as diverse as the huge collection of decorative art within it.

The Everton Library, Liverpool, opened in 1896. Its showy design, with lots of Jacobean details like mullioned windows and overhanging gables, was the work of Thomas Shelmerdine. The climax is the octagonal tower with its leaded spire piercing the skyline like a beacon of learning.

See also

Victorian parish churches, 56
Georgian houses, 138
Victorian country houses, 148
Museums and libraries, next page

Horniman Museum, Forest Hill
London

Tea importer and MP Frederick John Horniman chose Charles Harrison Townsend to design a museum in south London to house his collection of ethnography and natural history. When it opened in 1902 as the Horniman Free Museum it gave the capital the nearest thing it has to a great Art Nouveau building. The main block, with its segmental parapet, stands back from the street with the entrance above pavement level and reached by steps. The dominant feature is the extraordinary tower. At its base, this tower is square with curved corners, but at the top these corners transform themselves into round pinnacles with a circular parapet and cornice between them. It is a remarkable piece of architectural sleight of hand, and quite unlike anything else. Next to this tower the main museum building is rather less spectacular, like a large stone hall with its curving parapet. But it is wonderfully animated by the large mosaic by Robert Anning Bell who, like Townsend, was a member of the Art Workers' Guild. After this exterior, the interior is rather plain, but it provides a good neutral backdrop for the remarkable collection of artefacts from all over the world.

King's Lynn Library, King's Lynn
Norfolk

The library at King's Lynn was one of the many paid for by the Scottish-born philanthropist, Andrew Carnegie, who made a fortune in the United States. Thousands of unassuming, brick-built council- and Carnegie-funded public libraries are still serving local communities, but this one is unusually powerful architecturally. It was built in 1904–5 of random carstone with dressings of terracotta and this gives it a curious dark, brooding quality. H J Green was the architect, and he created an effective fan-shaped plan for the corner site, with three top-lit rooms spreading out from the entrance tower and lobby.

Central Library
Manchester

Vincent Harris chose the grand Roman style for his Central Library of 1930–4, in the process giving Manchester a vast Classical landmark to balance the famous monumental Gothic of the town hall. The Corinthian portico, Tuscan colonnade, and great shallow-domed roof create an image of a temple to all the gods of literature – could this be just too off-putting for a public library? But inside, the spaces are well planned, with book stacks beneath a large circular reading room: it seems to say that, if London's British Museum had one of those, Manchester should have one too.

Southfields Library
Leicester

To any London Underground traveller there is something curiously familiar about this branch library in Leicester. Designed in 1939 by Symington, Prince and Pike, it is reminiscent of the 1930s London Underground stations of Charles Holden – the use of brick, the circular issue hall, and the bands of windows are all common features. In addition, the Leicester architects may well have been influenced by modernist buildings farther afield. There are buildings in Holland with these features and the library work of the great Swedish designer Gunnar Apslund is a likely source too.

Southfields Library is a light and airy building and the red brick gives it a feeling of warmth. It is one of the acceptable, human faces of architecture's modernism and a visual asset to its neighbourhood. More provincial libraries should be designed with such care.

See also

Arts and Crafts parish churches, 60
Arts and Crafts houses, 156
Modernist houses, 164
Museums and libraries, previous page
Underground stations, 338

the success of the building.

broad piazza.

Long, low, horizontal hedges mirror the lines of the British Library beyond. This is a good example of what gardeners know as structural planting, complementing a modern building.

See also

Modernist houses, 164
The 20th-century factory, 226
Offices, 238
20th-century schools, 276

Recent buildings for education

Some of the most interesting late 20th-century buildings are universities, museums, and libraries. Educational expansion was especially prolific in the 1960s, while museums and galleries are now the new cathedrals – inspiring, high-profile public buildings that every architect wants to tackle. A new museum is the chance for an architect to do something different, and there were good opportunities in the flood of new projects in the late 20th century, leading up to the millennium.

St George's Hall, Liverpool

BUILDINGS FOR ENTERTAINMENT AND GATHERING

We take mass leisure for granted today, but it has not always been so. For much of our history, people have spent most of their lives working, and what little spare time they had amusing themselves around the hearth at home. For most, the only regular gathering-place was the local church or, for some, the guildhall, town hall, or market.

Since then, buildings for entertainment and gathering have often been places for the rich or privileged – or at least those who can claim membership of the middle class. Georgian assembly rooms, the buildings associated with our spas, and private halls for members of groups such as the Freemasons are typical examples.

But at different points in our history, the story of leisure has expanded, opening up new pastimes to more and more people and generating fresh architectural forms in the process. This happened in Elizabethan London, where theatrical companies such as Shakespeare's brought new life to the drama. Their main auditorium, a brilliant invention that was like a cross between an amphitheatre and the yard of a galleried inn, was a building type that was also used for spectacles such as bear-baiting.

Shakespeare's theatre, the Globe, provided true entertainment for the masses (standing room was available for a penny). Later, this role was taken by the music hall, which housed a variety of diversions: drinking, dancing, and theatre. Formal theatres were more exclusive and different in layout. Their interiors in particular became outstanding, especially during the theatre-building boom of the late 19th century, when a special brand of rococo, which blended plaster and papier-mâché decoration with gilding and painting, made theatres places of magic.

The layout of these theatres – with tiered seats, balconies, a proscenium arch, and a generous backstage area and fly tower for scenery – influenced another kind of mass-entertainment building: the cinema. Films as popular entertainment reached their heyday between the advent of sound in the late 1920s and the Second World War. The picture palaces where they were shown, many of them masterpieces of Art Deco or Moderne architecture, are now appreciated after decades of neglect.

Sport has provided another source of popular spectacle in the last 200 years and has produced building types of its own. The stadium, from stands with standing room only, to the safer, seat-filled structures of today, is a fine piece of engineering on the fringes of building. Cricket pavilions are usually more modest but more architectural. Both types are evocative of the cultures that produced them.

Another building type that encapsulates an era and an ethos is the swimming pool and bath complex. This has its origins in both the spa movement and the enthusiasm for hygiene in the Victorian period, when commissions for baths and wash-houses were established. The Victorians built indoor baths, but in the 1920s scientists recognised that fresh air and exercise are healthy, and millions decided that swimming in an open-air pool was the best way to achieve this. And so the lido was created, the characteristic pool of the 1920s and 1930s, with changing rooms, terraces, a café, engine house, and perhaps a multi-level diving board, surrounding the water. At many venues all these features were designed in contemporary style, with lots of white concrete.

So buildings for entertainment and gathering range from the most glamorous theatres to neglected structures like many lidos. The category also includes buildings such as village halls, which, although they are well looked after by their custodians, are frequently overlooked. They illustrate a bewildering variety of architectural forms, from the simple hall or pavilion to the 20th century's answer to accommodating everything from performance to painting: the arts centre. But, like a good arts centre, which can serve everyone from the rich to the unemployed, from beginners trying their hands at pottery or drawing to the most accomplished professionals, they have something in common. They bring people together, serve communities, and give them a source of pride.

First stages

The plays of Shakespeare and his contemporaries were put on in galleried, timber-framed outdoor theatres, a many-sided building type Shakespeare described, in *Henry V*, as a 'wooden O'. No wooden O's survive, although there is a superb modern reproduction on London's Bankside. But Shakespeare's company also had access to an indoor private theatre, a much smaller rectangular building, and this is the ancestor of the Georgian theatres that still exist in one or two English towns. In these

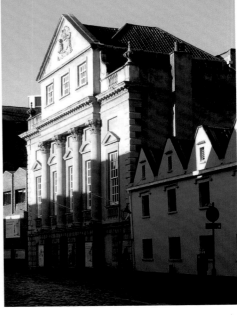

Shakespeare's Globe
London

This reproduction of the original 1599 Globe Theatre was built in the 1980s as a result of the vision and campaigning of American actor Sam Wanamaker. Its design was based on all the evidence that could be amassed as to the size, shape, and layout of the original – the discovery of the 1599 foundations, archaeological remains of the nearby Rose theatre, early illustrations, contemporary documents, and references in Shakespeare's plays. The result is a 20-sided oak-framed structure forming a galleried courtyard, into which protrudes a rectangular canopied stage decorated in rich English Renaissance style.

Since this is a working theatre, there are compromises. The seating capacity has to conform to today's health and safety standards. And to avoid the fate of the original Globe, which burned down when a canon misfired during a performance of Shakespeare's *Henry VIII*, the thatch is protected by fireboard and a sprinkler system – this is the first building to be thatched in London since the Great Fire of 1666. But compromises apart, this is still the nearest you can get to Shakespeare's original theatre. Actors and audiences alike find themselves seeing Shakespeare's plays in a new light as they experience them in conditions close to those for which they were written.

Theatre Royal
Bristol

Although much altered since it was built in 1764–6, the Theatre Royal contains Britain's oldest surviving theatre auditorium. It was funded by a group of 49 subscribers, who employed Thomas Paty to build it to plans based on those of the Theatre Royal, Drury Lane, London. Two tiers of boxes were built in a semicircle in front of a protruding stage apron. The stage and its proscenium doors have been replaced by a modern stage, but the box fronts survive, the seating behind them now arranged as dress and upper circles, with a later balcony level added above. In spite of these changes, the proportions of the semicircular auditorium still conjure up the atmosphere of an 18th-century theatre.

buildings, audience facilities such as boxes and balconies evolved and one can also trace the beginnings of theatrical features such as artificial lighting and the proscenium stage.

Market Cross, Bury St Edmunds
Suffolk

Robert Adam designed this dual-purpose building which was constructed in 1774–80 to provide a market hall on the ground floor and a theatre above. Adam used grey brick but picked out the rusticated ground floor and other details in stone. There are lots of typical Adam touches – such as swags and urns – and the capitals of the giant columns are Adam's personal version of the Ionic. There are similar capitals on the shafts of the venetian windows, all indications of the hand of this architect and master decorator. These windows admit lots of light to the upper floor, which has recently been used as an art gallery.

Georgian Theatre, Richmond
North Yorkshire

This tiny theatre by an unknown architect has an almost perfect Georgian interior. The audience in the pit sit on authentic 'knife-edge' backless benches. Above them is a tier of 11 boxes with playwrights' names over each. The lettering of the name of Shakespeare over the centre box is original. A further gallery level supported on Tuscan columns extends above the boxes. Today, with modern health and safety regulations, 220 people can sit in the auditorium, but early records show that 450 were crammed in during the building's early days. The little stage is in proportion with the rest of the building, only 24 ft (7.3 m) deep and 28 ft (8.5 m) in width.

This precious survival fell out of use as a theatre and was used as an auction room and later as a wine store. But in 1963 it was restored under the guidance of theatre-history experts Richard Southern and Richard Leacroft. Authentic Georgian paint colours – mostly blue-greens and reds – were used. There is an adjoining museum that contains a piece of early 19th-century scenery from another theatre – as rare a survival as the Georgian Theatre itself.

Carved relief panels at the Market Cross, Bury St Edmunds, depict masks, with one panel representing comedy, one tragedy.

See also

19th-century theatres

In the 19th century the theatre began to branch out architecturally. From the elegant, boxed, and rather boxy auditoria of the early part of the period, theatres broadened inside so that sightlines could be improved for bigger and bigger audiences. They became more fantastic too, with materials such as plaster and papier-mâché used to create all sorts of decorative masks, cherubs, flowers, swags, and similar motifs – all of which confirmed the theatre as a palace of entertainment. This trend came to a

Theatre Royal
London

The first theatre on this site was opened in 1720, so the house was already well established when it was rebuilt by John Nash in 1821. It retains its Nash façade on Haymarket. The central feature is a grand portico with six Corinthian columns set forward so that they come right to the edge of the pavement, ensuring that this building is an unmissable feature of the neighbourhood. When the sun catches the gilding on the Corinthian capitals, the eye is drawn to the building, and this very Classical façade reveals its showy side. Inside there is a fine auditorium of 1905 designed by C Stanley Peach.

Wilton's Music Hall
London

A giant music hall that began life in 1850, Wilton's is an example of how many 19th-century theatres are hardly noticeable from the outside. With the signs and posters gone, there is little apart from the decoration around the door and the iron lamp bracket to mark this east London building out from any other Whitechapel terraced house. Yet the proprietors claimed that they could seat 2,000 in the hall. This was the result of a major enlargement in 1859 when land at the rear of the building was acquired. The brickwork gives every sign that the hall was built in a hurry and on the cheap

– a fact that has not helped the recent custodians, who have tried to open the hall for occasional performances while campaigning for the restoration of this fragile building. But in spite of the structural problems, the hall is still beautiful inside. The audience sat in stalls and seats in the generous balconies supported by elegant spiral-twisted iron columns. Elegant carton-pierre balcony-fronts and an elliptical vaulted ceiling remain. There were many halls such as this in the late 19th century, although they fell out of fashion and mostly disappeared with the rise of the cinema.

One of the balcony fronts at Wilton's Music Hall is encrusted with leaf ornament and egg-and-dart, a motif drawn from Classical architecture. It glows, very much as it would have done under the flickering lights of a performance in the Victorian era.

climax at the end of the 19th century and the start of the 20th, in the work of designers such as theatre specialist Frank Matcham. In his work, a concern with the practicalities of the theatre went hand-in-hand with the desire to create the most luxurious and decorative interiors possible. Meanwhile, a parallel trend had begun, that of the popular theatre of music hall with auditoria no less supplying entertainment to the masses.

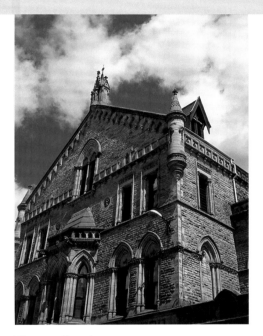

Theatre Royal
York

This theatre began life in the 18th century but was substantially rebuilt, with a new exterior of 1880 and a new auditorium interior of 1902. The façade is in a dramatic and rather muscular Gothic – the protruding corner turrets give it a hint of the Scottish baronial style and it seems to promise adventurous adaptations of the novels of Sir Walter Scott. Below the oriel there is a five-arched Gothic arcade, allowing people to shelter as they wait for admission, so the frontage is practical as well as dramatic.

Everyman Theatre, Cheltenham
Gloucestershire

Frank Matcham was the leading theatre architect of the Victorian and Edwardian periods and the Everyman, which was opened in 1891, is his earliest surviving theatre. It was originally called the New Theatre and Opera House, a name indicating a high-class venue, and there is still an orchestra pit to bear this out. The layout of the auditorium is typical Matcham, a small and intimate space with curving balcony fronts giving excellent sightlines. Much of the high-status decoration remains, again in a mode that is typical of the designer. There is a mass of painted panels, plaster swags, scrolls, and shells.

Angels above the boxes once carried house lights and boxes with columns and tied-back curtains look like miniature stages. The whole effect is one of fanciful rococo, exactly the right ambience in which to prepare for an evening's entertainment. The theatre was technologically advanced too. It was the first theatre with exit doors protected by the now ubiquitous crash bars and where there is now a central chandelier there was once a patent lamp called a sunburner, which lit the auditorium and helped the air to circulate.

See also

Cinemas

The first cinemas, built in the years before the First World War, were mostly small, and their façades could be decorated with a variety of rich motifs to symbolise the exotic entertainment available within – swags, Art Nouveau curlicues, or tiles. Plaster panels were the norm within. A new enthusiasm for cinema erupted with the arrival of the talkies after 1927, and plush super cinemas were built by chains such as Gaumont. Decoration was eclectic, ranging from Classical to Moorish. By the 1930s, Hollywood sophisticates had the industry under their thumbs, and sleek cinemas, in the style known as Moderne, mostly rather smaller than those of the 1920s, became fashionable. The Odeon chain dominated,

Kinema in the Woods, Woodhall Spa
Lincolnshire

Central cinema, Stamford
Lincolnshire

Today we are used to going to the movies in purpose-built cinemas, but there is a long tradition of cinemas in converted buildings, especially in small towns where the profits were not big enough to justify a brand-new picture palace. Most of these converted cinemas have long vanished, victims of the combined pressures of television and the more glamorous entertainments available in large towns and cities. But a few remain and one or two are visual delights. This surprising building began life as a concert pavilion, one of the structures associated with the spa at Woodhall, and was converted into a cinema in 1922. To convert the building, a corrugated-iron shed was built onto one end and a state-of-the-art rear projection-system, much praised by contemporaries, was installed. A sound projector followed in 1928 and this was only replaced 50 years later with electronically controlled projectors that still use traditional carbon-arc lamps. A large Compton Kinestra organ augments the entertainment. Lights and 1920s-style signage lift the profile of the building and the spirits of passers-by.

One kind of cinema design went for sophistication without the outré decoration that was popular in the early 1930s. Strong horizontal lines, here provided by mouldings, were a keynote – on other buildings similar lines were introduced through strips of windows. The windows themselves were usually metal framed. Walls could be of unfaced brick or covered in pale tiles – the Odeon chain favoured cream-coloured tiles. Decorative elaborations, such as the shafts on either side of this corner window, were kept to a minimum. This was a formula that produced sleek exteriors that promised the latest in entertainment – and without blowing the budget on lavish Egyptian details.

with streamlined, tile-clad exteriors and concealed lighting, coved ceilings, and more streamlining within. Cinema building stopped during the Second World War and when hostilities ended, rival entertainments saw scores of cinemas demolished or converted to restaurants and bingo halls. Few cinemas of architectural interest have been built since.

In 1934 the interior of the Odeon, Surbiton, Surrey, was new. Joseph Hill's Art Deco design emphasised the lines of the auditorium with strip lighting.

Odeon cinema
Leicester

The Odeon chain was owned by businessman Oscar Deutsch and the name is said to come from the phrase 'Oscar Deutsch Entertains Our Nation', although 'odeon' is also a Greek word for theatre. Between 1930 and the outbreak of the Second World War the chain opened 96 new cinemas in England. Most of them were built in a similar style, with streamlining, cream tiling, striking towers, and lettering often lit up in neon. The chain's success confirmed that cinema was the nation's favourite entertainment, and penetration into the suburbs meant that people did not have to go far to take in the latest that Hollywood or the British film industry had to offer.

Regal cinema, Melton Mowbray
Leicestershire

Some 1930s cinema design went for decorative motifs that were more Art Deco than Moderne. Here the tiles make interesting stepped and chevron patterns, there is a segmental arch, and the leaded window lights are designed in interesting patterns that have nothing to do with the modern or Moderne styles. This is the cinema as exotic location, redolent of adventure movies and historical dramas – and yet with its tile cladding somehow still up-to-date and high-tech. It sounds like a contradiction, but it sums up the marriage of technology and imagination that film represented, and still does.

It is also an example of how often one has to look up to get the best out of a cinema building. All too frequently, intent on getting inside, we rush past the posters towards the foyer and the flickering delights beyond, but often it is worth pausing to look at the cinema's façade, on which bits of early tiling or statuary may be visible, high up above the signs.

Large white fins, with smaller fins between them, are a dominant motif on Leicester's Odeon – and on many other cinemas built by the same chain.

See also

The suburbs and beyond, 166
The 20th-century factory, 226
19th-century theatres, 288

Concert buildings

Music was performed in church, in people's homes, and in buildings such as inns, but there were no dedicated concert buildings until impresarios such as Johann Peter Salomon began to put on musical performances in the 18th century at venues such as London's Hanover Square Rooms. The main survival from this period is the small Holywell Music Room in Oxford. Victorian halls could be much more ambitious, and designers tried new shapes, such as the oval of the Royal Albert Hall. More recently,

Holywell Music Room
Oxford

Oxford's Holywell Music Room was England's first purpose-designed stand-alone concert hall and was built, probably to the designs of Thomas Camplin, in 1742–8, although the porch and doorway were added later. It is a plain and simple building with a front like a chapel and an interior with rows of pew-like bench seats. Above hang a pair of chandeliers, used in Westminster Hall, London, at the coronation of George IV and later donated by the king. This compact interior, where no one is ever far from the performers, has been a popular venue for chamber music and recitals since it was built.

Musick Gallery, The Pantiles
Tunbridge Wells, Kent

Named for the terracotta tiles with which it was once paved, the Pantiles is in the centre of Tunbridge Wells and was a popular focus for visitors during the town's heyday as a spa from the 17th to 19th centuries. Musicians serenaded passers-by from this gallery with its early 19th-century iron balustrade, a forerunner of the later bandstands. The tradition of open-air performance was strong in Britain. From the 17th century on, dances and suites by the likes of Handel and Arne were played in London pleasure gardens such as Vauxhall, where music was performed on woodwind and brass instruments whose sound carried best outdoors.

Royal Albert Hall
London

Captain Francis Fowke, engineer and designer of the building for the 1862 London Exhibition, produced his design for the Albert Hall in 1864, the year before his death. The hall was one of a series of buildings that formed a 'cultural quarter' – known as Albertopolis – built under the aegis of Prince Albert after the Great Exhibition of 1851. Fowke's conception was daring: an elliptical roof measuring 219 ft (67 m) by 185 ft (56 m) covering an auditorium for 8,000 people. Red brick was enlivened with a terracotta frieze depicting a succession of heroes of arts and letters. The building was constructed after Fowke's death under the supervision of H Y D Scott.

A popular form of entertainment in the 19th century was provided by band concerts in public parks. Bands would play in purpose-built bandstands, usually supported on cast-iron columns and sometimes with wooden-panelled balustrades such as this late Victorian example in Clevedon, Somerset.

the science of acoustics has evolved, and has influenced the choice of materials and the overall form of the modern concert halls. Designers have discovered that the traditional 18th-century shoebox shape is acoustically one of the best.

Caryatids hold up the balcony in one of the interiors of St George's Hall, Liverpool.

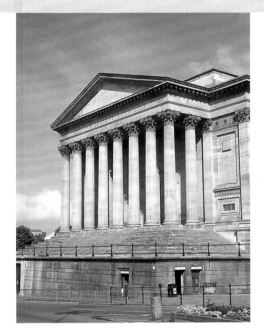

St George's Hall
Liverpool

This extraordinary building met twin needs for a concert hall and a courtroom. It was designed by a little-known architect from London, Harvey Lonsdale Elmes, who was just 25 years old when he won the competition to design the hall in 1839. It is a staggering design because of its size (bigger than St Paul's Cathedral), its prominent site, and its intensely Classical style, in fact a mix of Greek and Roman elements. But Elmes was not to see the completion of this triumphant building. He died in 1847 and the project was taken over by C R Cockerell. Elmes designed the exterior, but Cockerell had to do some of the interior designs, including the hall's vast floor, covered with tiles from the Minton factory.

The Sage, Gateshead
County Durham

This outstanding building by the River Tyne at Gateshead is the result of a collaboration between architects Foster and Partners and engineers Arup Acoustics. As one would expect from such a partnership, the building combines striking looks with excellent sound. The external appearance is dictated by the vast stainless-steel roof that curves to mirror the shapes of the famous Tyne bridges and seems to emerge out of the ground. Most visitors find that it looks remarkably at home for a vast building on an urban site that is already full of much-loved local scenery. Beneath the roof are two auditoria, a rehearsal space, and a 25-room music education centre.

This is where the partnership of architects and acousticians comes in. Surprisingly for such a modern-looking building, the main performance space is modelled on Vienna's Musikverein Hall, which takes the 'shoebox' form that gives the best concert acoustics. These are enhanced at the Sage by wooden surfaces, including ribbed ash on the walls and birch on the ceiling. But in a high-tech touch, the orchestra sits in a large parabolic dish to make the sound still clearer. Movable curtains and panels allow the users of the hall to make fine adjustments to the sound.

See also

Georgian houses, 138
Victorian country houses, 148
19th-century theatres, 288
Spa buildings, 296

Seaside piers

Piers were first built in the early 19th century to allow ships to deliver passengers to seaside resorts. Soon they were home to shops and eating-places too, and by the time Hastings Pier was built in 1869–72, with an oriental pavilion at its end, the pleasure pier had arrived. Designers such as pier expert Eugenius Birch had also perfected the networks of columns and struts that supported their masterpieces – cast iron for the uprights and wrought iron or steel, stronger in tension, for the beams and struts. The piers also rested on iron piles – wood had been tried but tended to be eaten

Eastbourne
East Sussex

Eugenius Birch, one of the most expert pier builders, used a clever support system for Eastbourne's pier, resting the supporting piles on cups rather like huge furniture castor cushions that sat on the bedrock. This system allows the structure to move slightly in response to currents and bad weather and has enabled the 1,000 ft (305 m)-long pier to survive rather well. It was only a particularly violent storm which succeeded in destroying the seaward end in 1877, but this was rebuilt. This entrance building is one of a number of additions that have appeared over the years. It was built in 1912 to give added shelter and sophistication, no doubt appreciated by the dancers arriving for the popular balls that took place here.

Great Yarmouth
Norfolk

There had been suggestions that Great Yarmouth should have a pier for landing and promenading in 1843. But it was almost ten years later when public subscriptions were invited to build a pier for the town. As a result, Great Yarmouth's Wellington Pier, the seventh in the country, was built in 1853 in tribute to the Duke of Wellington, who had died the previous year. At over 600 ft (183 m) long, with a 100 ft (30.5 m) promenading platform at the end, the wooden pier was a large if somewhat eccentric memorial to the duke. Adults paid one penny for admission and the pier proved popular until a rival pier, the Britannia, was erected in 1858. The early 20th century saw an upturn after the local authority took over in 1899.

They rebuilt the pier in the early years of the 20th century and commissioned the 1,000-seater Art Nouveau pavilion, which was designed by J W Cockrill using a steel-framed construction. The management put on improved entertainments here – including variety acts in the pavilion and firework displays outside – and later also acquired a second-hand winter garden building, which was bought from Torquay.

Variety, the hybrid popular entertainment of the mid-20th century, was the kind of diversion that best fitted the architecture and the audience at venues like the Wellington Pier.

away by marine worms. Up on deck, pier pavilions became exotic leisure centres, with ballrooms, theatres, and restaurants. Later came slot machines and other cheap entertainments, while some piers even had a winter garden; the complete entertainment experience.

Cromer
Norfolk

By the time Cromer Pier was built in 1900–1, owners were realising that a pier did not have to be long to be effective. Build a relatively short pier and you could avoid some of the maintenance problems that could bring these attractions to grief. So the Cromer Protection Commissioners went for a pier just 500 ft (152 m) in length. Their engineers, Douglass and Arnott, used quite a lot of steel in the structure – although it rests on iron piles – and built the pier relatively wide. All this meant that the Commissioners could reduce running costs, put on more attractions, and maximise income. They began with a simple bandstand before extending this to make a larger pavilion.

This was floored in maple wood for roller skating, but later was also used for concerts. The pier has worn well, in spite of occasional storm damage – notably in the severe storms that battered the east coast in 1953 – and the removal of decking during the Second World War to render the structure useless as an enemy landing platform.

Clevedon
Somerset

Completed in 1869, the delicate structure of Clevedon Pier was designed to cope with the strong currents of the Bristol Channel. The arches were made of reused rails from the failed South Wales Railway, bolted together in pairs. The resulting pier is 842 ft (257 m) in length from baronial-style tollhouse to pier head, where a new pagoda-style pavilion was built in 1891. The filigree structure of the pier itself, designed by John Grover and Richard Ward, survived until October 1970, when two sections collapsed into the sea. Since then the story of the pier has been one of further dilapidation, followed by triumphant restoration.

See also

Arcades, 196
The great termini, 332
Coastal buildings, 340

Spa buildings

Although the ancient Britons and Romans knew of the therapeutic qualities of the water of Bath, spas as resorts where healing and pleasure could be combined date mainly from the late 17th century. The most successful attracted royal patronage;

Queen Anne visited Bath and George III made Cheltenham famous. A flurry of pump rooms, assembly rooms, and fashionable shops and houses was the architectural result. Smaller towns with healing springs also expanded, and the wells of

Grand Pump Room, Bath
Somerset

Bath's Grand Pump Room was built next to the Roman baths to a design by Thomas Baldwin in 1790–5. It replaced an earlier pump room of 1704–6. The earliest part to be built was the elegant colonnade, with its pediment containing a pair of sphinxes and a bust of Hygeia, goddess of health. Various grand Classical façades followed. But the glory of the building is its interior with its giant Corinthian columns and coved ceiling. There are many delightful details, such as the little *oeils de boeuf* above the main windows and the apsidal ends, one with a bust of Beau Nash, Bath's 18th-century master of ceremonies.

Pittville Pump Room, Cheltenham
Gloucestershire

Cheltenham's most impressive surviving spa building is at one end of the town in the area called Pittville, after its developer Joseph Pitt. It stands in a landscaped park, laid out while the pump room was being built to the designs of local architect John Forbes in 1825–30. The building is in the Greek revival tradition, its Ionic columns copied from engravings by James 'Athenian' Stuart and Nicholas Revett, and its parapet supporting statues of Aesculapius, the Roman god of medicine, the goddess of health, Hygeia, and Hippocrates, the father of Greek medicine; they are modern copies of the originals. But in its green setting the pump room does not look as serious

as all this sounds, because the shallow lantern-topped dome and the statues break up its straight Grecian lines. Even so, it is grand enough to eclipse Cheltenham's other spas as it was no doubt meant to do in order to capture the town's competitive entertainment market. Inside, the main room has an interior designed by a London architect, J C Mead. There are more Ionic columns around a large main room (originally a ballroom but now used mainly for concerts). Above is a balcony, and the spectacle is completed by a beautiful domed ceiling, studded with Greek paterae.

An attached Ionic column is one of several holding up a rather plain frieze at Bath's Grand Pump Room. The somewhat severe style is in keeping with the Roman baths next door.

Malvern, the terraces of Buxton, and the extraordinary
spa buildings of Tenbury Wells survive to remind us
of the success of such places in the Georgian and,
especially, the Victorian periods.

Montpellier Pump Room and Rotunda
Cheltenham, Gloucestershire

In 1817 Cheltenham architect G A
Underwood built a long but rather modest
colonnaded room at Montpellier Spa, one
of the places where the town's visitors
could assemble and take the waters. To
make the building more magnificent, in
1825–6 the prolific architect J B Papworth
added this rotunda, a large copper-covered
dome, modelled on that of the Pantheon
in Rome. Its shallow but imposing form,
topped with lantern and weather vane,
rising gently above the surrounding
houses and shops, must have been an
effective landmark for its visitors. It is
now a bank.

Spa Building, Scarborough
North Yorkshire

Scarborough was a spa by 1700 and
developed as the country's first seaside
resort in the 19th century. The spa was a
popular venue for music-hall entertainment,
concerts, and dances. The present building
was put up in 1877–80 after its predecessor
was destroyed by fire. By this time the
railway was well established here and
made many Yorkshire coast resorts
accessible – Whitby, Robin Hood's Bay,
Filey, Bridlington, and Hornsea were
all on the timetable. So Scarborough
needed to keep its pre-eminent position
and a large spa building was in order. The
architects were Verity and Hunt, Frank
Thomas Verity being a theatre specialist.

At Scarborough they provided a terrace
commanding the sea, and gave the building
more than a little of the continental air –
the central roof is French in inspiration.
The rows of windows and the corner domes
are from the baroque tradition and their
hauteur seems to promise luxury within.

Village halls

Less often noticed than theatres and grand halls are the ubiquitous village halls, which cater for every occasion from parish meetings to wedding receptions, and which exist in their thousands. Most date from the late 19th or 20th centuries, and they come in every style to suit every locality. They are rarely elaborate or architect-designed buildings, although sometimes a local landlord or grandee donated land, building materials, and the services of the architect who was working on the local country house.

Euston Village Club, Euston Suffolk

Here is a timeless building serving a village in Suffolk, where sports groups and others can meet. With its sweeping roofs and bay windows this rear section behind the street frontage could be an addition in the Arts and Crafts tradition, though the white-painted walls could equally conceal a much earlier building. But age does not matter in a building such as this. Its importance is all to do with its social function and the way it fits into the village streetscape and village life.

Village hall, Madingley Cambridgeshire

A thatched roof makes this hall stand out from the crowd, its inviting texture reproduced on the roof above the little porch. This is a style that fits in with one local way of building in which houses have pitched roofs above white or colour-washed walls. The thin lines of the imitation timber frame are hardly convincing, and many vernacular buildings in this part of the country have not a timber frame but horizontal pentice boards that stick out like shelves to protect the clay walls. For all that, this charming hall manages to look the part.

Parish hall, Highnam Gloucestershire

The local landlord often contributed to the upkeep of facilities such as village halls, but it is unusual for the village bigwig to be the architect as well. But Sidney Gambier Parry came from an artistic family – his father painted the murals in the parish church – and he designed this parish hall in 1904. Parry would have known architects such as Detmar Blow and Guy Dawber, who worked in the Cotswolds Arts and Crafts tradition, but who added baroque and Classical elements to their buildings. Details such as the window, the keystone and the bay with its segmental top and ball finial are all part of this tradition.

The Women's Institute was founded in 1915 and still thrives today, doing charitable work, organising community events, and educating women. Originally strongest in country areas, Women's Institutes are still regular users of village halls, where their logo evokes memories of their meetings, markets, and other events.

But even these more pretentious halls consist of little more than a public room, toilets, and some simple catering facilities. Modest as they are, and varying from metal hut to thatched pavilion, they are often a source of justifiable local affection.

Village hall, Old Warden
Bedfordshire

With a medieval church, an 1870s Jacobean-style great house, and thatched cottages, Old Warden has an impressive architectural heritage. The village hall does its best to live up to this, with brick base, half-timbered upper walls, and curvaceous openwork bargeboards on the central gable that lift it above run-of-the-mill mock-Tudor. The white-painted dome-topped lantern that sits on the roof lifts it indeed, and is the sort of feature more often seen on high-status town halls. Buildings like this, so often seen in England's villages, are examples of the visual benefits of making an effort with modest means and everyday materials.

There is nothing over the top or monumental about it, but the building gives the impression that just a little extra care has been taken – and is still taken when it comes to upkeep. Framed by foliage, this village hall is an asset, both to the user and the admiring passer-by.

Church hall, Leverton
Lincolnshire

A wooden-frame structure clad in corrugated iron on a brick base, makes up this simplest of church hall in Lincolnshire. Buildings such as this are usually looked down on – after all, corrugated iron is not normally taken seriously as a building material: it is seen as fit only for sheds and the humbler structures put up by cash-strapped farmers. And yet this church hall does its job and manages as best it can to blend into the trees thanks to a coat of green paint. Advocates of honest building should not knock it.

Halls for gathering

In addition to the churches and town halls that have long provided room for meetings and other gatherings, all sorts of other buildings have evolved for meetings and assemblies of many kinds. Some, such as the numerous assembly rooms, are pleasure buildings, venues for balls and banquets. Many of these buildings are closely allied to the halls that were put up to house the balls and assemblies that took place at spa resorts. Others, such as Masonic halls, are for meetings and ceremonies. Both of these types offer architecture of great grandeur and interest.

Assembly Rooms
York

Masonic Hall, Cheltenham
Gloucestershire

York has some of the most magnificent assembly rooms, known to architectural historians as one of the earliest structures in the 18th-century Palladian style, and a source of pride to generations of city residents. At their heart is a central hall with its rows of closely spaced, marbled Corinthian columns, a fitting arena for the grandest of social occasions and ceremonies. The decoration is the epitome of Palladian taste – gold-tipped acanthus leaves on Corinthian capitals, touches of red and gold above, rows of niches behind the columns. It could be rather dark, but above the columns there is a clerestory where a row of windows, separated by white pilasters, throws light into the space below. This rich but restrained interior is the work of Lord Burlington, the pioneer of Palladian architecture, and is based on a structure described by the Roman architect and writer Vitruvius as an Egyptian Hall, although it is, of course, purely Classical. Burlington's design dates from 1730, about five years after he built Chiswick House. So York could claim to be at the cutting edge, and architects were eager to copy the details of Burlington's design.

Freemasonry, taking much of its symbolism from architecture and building, has been responsible for some interesting halls, and the little one at Cheltenham, dating from 1820–3, is amongst the best. It was designed by local architect G A Underwood, who had trained with Sir John Soane and who became a Mason in 1818. The hall combines almost blank walls (appropriately mysterious, perhaps, for a masonic building) with an almost windowless façade featuring masonic emblems, triangles, columns, empty niches, and blank panels of stone where we would expect to see glazing. It is an essay in stone and symbolism that must have given pleasure to mason and Mason alike.

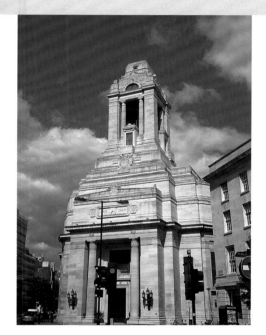

Freemasons' Hall, Great Queen Street London

This grandest of masonic halls, with its strong massing, looks like an Edwardian building. But it actually dates from 1927–33 and is a surprisingly old-fashioned building, even for such a tradition-conscious body as the Freemasons. Its architects, Ashley and Newman, clearly wanted to emphasise that tradition – after all, of the up-and-coming styles, Art Deco would have seemed too frivolous and modernist would have been too stripped down. Instead it is a Classical revival building that straddles its corner site and still stops passers-by in their tracks because of its sheer scale.

De La Warr Pavilion, Bexhill-on-Sea East Sussex

These curving windows and balconies belong to the De La Warr Pavilion, one of Britain's most striking 1930s modernist buildings. This view shows the part of the building that houses the staircase, which gives access to what was effectively a leisure centre before the term was coined; a complex housing a theatre, library, and cafés, together with areas where people can meet and enjoy the sea view. The idea, quite revolutionary at the time, came from Bexhill's Labour Party mayor, Earl de la Warr, and the Pavilion – the name seems inappropriate for this rather large building – was designed by émigré architects Erich Mendelsohn and Serge Chermayeff.

The building is lined with long strips of sea-view windows and balconies. Beneath the pale concrete cladding is a steel frame, prefabricated for speed and economy of construction. Curiously, then, there is a modern construction technique – steel framing – at the core of the design, but the building avoids the modernist doctrine of 'truth to materials' since the steel is hidden beneath the smooth, pale finish of the concrete.

See also

Palladian houses, 136
Modernist houses, 164
Spa buildings, 296
Village halls, 298
Coastal buildings, 340

Sports pavilions

Architects use the word 'pavilion' to describe any small ornamental building, often of lightweight structure, but most of us would look for a pavilion on a cricket ground. Sports pavilions come in all materials. Major grounds, rich clubs, and public schools often have a large building in brick that can offer hospitality to VIPs in addition to the usual facilities. At the other end of the scale, the humblest come in corrugated iron. In between there are countless wooden pavilions, varying in size and pretension,

Stanway
Gloucestershire

In the 1920s, scores of cricket teams were got together by the landed classes of England to play in the privileged setting of a country-house park. The writer James Barrie, friend and summer tenant of Lord Wemyss of Stanway, had this pavilion built in such a setting in 1925. He employed John Oakey, a builder from nearby Winchcombe, for the job, and Oakey obliged with a larch-clad thatch-roofed structure. Larch and thatch are not common materials in the Cotswolds, but a traditional touch was added by raising the little building off the ground on the kind of mushroom-like staddle-stones normally used for granaries.

Tillingham
Essex

Timber-clad and timeless, there are countless pavilions such as this one on village cricket grounds all over the country. Most offer just the basics – somewhere to change, toilet facilities, and often, as here, a veranda where members of the batting side can prepare themselves for the long walk to the middle. There are no architectural pretensions about such buildings: they are built to do a simple job on an often all-too-limited budget. But, to a local club, as John Parker said in his novel *The Village Cricket Match* (1977) about the fictional Sussex village Tillingfold, even the most basic pavilion is 'home'.

And it is homely architecture, simple and unpretentious but, with its overhanging canopy, somehow reminiscent of the colonial style of wooden bungalows and tiffin on the veranda. A comfortable place to return to, whether you've made 50 or you've just returned after the longest walk in the world – the trek back to the pavilion with a duck to your name.

from huts to ranches. At their best, finished in white, brown, or shades of green, these buildings fit comfortably into the landscape of the summer game to form the perfect symbol of England at play.

Uppingham School
Rutland

Cricket pavilions at their simplest provide somewhere for the players to change. But many go further than this, with a covered balcony area from which people can watch the game and dodge the rain showers that interrupt it, and also provide all sorts of additional rooms inside. A pavilion at a major public school often has all of these facilities, turning into a substantial building, and this is the case with this pavilion at Uppingham. In 1923, when it was built, cricket seemed the epitome of leisured old England and upper-class sportsmanship. The Arts and Crafts style was an idiom from the past by this time, but there were still builders who were pleased to turn their hand to this sort of work.

So it was thatch, mullions, and half-hipped roofs for the pavilion at Uppingham, with a pretty central turret, also thatched, to remind us that this was a cut above your average village cottage. The scoreboard is integrated into the design too, behind a pair of wooden doors that can be opened when it is in use. The perfect place to learn the virtues of sportsmanship and empire: play up, and play the game.

Bournville
Birmingham

When the Quaker chocolate manufacturer George Cadbury built his industrial village, Bournville, at the end of the 19th century, he wanted to house both factory and office workers, and to provide all the facilities they needed to improve themselves in body and mind, including sports grounds. The 1902 pavilion is built with a mixture of half-timbering and brick. The timbers are arranged in patterns that recall the dazzling Tudor houses of the West Midlands, but in an appropriate twist for this town of confectioners, they are a pleasant chocolatey-brown colour. As usual in Bournville, a public building is given special prominence, with an ornate turret roofed with a pointed hat of tiles.

The entrance front of the Uppingham pavilion is plainer than the side facing the sports ground, which is the true 'business end' of this kind of building. Simple Arabic numerals record the date of construction.

See also

Industrial villages and other alternatives, 150
Arts and Crafts houses, 156

Swimming pools

Bathing in the sea became popular in the 19th century, and there has been a long tradition of therapeutic bathing since spas became fashionable almost 200 years before that. Pleasure, health, and hygiene came together in Victorian public baths, palaces of iron and tile, many of which had complexes uniting swimming pools with slipper baths for cleansing, and even Turkish or Russian baths. The other great age of swimming was the 1920s and 1930s, when the continental vogue for open-air exercise spread to Britain and swimmers braved the cold or worshipped the sun in Art Deco lidos. The elegant

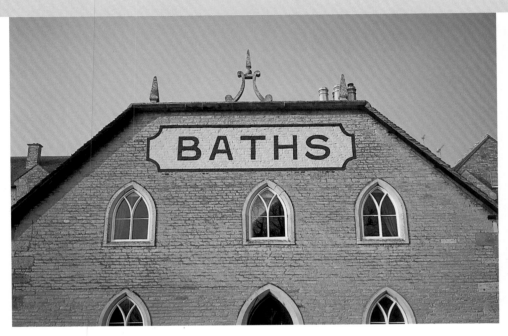

Stamford
Lincolnshire

Stamford today is still one of the most beautiful limestone towns in England, prosperous and picturesque. A clutch of medieval churches indicates its importance in the Middle Ages, while fine Georgian houses speak of its wealth in the 18th century, convenient as it was for the traffic on the Great North Road. It was prominent in the 19th century too, with its own newspapers, circulating libraries, and the like – together with facilities such as notably early public baths. The exterior of Stamford's baths, built in 1823, survives intact with its large sign, although the building is now a private house. The pointed windows still display the Y-tracery of 'Gothic'

buildings of the late 18th and early 19th centuries – the sort of design that was used on many a sham castle to evoke the age of chivalry. Similar tracery had been used in Hopkin's Hospital, a Stamford building of some 50 years earlier, showing the way in which the design endured. Here it is combined with the later-looking painted sign and a rather fanciful pinnacle to produce a frontage of great character.

Bournville
Birmingham

Cadbury's were famous for their concern for their workers' welfare, and one way in which this was evident was in the provision of sports and leisure facilities. Sports were believed to encourage good comradeship and to be improving for both body and spirit. Every young man or woman who came to work for the company was encouraged to learn to swim. Men had swimming lessons in an open-air pool, but by the early 20th century there was a heated indoor pool for women, whose sporting opportunities at Bournville were much greater than in most towns and villages of the time. The pool was built in a free Edwardian style to designs by G H Lewin in 1904.

In leafy Bournville even this name plaque is covered with foliage. The lettering, with its curving, slightly medieval looking capital A, is typical of the date: 1904.

lines and pale concrete finishes of these outdoor pools were perfect backdrops for human beauty, but many lidos were abandoned in the 1970s when swimmers demanded indoor comfort and governments demanded budget cuts. The ones that survive are now prized as pleasure architecture *par excellence*.

Victoria Baths
Manchester

Opened in 1906, this was one of the grandest of all municipal baths, offering swimming pools, Turkish baths, and regular bathrooms in a splendid building of striped brick and terracotta. Inside, three pools provided swimming for 'Males 1st class', 'Males 2nd class', and 'Women', with separate entrances for each group, to keep sexes and classes properly segregated. The glory of the interiors is the tiling, which is in the Art Nouveau style of the early 20th century. In the entrance area for 'Males 1st class' for example, with its Art Nouveau glazed decor, almost every surface – walls, columns, even banisters – is covered in glowing green tiles, some of which have floral or abstract decorations.

This tilework is beautiful, easy to clean, and ideal in an environment where there is lots of water. It also presents a conservation challenge, because in some parts of the building it conceals rusting ironwork that needs to be replaced. Although the usefulness of the slipper baths declined as bathrooms were installed in houses, Victoria Baths was popular with swimmers for most of the 20th century before closing in the 1990s. There is now hope for a new lease of life after the building won the first series of BBC TV's *Restoration* programme.

Peterborough Lido
Peterborough

The pool at Peterborough dates from 1936, the heyday of the lido, when Britain caught the fresh-air bug and embraced buildings that encouraged the outdoor life – in defiance of the climate. In spite of the brash modern signage, there is much remaining of the original, rather Italianate building, which involved five separate honorary architects. The lovely clock tower and row of windows survive and the replacement roof tiles give an idea of the original vibrant green. Inside there are sunbathing decks, pavilions, lawns, changing rooms, and two pools, one for adults and one for children.

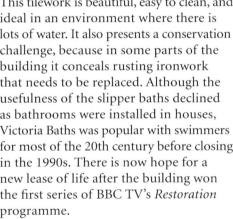

The original cast-iron detailing of the changing stalls, no doubt much-repainted, and fine Art Nouveau tilework survive at the Victoria Baths.

See also

Georgian Gothic parish churches, 50
Victorian country houses, 148
Industrial villages and other alternatives, 150
Modernist houses, 164

WEST COUNTRY ALES

1760

BEST IN THE WEST

Brewery sign, Winchcombe, Gloucestershire

BUILDINGS FOR HOSPITALITY

Since the time of the ancient Greeks at least, hospitality has been a virtue, and for centuries there have been buildings dedicated to offering travellers the hospitable facilities of a drink, a meal, and a bed for the night. It used to be said that in the Middle Ages there were alehouses, establishments that brewed and sold beer; taverns, where you could get a meal and more upmarket drinks such as wine; and inns, where you could find food, drink, a bed, and stabling for your horse. In truth the boundaries between such hostelries were blurred – it was the hospitality that mattered.

In those days people travelled less, and had less leisure time, than we do today. Many medieval travellers were on business connected with their lord or with the church, and many found hospitality in a manor house or monastery guest hall on the way. Numerous inns were owned by the church and connected with pilgrimage routes that crossed the country, such as the roads from Winchester and London to Canterbury.

The development of new or improved forms of transport – better roads in the 17th and 18th centuries, railways in the 19th – spawned new buildings for hospitality. Long-distance coaching services stimulated the development of the inn, with its stabling facilities. Inns developed into hotels, more luxurious establishments with a greater profusion of public rooms. More hotels were built as a result of social trends such as the habit of visiting spas or seaside resorts. And the railway companies added their share, to give their passengers somewhere to stay at the end of the line. Eating and drinking habits also changed, with the inn and tavern developing into the public house.

The pub is an architectural feast, too. The early buildings could be modest – a tavern or alehouse was typically part of the landlord's house where customers were served and inns were basically domestic courtyard buildings. Many of today's pubs still follow this pattern – vernacular buildings that fit into landscape and townscape as if they have always been there. Indeed some landlords claim their buildings have almost always been there: the competition to be 'Britain's oldest pub' is fierce and inconclusive.

But hotels were different. They were grand from the start, when owners added luxurious ballrooms and plush lounges to inns. And so it has continued with countless purpose-built examples – Grecian Regency pleasure temples, brick Victorian railway hotels, Edwardian baroque palaces (sometimes called The Palace), Moderne creations such as London's Strand Palace or the Dorchester, and plush, high-rise Hiltons. All are designed to make the guest feel important, pampered, swathed in luxury. Technology was as important as architecture, and these buildings vied to provide the latest – lifts to all floors, bathrooms, WCs, the latest in heating and ventilation, winter gardens, and hairdressing salons with mechanical hairbrushes.

Smaller establishments could not compete with all this. Pubs, after all, were for the working classes whereas hotels were for those with more money and pretensions. But in the Victorian period, the pubs made up for it with decorative swagger. Wood and tile, glass and brass sparkle in Victorian pubs. Classic examples such as the Lion and the Philharmonic in Liverpool are justly famous. Many others have vanished, because the licensed trade, like retailing, is the victim, as well as the beneficiary, of frequent changes in design fashion. But we are fortunate that a number of these gin palaces, true temples to drinking, have survived in our large cities. If they looked mainly to the lower orders for their clientele, they had their gradations of social class, too – big pubs were divided into numerous bars, separated by partitions and 'snob screens' (translucent eye-level panels), each catering for different segments of society.

Early inns

Although a number of English inns claim origins in the early Middle Ages, few of the actual buildings are older than late medieval. By this time a pattern had evolved, with most inns built around a courtyard with an archway giving access from the street. They are usually vernacular buildings that have evolved over the years, with extra rooms and wings added according to need and with little thought to aesthetics. But they often display signs of pretension – a column here, a carving or piece of moulding there – that draw attention to the inn. Such buildings had to catch the eye of the traveller, and they continue to do so.

Angel and Royal Hotel, Grantham
Lincolnshire

Hospitality began early on this site. It belonged to the religious order of knights, the Templars and Hospitallers, in the Middle Ages, when it was certainly a place where travellers could stay. A 13th-century cellar dates from this time. But by the 15th century it was a sizeable inn with this magnificent frontage, carved with figures and heraldry. A W N Pugin admired this façade and included it in his 1836 book *Contrasts* as a prime example of late Gothic domestic building. And visitors still admire it, with its delightful asymmetrical proportions, its carved parapet, and its welcoming entrance, as one of the very few medieval inns that is largely intact.

George, Southwark
London

The George is a courtyard inn and is one of the few of its type that still has upper galleries that gave access to the rooms. Many parts of its structure, such as these gallery columns and railings, probably date from the 17th century, when the building was famous as a coaching inn on the route from London to Kent. The balconies also gave a good view of the courtyard, a fact that was exploited when theatrical performances were held in the yard in the 16th and 17th centuries. Today the yard provides an excellent opportunity to extend the drinking area outdoors.

New Inn
Gloucester

Gloucester's New Inn was originally built in the mid-15th century by a monk of the city's abbey called John de Twynyng, no doubt to house pilgrims visiting the tomb of Edward II in Gloucester Abbey (now the cathedral). Monastic building projects such as this were not uncommon in the late Middle Ages, because they allowed abbeys to make money from their property while extending the hospitality they offered to visitors and travellers. Many of the galleries at the New Inn remain, together with a lot of early timber framing, although there have also been many alterations, from 18th- and 19th-century sash windows to still later signs.

Bull Hotel, Long Melford
Suffolk

In a town of notable timber-framed buildings, the Bull stands out. Its protruding, or jettied, upper storeys indicate that this was always a prominent building – only those with a long purse could afford the extra timber involved in building a jetty, and this was recognised in the late Middle Ages as a way of showing one's wealth and importance. Like nearly all early inns, the building has been extended and otherwise altered over the centuries: there are sections of white-painted brick among the timber-framing. But the overall effect is still both unified and welcoming.

Talbot, Oundle
Northamptonshire

The Talbot has dominated the centre of Oundle since 1626. It is impressive both because it is very well preserved, with lots of Jacobean windows with their mullions still intact, and because lots of care was lavished on its design. Like so many Northamptonshire buildings it shows glorious use of stone – from those mullions to the ball finials, from the lozenge-shaped panels to the round arch over the central window. It is all straight out of the grammar book of Jacobean architecture, but with delightful individual touches, such as the way the lower corners of the dormer windows are bracketed out with an elegant scroll shape.

So although its stone frontage fits superbly into its old town, the Talbot is a far cry from the inn as vernacular architecture – it was built with special care, by someone who wanted the best and most fashionable of design in 1626. Without the central archway it could almost be a small country house.

The Talbot retains its old mounting block so that riders can easily be up and away.

See also

From tavern to pub

The vernacular pub, combining local building style with the individual imprint of landlord (and often local clientele), is one of the joys of English building. Simple exterior architecture is often complemented by an unpretentious interior, perhaps with wooden boards or stone flags on the floor, wooden panelling or plain walls, and most of the decorative interest provided by the impedimenta of the drinks trade, from the pumps and their labels to jugs and glasses. A few landlords, in reaction against the corporate decoration of today's franchises (books by the yard, farm tools or garden implements), display personal collections – the multitude of mugs at the Falkland Arms is just one example.

Three Chimneys, Biddenden
Kent

The earliest part of the timber-framed Three Chimneys dates from 1420 and, like many a country pub, it has grown from a vernacular structure that could be a private house. The domestic scale and local 'fit' of the architecture began as convenience – this was just how people built houses – but today this building attracts the tourist who wants to eat and drink in countrified surroundings, while puzzling about the name of the pub. It comes from the 18th century, when French prisoners of war were allowed to walk from nearby Sissinghurst Castle to the junction of the three ways ('les trois chemins').

Falkland Arms, Great Tew
Oxfordshire

An inn since at least the 16th century, the Falkland Arms, like the Three Chimneys, shows how the smaller village hostelry can be very similar in form to a cottage or farmhouse, with space for eating and drinking downstairs, and bedrooms above. It became the Falkland Arms in honour of Lucius Cary, Lord Falkland, a cultivated aristocrat who was a friend to poets such as Ben Jonson and Edmund Waller, whom he entertained at Great Tew Manor in the 17th century. Falkland was killed in the Civil War but his name lives on among literary scholars and drinkers at this pub. The accommodation now spills over into the thatched cottage next door, a building that is typical of the style of Great Tew, which was developed as a model estate village around the time that horticulturalist, writer, and designer John Claudius Loudon worked there in 1809–11. The blend of dark evergreens, yellowish-brown ironstone, thatched roofs, Gothic porches, and curving lanes is the perfect Picturesque setting, drawing in travellers on the road between Chipping Norton and Banbury who might otherwise pass the village by.

Brewery signs enliven the walls of many an inn and pub. Some are painted on to embellish the flat surface of bricks or tiles. Others are examples of ceramic art.

A brewer's dray delivers to the Waggon and Horses, Haddenham, Buckinghamshire, in 1900. This is one of thousands of traditional pubs that disappeared during the 20th century.

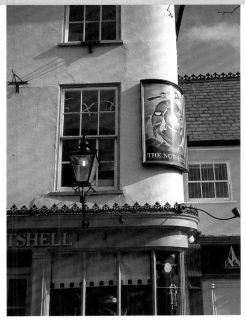

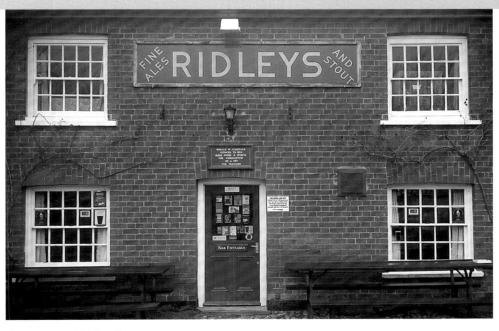

Nutshell, Bury St Edmunds
Suffolk

This claims to be Britain's smallest pub, and at 15 x 7 ft (4.5 x 2 m) it is likely to have few challengers. It is a timber-framed structure that appears to have been stuck on to the adjoining buildings, and that is more or less how it began. In 1857 John Stebbings, a Bury St Edmunds pawnbroker, was expanding his small business empire. He went into the greengrocery business and then decided to sell drink as well. This tiny pub with its pleasant curving frontage is the result. On its modern sign great tits take a drink from a coconut shell – what else?

Compasses, Littley Green
Essex

Pub architecture at its simplest is exemplified by the Compasses. Once more, the form is basically domestic. As with many such buildings, it is easy to believe that this one started out as a private house before becoming a public one. And the ingredients, red-brick walls with white sash windows, are unpretentious to say the least. It is all set off by the signage, a job done here by boards screwed to the wall, with lettering that is again admirably simple and a colour scheme in which the green brewery sign mirrors the green door. We expect a simple, welcoming interior with a tiled floor and

that is what we get, for in a good pub, the label on the bottle should tell us all we need to know about the contents. From small-paned sash windows to neatly bonded bricks the Compasses is so unremarkable that most passers-by must ignore it – supposing, that is, that many passers-by come to this quiet bit of Essex. But like many a country pub, it is an example of an ordinary building that repays more than a casual glance.

A delightful variant on the hanging sign is the plaster plaque. This example at the Rising Sun, Wellingborough, Northamptonshire, is brightly painted and framed in a surround with a curving top that exactly contains the corona of orange rays. The sign provides both visual stimulation and eye-catching publicity on its corner site.

See also
Vernacular houses, 110
Early inns, 308

The pub comes of age

Alcohol brought social problems as well as pleasures. Cheap gin, combined with a tax that made beer expensive, sent many of the poor off the rails in the early 19th century, and the government responded with the 1830 Beer Act, which abolished the tax and allowed anyone with a two-guinea licence to sell beer. Not only beer houses (selling beer only) but also larger licensed premises flourished and the Victorian era became the heyday of the pub. A host of new decorative resources (especially the combination

Larrik, Crawford Place
London

Corner sites were favoured by publicans because potential drinkers could see their establishment from several directions. This corner pub advertises its presence with elaborate gables (Queen Anne Dutch style, but with extra elaborations concealing chimneys behind) and a magnificent bow window, breaking out from the doorway like a clam shell and culminating in a bell-shaped cupola with a large ball finial. Features such as this were not unusual in the more ambitious pubs of the late Victorian building boom. They take the architecture of contemporary houses and mansion flats and give it an extra joyous showy twist or two.

Philharmonic
Liverpool

Named for the nearby concert hall, the Philharmonic was designed by virtuoso pub architect Walter W Thomas for local brewer Robert Cain. Behind a façade of stepped gables and ogee-shaped domes, the interior is the quintessence of bar design of the very end of the 19th century, a shrine to drinking. Thomas and a group of designers from the city's School of Architecture and Applied Arts ran the gamut of interior decoration: repoussé copper panels, decorative plasterwork, brasswork, tiles, frosted-glass lampshades, heraldic glass, the eagle over the clock – and behind the scenes some of the best sanitary ware in Liverpool.

The wall tiling in the Philharmonic is especially notable. It covers a range from a Classical egg-and-dart frieze to a cable moulding and a kind of stylised foliage that seems to come from the Arts and Crafts tradition. Above are wall coverings in a floral pattern that comes from Art Nouveau and another that suggests William Morris. It is a bizarre mixture, but it works in the context of an interior that displays such a joy in rich decoration from every available source.

Two examples of Victorian pub tiling show Classical friezes from the Philharmonic in Liverpool and fishing birds from the Old Bell, St Bride's Avenue, London. Firms such as Simpson, Doulton, and Burmantoft supplied tiles, either painted or with relief decoration.

of engraved glass and gas lighting) gave city pubs their characteristic stamp and decorative fragments – windows engraved with 'smoke room' or 'parlour', patches of riotous tilework – remain to enliven many a pub otherwise altered beyond recognition.

Black Friar, Queen Victoria Street London

This city pub takes superb advantage of its corner site, which is fittingly enough opposite Blackfriars Station. It was originally a Victorian pub of 1875, but it was made over in a new style in the early years of the 20th century. Pub enthusiasts get angry these days at makeovers, but the Black Friar was in the hands of Arts and Crafts architect H Fuller Clark. Clark installed the sculpture of the friar, and in fact there are images of friars all over the interior, pointing the way to the different bars, preparing drinks, and acting as if they have had one too many.

Chequered Skipper, Ashton Northamptonshire

From the same period as Liverpool's Philharmonic comes the Chequered Skipper, a pub in a model village built in 1900 by local landlord Charles Rothschild of the great banking family. The building is just as much at home in its locality as the Philharmonic, being built in a vernacular style of stone and thatch, with just enough in the way of curving roofs and dormers to give it a Picturesque air. The pub, which takes its name from a rare local butterfly, is part of a wider scheme in which a landlord showed that he could do things properly – cottages with bathrooms and an electricity supply, delivered to the village by concealed underground wires.

Settlement (formerly the Skittles) Letchworth, Hertfordshire

The Arts and Crafts style, with its plunging roofs and tall chimneys, was chosen for the Skittles in the garden city of Letchworth to create a pub that blended in with the surrounding domestic architecture. But the Skittles was not famous for its architecture but for being the pub without alcohol – locals voted to have a 'dry' pub where they could relax, enjoy pub games such as billiards, and drink hot chocolate, Bovril, or lemonade. This curious anomaly still remained when in 1923 the building became the Settlement, an adult education centre, while the Bovril drinking carried on at another venue until the 1950s.

This beautiful pierced copper sign is one of a host of telling details at the Black Friar, in which period letter forms with bulging, rounded letters fittingly mirror full-figured friars.

See also

Arts and Crafts houses, 156
The art of display, 200
From tavern to pub, 310
Hospitals, 320

Hotels

Many inns became hotels when the landlord added some luxurious public rooms – the Lion Hotel in Shrewsbury, for example, acquired an elegant ballroom in the late 1770s and many others followed, some adding upmarket exterior features such as porticoes. In spite of this added luxury, many hotels still looked like inns, with their courtyards and organic extensions. But the Victorian building boom brought countless purpose-built hotels – for business travellers, railway users, and visitors to the seaside.

Swan Hotel, Southwold
Suffolk

Southwold was a fishing and local trading centre in the 17th and 18th centuries. When there was a fire in the town in 1659, the main inn, the Swan was soon rebuilt. At some point during the next century or so, the Swan made the transformation from inn to hotel, providing upgraded and more luxurious accommodation that was enthusiastically taken up when Southwold became a seaside resort in the 19th century. The changes to the building would not have been seismic – a little more comfort and some careful expansion could do the trick. And the expansions, when they came, were done with care and discretion. The white pedimented bays, for example, look Georgian, but were actually added in the 19th century, while the addition to the left was made in 1938. So, like many a country-town hotel, this is a conservative building, built the way it is to fit with the tastes of the locals and the style of the buildings round about.

Swan Hotel, Bedford
Bedfordshire

Overlooking the River Ouse, the Swan was built in 1794 for the 5th Duke of Bedford. The architect was Henry Holland, who had worked at the Duke's vast country house, Woburn Abbey, and went on to design a number of inns and other buildings for his noble client, of which this is one of the grandest and most Classical. The front shows Holland's varied way with window shapes – the semicircular opening in the pediment is a pleasant touch – and plain, unfluted Ionic columns. It makes a fitting frame for the Boer War memorial that now stands in front.

A 'Prince of Wales feathers' sign in the form of a lamp lights guests towards their beds at the Feathers Hotel in Ledbury, Herefordshire, a practical and attractive touch.

These buildings were often huge and designed in a Classical or Renaissance style, chateaux with mansard and pavilion roofs looming over the skylines of Leeds and Scarborough. Gothic hotels were rare until Scott's phantasmagoric Midland Grand showed the way.

This photograph of a bathroom at the Metropole Hotel, London, shows the standard of facilities expected in a luxury establishment in 1914.

John Dower House, Cheltenham
Gloucestershire

This building began life as a hotel, put up in around 1820 to profit from the influx of visitors arriving at the then fashionable spa. Like many of Cheltenham's better buildings, it is faced in ashlar and adorned with wrought iron, and the interior in 1827 was luxurious enough to attract Princess Adelaide of Saxe-Meiningen, the future queen of William IV. The proprietors put up these beautiful royal arms above the Ionic portico and they have remained there ever since. But the building did not continue as a hotel for long after the Princess's visit – it has since been a police station and, more recently, offices.

Grand Hotel, Scarborough
North Yorkshire

This vast hotel dominates the coastal town of Scarborough. It was completed in 1867 to the design of Cuthbert Brodrick, architect of various other monumental Yorkshire structures, such as Leeds Town Hall. The high mansard roofs and truncated domes give the building a continental flavour: Mixed Renaissance was the Victorian label for the style. But the main impression is of sheer size – it was originally supposed to have had 365 bedrooms, 52 chimneys, and 12 floors, although such figures are apt to be adjusted to make a plausible myth. The hotel cost around £66,000 to build and the lavish interiors include a huge sweeping staircase.

Midland Grand Hotel, St Pancras
London

The train shed at St Pancras Station is fronted by the grandest of station hotels, designed by George Gilbert Scott, designer of the Albert Memorial among others, in the most eclectic and extrovert Gothic in 1866. It makes the most of a difficult site, turning the corner of Euston and Midland Roads with a collection of turrets, spires, and stepped gables that must have beggared even Victorian belief. The combination of polychrome brick and marble shafts, together with swanky features such as the clock towers in Big Ben style, exude richness. But the fashion did not last. Soon hotels such as the Savoy were offering greater sophistication and better plumbing.

The interior decoration in the Midland Grand Hotel at St Pancas is lavish, especially in public areas such as the staircase. Heraldry, depictions of the virtues, and other subjects catch the eye with their colours, which are still bright.

THE ROYAL
TAL FOR CHI

Royal Waterloo Hospital, London

BUILDINGS FOR CARING AND CONFINEMENT

Hospitals and prisons are our crisis buildings, designed to hold large numbers of people in a controlled environment until they are cured of their disease or have served their due term of imprisonment. This similarity of purpose means that there are architectural similarities between the two building types – the provision of a similar mix of communal and separate spaces, the use of devices allowing inmates to be observed by staff, and the common prioritising of practicality over decoration.

But the parallels have not always been so close. The prison has its origins in the medieval lock-up, a small building where wrongdoers could be held for short periods. Hospitals, by contrast, began in monasteries and in charitable institutions – almshouses and the like – set up to care for those in need. In the Middle Ages there were hundreds of such institutions, known variously as hospitals, spitals, houses of alms, or colleges, and many were indistinguishable from monasteries. Some were isolated leper hospitals, others were in towns and cared for the sick and aged.

From the 17th century onward, though, there were big changes. The beginnings of modern science, together with the post-dissolution disappearance of monastic infirmaries, led to the beginnings of the modern hospital. There are still remains of some of the 18th-century hospitals, but the real roots of the health service as we know it today lie in the 19th century. With the Victorian period came a burgeoning of varying theories about how to run and design hospitals, together with key advances in medicine. There was also more specialisation, and more hospitals specifically designed to suit different medical disciplines and the needs of different-sized communities.

Many of these buildings were enormous, especially the pavilion hospitals such as London's St Thomas's, built to provide a light, well-ventilated environment for thousands of patients in what Dickens described as a 'great and dirty city'. Such structures were buildings of pride, too, in an age when developments such as antiseptics gave patients better and better chances of survival. The resulting optimism is sometimes expressed in the scale and exuberance of the hospitals' architecture.

With prisons it is in some ways a similar story. Frequent attempts at prison reform were linked with surprisingly optimistic-looking buildings and gradually led to better conditions and to new theories about prison layout. The most famous of these are the reforms of Bedfordshire squire John Howard, who in his 1777 book, *The State of the Prisons*, exposed the barbaric conditions in prisons. Howard advocated healthier gaols, with segregation of the sexes, improved heating and ventilation, and better supervision. Allied to these recommendations are late 18th- and 19th-century attempts to design what they called panopticon prisons, in which cell blocks could be viewed from a central command centre, where the all-seeing governor presided.

There are still many surviving prison wings from this era, but this is hardly accessible architecture. Most of us are aware of prisons because of their entrances, which, in many cases, use either the vocabulary of robust Classicism (rusticated masonry, blank walls, empty niches) or of medieval castle architecture (turrets, battlements, arrow loops) to create an image of safety and security. This is ironic, given that medieval castles on the whole were not prisons – the Middle Ages usually dealt with criminals by corporal punishment, fines, or execution, except in the monasteries, where prisons seem to have been widespread. The later use of Norman-style castle architecture for prisons is a tribute to the enduring power of the Middle Ages and its myths.

Something of the life of those who lived in confinement, though, can be imagined at places such as Lincoln Castle, where a secure chapel with lockable pews is preserved, and at a National Trust property, Southwell Workhouse. The workhouse, which developed after the infamous Poor Law of 1834 as a way of coping with the poor and destitute, was only a little better than a prison. Inmates lived in a harsh, secure environment, men and women were segregated, and the work was hard. Clean brick walls and domestic-looking sash windows conceal this darker side of our heritage.

Almshouses and early hospitals

The first English hospitals of which we have much knowledge were Christian foundations run by monks or priests who were drawn to the work by their ethic of charity, their education, and their possession of holy relics attributed with healing powers. They cared for the aged as well as the sick, and an early hospital could be more like an almshouse than a place of healing. Many of these buildings were simple structures like small houses, some were church-like (with a hall or nave for the patients, a chancel for worship) and

St Cross, Winchester
Hampshire

Bede House, Higham Ferrers
Northamptonshire

In around 1136, Henry of Blois, Bishop of Winchester, founded this hospital, partly to provide a daily meal for 100 poor men, who were also allowed to take away any leftover food. Stew was served up from a 'hundred-men pot' with a 'hundred-men ladle' in the great 'hundred-men's hall' near the entrance gatehouse. In addition there was a brethren's hall, in which the ordinary inmates of the hospital took their meals. In 1443–6 the bishop's hospital was expanded, when it became an almshouse for the former servants of Henry, Cardinal Beaufort and other impoverished men of gentry rank, the 'noble poor'.

Much of the structure of Cardinal Beaufort's time survives with a 'cell' consisting of living room, bedroom, and privy for each inmate. The Beaufort family stamped their identity on the building. Their arms can be found in the spandrels of the entrance arch and a kneeling image of Cardinal Beaufort is set in a niche in the gatehouse. In addition there are carved heads that are said to depict Henry IV, John of Gaunt, and Katherine Swynford, wife of Gaunt and mother of Cardinal Beaufort.

Henry Chichele, Archbishop of Canterbury in the early 15th century and native of Higham Ferrers, founded the Bede House in the 1420s. There were to be 12 bedesmen all over 50 years old, and the eldest of them was appointed prior, with the responsibility of ensuring that all the inhabitants obeyed the rules of the house and attended Evensong daily. The form of the building was church-like, with a main hall divided by partitions into cubicles and a chapel at one end. The glory of the building remains its two-tone masonry, in which ironstone and grey stone are used in bands in the local manner.

some were large complexes with halls for men and women, a chapel, and various service buildings. As time went by, foundations for the aged increasingly provided separate accommodation for each inmate, and the almshouse we know today evolved.

Carre's Hospital, Sleaford
Lincolnshire

The tradition of the almshouse was still very much alive in the 19th century, when the draconian Poor Laws of 1834 sent the homeless to the workhouse. Life in an almshouse, with the special blend of personal space and communal life that it brought, was far preferable, and places in such charitable institutions were eagerly sought. Many towns had their benefactors, and many, such as Sleaford, were lucky to find a family that would found a grammar school as well as an almshouse. Carre's Hospital began in 1636, 32 years after the school, and by 1830 it was due for a rebuild. Using a Tudor-Gothic style, H E Kendall

took the hospital into the 19th century. It is built of creamy limestone, which is also the material of Oxford colleges, and the building's strong roof line, with castellated parapet and tall Tudor-style chimneys, gives the hospital some of the grandeur of Oxford and Cambridge college buildings. This is an effect that is enhanced by a Perpendicular chapel with high window and crocketed pinnacles. But the little stone porches add a more friendly, domestic note, making the place look more like the refuge for retirement that it is.

Christian Union Almshouses, Crawford Place
London

Many almshouses of the 19th century had a Christian connection and included religious clauses in their regulations. The Christian Union Almshouses, for example, were controlled by a charity set up in 1832. The houses were meant to accommodate 60 people of 60 years old or more. The inmates were to be Protestants, and had to have an income of at least 4s 6d per week. Single men and widowers were not admitted. Those who fitted the bill took advantage of accommodation in this neo-Classical building in central London. Rules and regulations notwithstanding, it was an attractive alternative to the workhouse.

House numbers at the Christian Union Almshouses are painted within a smart shield, a fancifully Gothic detail on this Classical column.

See also

Hospitals

The dissolution of the monasteries in the 15th century left England short of hospitals and there were still gaps in the late 17th century when, looking to the more impressive provision in Europe, the crown began to build big military hospitals in London at Greenwich and at Chelsea. Local hospitals, by contrast, were usually supplied by charitable institutions.

Their buildings grew as time and money permitted and often had quite haphazard plans as physicians and builders learned what was needed. Things changed in the Victorian period. A rapidly rising population and the pressing need to treat a range of diseases from tuberculosis to mental disorders meant that hundreds of hospitals were built during

Guy's Hospital, Southwark London

Thomas Guy, who had grown rich selling South Sea stocks, founded his hospital to care for the sick, especially those, such as the lunatic and incurable, who were not admitted to nearby St Thomas's Hospital. Thomas Dance designed the original buildings in 1722. He ranged the wards around a double courtyard – a layout that reflected St Thomas's and innumerable older colleges and almshouses. But if it looked traditional, Guy's was larger than normal – the idea was to treat up to 400 patients at a time, and the grandeur of Dance's buildings and the later entrance by Richard Jupp reflected this ambition.

St John's Hospital, Bracebridge Heath Lincolnshire

Part of the 19th-century boom in hospital building was in response to the need for institutions to care for the mentally ill. Started in 1849 and repeatedly extended over the decades, St John's is typical of the hundreds of 19th-century hospitals for the mentally ill. The original design was supervised by the county surveyor, for this was originally the County Pauper Lunatic Asylum. The style he chose is the early Victorian idea of Palladian, so the centre bays have venetian windows, heavy quoins, and triangular pediments. The plan is a series of pavilions, sprawling over a huge site and overlooked by a tower like an Italian campanile.

By building in sections like this, and keeping the structure low-rise, the architects stopped the asylum being too overwhelming. The pavilion hospital was thought to have health advantages too. Pavilion wings were built with windows on either side of the ward so that there was good ventilation, which the Victorians saw as vital for health. So it was not just hospitals for the mentally ill that were built on a pavilion plan. Many of the larger infirmaries and sanatoria were built along the same lines, sometimes on a large scale, as in London's St Thomas's Hospital.

The colonnaded courtyard at the heart of the old Guy's Hospital is still sometimes an oasis of quiet.

the Victorian period. New developments in medicine and nursing, from the lessons of Florence Nightingale's work in the Crimea to advances in anaesthesia and antisepsis, gave patients more hope. And from the early 19th century, local boards of health brought increased organisation to the building and running of hospitals. All this resulted in an explosion of hospital building. Cities gained huge new pavilion hospitals. Cottage hospitals were built to serve smaller communities, and sufferers from infectious diseases were isolated in sanatoria.

Mundesley Sanatorium, Mundesley Norfolk

This remarkable building was part of a wave of hospitals built in the late 19th and early 20th centuries to treat tuberculosis. It is said to have been designed by its founder, Dr F W Burton-Fanning, and was built in 1899 by Boulton & Paul, producers of temporary wooden buildings. The style was no doubt intended to recall the chalets amongst the forests of Switzerland where rich sufferers of tuberculosis went for treatment in the fragrant, pine-scented atmosphere. The generous, south-facing windows certainly provided plenty of sun and air, held to be good for the disease. Further therapy was provided by little sleeping chalets, which could be turned on wheels away from the wind.

Royal Waterloo Hospital London

Covered in ceramic decoration with inscriptions declaring its name, its voluntary status, and its royal patrons, this hospital seems to typify Edwardian optimism. Originally built in 1823 as a charitable hospital for women and children, it was completely rebuilt in 1903–5. The layout, with multiple loggias, was by architect M S Nicholson and much of the ceramic decoration came from Doulton's Lambeth factory, not far up the river from the Waterloo area. Some of this ornament – notably the green-cladding of the entrance porch – was donated by the Doulton family themselves. The tilework continued inside, too. The children's ward, for example, had tile panels with nursery-rhyme subjects which were removed to St Thomas's Hospital after this building closed. The optimism comes not just from the decoration but from the notion, which must be embodied in the design, that the fresh, health-giving air implied by the long balconies could in any way be had in the smoggy and soot-ridden atmosphere of central London. The hospital closed in 1936, after which the building became a campus of the Schiller University.

See also

The pub comes of age, 312
Almshouses and early hospitals, 318

Prisons

Inmates did not expect to spend long in a medieval lock-up, but when similar cramped and insanitary conditions were used for long-term imprisonment, the result was inhuman. The man who publicised this was the Bedfordshire squire and High Sheriff, John Howard, who wrote and campaigned for better prisons in the 18th century. Howard found widespread gaol fever and inmates chained and suffocating in stench. He made his discoveries public in his book *The State of the Prisons* (1777) and the campaign for reform began to gain momentum. Reform continued into the 19th century, as more and more offences were dealt with by imprisonment rather than with the death penalty. This led to the

Hexham Old Gaol
Northumberland

The Old Gaol at Hexham was built in 1330–2 and its stone walls, almost uninterrupted by windows, look a picture of medieval maximum security. The interior has been altered but originally had a pair of dour barrel-vaulted rooms on the ground floor, plus single rooms on the two floors above. The only home comfort was a garderobe of the kind found in castles. The gaol is a rare survival and must have been necessary in an area not far south of Hadrian's Wall, where there is a long history of border disputes, raids, and wars.

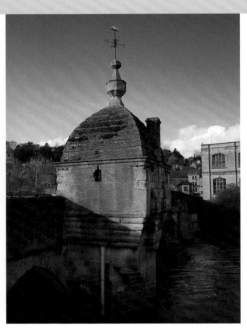

Bradford-on-Avon
Wiltshire

In the Middle Ages, local wrongdoers could be detained in the town or village lock-up, which was usually nothing more than a single secure cell where drunkards dried out, hotheads cooled down, and those accused of more serious crimes awaited an appearance before the magistrate. One of the most famous lock-ups is the Jacobean one on the town bridge in Bradford-on-Avon. This began life in the medieval period as a chapel. The curving pavilion-style stone roof, ball finial, and tiny barred window probably date from the 17th century, when the bridge was refurbished.

Northleach House of Correction
Gloucestershire

This is one of four prisons built in the late 18th century by Sir George Onesiphorous Paul, a local manufacturer and philanthropist. It was originally built around five sides of an octagon, but only the front block remains, which was partially rebuilt in the 19th century. The centre section, in the foreground, contained the keeper's house. A long, almost windowless, wall connects this to the women's wing, its distinctive cross-shaped windows recalling a medieval castle. Since this building ceased to be a prison in the early 20th century it has housed in turn a police station, a museum, and offices.

need for more and larger prisons, and to new ideas about prison design. The philosopher Jeremy Bentham publicised the panopticon, with cells arranged in a circle or polygon surrounding a central observation platform. An alternative was the radial layout, in which wings extended from a central observation point. Theorists also espoused better conditions, for example promoting central heating and running water to benefit the health of prisoners. In the 20th century, prison builders have dropped these complex plans, adopting separate wings, sometimes linked by a spine service building in an arrangement similar to a pavilion hospital.

HMP Leicester
Leicester

This piece of municipal pomp was built by Leicestershire county surveyor, William Parsons, in 1825–8. Many prison architects made a special feature of the gatehouse, conjuring up imagery of castles and creating an appropriate atmosphere of security. The main part of the building is faced with stone (the rest is in cheaper, more utilitarian brick) and the pair of round towers and portcullis get the message across. Inside the gatehouse are cells that were intended for difficult inmates. Behind it was a radially planned complex with six prison wings around a central octagon, from which the governor kept watch.

Harperley Prison Camp
County Durham

Prisoners of war at Harperley and many similar, now demolished, Second World War prison camps, lived in very basic huts. The main thing that drove this rough-and-ready architecture was the need to build quickly, so many camps used a new, prefabricated form of construction. The key element in the system was a concrete post with grooves along the edge. Once the posts were erected, concrete slabs could be slid into the grooves to form the infill. Standard window frames filled gaps between the slabs. Buildings such as this could be put up on a prepared base in a few hours by unskilled labour.

Often it was the prisoners themselves who slotted together the components to make the huts where they were to live. This rough-and-ready architecture is not the only evidence of the prisoners' handiwork at Harperley. The inmates got permission to create a prison theatre, and some of the painted decoration that they created still exists. Remains such as these make Harperley, already one of only a handful of surviving Second World War camps, a very precious survival.

These flat tiles, laid in overlapping courses like bricks, are one of the materials used for infilling the walls of Harperley's prison huts.

WAITING ROOM

Station waiting room, Wansford, Peterborough

BUILDINGS FOR TRANSPORT

With the industrial revolution came a rush of new developments in transport – canals on which the coal for steam engines and furnaces was carried, followed by improved roads and the railways that transformed Victorian Britain. Still later came the motor car and aeroplane, and all these changes have meant that the last two centuries have been a period of unprecedented change in our mobility. A variety of new building types came with these developments: railway stations, signal boxes, airports, hangars, garages, and filling stations. And all sorts of structures, from modest sheds to vast lighthouses, stand tribute to our continuing use of the sea.

Some would deny that some of these buildings are architecture at all: filling stations, for example, are ephemeral and gaudy, and an air of the ephemeral hangs about many of the buildings associated with transport. Petrol stations seem often to be more about advertising than architecture, airports can feel like hastily assembled clusters of cheap buildings, and we even tend to take railway stations for granted. But they are all part of our rich and diverse built environment and even architects of the calibre and inventiveness of Wallis Gilbert and Clough Williams-Ellis designed garages: they would have had no truck with snobbish distinctions between architecture and building.

Look up and around you, and these vibrant buildings engage the eye and mind. Railway stations alone draw on the whole gamut of styles from Gothic to international modern, and speak eloquently about the values and interests of our ancestors, especially those of the Victorian period when most of them were built. This is true most obviously of the giant metropolitan termini, which, with their glass and iron roofs, are acknowledged engineering masterpieces. Their broad single spans are practical, adaptable, and simply breathtaking.

But also memorable are the countless little stations, designed to look like houses or huts and built of humble materials such as wood or brick. Many of these simple and unregarded structures have been sheltering passengers for 150 years. When they were built, they too seemed like advertising hoardings, decked out in the livery of the railway company. Now they are covered in modern signs and their fittings are often the same in Yorkshire as in Cornwall. But much of their Victorian architecture, and some of those early fittings and signs, remain, making these small stations excellent examples of a quality beloved of both planners and travellers – local distinctiveness.

Some of this kind of building is so humble that it is easy to miss except by the most inquisitive of architectural snoopers. The railways have wonderful examples of Victorian working buildings, and thankfully railway preservation societies do a good job restoring and using them. And many humble transport buildings are still in use. Many people walk quickly past fishermen's sheds and net stores on the way to the beach. Yet these simple wooden buildings are as well fitted to their purpose as a modernist factory – and locally distinctive to boot.

Airport buildings, by contrast, are usually built in an up-to-date idiom. There are still a few survivors from the early years of commercial aviation, structures in the Moderne idiom of the 1930s, with strip windows and pale rendered walls. Today, in the era of mass air travel, the emphasis is more on handling large numbers of people, and the results are often anonymous and bland.

The motor industry, too, has mostly shunned traditionalism and its buildings usually want to look modern. London once had many Art Deco and Moderne garages and motor showrooms, such as Wallis Gilbert's Daimler Car Hire Garage, in Herbrand Street, basically an early multi-storey car park with all the design pizzazz of an Odeon cinema. The few such buildings that survive look quaint – and also solid – beside the plastic-faced filling stations where we refuel today. But they still work and probably will go on doing so for years.

And if all this still sounds like nostalgia, take a trip on London's underground. Here, good design has been a watchword for generations. The network's typography, mapping, signs, and station layouts are still the envy of many other capital cities. From the station buildings that sometimes tower above ground, to the deepest platforms on the tube, London's underground truly shows us the way to go.

Small stations

The Victorians built hundreds of small railway stations, often only a few miles apart from one another to make them easy to get to on foot. Their varied styles reflect the financial resources and the tastes of the builders of each line. Some railways built elaborate stations in the *cottage orné* style (some remain in Yorkshire and Bedfordshire). Others, such as the Midland Railway, liked buildings with decorative bargeboards. Some designed simple brick buildings like ordinary houses, or favoured an Italianate or Tudor style. Many of these stations were very simple, providing only a ticket office and some shelter for

Millbrook
Bedfordshire

In the 1840s the railway still seemed an alien force, invading the peace of the countryside with steel and steam. One way to make it fit in better was to design the stations in a 'countrified' style such as the *cottage orné* Picturesque of the Bedford Railway, which blends well with the home counties' scene of villages and trees. Half-timbered walls, steep gables, tall chimneys, and ornate openwork bargeboards make Millbrook (1846) typical. But the colour scheme – white timbers set against darker infill – provides an added surprise, reminding us after all that this is a consciously Picturesque building, not an ancient cottage.

Charlbury
Oxfordshire

This station serves a small town in the northern Cotswolds on the line between Oxford and Worcester. It was built in 1853 on the Oxford, Worcester and Wolverhampton Railway, which was engineered by Isambard Kingdom Brunel. It was a broad-gauge line such as the same engineer's Great Western Railway. The line did not have adequate capital to build the monumental stone stations one might expect in the Cotswolds, so the stations were built of wood. In spite of the unpromising material, Brunel managed to keep to his favoured Italianate style, the round-headed windows surrounded by timber in a different colour.

There is a very shallow-pitched hipped roof covering both the station block itself and the canopies, and the whole station, now restored, produces the pleasing effect of working with economical means. Evocative furnishings such as Great Western Railway platform benches survive to add to the period atmosphere. Charlbury is now the only station on the line where the original wooden building is preserved. Most of the smaller stations on the line have been rebuilt and some have been closed.

On a traditional station awning, valances along the edge were designed to protect waiting passengers from rain, steam, and speeding soot particles. They come in hundreds of different fretwork patterns, an endless delight of repeated shapes. These examples are at Thetford, Norfolk, and at Oakham, Rutland.

the passengers, and if money was tight they might be built of wood or even corrugated iron. Smallest of all were the unmanned halts, with perhaps only the most basic hut on the platform.

Denham Golf Club
Buckinghamshire

The golf club at Denham was founded in 1910 and soon acquired its own station, within walking distance of the fairways and club house. A pair of corrugated metal shelters form a most minimal station. And yet thought went into even these very basic sheds. The curve of their galvanised, hipped roofs goes beyond the utilitarian and creates an effect reminiscent of an oriental temple or pagoda. As the ridges catch the sunlight, one is tempted to describe them, bearing in mind the destination of many of the station's users, as a pair of simple pavilions. In fact they were not only used at this golf club station.

They were made to a standard design, known as the pagoda shelter, that was used in a number of places by the Great Western Railway from about 1904 onwards. It was useful to have a prefabricated module available that could be cheaply installed and sometimes several shelters were used in a row on the same platform.

Rothley
Leicestershire

Rothley was on a line opened in 1899 to form a fast link from Manchester to Marylebone, London. Although the line has gone, this station has been restored as part of a preserved section. The place is full of telling details, such as the covered stairway to the overbridge, glazed for a good view as the passenger rushes for a train, its bricks and cream paintwork lovingly maintained and not so different from the way they were in the early 20th century. Elsewhere there are lots of well-restored details, including good examples of the painted lettering that once made railways treasuries of graphic design.

Town stations

Market towns and smaller industrial settlements usually had smaller stations than major cities, but these were still built to high standards. Frequently there was an effort to make the station fit into the townscape by using local materials, often a concession to those who did not want the dirty, steaming 'iron horse' anywhere near their homes. There were plenty of styles that could be adapted to produce a station that created the required impression of local identity (Tudor or enlarged cottage) or urban gravitas (Gothic or French Renaissance). Fine ironwork or ceramic decoration

Wellingborough
Northamptonshire

The Midland Railway liked its small stations to be built from local materials, often in a cottage-like style. On the Leicester to Hitchin line there are a number of stations in a variety of materials mostly with round-headed Norman-looking windows. Wellingborough, designed by C H Driver in 1857, is one of the finest, the pale arches and carved bargeboards standing out against the red brick. Looking more closely, one can see that the arches, apparently carved with the Norman zigzag motif, are actually made up of alternating pale and dark bricks. The patterns of lozenges and hexagons created by the glazing bars make more patterns of light and dark.

Stamford
Lincolnshire

A stone station for a stone town: silver-grey limestone was the obvious choice for the new station serving the unspoilt stone town of Stamford when the railway came in 1846. Architect Sancton Wood, who also designed Dublin's Kingsbridge (now Heuston) Station, obliged with a neo-Tudor building boasting a rather serious bell turret. Take away the platform awning and it could almost be a manor house. This manorial decorum was commissioned by the Syston & Peterborough Railway, but the Midland took over before the station opened in 1848. The initials SPR are, however, preserved on the weathervane.

Hertford East
Hertfordshire

A county town demanded a large station, with *portes cochères* (drive-through porches) beneath which well-heeled travellers could get out of their carriages in the dry. In 1888, when Hertford station was built, the best style for this seemed to be Free Renaissance, the idiom of numerous town halls and one that could evoke the golden age of the Tudors. The result is an attractive building designed by W N Ashbee (head of the Great Eastern Railway's architectural department), with curvaceous gables, openwork parapets, and lots of brick with stone dressings. The dominant feature though, is the large *porte cochère* with its inviting elliptical arches.

Wellingborough station has beautiful platform awnings supported by slender iron columns and decorated with spiralling fronds of cast-iron foliage. In the wake of the Great Exhibition at the Crystal Palace (1851), the virtuoso effects possible with cast iron were being exploited in buildings great and small during the 1850s.

provided an added touch of quality and ornately shaped valances (different patterns for different lines) added to the effect. Many communities are now rightly fond of the stations that Victorian NIMBYs shunned.

Market Harborough
Leicestershire

Queen Anne, the revivalist style with sash windows, hipped roofs, and tall chimneys, seemed right for the station at Market Harborough, built in 1884. The building was a joint station that saw the Midland Railway collaborate with the London & North Western on its construction. It was partly a case of fitting the station to the town – Market Harborough is a historic town rich in Georgian buildings and the Queen Anne red-brick and stone pilasters harmonise well with these. But this station is not simply a sop to fashion. It is a carefully worked-out design with several delightful details, especially the

little dormer with its curving pediment and brackets, the pale edges setting off the brickwork like a picture frame, and the graceful roof line with its twin leaded finials. The station was restored in the 1970s and is an ornament to town and railway alike.

Great Malvern
Worcestershire

Already well developed as a fashionable spa by the time the railway arrived in 1860, Malvern got the station it deserved, a highly decorated concoction in purplish Malvern stone with French Gothic details. It was designed by E W Elmslie, who was also working on two hotels in the town at the time. When Elmslie's station buildings were finally complete in 1862, passengers could marvel at the random rubble masonry like vertical crazy paving and the crisply carved pale stone dressings – just the kind of visual environment they would find in their hotel.

One of the chief glories of Great Malvern station is its ironwork. In all there are 40 columns holding up the awnings, each with a different iron capital depicting foliage. The leaves of Malvern are a fitting tribute to the laurels and pines of the town's gardens and parks. Other iron structures include a built-in weighing machine.

See also

Grand stations

To serve larger towns and cities, the railway companies built stations that were one step down in size from the great termini. These buildings usually lacked the vast arching train sheds of London's stations at Paddington or King's Cross, often featuring platform roofs supported by the buildings and rows of iron columns. The structures were often monumental – Classical designs by architects such as Sir William Tite or Francis Thompson were favoured. Alternatively they could make their mark with extravagant

Monkwearmouth
County Durham

Although not a large station, Monkwearmouth was built in the most grandiose of Classical styles, with a big Ionic portico, to a design by Thomas Moore. The reason for the grandeur was that the station was built to mark the election of George Hudson as MP for Sunderland in 1845. Hudson, known as the 'Railway King', by this time owned around half the track in England and was in the process of becoming the first railway millionaire. Monkwearmouth (now a museum) opened as his noble memorial in 1848, but seven years later Hudson was forced to leave the country in shame as his business empire, built on dodgy dealings, collapsed.

Eastbourne
East Sussex

Eastbourne grew with the railway and the station grew with the town. The station opened in 1866 as part of the London, Brighton & South Coast Railway. There had been a station at nearby Polegate before, and as Eastbourne grew it got its own branch line. The buildings were expanded 20 years later and, as the town continued to grow as a resort, again in the 1930s. The original double front still impresses, and is more dramatic than a visitor might expect who comes to Eastbourne thinking that the town is all buttoned-up respectability. The frontage has as a corner focal point a clock tower corbelled out of the wall, its heavy cornices and coat of arms proclaiming its importance. On either side is a pair of very different roofs: one is a pavilion roof covered with fish-scale tiles, the other a hipped roof above a rectangular clerestory to throw light on to the concourse below. Many of these motifs are drawn from the French Renaissance style, but the building is too eclectic and full of incident to pin down. Better by far to enjoy it in all its diversity.

Time is of the essence on the railway, and the train companies often built clocks into their stations. These examples come from Bath, Somerset, and Scarborough, North Yorkshire.

Birds, fruit, and fish whose tails seem to turn into foliage, are some of the motifs on the wall plaques at Leicester London Road, as if the railway is meant to transport one into a world of mythical beasts.

details and decoration, such as some of the stations on the Midland or South-Western Railways. Either way, these stations were effective advertisements for the railways that they served.

Leicester London Road
Leicester

For his 1892 rebuild of Leicester London Road station, Charles Trubshaw used brick and terracotta to create an imposing impression – here was a station that was worthy of prosperous, late 19th-century Leicester. A row of urns on the parapet, together with the domed clock tower, added to the impression. But most striking of all are the entrances and exits – separate ones for arrivals and departures, each with an arch tall and wide enough for the largest Victorian carriage or omnibus. But it was not all front. The station's public areas were designed to give plenty of circulation space, well lit by glass roofs.

Manchester Piccadilly
Manchester

This major Manchester station has a long history of change and modernisation. Originally called London Road, the station was opened by the Manchester & Birmingham Railway in 1842. It underwent various 19th-century extensions before a rebuild in 1866, when it acquired a trussed-arch roof that was 680 ft (207 m) in length. Further arch spans were added in 1881 to make a covered area some 280 ft (85 m) wide. There was a major remodelling in 1960, when the station was renamed Manchester Piccadilly, and yet more modernisation in 1998–2000. As this history suggests, the fabric of the station is of various

dates and styles. The concourse is modern, but there are still train sheds of the 1880s with their cast-iron columns and just one of the Victorian warehouses and goods stores, a seven-storey warehouse of 1876, survives nearby. There is also a fine new train shed, its roof shown in this picture, which is very much in the spirit of the old ones.

The entrance and exit arches at Leicester London Road are all signed with ornate Victorian lettering through which weaves spiralling foliage decoration.

See also

The great termini

As the railway boom accelerated through the 1850s and 1860s, the railway companies began to build great terminal stations at the ends of their lines. Since many routes ended in the capital, lots of these stations were built in London, where most of them are still serving travellers today. The largest have enormous arching train sheds roofed in glass on an iron framework that were the product of collaboration between architects and engineers who used the latest Victorian technology. They have, with their arches and columns not to mention their size and grandeur, inevitably been compared to cathedrals.

York Station
York

Bristol Temple Meads
Bristol

Thomas Prosser designed York Station for the North Eastern Railway and it was completed by William Peachey in 1877, immediately impressing travellers with its spacious quartet of iron roof spans sitting on rows of Corinthian columns and complemented by colourful NER coats of arms. A first arrival at York is unforgettable because of the way the roof spans curve gently, making the already impressive engineering of columns and trusses into a masterpiece of precision. The light can create dramatic shadows and highlights as the sun shines through the roof, illuminating the wedges and slivers of glass between the dark trusses.

It is worth walking to the ends of the platforms because this is where the effect of light and shadow is strongest of all. Here there are sweeping glass end-screens that add to the pattern of line and light. The structure of these screens consists of three curving transoms, which follow the line of the roof, together with a multitude of radiating glazing bars. The city of York has many other joys for railway enthusiasts because it is also the home of the National Railway Museum, a vast collection containing everything from station signs to Queen Victoria's railway carriage.

This station was begun by Isambard Kingdom Brunel in 1840 and extended between 1865 and 1878, when the architect was Sir Matthew Digby Wyatt. Wyatt's golden stone front forms the station entrance and is still the scene of bustling activity. Wyatt adopted a turreted and pinnacled late Gothic style that owes something to French Gothic and something to English Perpendicular. The central tower was originally topped by a truncated spire and the pinnacles at each corner of the tower were crocketed. These elaborations were removed during a refurbishment in the 1930s, but the tower is still a striking city landmark.

With long-distance railways came the standardised time needed for a consistent timetable, and clocks began to appear on station platforms everywhere. This electric clock with heraldic adornment is from York. Smaller stations usually had off-the-shelf models with wooden cases.

The train shed in the old part of Temple Meads station at Bristol, with its hammer-beam roof, is no longer used by travellers.

Kings Cross
London

The first large London terminus was Kings Cross (1852), designed by Lewis Cubitt, the architect member of the great London family of builders and developers. The frontage is simple and functional, with a pair of arches that match the ends of the double-span train-shed roof behind. Lest this composition seemed overly simple (and in part it resembles the functional monumentality of the power stations of the 1920s) Cubitt added a little clock tower to the skyline. The lower part of the façade, which originally featured a row of arches, has long been obscured by modern buildings containing booking halls, shops and other paraphernalia.

Paddington
London

The Great Western Railway's London terminus was built in 1854 to replace a temporary station that had been put up nearby 16 years earlier. The great train shed, with its three sweeping iron-and-glass roofs (the picture shows the central one) was the brainchild of Isambard Kingdom Brunel and Sir Matthew Digby Wyatt. Engineer and architect produced a harmonious structure, the iron ribs running down to paired braced girders that rest on dozens of slender columns. Brunel's roof looks beautifully light, an effect enhanced by the decorative holes punched through the ribs. Wyatt's decoration shows great flair, especially the curling ironwork in the end screen.

An unusual feature of Paddington's train shed is that it has a pair of transepts running at right-angles to the line. These open up the space in the train shed in a way that is virtually unique and must have reminded Victorians of the Crystal Palace. Their purpose was to house machinery that was intended to move locomotives from one line to another. This machinery was never installed, but the transepts remain to make this one of the most spacious of the great termini.

See also

Arcades, 196
Hotels, 314
Small stations, 326
Town stations, 328
Grand stations, 330
Modern stations, 334
Greenhouses, 352

Modern stations

Our railway system is the product of the Victorian era, and its story since has been mainly one of contraction. But a number of new stations were built in the 20th century, some as upgrades of earlier ones, others for new lines or new towns. One or two 1930s stations, combining the white concrete of modernism with details that remind one of early radio sets, stand out. Another building period was the 1960s and 1970s, when fresh ideas about passenger handling and facilities failed in many cases to generate buildings

Surbiton
Surrey

Commuters returning to this leafy London suburb in the 1930s must have felt the shock of the new – Surbiton station was the first outbreak of modernism on the overground. It was the result of a modernisation campaign on the Southern Railway, with electrification of the lines and the appearance from 1937 of dazzling white stations. Buildings such as these perhaps owed more to the Moderne style of recent cinemas than to the pared-down architecture of hard-core modernist architects such as Le Corbusier. Motifs such as the horizontal ribbing at the top of the tower act almost like go-faster stripes, suggesting that the railway is clean, new, and efficient.

Harlow Town
Essex

Harlow was a new town, developed through the 1950s, and its station is in keeping with this newness, very much in the tradition of post-war modernism, but neither as dull nor as inhuman as that might suggest. The structure shows how post-war architects often liked to think of buildings in terms of overlapping slabs. Here there are three slabs, one extending over the track and two running below it. The two main slabs are constructed from bands of pale brick, dark green fascia boarding, and strip windows and these elements work together to produce an effect that is simple and expresses the function of the different parts of the building – the upper slab containing a bridge over the platforms, the middle one lighting the booking hall, and so on. This all works well from a distance, creating a geometrical pattern by day and looking good when lit up at night. Close to, details such as the careful lettering enhance the building further.

Architecture meets the bicycle shed: simple sans serif lettering shows the way to the cycle racks at Harlow Town station.

of distinction. But today architects are turning to transport with new interest and an awareness that a high-tech style and attention to the quality of materials can produce inspiring structures – some recent light-rail stations augur well for the future.

Coventry
Warwickshire

British Railways felt bomb-damaged Coventry deserved a special effort when they built its new station in 1961–2. So the building was well funded and the high-quality materials that are needed for the pared-back modernist style of the 1960s to work were made available. From a distance, it does seem rather forbidding, but once one gets near the entrance, the timber ceilings and white-tiled walls look more inviting. There is a spacious, high booking hall, and the signs have been praised for their clarity – special care was taken because this was a pilot scheme for a new system, also to be used in motorway service stations.

Banbury
Oxfordshire

The railway came to this Oxfordshire town in 1850 and by the 1940s, the original fabric of the station was shaking worryingly as fast trains went through. But the war, and post-war austerity, prevented the necessary repair work, the building deteriorated further, and the frail, old roof finally had to be removed in 1953 for safety reasons. So in the late 1950s, a much-needed station reconstruction was begun, one of the first such rebuilds to take place after the end of the Second World War, with a bright, new station emerging from the scaffolding in 1959. While the engineers were at work they lengthened the platforms as well as building an integrated footbridge and lift towers. The most striking part of the station, though, was the entrance building, a clean-looking, modern composition incorporating a great deal of glass together with prefabricated panels and brickwork. It has worn well.

Trackside buildings

The railways spawned a host of buildings, from trackside warehouses to plate-layers' huts, that were used mainly by railway staff and were scarcely noticed by passengers. Many of these are still unnoticed or inaccessible. Those that are on the beaten track are mostly visible from the outside, where fine Victorian brickwork or even early advertising lettering may be there to admire. Perhaps the most common of these buildings is a type unique to the railways – the signal box.

Signal box, Culgaith
Cumbria

Water tower, Kemble
Gloucestershire

Although signalling is now more about electronic displays and switches than levers and mechanics, many of the old signal boxes remain, especially on the quieter lines away from intercity routes. They can often be seen from level crossings as well as from passing trains. Signal-box design evolved from the 1860s onwards and the classic layout has a first-floor operations room with windows around at least three sides and a locking room below. Occasionally a taller box was built, to give the signal operator a long view where a main line and branch line joined. Some are brick buildings with a pitched roof and ornate bargeboards.

Many, such as this one at Culgaith on the Settle & Carlisle line, have wooden walls and a hipped roof. A wooden box lends itself to paintwork in the livery of its railway company – this one is in the colours of the Midland Railway and many other early liveries are preserved on wooden signal boxes around the country. Railway preservation societies have long recognised the value and interest of these once ignored trackside structures, and a number of early signal boxes are now listed buildings.

Steam engines needed water, and water towers were a frequent sight on the early railways. This one is on Brunel's Great Western line of 1840–5, and the vast cast-iron tank and pillars (with an attractive interlacing circle pattern on the beam beneath the tank) speak the structural language of the terminus at Paddington rather than that of the neighbouring Cotswold-stone station. Originally fed by a spring that was found during the construction of the station, the tank was big enough to supply both the village and the GWR works in Swindon, about 10 miles away.

Rows of levers control the signals in a traditional signal box such as Culgaith.

Many of these are unassuming but very durable. Design variations favoured by the different Victorian railway companies can still be seen from Cornwall to the north-east.

Goods shed, Wellingborough
Northamptonshire

The goods shed at Wellingborough is designed using the same brickwork as the main station, with dark and light bricks used to produce patterns above the doors and windows and in the arches. There is also a brick dentil course beneath the eaves. All this makes a utilitarian building special and draws the whole station complex together visually – a tribute to the design thinking of the Midland Railway and its architect C H Driver. The interior of this building is interesting, too. It contains a pair of original cast-iron hand cranes. These impressive machines are built in as part of the shed's structure.

Coalyard store, Rothley
Leicestershire

Many trackside buildings are described as 'sheds' and there is an enormous range of such structures. The largest are the engine sheds, where locomotives were maintained and serviced. These were usually long, rectangular buildings, with track running through them, but sometimes they are roundhouses, incorporating a turntable. These are by necessity large buildings, but smaller trackside sheds can be just as interesting. This simple brick coalyard store, for example, is one of the preserved railway buildings at Rothley, a station on the line between Manchester and Marylebone,

London. Old stations were often surrounded by such working buildings, slate-roofed brick sheds of little or no architectural distinction. This one is made into a visual delight by the lettering across wall and door, a memory of a business from the early 20th century that relied on the railway to transport its goods. The lettering is everything it should be – simple sans serif capitals given period flavour by the superior letters in 'Ltd' and the inevitable square full stop.

Cast-iron signs were everywhere on the Victorian railway and, although most have found their way into the hands of collectors and railway enthusiasts, some still survive to warn passengers of the dangers of crossing the line. The letters could be picked out in railway livery or plain black and white.

See also

Underground stations

London's underground system has become famous for good design. Attention to everything visual on the underground began with the work of architect Leslie Green, designer of the oxblood-tile-clad stations that can still be found all over the capital. But the design ethic found its greatest advocate in

Frank Pick, who eventually became the managing director of the Underground Group and put design at the forefront of the organisation in the 1920s and 1930s. Pick commissioned calligrapher Edward Johnston to create the display typeface still used on the tube. He also worked with architect Charles

Kentish Town

Covered in rich oxblood-coloured tiles, the underground stations designed by Leslie Green are still instantly recognisable. Green, architect to the Underground Electric Railways Company of London, created a 'corporate identity' for London's underground between 1903 and 1908, before anyone had heard of the term. Kentish Town, opened in 1907, displays the arched windows (with egg and dart moulding and tile 'keystone'), tiled station name, and tiles typical of Green's stations. The blue sign is recent, but it bears the roundel that has become the symbol of the underground. Roundel signs with a red disc and blue name board appeared in 1908.

The disc was replaced by a red ring in the 1920s, one of the design innovations commissioned by Frank Pick from Edward Johnston. Now single-colour versions of the symbol are often used and they are still instantly recognisable. Below ground the majority of the passages and stairways at this station still bear some of the design symbolism of the early years – they are tiled in the original cream and brown colour scheme of the Charing Cross, Euston & Hampstead Railway.

Chalk Farm

This 1907 station is another of Leslie Green's designs that retains many original features. The glazed faience tiling, chosen by Green because it was cheap, quick to install, and allowed decoration and mouldings to be fitted easily, here covers a corner building. Where the station turns the corner, the tiling is especially ornate, with pediment, scroll brackets, cornices, and pilasters all done in oxblood. Tile firms such as Burmantoft's, who supplied the covering, boasted that their products were appearing all over London – Burmantoft's even gave their oxblood tiles an up-market French name: they became 'sang de boeuf'. Edward Johnston's 'UNDERGROUND' motif, with its pecked lettering, also lent itself to reproduction in tiled form.

This is the most familiar form of the underground's roundel sign, with the red ring – a design described by Edward Johnston as the 'bull's-eye'. Here the station name is edged with a moulded surround like a picture frame.

Holden, who designed London Transport's headquarters at St James's Park and epoch-making modernist stations on the Piccadilly Line. The meticulous attention to detail in the recent Jubilee Line extension stations is a fitting tribute to the work of Pick and Holden.

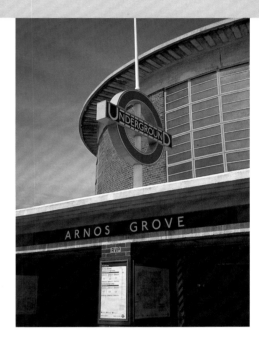

Kentish Town

A coherent colour scheme was an important feature of the underground network almost from the beginning. This station was opened in 1907 as part of the Charing Cross, Euston & Hampstead Railway, and had cream-tiled walls picked out in brown. (Brown is now the colour of the Bakerloo Line.) Part of the tilers' job was to include the station name, in big capitals six tiles high, on the platform walls. These remain at some stations, although here they have been replaced by the modern strip signs just above eye level.

Golders Green

By 1911 the Charing Cross, Euston & Hampstead Railway had reached beyond Hampstead to Golders Green, where its station was at ground level. When the station was built there were few houses here, but the presence of a transport link stimulated development and in a few years, many were benefiting from the fast trains to central London. The architecture of this ground-level station is very much drawn from that of the overground railways, with its iron structure and fancy valances. But some details seem designed for the underground, such as the seat backs that reflect the shape of the roundel sign.

Arnos Grove

The work of Charles Holden, consulting architect to the Underground Group and then to London Transport between the 1920s and early 1950s, transformed the underground network. He designed many modern stations, most famously on the Piccadilly Line but also on the Northern. They are known for their tall, spacious ticket halls with big, metal-framed windows, modern ticket booths with curving corners, and glazed waiting rooms with extensive views out so that passengers could see their trains approaching. Whether working in brick, concrete, or the rich woods of some of the booking halls, Holden identified the underground with the best modern design.

Coastal buildings

England's seaside towns are places of work as well as of leisure. They have a host of buildings, such as boathouses, net stores, and sail lofts, that are purely practical and often unremarkable, but which, with their white paint and, often, weatherboarding, make the coastal scene what it is. Now and then they also exhibit one of those flashes of inspiration that add to local distinctiveness and make the seaside special. The unique netshops at Hastings and the boat-hull sheds of Lindisfarne are two examples.

Net stores, Hastings
East Sussex

The net stores or deezes of Hastings, slim towers like etiolated sheds on the foreshore near the 1854 fishermen's church, are unique. Since the 17th century the fishermen of the town have hauled their boats up here (there is no harbour), and dried their nets in these buildings, which are weatherboarded and tarred against the elements. These exceptional little structures are all individually built – such oddities could not come from a sectional building catalogue – and are all different heights. They were rebuilt in the 20th century after a fire and so carry on into the 21st, the most distinctive buildings in the town.

Huer's House, Newquay
Cornwall

Cornwall is not all neat terraces of fishing-village houses – this building in Newquay is very different from the usual local house, but still has a close connection with the sea. One of the most important industries in 19th-century Newquay was pilchard fishing, but the pilchards came and went unpredictably in their large shoals and fishermen could often launch their boats in vain. The solution was to employ a huer, or lookout, who stood watch at this house. The house is naturally dominated by its little lookout tower, providing a vantage point to scan the sea. But the curving walls, battlements and diamond-shaped openings of the building's lower portion are just as striking, making this Cornish curiosity a notable example of seaside picturesque. The huer would scan the sea for the fish, looking for a tell-tale reddening of the water, indicating a shoal of pilchards. As soon as he spotted the reddening, he would make a great cry of 'Heva, heva!', and the boats of Newquay would launch in pursuit, seine nets at the ready.

Spindly sans serif letters send out a simple message on a fish hut at Dunwich, Suffolk: it does what it says on the wall.

They are beautifully simple, ingenious, perfectly adapted to their purpose, and made with the most economical of materials – local heroes in the world of buildings.

Fishermen's sheds, Lindisfarne
Northumberland

This windswept coastal scene looks like a stage set for Benjamin Britten's opera *Peter Grimes*, but it is part of the Northumberland coast, not the Suffolk world of Britten, that is pictured here. With roofs made in the ogee shape of upturned boat hulls (these examples started out as actual boats), these fishermen's sheds on the shore of Holy Island have an unmistakeable nautical feel. Long and low, they hug the landscape, although their pitch-black colouring hardly helps them blend into this terrain of sand and sparse grass. But these are practical working buildings. Those that began life as boats are inspired bits of recycling and their usefulness should attract our praise. The artist Simon Starling won the 2005 Turner Prize for a project that involved turning a shed into a boat and back again, and these Lindisfarne sheds seem just as interesting. Their practicality is enhanced because they are aerodynamically efficient – the biting wind blows over their curves without blowing them down.

Yacht stores, Tollesbury
Essex

Tollesbury, on the Blackwater estuary, has always looked to the sea for its economy, for oyster fishing, yachting, boat building, and smuggling. In 1904 the Tollesbury Yacht Berthing Company bought and erected these neat weatherboarded yacht stores (sometimes known as sail lofts) and they have formed the focal point of the waterfront here ever since. They have seen prosperity, when a 1920s America's Cup contender was built here, before a decline in the post-war period. But now they are restored and painted once more in their original pale colour.

See also

Seaside piers, 294
Halls for gathering, 300
Coastal buildings, next page
Lighthouses, 344

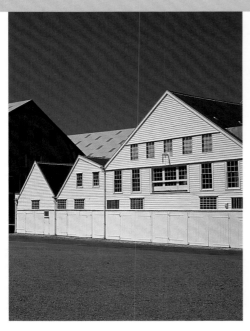

Chatham Historic Dockyard
Kent

The naval dockyard at Chatham has been building ships since the 16th century and expanded vastly during the 18th and 19th centuries. Many of the remaining buildings date from the 1700s, including this row of 1750s timber-framed buildings. They were originally built of reused ship timbers for the making and storing of masts. Later in the 18th century the taller central block was converted for various trades involved in making ships' fittings – capstan making, pump making, and wheelwrighting. These large workshops, timber-framed and clad, are the ancestors of countless modern factory buildings, sheds that provide lots of floor space within simple, easily erected structures.

King's Lynn Customs House
Norfolk

The Customs House at King's Lynn is one of the town's most beautiful and prominent buildings, standing on the Purfleet Quay looking towards the Wash, and is testimony to Lynn's long trading history. It was built in 1683 as a merchants' exchange, and where there are now round-headed windows there were originally arches open to the street. It is therefore in the tradition of English town hall buildings with arches below and a room above, a building type of which Abingdon has a famous example. Lynn's Custom House, though, is less grand than Abingdon's town hall. It was designed by a local architect, Henry Bell, who was alderman and mayor of Lynn; he was no doubt influenced by Wren, as the restrained Classical details and delightful lantern (itself like a miniature building) show. But Bell must also have known about Dutch architecture – the Customs House has been compared to buildings in Amsterdam and Haarlem. But one detail is incorrigibly English: the customs house proudly displays a statue of Charles II, who was on the throne when the building was first constructed.

Lifeboat station, Rye Harbour
Kent

There is a tradition of wooden seaside buildings, cheap and easy to erect and kept painted to protect them from the water and salt. Lifeboat stations are often built in this way and the one at Rye Harbour is a recent example that keeps the tradition going. With its shiny blue boards and white window surrounds it looks every inch a seaside building, the sort of bright splash of colour everyone appreciates when they go down to the sea. But such a structure is also practical, providing a launching platform and protecting the boat from the elements – from salt to sun.

Lifeboat station, Wells-next-the-Sea
Norfolk

Wells is next to the North Sea and developed as a busy port, its trade encouraged by the Great Eastern Railway. Then, attracting a different sort of visitor, it became a seaside resort, and diehard holiday-makers withstood bitter east winds on the beach before diving into the amusement arcades. This far northern coast of Norfolk needed a lifeboat station and for years Wells had a corrugated-iron one. When its corroded walls needed replacing, a kind of homage to the old building was put up, a simple practical structure clad in ridged metal with some of the original building of 1895 preserved inside. Painted in bright colours, its ridges catch the light and shade effectively, so that it is both easy to spot and a pleasure to look at. It is another example of how, beside the sea, a cheap, unpretentious building can be a visual asset – and a brightly dazzling advertisement for the life-saving work of the RNLI, an emergency service all too often ignored.

The National Institution for the Preservation of Life from Shipwreck (later the Royal National Lifeboat Institution) was founded by William Hillary in 1824 as a charity to save lives at sea. This RNLI crown and anchor badge is from the old lifeboat station at Aldeburgh, Suffolk, but a flag symbol, also incorporating a crown and anchor, is now used more widely.

See also

Seaside piers, 294
Coastal buildings, previous page
Lighthouses, 344

Lighthouses

Since people went to sea there has been a need for lighthouses, and the remains of a Roman example survive at Dover Castle. By the 17th century the Corporation of Trinity House (which began as a guild of mariners) was building lighthouses, and so were a number of private individuals. In 1836 Trinity House took over the private lights and since then has administered the lighthouses of Britain. By this time the challenge of building lights on rocks and islets had been met. One of the most famous was the much-rebuilt Eddystone Lighthouse, south-west of Plymouth, where in 1756–9 John Smeaton

Flamborough Head
East Yorkshire

The headland at Flamborough extends out into the sea north of Bridlington and is an obvious place for a lighthouse. The first one was this octagonal tower, built from the local chalk of the headland itself, by Sir John Clayton, who had received letters patent in 1674 to build five lighthouses at various sites. Even in its present stumpy state, without a light, this early structure still looks every inch a lighthouse. But the 79 ft (24 m)-high tower never seems to have been lit, perhaps because Clayton's letters patent included no provision for a light levy to fund the building's upkeep.

South Foreland
near St Margaret's at Cliffe, Kent

In 1793, when the South Foreland light was built, sham Gothic and Norman castles were popular as eye-catchers, and it seemed fitting to build the new tower as if it were a castle, with mock machicolations and round-headed doorway. But this antique-looking building was the home of hi-tech experiments. Michael Faraday, the 19th-century electricity pioneer, was scientific adviser to Trinity House which ran the lighthouses. He experimented with electricity here and South Foreland was the first lighthouse with an electrically powered lamp. The light was visible for about 26 miles (42 km). In 1898, South Foreland was the site of Marconi's experiments with wireless telegraphy.

Burnham-on-Sea
Somerset

Burnham once had another light, called the Pillar Lighthouse, but it was built too low to cope with the large difference between the highest and lowest tides. So in 1832 this wooden structure was built to provide added protection. The lighthouse played a different role in the town's history when a local clergyman decided to try to turn Burnham into a spa. With the lighthouse used as a marker, passing ships were stopped and made to pay a toll. The money went towards sinking wells, but Burnham's spa got no further than this. The lighthouse-on-legs remained, and is still a valued signpost for shipping.

This is the lamp room at North Foreland Lighthouse in Kent. Banks of lenses are designed to magnify the already intense light from the tiny bulbs so that the light can carry for miles.

used interlocking stone blocks and a tapering design that was very stable and much copied. Dozens more lighthouses followed in the 19th century, ranging from solid stone or concrete towers to openwork structures of cast iron. Today the lights are unmanned and automatic.

Although modern navigational aids make them increasingly redundant, these traditional coastal structures are still much loved.

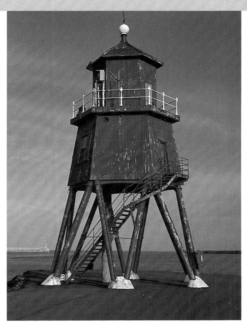

Watchet
Somerset

This compact little lighthouse is only 22 ft (6.7 m) tall but its light can still be seen 10 miles (16 km) out to sea. In 1862, when the builders decided they needed quite a short lighthouse they realised they could build it from a 'modern' material – cast iron. With its cheery red paint and ornate weathervane it has been pleasing visitors, as well as doing the useful job of warning shipping, ever since.

Herd Groyne Light, South Shields
Northumberland

The River Tyne was once a major artery, for both new ships and old, but also a foggy one. This utilitarian structure was put into use in 1882, resembling a corrugated-iron alien on metal legs looking out to sea or contemplating conquest of the opposite bank of the river. It has been serving shipping ever since. At 48 ft (14.6 m) high it is perhaps taller than it seems at first glance and casts a light that is visible for 13 miles (21 km). Just in sight next to the railings is the bell that is rung every five seconds when the fog comes down and the light is no longer visible.

Spurn Head
East Yorkshire

Fragile Spurn Head, a narrow, 3-mile-long spit of sand and gravel at the mouth of the River Humber on Yorkshire's east coast, is the product of the sea erosion that also threatens to destroy it. In 1776, renowned lighthouse engineer John Smeaton built two lights here, and this one replaced his high light in 1895. The remains of Smeaton's old high light are next to this black-and-white tower, which is some 120 ft (37 m) high and threw its light about 17 miles (27 km) out to sea. The lighthouse was abandoned in 1985 and the area is now a nature reserve, but the tower is still a useful landmark to shipping in the River Humber's muddy channels.

Francis Pickernell's lighthouse of 1835 takes the form of a Doric column supporting an octagonal lantern, an unusual architectural form that makes a dramatic feature in the historic Yorkshire town of Whitby.

See also

Seaside piers, 294
Coastal buildings, 340

Garages and filling stations

The motor car sometimes seems to be the enemy of architecture: many buildings have been knocked down to make way for roads. But builders quickly realised that cars needed housing and maintaining and by the time vehicles became numerous there were many Art Deco garages offering service and fuel, their curves and angles exactly in keeping with the lines of a Jowett or a Humber. There was also a healthy tradition of modifying existing buildings – from sheds to coach houses – for the motor car.

**Store Street Service Station
London**

Within close range of the once numerous furniture vans of the Tottenham Court Road, this small service station – one of several built in the area – preserves its 1930s style. It has an elegant fascia, complete with architectural acanthus motif and stepped panel to set off the sign, behind the forecourt. The hi-tech, fashion-conscious world of the motor trade has not preserved many early garages and filling stations, although they have perhaps missed a trick, since such buildings convey images of both style and service. This garage has changed its colour scheme in recent years, but still flies the flag of tradition and flair.

**Stokes Garage, Stockbridge
Hampshire**

This is an extraordinary combination, a Protean building indeed. Victorian or Edwardian sash- and bay-windows are overlaid with a mixture of Swiss-cottage-like boarding, iron balustrades, and valances imitated from railway station architecture. A variety of tyres, petrol pumps, and other impedimenta adds to the mixture, but a unifying paint scheme pulls everything together visually. It is an example of the sort of rugged individualism that is all too rare nowadays, assaulted as it is on either side by planning regulations which are interpreted as quashing the unusual, and by conglomerates which take over premises and impose their all too often ill-adapted house style. On the one hand, big oil companies like to present a standardised, unified image. On the other, our virtuous respect for local identity and neighbourhood style makes us want buildings like filling stations to 'blend in'. This garage resolutely refuses to blend with anything, but it is refreshing as a result. As a counter to modern blandness, we need buildings such as this garage more than we know.

The AA began to erect wooden, sentry-box-style telephone kiosks in 1911 so that members could call for assistance. This style of black and yellow gable-topped box was introduced in 1955. Once there were more than 2,000 of these boxes; in the year 2000 only 22 remained.

Raised lettering and recessed bands of colour enhance the lively surface of the tile-clad walls of the Michelin Building in London.

Sadly most old garages have been upgraded out of existence. The remaining few, tucked away in corners of countryside and city, should be celebrated.

By 1907 Mitchell's Motors in London's Wardour Street had installed the latest lift to move cars from floor to floor.

Much Marcle Garage
Herefordshire

In the 1920s, the internal combustion engine was too new for there to be anything like a standard filling station or garage. In fact there had not been roadside filling stations at all for very long. The AA opened the first one, in a wooden shed at Aldermaston in Berkshire, in 1920. Elsewhere, the motorist often had to pull in at pumps outside hotels and other establishments. This utilitarian structure, built in 1926, was one answer to what a garage should be like, with a tall entrance to take the lorries of Weston's, local makers of cider and perry, which were serviced here.

With walls clad in wood and corrugated iron, it is a long way from the Herefordshire black-and-white vernacular, owing more to the traditions of the aircraft hangar or the Dutch barn. But it proved durable and was still fitting tyres in 2005.

Michelin Building, Fulham Road
London

This building was designed as a drive-in hymn of praise to Michelin tyres in 1905 (and extended in 1910) by French Art Nouveau architect François Espinasse. Stained-glass Michelin men and lamps like heaps of tyres enlivened its façades and some of these were restored in the 1980s by Terence Conran to create a restaurant, shop, and offices. With its tiled decoration, twirling monogrammed ironwork, bold lettering, and unusual roof line it was the ultimate urban eye-catcher, long a talking point in the salubrious Fulham Road. Few London buildings are as over-the-top as this, even those from the era of Postmodernism.

Tile panels at the Michelin Building depict motor-racing scenes from the 1900s, evoking the excitement of travelling at speed in the powerful early Naudin and Mercedes Benz.

See also

Stables, 248
Cinemas, 290
Airports and allied buildings, 348

Airports and allied buildings

Air travel has grown quickly over the last hundred years, and airport buildings have sometimes struggled to keep up. As a result many airports are chaotic-looking jumbles of buildings, put up over the decades as the numbers and needs of travellers have demanded. Ironically they are in a way quite simple structures that work in a similar way to railway stations, with landside and airside facilities mirroring booking halls and platforms. Occasionally, one can still find buildings from the early decades of air travel that actually look this simple, white and pure and almost as streamlined as contemporary aircraft. Early hangars,

Airship hangars, Cardington
Bedfordshire

The first of these awesome steel-framed, corrugated-iron-clad buildings was designed and built by A J Main and Co – known as manufacturers of more modest prefabricated buildings such as Dutch barns – for the aircraft manufacturer Shorts in 1916–17. It was extended in 1926–7 for the manufacture of the vast R101 airship. By this time the building was 812 ft (247 m) in length, but even this was only slightly longer than the airship it housed. The pair of vast motorised metal doors, each weighing 940 tons, provide an entrance 180 ft (55 m) square, which was again just large enough to accommodate the girth of the R101 and the men and equipment who built it.

The second shed, similar in size, was brought to the site from Norfolk in 1928 to house the R100. The space inside these buildings is cathedral-like in its size and proportions, but even Winchester Cathedral, the longest of the medieval Gothic churches, is only 556 ft (170 m) long.

Sywell Aerodrome
Northamptonshire

Opened in the 1920s with the slogan 'You can fly well at Sywell', this aerodrome quickly became a popular destination for many who flew their own light aircraft. It played an important role training Second World War pilots and still boasts a well-used grass runway. The aerodrome has buildings from the first heyday of aviation, when Art Deco and modern architecture seemed to symbolise the up-to-the-minute image of air travel. White concrete and plaster details contrast with brick and the view of aircraft taking off and landing is through the classic metal-framed windows of the period.

This Nissen hut is at Sywell, where it now forms part of an aviation museum. Although most Nissen huts had windows only in the ends, this one has had windows skilfully inserted in the sides.

both basic rectilinear sheds and the more aerodynamic lamella (or segmental-roofed) designs, have a similar simple fit of form and function. Recent terminals, such as Stansted or Bristol, carefully built and planned, functional and elegant, live up to this early promise.

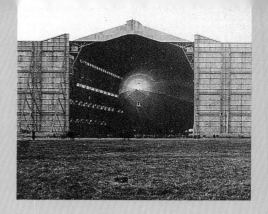

An early 20th-century photograph shows the Cardington hangars with their doors open to reveal the monstrous airships inside. Tiny human figures can just be made out near the doors.

Aircraft hangar, Warrington
Cheshire

In the 1930s and 1940s, the Royal Air Force built many blister hangars, buildings with a low profile and gently curving segmental roof like this one at the former Burtonwood air base. Their ancestor was the Nissen hut, invented during the First World War by engineering officer P N Nissen as a temporary building that could be rapidly erected by unskilled workers or soldiers to provide accommodation for everything from men to machines. Nissen huts were covered with bent corrugated iron and provided plenty of interior space. The doors and windows were normally in the end panels. These spacious hangars were built in a similar way. They could be put up quickly and cheaply, and were easy to camouflage so they could not be seen from the air. Most were clad in corrugated iron supported on steel trusses. Many of these hangars have survived. They are still valued for their spaciousness and minimal impact on the landscape and are used not just for housing aircraft but also as workshops, factories, garages, and storage units.

Stansted Airport
Essex

After air travel expanded and lost its romance, international airports got big and soulless. They were meant to handle large numbers of people efficiently but most failed, with a confusion of signs, endless walks, and tawdry shopping areas. The biggest airports also expanded rather haphazardly. Stansted offered a chance to build a new terminal from scratch and Norman Foster, designer of many prestigious buildings, got the job. He produced one vast room, with a high roof held up on these posts and struts, that seemed to recall the sheds of early aviation, but was ultra-modern at the same time. Most passengers enjoy using this clear, simple, spacious terminal.

Buxton Memorial Fountain,
Victoria Tower Gardens, London

LANDSCAPE PAVILIONS

All buildings have a context and many churches, country houses, and even factories owe their appeal to their setting in a landscape. But there are also buildings whose very reason for being is their relationship with a designed landscape. These are structures such as the greenhouses and pavilions that enliven country parks and public gardens, the lodges which owners of big houses like to build at their gates, towers placed in the landscape from which people could admire the view, and the innumerable memorial buildings in cemeteries and parks.

These are a mixed bunch, but they are mostly comparatively small and have in common this interaction with a designed landscape that has made them the interest of architects and, especially, gardeners. The British are enthusiastic gardeners and gardens provide colourful and delightful contexts for all sorts of buildings, from cottages to country houses. A garden can tell us a lot about the way its owners thought about their house, but gardens, by their very nature, change continuously.

Garden history can be hard to unpick, although, thanks to today's historians, archaeologists, and plant experts we know more about it than ever before. Vital clues to the way past people saw their gardens are provided by the buildings they erected in them, structures that are often longer lasting than the plants they were designed to complement.

Apart from the usually hidden stores and potting sheds, most garden buildings were designed to be seen and admired. None more amazed the eye than the generations of greenhouses that gardeners have built since the 17th century. These structures got bigger and bigger as resources, enthusiasm, and glass-and-iron technology permitted, until Joseph Paxton, the Duke of Devonshire's gardener at Chatsworth House, Derbyshire, was designing houses in the mid-19th century that could accommodate tall pines or vast water lilies. What began as the preserve of dukes and kings soon became part of the tradition of public parks and gardens, an education for us all, a world under glass.

Buildings such as the Palm House at Kew Gardens in London could be huge, but most garden structures were smaller and built as much for visual as for practical effect. These were the multitude of pavilions and eye-catching temples that people put up to act as focal points and shelters from the 18th century onwards. Such structures were of varied styles and evoked a variety of values and interests. Grecian temples in a landscape garden could call to mind a Classical Arcadia. Picturesque farm buildings could evoke the kind of pastoral paradise that saw 18th-century aristocrats dressing up as shepherds. A fragment of a 'Gothic ruin' could stand for the age of chivalry and the long history of a noble family. An Egyptian temple or Chinese pagoda could remind visitors that their host was up on the latest aesthetic fashion.

But some of these buildings seem to go further, to be the product of some wilful eccentricity. The eccentricity, for example, that leads a rich landowner to build an apparently purposeless tower. If such buildings seem to be expressions of sheer ego, they are also among our most generously giving of buildings; while English families hide their country houses up long drives or in quiet valleys, their towers, boastfully tall, are often sited on hilltops. Seen from afar, many an eccentric tower enlivens a view or provides a landmark on a journey. Many of our more privileged families have pulled off a similar trick with their memorial buildings, monuments and mausolea that combine tomb and landmark in a grand architectural gesture. Such structures began as expressions of grandeur and family power, but now we can all appreciate their art and their relationship with the landscape.

The frequently odd size or shape also stimulates our curiosity. Such buildings want us to be curious, to ask questions about their purpose and history, and to get us interested in our past. They demand not to be taken for granted. And that is a lesson for how we should look at all our buildings, small and large, new and old.

Greenhouses

It is said that Sir Walter Raleigh introduced the first orange seeds to Britain in the 16th century. Since then the British have been obsessed with finding ever more rare and interesting plants from all over the world. By the late 17th century the grandest houses, such as Hampton Court Palace, had orangeries, large heated rooms with big windows, for growing exotic plants. Greenhouses evolved from these buildings, with ever bigger panes of glass and ever narrower glazing bars, to let in the maximum amount of light. The Victorian period was the golden age of the large greenhouse, with the work of Joseph

Camellia house, Wollaton Hall
Nottinghamshire

One of the earliest surviving prefabricated metal structures is the camellia house at Wollaton, which was made in 1823 in the workshop of Thomas Clark of Birmingham, supplier of glasshouses to the nobility and sashes to Queen Victoria's kitchen garden at Frogmore, Berkshire. The façade of engaged columns and glazing bars conceals an interior in which iron columns (doubling as rainwater pipes) support a roof that is part glazed pyramids, part sheet-iron barrel vault. Although the house may have begun life as a hothouse for tropical plants, the partly vaulted roof made it more suitable for cold-house plants such as camellias.

Conservatory, Wentworth Castle
South Yorkshire

By the 1840s, when the Wentworth conservatory was built, explorers were scouring the world for exotic plants that British gardeners could cultivate. In the wake of innovators such as Joseph Paxton, builders were turning out increasingly delicate, filigree structures using cast iron. At Wentworth the conservatory has a trio of pitched roofs, the central one higher and extended with a miniature clerestory. This entire structure is made of the most slender glazing bars to let in maximum light to the tropical plants inside. There is little decoration, save a few iron brackets with spiralling foliage – the iron and glass were intended to form a backdrop to the main point of interest – the plants.

A lot of the interior innovations were concealed so that the plants could be allowed to dominate. Rainwater from the roof was collected and flowed down hollow cast-iron columns to underground tanks, from where it could be collected for watering. Underfloor heating pipes kept the greenhouse warm, so that exotic specimens could thrive. It was a triumph of technology, but also very fragile – the thin glazing bars, structural movement, and the proximity of iron and water has led to a host of conservation challenges.

Slender iron columns support pitched roofs of glass that let natural light flood into the camellia house at Wollaton.

Paxton at Chatsworth and London's Crystal Palace leading the way. With their powerful stoves and prefabricated structures, the greenhouses of the 19th century are some of the most revolutionary buildings of their time.

Palm House, Kew Gardens
London

This huge greenhouse of 1845–8, 362 ft (110 m) long and 63 ft (19 m) high, its curving form uniquely beautiful, is one of the great English buildings. Its design was the result of collaboration and dispute between Richard Turner (designer-contractor) and Decimus Burton (architect), and historians have argued at length about the contributions of the two men. Burton did an initial design, which Kew's director rejected because it had too many columns. Burton agreed to revise his design, but Turner came up with an alternative, criticising Burton's 'Ecclesiastical or Gothic style' in the process. The result seems to have been a compromise between the two rivals, with Turner providing the overall layout and Burton contributing much to the visual appearance of the central section of the Palm House. Indeed a building like this demanded the skill sets of both men – Turner's engineering expertise and Burton's flair with decoration and proportion. The wrought-iron framework is epoch-making because it is the first to use I-section ribs, which Turner prefabricated. Wrought-iron tie rods inside cast-iron tubes were used to brace the ribs, the tie rods being pulled taut once they were assembled. This was another innovative engineering solution, later used in a number of railway stations.

Temperate House, Kew Gardens
London

The Temperate House was built when Parliament made a special grant of £10,000 for the purpose in 1859. Decimus Burton was the architect, planning a 212 ft (65 m) central greenhouse flanked by two octagonal houses and a further pair of rectilinear buildings. Altogether it is roughly twice the size of Kew's Palm House and beautifully sited on a low grass platform and masonry base. Because Burton was allowed more freedom than in the design of the Palm House, there are plenty of grand architectural gestures, from the entrance portico to rows of urns. But the needs of the plants were not forgotten, and Burton built in an effective ventilation system.

Plants spread their leaves against a background of glazing bars inside the Temperate House at Kew.

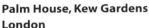

Garden pavilions

For centuries, gardeners have liked to complement their gardens with ornamental buildings. Most of these are on a fairly small scale. Many date from the 18th century, when people became aware as never before of the range of past architectural styles. Various forms of Classicism, from Italian-sourced Palladianism to the close study of ancient Greek ruins, were joined by explorations of medieval architecture and, most exotic of all, experiments in the Chinese style. The landscape garden was in vogue too, and its vistas and viewpoints made ideal settings for miniature temples, pagodas, and

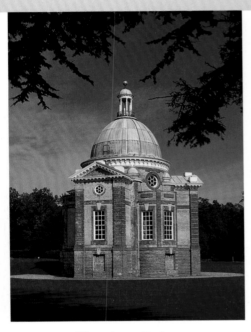

Garden pavilion, Wrest Park
Bedfordshire

Thomas Archer's design for this little pavilion, built in 1709–11, is about as baroque as English architecture gets, a building that would feel at home in a palace garden in Prague or Vienna. The basic plan is circular and the building is full of rounded motifs – the round windows, the dome, the lantern topped by its own tiny dome, the golden ball finial. From the central circle project three semicircular and three square bays (one of the latter housing the doorway), a plan that somehow suggests movement as the visitor walks around to see how the building works. How different, how much more stable, and how less baroque it would have been if there had been even numbers of bays. A delight, all the way round.

Temple of the Four Winds, Castle Howard
North Yorkshire

The vast mansion at Castle Howard is set in a spacious park, and these grounds are full of interesting structures – various gates, a garden house, an obelisk, several pyramids, a famous mausoleum, and this remarkable temple. John Vanbrugh based this garden building on Palladio's famous Villa Capra, the house that inspired Lord Burlington's Chiswick House, which in turn started the Palladian movement in Britain. Both Chiswick and this temple date from the 1720s, showing that Vanbrugh was more than capable of keeping up with architectural ideas and fashions. But Vanbrugh, typically, departed further from the original than had Lord Burlington. He kept Palladio's four porticoes and dome, but his little temple is higher in proportion to its width than the original villa – there is only space enough for a single room inside. In this way, Vanbrugh was able to make the building do the job he wanted – to stand out on its eminence in the park, a true eye-catcher.

Sunlight falls on shutters and painted walls in the pavilion at Wrest Park.

pavilions in these different styles. Mostly, then, these delightful buildings were put there to enhance the view, to mark the climax of a vista, to catch the eye. They were also cultural markers, showing the taste and ideas of their owners.

**Pavilion, Holkham Hall
Norfolk**

This little Tuscan pavilion is in the grounds of Holkham Hall. Its plain Classicism is very much in tune with the stern Palladian grandeur of the house and it is well set amongst the garden's deep green trees. Little Italianate buildings such as this seem foreign in the English landscape, yet they were eminently practical – equipped with a bench they were ideal to take a rest during a stroll through the grounds, or to shelter from the rain.

**Moorish Temple, Elvaston Castle
Derbyshire**

Moorish Temple is a misnomer: this weird garden building of 1860 is more a mixture of Chinese and Gothic, with a little Islamic influence thrown in. There is also a round window with cross-banded tracery that comes from none of these traditions. The little gem is a typically Victorian eclectic mixture, but even the Victorians would only go this far in a garden building, a form of architecture in which it was acceptable to be frivolous. It was built by the Earl of Harrington, who was a collector, eccentric, and garden maker and created several follies in his estate at Elvaston Castle.

**Round Tower, Hartwell
Buckinghamshire**

The mid-18th-century fashion for Gothic architecture inspired all sorts of garden buildings and they were not all large sham castles. Aristocratic gardeners built Gothic pavilions, too, such as this little round tower, now surrounded by scrub and trees, but still just tall enough to make an impression on the landscape. Unlike the sham castles favoured by many garden builders, this kind of building was not designed to look like a specific sort of structure from the chivalric past. It was simply a piece of Gothic fancy, with charming quatrefoil windows and mock battlements to give a medieval feel.

See also

Landscape towers

Outlandish towers poking up through trees or crowning the tops of hills were among the favourite architectural whimsies perpetrated by the rich from the 18th century onwards. Many are garden buildings on a large scale, elaborate platforms from which one can admire the view or elicit admiration from passers-by, some seem to have no obvious function other than to amaze. If they began as the follies of the rich, many are now accessible to anyone who wants to climb their stairs and work out how far they can see on a clear day.

Sturt's Folly, Horton
Dorset

Built probably in the mid-18th century for a member of the Sturt family, this tower was said to have been originally intended to be used as an observatory before becoming a platform for admiring the surrounding landscape. The building's style is bizarre, a mixture of pedimented Classical and pointed Gothic. Its shape is difficult to define – a kind of hexagon with round corner turrets that make it seem triangular. Its material, brick, is surprising. And its architect is unknown. The overall effect is one of studied ugliness and perhaps deliberate mystery as to the building's exact purpose.

Old John, Bradgate Park
Leicester

The sham medieval tower known as Old John was built in 1786. It is said to be a memorial to a miller, the eponymous John, who was employed by the Earl of Stamford. The story goes that the Earl's staff had built a bonfire to celebrate his son's coming of age. At the centre of this bonfire was an old flagpole, which fell over, hit miller John, and killed him. And so, it is said, the tower was built on the site of John's mill. Even if one disbelieves the story, it is still possible to enjoy this bit of fake-medievalism – battlements, blocked windows, pointed opening, 'ruined' archway, and all – on its rise in Leicester's Bradgate Park. And the tower was not all faux-medieval fancy. In the 19th century, as in the Middle Ages, Bradgate Park was in the heart of East Midlands hunting country. A tower atop a 700-ft (213-m) hill formed an ideal vantage point and it was also a favoured rest and refreshment point for the huntsmen. Now walkers come to enjoy the view.

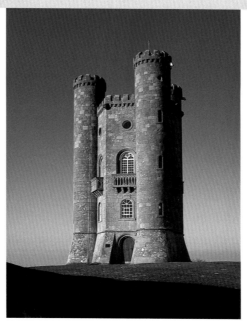

Brizlee Tower, Alnwick
Northumberland

A story went the rounds that this tower was designed by the Duke of Northumberland, the owner of Alnwick Castle, or better still that it was based on a confection made by his pastry cook. But it was probably designed by the most famous architects of the time, the Adam brothers. Finished in 1781 it is some 80 ft (24 m) tall and stands on top of a hill. Crocketed and gabled doorways and window openings give the tower an over-the-top Gothic style, as do the openwork balustrades around the balconies. At the very top is a brazier-like basket, as if the building is a kind of stranded lighthouse.

Broadway Tower
Worcestershire

James Wyatt designed Broadway Tower in 1794 as a landmark that could be seen from Croome Court, the house of his client the Earl of Coventry, 15 miles (24 km) away. From its hilltop setting, just 1,000 ft (305 metres) above sea level, the views are breathtaking, and stories abound of the number of counties one can see from the top. Wyatt described the building as a Saxon tower, although its turrets and battlements make it look more Norman. But as with 18th-century Gothic, Wyatt's version of a castle is a free interpretation. The key features are the inauthentically big windows, from which to admire the scenery.

Lord Berners's Folly, Faringdon
Oxfordshire

The 14th Baron Berners devoted his life to eccentricity, writing witty if gnomic music, dying his doves in rainbow colours, and generally standing at a slight angle to the universe. He built his tower, which was designed by Trenwith Wills and Lord Gerald Wellesley, in 1935, in the face of local opposition. This has, with time, turned to admiration, and in spite of the loss of the original cream colourwash, the restored structure now looks quite mellow seen through the screen of nearby trees. Now locals and visitors alike climb eagerly to the viewing room at the top.

See also

Lodges

Every building needs an entrance and every garden a gate. These rules of private property come together in the lodge, the building on the edge of a park or garden that stands by the gate and is traditionally the home of a porter or gatekeeper, who can police the comings and goings. But it is also of huge symbolic significance because it is often the first inkling one gets that beyond the gates and park wall is an important building such as a country house. The lodge is, in other words, the public face of the

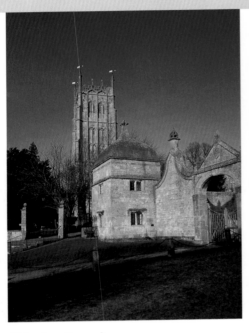

Chipping Campden
Gloucestershire

Sir Baptist Hicks was the Jacobean lord of Chipping Campden who endowed his town with almshouses and a market house. He built his home on the edge of the town but it was destroyed in the Civil War. One of the retreating Royalists lamented the loss of the house, 'which was so faire'. The earthworks of the garden can be found, two banqueting houses, and some fragments of wall. But amongst the most interesting remains are a pair of entrance lodges on either side of the gate. Their roofs curve in ogee form to a finial, a beautiful 17th-century touch.

Clumber Park
Nottinghamshire

In 1770 the first Duke of Newcastle built himself a house at Clumber Park, an area that had been part of Sherwood Forest. His architect was Stephen Wright, a Palladian who had worked for William Kent, but nothing remains of the house – it was rebuilt after a fire in the Victorian period before being pulled down just before the Second World War. These lodges survive on the western side of the park, on the way to the village of Carburton. Their strong, plain, confident design gives one an idea of the sort of house that Wright must have built for the duke.

This situation, where lodges survive a lost country house, is not unusual. Thousands of great houses were demolished in the middle years of the 20th century, as increasing repair bills and death duties took their toll, and ways of rural life changed beyond recognition. But the demolition men frequently left the gate lodges alone. These small buildings often made decent small houses for remaining estate workers – or for people who got the chance to buy them on the open market. For anyone interested in architecture or the history of the countryside, they are priceless evidence when tracing vanished houses and forgotten estates.

Impressive stone gateways are a pervasive feature of Clumber Park. The urn-topped pier of about 1700 is part of the park's Normanton Gate and was moved here from Shire Oaks Hall. The broader pier – from the Drayton Gate – features weighty baroque details, such as the big blind arch and heavy rustication, from some 60 years later.

house or mansion. And so owners and architects made the effort to make their lodges special, making the story of these buildings like a history of grand architecture in miniature.

Stoke Edith
Herefordshire

This lodge served another vanished house. Stoke Edith Park was lost in a fire in 1927, leaving this little domed building stranded among the hop country between Ledbury and Hereford. It is probably the work of William Wilkins. This architect is best known for large-scale buildings such as London's National Gallery and various additions to the colleges in Cambridge, and the lodge would have been built in the early 19th century, when the grounds of Stoke Edith Park were being landscaped by Humphry Repton. It is a refreshing little building with its unusual plan (an octagon with protruding bays) and chimney in the middle of the dome.

Easton Neston
Northamptonshire

'And now for something really impressive', this combination of triumphal arch, columned screen, urns, heraldic beasts, and twin lodges seems to proclaim. It was built in 1822 as an entrance for Easton Neston, which had been designed in the previous century by Nicholas Hawksmoor. The most surprising thing about it is that it is built of Coade Stone. Coade Stone was an artificial stone that was invented by Eleanor Coade in the 1770s and produced at first by her firm and later by Coade and Sealy in London. It was especially popular for producing ornamental elements such as urns because it could be cast.

Here it manages to look genuine even in Northamptonshire – a county rich in its own local stone. It has worn well and now does duty as the entrance both to the grand house and to Towcester Racecourse.

See also

Tudor and Jacobean houses, 122
Baroque houses, 134
Georgian houses, 138
Regency town houses, 144
Lodges, next page

Lodges (continued)

Leigh
Kent

Industrialist and philanthropist Samuel Morley, who made a fortune in the hosiery business and spent much of his money on good works, restored Hall Place in Kent and built much of the neighbouring village of Leigh. He found the house fire-damaged, so went to work recreating it in the Victorian version of the original Elizabethan red brick. His lodges are tall Tudor-revival structures, their brickwork relieved by dressings of stone and on some walls by diaper patterns. A lodge-keeper could live in some comfort here, as the philanthropic Morley no doubt intended.

Childwickbury
Hertfordshire

The big house at Childwickbury is a 17th- and 18th-century building that was restored and refaced by the great Victorian architect George Gilbert Scott in 1854. This lodge came later, in 1897, and its date is commemorated in ornate numerals in the richly moulded terracotta panel above the large upstairs window. It is an amazing late Victorian confection, almost like a miniature mansion. Its plum-coloured brick and yellow terracotta stand out beside the road near St Albans, making the visitor pause to admire the collection of finials and decorative panels, not to mention the architectural forms of porch, turret, conical roof, and chimney.

Eaton Hall
Cheshire

All that remains of the original Eaton Hall, the house designed by Alfred Waterhouse for the Duke of Westminster, are the chapel, stables, and clock tower, which had a carillon that played 'Home, Sweet Home' whenever the duke returned. But there are also the lodges, including the magnificent North Lodge of 1881. For this building Waterhouse composed a cluster of round towers to create an effect akin to a French castle from an illuminated manuscript. The pointing conical roofs are reflected in the spirelets that top the gate piers and the gate and lodge together are a good example of the romantic late Victorian view of the Middle Ages.

This is another of the lodges at Eaton Hall, an eccentric mixture of corbelled-out corner turrets, chimneys, and half-timbering.

Pipewell
Northamptonshire

Not every lodge is brash and bold. This one is hidden away amongst trees and bushes and its restrained Gothic-revival architecture is a far cry from the loud visual language of Childwickbury or Eaton Hall. There are big parapets, the odd finial, and some ornate tiles on the roof, but none of this seems showy. The lodge does not have to explode from the countryside, it can blend in.

Victoria Park
Leicester

One can often think of a lodge as a pavilion, a small, ornamental building. But the lodges Edwin Lutyens designed for Leicester's Victoria Park are each made up of four linked pavilions. The architect had already worked in Leicester before, coming to design the city's imposing war memorial, a large domed arch. Then, he had to be serious, but with these little lodges, he could afford to be rather more light-hearted. So Lutyens, an architect with a famous visual sense of humour, was up to his tricks. The lodges look at first glance highly serious, with their strong-looking Classical quoins and window surrounds. But the playful architect topped them not with a pediment, as one would expect with such a Classical building, but with little flattened pyramidal roofs and exaggeratedly tall chimneys, as if to point out that they are only garden buildings, after all.

See also

Victorian country houses, 148
Edwin Lutyens, 158
Lodges, previous page

Memorial buildings

There is an entire architecture of last things – the tombs, mausolea, lych-gates, and memorials that furnish our churchyards and cemeteries. It has existed since the Middle Ages, but the richest heritage of actual memorial buildings is strongest in the 18th and 19th centuries, when high-ranking families began to build mausolea, partly in response to a lack of burial space inside parish churches, partly as a result of the influence of Vanbrugh, who had seen these structures on his travels in India. However they began, such buildings became family status symbols, grander and more serious than any Classical garden building.

Severndroog Castle, Greenwich
London

The original castle of Severndroog was a pirate fortress off the coast of India, which was 'cleaned up' by the naval hero Sir William James, who routed the pirates, retired to his home in Eltham, Kent, and died in 1778. His widow had this tower built to commemorate her husband. One room contained a museum about James's life, another had a painted ceiling that told the story of his battle against the pirates. And the tall tower could also be used to admire the surroundings, with views all over London from the top. The exhibits have long gone but the memorial building remains.

Darnley Mausoleum, Cobham
Kent

This is one of the greatest of mausolea, built by James Wyatt in the 1780s for the Earl of Darnley and his family of nearby Cobham Hall. Wyatt virtually defined the mausoleum as an architectural form in this building, including many key motifs: the pyramidal roof, the stone coffins placed above the entablature, the funereal emblems such as extinguished torches. Such a building was full of allusions. The pyramidal roof, for example, refers not only to the ancient Egyptian cult of the dead but also to the similarly roofed tomb of Mausolus at Halicarnassus. This long-decayed funereal triumph is being restored at the time of writing.

Highgate Cemetery
London

Begun in 1838, Highgate is the most famous of the seven commercial cemeteries that were established in London at about this time. It is the resting place of a host of famous Victorians, from Michael Faraday to Karl Marx. The cemetery was laid out by owner-architect Stephen Geary, an enthusiast for Gothic and Egyptian architecture, and is full of outstanding chapels, mausolea, and catacombs ingeniously arranged on a series of changing levels and curving pathways. These are the entrances to the Cedar of Lebanon Catacombs, originally built around a tree, which no longer stands. Although they look Classical, they are near the more exotic Egyptian Avenue.

Lotus columns adorn Highgate Cemetery's Egyptian Avenue.

The middle classes built these elaborate roofed tombs too, if they were rich enough, although in the Victorian period they were more likely to be buried in one of the great cemeteries where the buildings, with typical Victorian copiousness, were in all sorts of styles, from Romanesque and Gothic to Classical and Egyptian.

Watts Chapel, Compton
Surrey

Ashton Memorial, Williamson Park, Lancaster
Lancashire

Mary, the wife of the late 19th-century painter G F Watts, designed this memorial chapel for her husband in 1896 in a curious mix of Italian Renaissance and Celtic revival styles. The plan is clearly symbolic – a circle intersected by a cross – standing for eternity underpinned by Christian faith. The decoration, by contrast, seems less assured, looking as if Art Nouveau curves are trying to break loose from a Celtic manuscript. But it still achieves a fascinating fusion of styles that could only come from England at the turn of the 20th century. The interior, completed a few years later, is decorated in a more full-blown Art Nouveau style.

On its hilltop site the gleaming white Ashton Memorial catches the sun and is visible for miles. It was built as a memorial to his family and especially his wife, by linoleum millionaire James Williamson II, Lord Ashton. Ashton's firm once employed around one quarter of the workers of Lancaster. He commissioned the baroque architect John Belcher, whose 1904 design was finally built in 1907–9 and is the swansong of the Edwardian baroque. More ornate than the grandest of town halls, it has a dome to rival London's St Paul's Cathedral (or St Peter's in Rome) and statues glorifying science, art, commerce, and industry.

The setting of the memorial is Lancaster's Williamson Park, which was given to the city in 1880 by Ashton's father. In making this donation, the elder Ashton was in line with late Victorian fashion. Few towns had public parks before the mid-19th century, and benefactors such as Ashton rushed to fill this gap in the late Victorian period. The memorial was the bright white icing on the cake.

Art Nouveau viewed through the Celtic fringe: the decoration of the Watts Chapel.

See also

Georgian Gothic parish churches, 50
The Picturesque and exotic, 146
Landscape towers, 356

TIMELINE

This timeline shows the approximate
dates of major architectural styles
and the life dates of some important
architects alongside key historical eras.
The dates of the architectural styles
are always approximate – there are
sometimes early precursors, as well
as examples that appear long after
the style has fallen from fashion.

HISTORICAL ERAS

600 – 1066 Saxon

1066 – 1485 Medieval

1485 – 1603 Tudor

1603 – 1714 Stuart

1649 – 60 Commonwealth

1714 – 1830 Georgian

1830 – 7 William IV

1837 – 1901 Victorian

1901 – 99 20th century

ARCHITECTURAL STYLES	MAJOR ARCHITECTS
600 – 1066 Saxon	
1066 – 1200 Norman	
1200 – 1300 Early English Gothic	
1300 – 1400 Decorated Gothic	
1400 – 1500 Perpendicular Gothic	
1500 – 1603 Tudor	1535 – 1614 Robert Smythson
1500 – 1700 Gothic survival	
1530 – 1640 Renaissance	
1603 – 25 Jacobean	
1610 – 1700 Stuart Classical	1573 – 1652 Inigo Jones
	1611 – 72 John Webb
	1620 – 85 Sir Roger Pratt
	1632 – 1723 Sir Christopher Wren
1690 – 1730 English baroque	1650 – 1719 William Talman
	1661 – 1736 Nicholas Hawksmoor
	1664 – 1726 Sir John Vanbrugh
	1668 – 1743 Thomas Archer
1700 – 1900 Gothic revival	
1714 – 1820 Georgian	1676 – 1729 Colen Campbell
1720 – 60 Palladian	1682 – 1754 James Gibbs
1730 – 70 Rococo	1685 – 1748 William Kent
	1686 – 1746 Giacomo Leoni
1760 – 1830 Classical revival	1717 – 88 James Stuart
	1723 – 96 Sir William Chambers
	1728 – 92 Robert Adam
	1739 – 1808 Joseph Bonomi
1770 – 1840 Picturesque	1746 – 1813 James Wyatt
1800 – 40 Regency	1752 – 1835 John Nash
	1753 – 1837 Sir John Soane
	1775 – 1847 J B Papworth
	1778 – 1839 William Wilkins
	1781 – 1867 Sir Robert Smirke
1837 – 1901 Victorian	1795 – 1860 Sir Charles Barry
	1803 – 65 Sir Joseph Paxton
	1811 – 78 Sir George Gilbert Scott
	1812 – 52 A W N Pugin
	1814 – 1900 William Butterfield
	1817 – 97 J L Pearson
	1820 – 77 Sir Matthew Digby Wyatt
	1822 – 1905 Cuthbert Brodrick
	1824 – 81 George Edmund Street
	1827 – 1907 G F Bodley
	1830 – 1905 Alfred Waterhouse
	1831 – 1912 R Norman Shaw
1860 – 1900 Old English	
1870 – 1900 Queen Anne	1831 – 1915 Philip Webb
1880 – 1920 Arts and Crafts	1849 – 1930 Sir Aston Webb
	1851 – 1928 Charles Harrison Townsend
	1857 – 1941 C F A Voysey
1900 – 10 Art Nouveau	1863 – 1940 Raymond Unwin
1925 – 40 Art Deco	1864 – 1960 Sir Ninian Comper
	1869 – 1944 Sir Edwin Lutyens
	1875 – 1960 Charles Holden
	1880 – 1960 Sir Giles Gilbert Scott
1925 – Modernism	1901 – 90 Berthold Lubetkin
	1907 – 76 Sir Basil Spence
	1914 – 2001 Sir Denys Lasdun
1955 – 75 Brutalism	1926 – 92 James Stirling
1975 – High Tech	1933 – Richard Rogers (Lord Rogers)
	1935 – Sir Norman Foster
1980 – Postmodernism	

GLOSSARY

Cross references are in *italic* type

aisle Part of a church, parallel to the nave and separated from it by a row of arches.

alabaster White form of the mineral gypsum, often carved into ornaments.

ambulatory Passage encircling the east end of a large church.

anthemion Ornament, used in Classical architecture, based on the flower and leaves of the honeysuckle.

apse Rounded or polygonal end to part of a church, especially the chancel.

arcade 1 Row of arches supported by piers or columns; 2 covered passage with shops.

architrave 1 Moulding surrounding a door or window; 2 lower part of an *entablature*.

arrow loop Narrow opening in the wall of a castle through which an archer could shoot while remaining largely protected from enemy arrows.

Art Deco Style of architecture and design fashionable in the 1920s and 1930s and typified by geometrical shapes and sometimes by ornamental motifs drawn from ancient Egypt.

Art Nouveau Style of architecture and design fashionable in the early 20th century and characterised by flowing lines, whiplash curves, and floral decoration.

ashlar Blocks of masonry finished to an even surface and laid in courses with vertical joints.

bailey Open space in a castle, usually surrounded by protective walls and a ditch.

baluster One of a series of posts supporting a rail to make a banister.

banded rustication See *rustication*.

bargeboards Boards fitted against the sloping edge of a roof.

baroque Style of architecture marked by its elaborate decoration, large masses, and enthusiastic use of curves, fashionable in England in the late 17th and early 18th centuries and again during the Edwardian period; English baroque architecture is sometimes termed 'baroque Classicism' because it is more restrained than baroque in continental Europe.

barrel vault Vault in the form of a continuous half-cylinder; also called a tunnel vault.

bar tracery Window tracery in which the glazed sections in the head of the window are separated by narrow bars of stone.

base Lower portion of a column or pier.

basilica Roman meeting hall, usually oblong with aisles; or a church based on this design.

bastion Projecting part of a castle or town wall, offering various lines of fire to defenders.

bastle Form of fortified house local to northern England.

batter Sloping face of a wall.

battlements Parapet with alternating gaps and raised portions.

bay One vertical section or division of a building, defined by the layout of the windows, buttresses, vaulting, arches, or similar repeated structural elements.

beakhead Decorative motif used in Norman architecture consisting of repeated human or animal heads, each bearing a downward pointing beak.

bellcote Small turret or framework on the roof or gable of a church, containing one or two bells.

bell opening Pierced or louvred window-like opening in a tower, designed to allow the sound of the bells to carry.

blind Term used to describe features, such as arches or windows, that are blocked or blank.

blind arcade Series of decorative blank arches attached to the surface of a wall.

bond Way in which courses of bricks are laid out, creating patterns made up of the headers (ends) and stretchers (sides) of the bricks.

boss Decorative stone placed at the meeting place of the ribs in a vault.

box pew Fitted church seat with high wooden surround and small door.

bressummer Heavy beam carrying the weight of the wall above in a timber-framed building.

broach spire Octagonal spire with inclined mass of masonry abutting on the base of four of its sides.

buttress Support built against a wall.

Byzantine Style of architecture imitating the buildings of the Byzantine Empire, the empire that developed in Eastern Europe, Turkey, and the Mediterranean after the fall of Rome in the 7th century.

cable Type of moulding in the form of a rope; used in Norman architecture.

canted Having an oblique or sloping edge or line.

capital The upper part, or head, of a column.

carrel Alcove containing a desk for study.

carton-pierre Material similar to papier-mâché, made by mixing paper, plaster, glue and a whitener of chalk or whitewash; used to produce decorative mouldings in some interiors.

cartouche Decorative panel.

caryatid Sculpture of a standing woman used as a support or column.

casemate Vaulted room in a fort, often used to house a gun.

chancel Eastern wing of a church, where the altar is placed.

chancel arch Arch at the point where the nave and chancel of a church meet.

chevron Moulding in the form of a zigzag; used in Norman architecture.

choir Part of the eastern wing of a church where the choir sit.

cinquefoil See *foil.*

Classical Term used to describe architecture influenced by ancient Greek or Roman building styles, typified by the use of the *orders*; English Classical architecture takes many forms, from the Italian-influenced *Palladian* style of the 17th and 18th centuries to the *Greek revival* of the 19th century.

clerestory Row of windows placed on an upper level, usually above the arcade in a church.

cloister Quadrangle giving access to the domestic parts of a monastery and linking these with the church.

Coade Stone Artificial cast stone, named after its 18th-century inventor Eleanor Coade and used widely for ornamentation on 18th- and 19th- century buildings.

cob Mixture of clay and straw used for walling.

collegiate church Church staffed by a number of priests or canons living communally.

column Upright support, usually of round cross-section.

Composite Order of Classical architecture combining elements of the Ionic and Corinthian orders.

corbel Block projecting from a wall, designed to support some other structural element.

Corinthian Order of Classical architecture characterised by its ornate capitals encrusted with acanthus leaves.

cornice 1 Ornamental moulding running along the top of a wall; 2 upper part of an *entablature.*

cottage orné Building deliberately designed to look countrified and cottage-like, with thatched roof, asymmetrical plan, and rustic features; style of building developed in the late 18th and early 19th centuries.

crenel Opening or gap in a battlement or crenellation.

crenellation Parapet with alternating gaps and raised portions.

crocket Small, repeated decorative motif along the edge of a spire, pinnacle, or moulding.

cruciform Cross-shaped.

crucks Matched pairs of timbers, arranged in an inverted V-shape, to form the structural support for a wood-framed building.

cupola Dome, especially a small one on top of a roof or turret.

curtain wall Outer wall of a castle.

cusp Projecting point used to divide shapes in window tracery.

dado The lower part of an interior wall, roughly from floor to waist height, often topped with a moulding called a dado rail.

Decorated Style of Gothic architecture fashionable in England in the late 13th and 14th centuries, characterised by more lavish ornament than in the previous phase of Gothic.

dentils Small, regularly spaced blocks of stone used in the cornices of some Classical buildings.

diaper Lozenge or diamond shape, repeated to form a decorative pattern.

dissolution The closure of the English monasteries, instigated by Henry VIII in the 1530s and 1540s.

dogtooth Decorative motif, used in Gothic architecture, consisting of a repeated four-pointed star-like design.

Doric Order of Classical architecture characterised by its minimal capitals and the lack of a separate base to the columns.

dormer Window with a small gable projecting from a sloping roof.

dormitory Communal sleeping room, especially in a monastery; sometimes known as the dorter.

dressed Of stone, having a finely finished face.

dripstone See *hood-mould.*

drum Cylindrical feature supporting a dome.

Early English First phase of English Gothic architecture, fashionable mainly in the 13th century and typified by features such as lancet windows and stiff-leaf ornament.

egg and dart Decorative moulding made up of repeating and alternating ovals and arrowheads; used in Classical architecture.

elevation One side or façade of a building; or a drawing of one such side.

embrasure Small opening on the wall of a castle or fort, usually splayed on the inside, to provide a point from which an archer or artilleryman may shoot.

enfilade Series of rooms arranged so that the internal doors align, providing a vista from the first room to the last.

entablature Upper part of an order, running horizontally above the columns that support it and consisting of three bands: architrave, frieze, and cornice.

escutcheon Metal plate protecting a keyhole.

faience Glazed ceramics used as decoration on a building.

fanlight Window directly above a door.

fan vault Vault in which the ribs combine to make cone-like shapes resembling fans.

finial Small ornament, such as a ball or fleur de lys, at the top of a roof, pinnacle, or other feature.

flèche Small narrow spire on top of a roof.

flushwork Decorative use of flint and stone to make patterns on the surface of a wall.

foil Circle divided by cusps into several lobe-shaped sections and named according to the number of sections, for example trefoil (three sections), quatrefoil (four sections), cinquefoil (five sections), and so on.

forebuilding Structure at the front of a castle keep or tower containing the main entrance.

frieze Middle section of an *entablature*.

gable Portion of the wall at one end of a pitched-roofed building that is usually triangular but may be in a decorative form such as stepped or curved.

gablet Miniature gable.

garderobe Form of lavatory in medieval houses and castles.

gargoyle Water spout projecting from the side of a building, often carved into a grotesque or amusing head.

garth Garden or lawn area in the middle of a monastic cloister.

gazebo Small summerhouse or garden building, designed to be ornamental, offer shelter, and provide a place to admire the view.

Georgian Term used to describe the architecture current during the reigns of George I and II, and the first part of the reign of George III (roughly 1714–1811), which is mainly Classical in inspiration.

glazing bar Slender divider (traditionally of wood) between the panes of a window.

Gothic Overall term referring to the various kinds of architecture developed in the Middle Ages, roughly during the 13th, 14th, and 15th centuries, typified by the use of pointed arches and in greater churches also by the use of flying buttresses and stone vaults.

Gothic revival The renewed fashion for Gothic architecture during the 18th and, especially, 19th centuries.

Gothic survival The phenomenon of Gothic-style building that persisted after the fashion for the style waned in the 16th century.

Gothick Term sometimes used for the revived Gothic style of the 18th century, in which more emphasis is placed on ornamental than on structural elements.

Greek revival Architecture inspired by the interest in the ruins of ancient Athens, especially between the 1780s and 1820s.

groin Pronounced edge formed where two surfaces meet in a vault that does not have ribs.

gun loop Small opening in the wall of a castle or fort through which a defender could shoot while remaining largely protected from enemy fire.

half-timbered See *timber-framed*.

hammer beam Horizontal arched bracket supporting the braces and struts in some medieval roofs.

herringbone Type of masonry in which the stones or bricks in the courses are laid at a diagonal angle with alternate courses in opposite directions, to produce an effect that looks like the bones of a fish.

hipped roof Type of roof with sloping, rather than vertical, ends.

hood-mould Projecting moulding above an arch, doorway, or window, designed to throw off the rain; also known as a dripstone.

impost Bracket-like structure projecting from a wall to support an arch.

Ionic Order of Classical architecture characterised by capitals bearing a scroll-like design.

Jacobean The period when England was ruled by James I, and the style of architecture prevalent then and in the early 17th century.

jamb Straight side of a doorway or window.

jetty Projecting upper storey of a timber-framed building.

keep Main, usually free-standing, tower of a castle; also called the great tower.

keystone Central stone of an arch or vault.

king post Upright post in a timber-framed roof.

lancet Narrow window with a pointed top.

lantern Open or glazed turret at the top of a roof or dome.

lierne Subsidiary vaulting rib that does not spring from one of the main structural points in the vault.

light Vertical subdivision of a window.

linenfold panelling Form of decoration, usually in wood, imitating folded cloth, and found in Jacobean interiors.

lintel Horizontal beam above a door, window, or other opening.

long and short quoins Alternating short and long corner stones.

longhouse Traditional form of rural house in parts of northern England, consisting of a long, low structure with accommodation at one end for people and at the other for animals.

loop Slit or similar opening in a castle wall through which a defender can shoot.

lozenge Diamond-shaped decorative motif.

lucam Structure projecting from the upper outer wall of a mill or warehouse and containing a hoist.

lucarne Opening, like a small dormer window, in a roof or spire.

machicolation Projecting parapet along the top of a castle wall, with holes that allow missiles to be dropped on enemies below.

mansard roof Roof with a double slope, the lower section sloping more steeply, usually to accommodate rooms inside.

mausoleum Large, high-status tomb, often accommodating many members of a single family.

merlon Upright portion of a crenellation or battlement.

Moderne Style of architecture popular in the 1930s, more flexible and ornamental than the modernist style.

modernist Style of architecture and design widespread in the early and mid-20th century, in which ornament was banished and modern materials, such as concrete, steel, and glass, dominated building construction

mosque Muslim place of worship.

motte Artificial mound on which was built the main stronghold of an early medieval motte-and-bailey castle.

moulding Ornamental carving applied to the projecting sections of an arch, doorway, window, wall, or other architectural feature.

mullion Upright member dividing a window into vertical lights.

murder holes Small openings in the ceiling of a castle gatehouse, allowing missiles to be dropped on attackers below.

narthex Entrance chamber, like an enlarged porch, sometimes found at the western end of a church.

nave Main western wing of a church.

Norman Style of architecture prevalent in the decades after the Norman conquest of England (1066), based on the architecture of Normandy and featuring semicircular arches, thick walls, small windows, and barrel vaults.

oeil de boeuf Small round or oval window.

ogee Double curve, with convex and concave parts, making up an arch or other opening.

openwork Term used to describe a screen, parapet, or similar structure that is pierced to form a decorative design.

orangery Garden building with glazing along the southern side, designed for growing oranges but often also used as a greenhouse for other plants.

order 1 In Classical architecture, one of the five accepted style of architecture defined by the appearance of the column, its capital, and the entablature above it; the five Classical orders are the *Tuscan, Doric, Ionic, Corinthian*, and *Composite*; 2 more generally, one of a series of concentric arches, around a doorway or similar feature.

oriel Projecting bay window on an upper storey.

palisade Strong fence made of wooden stakes.

Palladian Style of architecture inspired by Roman buildings as described by the Italian Renaissance architect Andrea Palladio and characterised by simple Classical façades, rusticated lower floors, and plain Tuscan porticoes; there were two phases of Palladian architecture in England, in the early 17th century (with the work of Inigo Jones) and in the 18th century (under the influence of Lord Burlington and William Kent).

panopticon Type of layout, devised in the late 18th century and most commonly used for prisons, in which a central observation post allows staff to keep watch on the surrounding cells or wings.

pantile Clay roof tile with a cross-section in an S-shape.

pargetting Form of highly ornate plasterwork traditionally used on outside walls in East Anglia.

patera Small, round, slightly raised decoration used in Classical architecture, often taking the form of a flower.

pavilion 1 Small, ornamental building, often lightly constructed; 2 building providing changing and other facilities on a sports field.

pavilion hospital Hospital planned as a series of separate, almost free-standing, wings (the pavilions) connected by a narrow communicating 'spine'.

pediment Low-pitched gable above a portico in Classical architecture.

Perpendicular The third and final phase of Gothic architecture in England, popular in the 15th century and typified by straight verticals, a panelling effect on walls, and fan vaulting.

pellet Ornamental motif used in Norman architecture, consisting of repeated ovals in low relief.

pendant Decorative feature hanging from a ceiling.

piano nobile Main floor of a building, containing reception rooms, usually above a semi-basement or ground floor.

Picturesque Movement in architecture that emerged in the late 18th century in which buildings were designed as if they had come out of a picture; prevailing elements included asymmetrical façades and the use of the *cottage orné*.

pier Solid support built of stone or brick.

pilaster Decorative, column-like feature projecting only slightly from a wall.

pillbox Small enclosed fortification made of reinforced concrete; widely used during the Second World War.

pinnacle Small, decorative structure like a miniature tower or spire.

plate tracery Style of tracery in which openings are cut into the solid stone of a window head.

plinth Projecting base of a wall.

polychrome Multi-coloured.

portcullis Reinforced gate designed to slide up and down to provide added strength and security at the entrance to a castle.

portico Porch-like structure, usually with columns supporting a pediment, on the front of a Classical building.

porticus Small side-room in a church of the Saxon period.

precinct In a monastery, the walled area containing the monastic buildings.

proscenium arch In a theatre, the arch that frames the stage and distinguishes it visually from the auditorium.

purlin Horizontal beam connecting the main structural elements – such as the trusses – and supporting the common rafters in a roof.

putti Cherub-like figures of children as portrayed in painting and sculpture.

quadrangle Four-sided courtyard of the kind often found in colleges and schools.

quatrefoil See *foil*.

Queen Anne Term used to describe buildings of the late 19th century characterised by brick walls dressed with stone and ornate, Dutch-style gables, which was a revival and adaptation of the building style of the period at the beginning of the 18th century when Anne was on the throne.

quoins Dressed stones at the corners of a building.

range Row or line of linked buildings, such as those along one side of a courtyard.

refectory Communal dining room, especially in a monastery; sometimes known as the frater.

Regency The architecture of the period during which the future George IV acted as Prince Regent and the years immediately afterwards. It is best known for elegant terraces and crescents and for buildings with an exotic influence, such as the Prince's Royal Pavilion at Brighton, East Sussex.

relieving arch Strong arch built into a wall above a window or door, to take some of the weight of the masonry above.

render To plaster the outer wall of a building.

repoussé Term used to describe a decorative relief on sheet metal that has been produced by hammering the design from the underside.

reredos Screen, usually decorated, behind an altar in a church.

rib Projecting band of stone in a vault.

rococo Style of architecture and interior decoration used occasionally in the 18th century and typified by a lightness of touch and a use of motifs such as S-curves, shells, and flowers.

roll moulding Moulding with a rounded profile, either semicircular or larger.

rood Statue of the Crucifixion, flanked by figures of St Mary and St John, placed above the chancel arch in churches in the Middle Ages.

rood screen Screen beneath the rood, separating the nave and chancel of a church.

rose window Round window used in medieval architecture.

roundel Circular panel, often slightly raised, bearing decorative symbols or images.

rubble masonry Masonry consisting of irregularly shaped stones, which may or may not be laid in courses.

rustication Masonry consisting of large blocks separated by deeply cut joints; or plasterwork made to simulate such masonry; banded rustication consists of stretches of masonry with deep horizontal joints only, to give the effect of strips of stone.

saddleback roof Small pitched roof on top of a tower.

sash window Window made up of vertically sliding sections called sashes.

scalloped Decoration, sometimes used on capitals, resembling the ridges of a shell.

screens passage Passage at one end of a medieval hall, giving access to the service rooms of the house and separated from the hall itself by a wooden screen.

segmental Term used to describe an arch or similar feature shaped like a segment, that is a curve consisting of part of a circle less than a semicircle.

shaft Slender column attached to a pier, doorway, or window.

solar Private chamber or living room in a medieval house.

spandrels Triangular spaces on either side of the head of an arch.

springing The point at which an arch or vault joins its supports.

staddle-stones Mushroom-shaped stones used to support granaries or similar farm buildings, to protect the contents from rats and mice.

stallriser The section of a shop front between the ground and the base of the window.

steeple Structure consisting of the tower and spire of a church together.

stiff leaf Form of stylised carved foliage used as ornament in early Gothic architecture.

strapwork Form of ornament popular in the Jacobean period consisting of slightly raised bands that resemble straps of leather, applied to such surfaces as plaster ceilings and carved screens.

string-course Continuous horizontal band of masonry projecting slightly from a wall.

Stuart The dynasty of rulers on the throne between 1603 and 1714, and the architecture of this period.

stucco Plaster covering the walls of buildings, especially on the exterior.

swag Ornamental carving or moulding of a piece of cloth or bunch of fruit or flowers draped over two supports.

synagogue Jewish place of worship and religious instruction.

term Sculpture consisting of an armless bust on top of a square pillar.

thermal window Semicircular window divided into three lights, so-called because such windows were used in the baths of Diocletian in Rome.

three-decker pulpit Large pulpit with three levels, containing the clerk's desk, the lectern, and the pulpit itself.

tile hanging Wall cladding consisting of rows of tiles attached to a timber frame.

timber-framed Form of construction in which a framework of timber is filled with some other material, such as bricks or plaster.

tracery Ornamental stonework in the head of a window, providing one of the main ornamental features of Gothic architecture.

transept Spaces in a church set at right-angles to the nave and chancel, making up the 'arms' of a cross-shaped plan.

transom Horizontal member set across a window.

trefoil See *foil*.

triforium Arched gallery above the arcade in some large churches.

truss Framework designed to span a space, especially in a roof.

Tuscan Order of Classical architecture characterised by its very plain capitals and the lack of flutes on the columns.

turret Small tower, usually designed to be ornamental, defensive, or to contain a staircase.

tympanum Semicircular area above the lintel of a doorway, often decoratively carved.

undercroft Vaulted room either below ground or below a main room.

valance Decorative edging along the side of an overhanging canopy or similar structure.

vault Ceiling or roof in the form of an arched structure, usually in stone or brick but sometimes in wood or plaster designed to imitate masonry.

venetian window Three-part window with a central, arch-topped section flanked by two slightly lower rectangular sections.

vermiculation Ornament carved in blocks of masonry consisting of twisting channels like the burrows of worms.

vernacular The local way of building; the form taken by ordinary buildings, such as traditional houses and barns, built with local materials.

villa 1 Country house designed in imitation of an Italian country residence in the Palladian style; 2 a superior detached house, usually on the edge of a town.

volute Spiral scroll as used on capitals of the *Ionic* order.

voussoir Wedge-shaped stone forming part of an arch.

wattle and daub Walling material consisting of a mud or clay plaster (daub) over a network of twigs (wattle), used between the wooden posts and beams of a timber-framed building.

weatherboarding Overlapping boards attached to the framework of a timber-framed building to form a protective cladding.

FURTHER READING

There are thousands of books about English buildings. This list contains a small selection, mostly ones that are specifically relevant to the chapters in this book. In addition to these there are many general histories of architecture. The best history of world architecture is Sir Banister Fletcher's *A History of Architecture,* which has been published in many editions, the most recent edited by Dan Cruikshank. One of the best sources of information about English buildings is the *Buildings of England* series, containing at least one volume for each county, originally written and edited by Nikolaus Pevsner and now being reissued in updated form. There is also a growing series of *Pevsner City Guides.* For briefer information on the buildings but more contextual information on landscape and history, the *Shell Guides to the English Counties,* originally edited by John Betjeman and John Piper, are still both useful and inspiring, although they are no longer in print.

General

Brabbs, D *et al* 2001. *England's Heritage.* London: Cassell

Brunskill, R 1987 (3rd edition) *Illustrated Handbook of Vernacular Architecture.* London: Faber

Clifton-Taylor, A 1987 (4th edition) *The Pattern of English Building.* London: Faber

Cruickshank, D (ed) 1996 (20th edition) *Sir Banister Fletcher's A History of Architecture.* Oxford: Architectural Press

Forsyth, A 1982 *Buildings for the Age: New building types 1900–1939.* London: Royal Commission on the Historical Monuments of England

Pevsner, N Various dates *Buildings of England.* Harmondsworth: Penguin and London: Yale University Press

Pevsner, N 1976 *A History of Building Types.* London: Thames & Hudson

Wood, E S 1995 *Historical Britain.* London: Harvill Press

Parish churches

Betjeman, J (ed) 2 vols 1968 *Collins Pocket Guide to English Parish Churches.* London: Collins

Friar, S 1996 *A Companion to the English Parish Church.* Stroud: Alan Sutton

Jenkins, S 2002 *England's Thousand Best Churches.* London: Penguin

Morris, R 1989 *Churches in the Landscape.* London: Dent

NADFAS 1993 *Inside Churches: A guide to church furnishings.* London: NADFAS

Platt, C 1981 *The Parish Churches of Medieval England.* London: Secker & Warburg

Smith, E *et al* 1976 *English Parish Churches.* London: Thames & Hudson

Greater churches

Clifton-Taylor, A 1967 *The Cathedrals of England.* London: Thames & Hudson

Wilson, C 1990 *The Gothic Cathedral.* London: Thames & Hudson

Other places of worship

Barton, D A 1975 *Discovering Chapels and Meeting Houses.* Aylesbury: Shire Publications

Kadish, Sharman (ed) 1996 *Building Jerusalem: Jewish architecture in Britain.* London: Valentine Mitchell

Lidbetter, H 1979 *The Friends Meeting House.* York: Sessions

Lindley, K 1969 *Chapels and Meeting Houses.* London: J Baker

Stell, C 1986 *An Inventory of Nonconformist Chapels and Meeting-houses in Central England.* London: HMSO

— 1991 *An Inventory of Nonconformist Chapels and Meeting-houses in South-west England.* London: HMSO

— 1994 *An Inventory of Nonconformist Chapels and Meeting-houses in the North of England.* London: HMSO

— 2002 *An Inventory of Nonconformist Chapels and Meeting-houses in Eastern England.* London: English Heritage

Monastic buildings

Aston, M 2000 *Monasteries in the Landscape.* Stroud: Tempus

Butler, L and Given-Wilson, C 1983 *Medieval Monasteries of Great Britain.* London: Joseph

Coppack, G 1990 *English Heritage Book of Abbeys and Priories.* London: Batsford

Platt, C 1984 *The Abbeys and Priories of Medieval England.* London: Secker & Warburg

Robinson, D (ed) 1998 *The Cistercian Abbeys of Britain.* London: Batsford

Houses

Airs, M 1995 *The Tudor and Jacobean Country House: A building history.* Stroud: Sutton

Aslet, C and Powers, A 1985 *The National Trust Book of the English House.* Harmondsworth: Viking

Ayres, J 1981 *The Shell Book of the Home in Britain.* London: Faber

Bell, Y 2005 *The Edwardian Home.* Princes Risborough: Shire

Durant, D N 1996 *Life in the Country House: A historical dictionary.* London: Murray

Girouard, M 1978 *Life in the English Country House.* New Haven & London: Yale University Press

— 1979 *The Victorian Country House.* New Haven & London: Yale University Press

Hoskins, L et al 2003 *Little Palaces: House and home in the inter-war suburbs.* London: Middlesex University Press

Jackson-Stops, G and Pipkin, J 1985 *The English Country House: A Grand Tour.* London: National Trust/Weidenfeld & Nicolson

Jenkins, S 2003 *England's Thousand Best Houses.* London: Allen Lane

Lloyd, N 1931 *A History of the English House.* London: Architectural Press

Mercer, E 1975 *English Vernacular Houses.* London: HMSO

Muthesius, H, (trans and ed Sharp, D) 1979 *The English House.* London: Crosby Lockwood Staples

Osband, L 1991 *Victorian House Style.* Newton Abbot: David & Charles

Parissien, S 1995 *The Georgian Group Book of The Georgian House.* London: Aurum

Penoyre, J and J 1978 *Houses in the Landscape.* London: Faber

Vale, B 1995 *Prefabs.* London: Spon

Wood, M 1965 *The English Mediaeval House.* London: Phoenix House

Castles

Brown, R A 1976 (3rd edition, revised) *English Castles.* London: Batsford

Fry, P S 1980 *The David and Charles Book of Castles.* Newton Abbot: David & Charles

McNeill, T 1992 *English Heritage Book of Castles.* London: Batsford

Morris, M 2003 *Castle: A history of buildings that shaped medieval Britain.* London: Channel 4

Toy, S 1966 (4th edition) *The Castles of Great Britain.* London: Heinemann

Fortifications

Hughes, Q 1974 *Military Architecture.* London: H Evelyn

Kightly, C 1979 *Strongholds of the Realm.* London: Thames & Hudson

Turner, H L 1971 *Town Defences in England and Wales.* Hamden, Connecticut: Archon Books

Buildings for commerce

Evans, B and Lawson, A 1981 *A Nation of Shopkeepers.* London: Plexus

Geist, J F 1983 *Arcades: The history of a building type.* Cambridge, Massachusetts & London: MIT Press

Lindley, K 1973 *Seaside Architecture.* London: H Evelyn

Morrison, K A 2003 *English Shops and Shopping.* New Haven & London: Yale University Press

Pearson, L 2002 *Piers and Other Seaside Architecture.* Princes Risborough: Shire

Powers, A 1989 *Shop Fronts.* London: Chatto & Windus

Schmiechen, J and Carls, K 1999 *The British Market Hall: A social and architectural history*. New Haven & London: Yale University Press

Buildings for industry

Beedell, S 1975 *Windmills*. Newton Abbot: David & Charles

Brown, R J 1976 *Windmills of England*. London: Hale

Burton, A 2002 *The Daily Telegraph Guide to Britain's Working Past*. London: Aurum

Cossons, N 1987 (2nd edition) *The BP Book of Industrial Archaeology*. Newton Abbot: David & Charles

Jones, E 1985 *Industrial Architecture in Britain 1750–1939*. London: Batsford

Pragnell, H 2000 *Industrial Britain*. London: Ellipsis

Reynolds, J 1970 *Windmills and Watermills*. London: H Evelyn

Tann, J 1970 *The Development of the Factory*. London: Cornmarket Press

Farm buildings

Brigden, R 1986 *Victorian Farms*. Marlborough: Crowood

Brunskill, R W 1987 *Traditional Farm Buildings of Britain*. London: Gollancz

Darley, G 1982 *The National Trust Book of the Farm*. London: National Trust

Harvey, N 1984 (2nd edition) *A History of Farm Buildings in England and Wales*. Newton Abbot: David & Charles

Martins, S Wade 2002 *The English Model Farm: Building the agricultural ideal 1700–1914*. Macclesfield: Windgather

Woodforde, J 1983 *Farm Buildings in England and Wales*. London: Routledge & Kegan Paul

Worsley, G 2004 *The British Stable*. New Haven & London: Yale University Press

Buildings for government

Cotton, A C 1936 *Town Halls*. London: Architectural Press

Buildings for education

Ministry of Education 1957 *The Story of Post-War School Building*. London: HMSO

May, T 2004 *The Victorian Schoolroom*. Princes Risborough: Shire

Robson, E R 1874 *School Architecture*. London: John Murray

Seaborne, M 2 vols 1971 and 1977 *The English School: Its architecture and organisation*. London: Routledge & Kegan Paul

Sharp, P and Hatt, E M 1964 *Museums*. London: Chatto & Windus

Buildings for entertainment and gathering

Adamson, S H 1977 *Seaside Piers*. London: Batsford

Atwell, D 1980 *Cathedrals of the Movies*. London: Architectural Press

Binney, M 1982 *Taking the Plunge: The architecture of bathing*. London: SAVE Britain's Heritage

Earl, J and Sell, M 2000 *The Theatres Trust Guide to British Theatres 1750–1950*. London: A & C Black

Earl, J 2005 *British Theatres and Music Halls*. Princes Risborough: Shire

Glasstone, V 1975 *Victorian and Edwardian Theatres*. London: Thames & Hudson

Gray, R 1996 *Cinemas in Britain: One hundred years of cinema architecture*. London: Lund Humphries

Harwood, E 1999 *Picture Palaces: New life for old cinemas* London: English Heritage

Leacroft, R 1988 *The Development of the English Playhouse*. London: Methuen

Southern, R 1970 *The Victorian Theatre: A pictorial survey*. Newton Abbot: David & Charles

Buildings for hospitality

Boniface, P 1981 *Hotels and Restaurants*. London: HMSO

Brandwood, G, Davison, A, and Slaughter, M 2004 *Licensed to Sell: The history and heritage of the public house*. Swindon: English Heritage

Girouard, M 1984 *Victorian Pubs*. London: Yale University Press

Haydon, P 1995 *The English Pub*. London: Robert Hale

Richardson, Sir A E 1948 (5th edition) *The Old Inns of England*. London: Batsford

Binney, M 1983 *Time Gentlemen Please!* London: SAVE Britain's Heritage

Buildings for caring and confinement

Bailey, B 1988 *Almshouses*. London: Hale

Brodie, A et al 2002 *English Prisons: An architectural history*. Swindon: English Heritage

Godfrey, W H 1955 *The English Almshouse*. London: Faber

Hallett, A 2004 *Almshouses*. Princes Risborough: Shire

Mitton, L 2001 *The Victorian Hospital*. Princes Risborough: Shire

Morrison, K 1999 *The Workhouse: A study of poor-law buildings*. Swindon: English Heritage

Orme, N and Webster, M 1995 *The English Hospital 1070–1570*. New Haven & London: Yale University Press

Richardson, H (ed) 1998 *English Hospitals 1660–1948: A survey of their architecture and design*. Swindon: Royal Commission on the Historical Monuments of England

Stevenson, C 2000 *Medicine and Magnificence: British hospital and asylum architecture 1600–1815*. New Haven & London: Yale University Press

Taylor, J 1991 *Hospital and Asylum Architecture in England 1840–1914*. London: Mansell

Buildings for transport

Betjeman, J and Gay, T 1978 *London's Historic Railway Stations*. London: John Murray

Biddle, G *et al* 1983 *The Railway Heritage of Britain*. London: Joseph

Biddle, G 2003 *Britain's Historic Railway Buildings: An Oxford gazetteer of structures and sites*. Oxford: Oxford University Press

Binney, M and Pearce, D (eds) 1985 *Railway Architecture*. London: Bloomsbury Books

Hague, D B and Christie, R 1975 *Lighthouses*. Llandysul: Gomer Press

Holder, J and Parissien, S (eds) 2004 *The Architecture of British Transport in the Twentieth Century*. New Haven and London: Yale University Press

Leboff, D 2002 *The Underground Stations of Leslie Green*. Harrow Weald: Capital Transport

Parissien, S 1997 *Station to Station*. London: Phaidon

Taylor, S (ed) 2003 *The Moving Metropolis*. London: Laurence King

Landscape pavilions

Casson, H (ed) 1963 *Follies*. London: Chatto & Windus

Headley, G and Meulenkamp, W 1999 *Follies, Grottoes and Garden Buildings*. London: Aurum

Hix, J 1996 *The Glasshouse*. London: Phaidon

Mowl, T and Earnshaw, B 1985 *Trumpet at a Distance Gate: The lodge as prelude to the country house*. London: Waterstone

WEB RESOURCES

http://www.english-heritage.org.uk
English Heritage

http://www.nationaltrust.org.uk
The National Trust

http://www.architecture.com
Extensive architectural site,
run by the RIBA

http://www.lookingatbuildings.org.uk
Comprehensive site created under the
auspices of the Pevsner guides; with
information on building types, major
cities, glossary, index of architects, etc

http://viewfinder.english-heritage.org.uk
Online image resource for English
historic sites and buildings

http://www.spab.org.uk
The Society for the Protection of
Ancient Buildings

http://www.savebritainsheritage.org
SAVE Britain's Heritage

http://www.georgiangroup.org.uk
The Georgian Group

http://www.victorian-society.org.uk
The Victorian Society

http://www.c20society.org.uk
The Twentieth Century Society

http://www.hct.org.uk
Historic Chapels Trust

http://visitchurches.org.uk
Churches Conservation Trust

http://ecclsoc.org
Ecclesiological Society

http://www.hha.org.uk
The Historic Houses Association

http://www.hudsons.co.uk
Hudson's: directory publishers providing
links to web sites on heritage and historic
houses

http://www2.glos.ac.uk/hfbg
The Historic Farm Buildings Group

http://www.industrialheritage.org.uk
Industrial heritage resources

http://www.theatrestrust.org.uk/main/index.html
The Theatres Trust

http://www.heritage.co.uk/follies/index.html
The Folly Fellowship

http://www.mausolea-monuments.org.uk
The Mausolea and Monuments Trust

INDEX

Page numbers in **bold** type refer to main, illustrated entries.

ACKNOWLEDGEMENTS

Philip Wilkinson

Thanks first of all to Peter Ashley. His revelatory photographs speak volumes about the buildings they portray and his ceaseless explorations off Britain's beaten tracks and down its alleys have yielded many of the most interesting buildings featured here. Many others have helped along the way. Thanks to: Philip Bernays, John Brooks, Val Horsler, David Johnston, David Pearson, James Wingate, and Sugra Zaman for advice, assistance, and support during the writing of the text; to the staffs of the library of the RIBA, London, the Bodleian Library, Oxford, and the Public Search Room at the NMR, Swindon, for research facilities and answering endless queries; to Janet Hadley for her editing and Philip Jansseune for his design and Mark Healey and Gillian Modrate for freelance design help; and to the staff of English Heritage Publishing, especially Rob Richardson and Adèle Campbell for their faith in the book and Susan Kelleher and René Rodgers for their painstaking work in bringing the work to publication.

Peter Ashley

This is my third collaboration with Philip Wilkinson. I couldn't wish for a more companionable, patient and understanding friend to work with on a project of this scale. I am also deeply indebted to English Heritage and the National Trust, not just as organisations, but also as individuals who made me welcome and put up with me running madly around the properties in their custodianship.

Many other people helped me in my sometimes seemingly interminable quest, but in particular I would like to thank in alphabetical order: Lucy Bland, Caius College Cambridge, Canterbury Cathedral, Castle Howard, Ptolemy Dean, Durham Cathedral, Everyman Theatre Cheltenham, Rupert Farnsworth, Girton College Cambridge, Richard Gregory, Laura Hannaway, Hartwell House Hotel, Hodder Headline, Holkham Hall, Hook Norton Brewery, Val Horsler, Susan Kelleher, Kew Gardens, Multiprint of Peterborough, Lady Nutting, Octagon Chapel Norwich, Nick Patterson-Gordon, Penshurst Place, Revd John Quarrell, Biff Raven-Hill, Rob Richardson, René Rodgers, Ruddle Wilkinson, Margaret Shepherd, Karen Southwell, David Stanhope, Wilton House.